OBD-I & OBD-II

A COMPLETE GUIDE TO DIAGNOSIS, REPAIR, AND EMISSIONS COMPLIANCE

Greg Banish

S-A DESIGN

CarTech®

CarTech®

CarTech®, Inc.
6118 Main Street
North Branch, MN 55056
Phone: 651-277-1200 or 800-551-4754
Fax: 651-277-1203
www.cartechbooks.com

Edit by Bob Wilson
Layout by Connie DeFlorin

ISBN 978-1-61325-752-4
Item No. SA532

Library of Congress Cataloging-in-Publication Data Available

Written, edited, and designed in the U.S.A.
Printed in China
10 9 8 7 6 5 4 3 2 1

All photos are courtesy of Greg Banish unless otherwise noted.

DISTRIBUTION BY:

Europe
PGUK
63 Hatton Garden
London EC1N 8LE, England
Phone: 020 7061 1980 • Fax: 020 7242 3725
www.pguk.co.uk

Australia
Renniks Publications Ltd.
3/37-39 Green Street
Banksmeadow, NSW 2109, Australia
Phone: 2 9695 7055 • Fax: 2 9695 7355
www.renniks.com

Canada
Login Canada
300 Saulteaux Crescent
Winnipeg, MB, R3J 3T2 Canada
Phone: 800 665 1148 • Fax: 800 665 0103
www.lb.ca

CONTENTS

Preface

I wrote my first book more than 16 years ago. With heavy theoretical schooling and solid practical experience from the shop, I put some of the hard lessons that I learned about the ECU's operation into one comprehensive text to be shared with others who really wanted to learn. What eventually became CarTech's *Engine Management: Advanced Tuning* was written in a timeless manner, focusing on the science and facts that don't change. As expected, the industry continued to adapt to new technologies and hardware, but the information in that book stood the test of time.

My first two books continue to sell well today because of an unrelenting focus on the underlying fundamentals that can be applied to any engine control unit (ECU). These books opened the door for many incredible opportunities over the years. I was invited to speak at events, host live classes through my company, Calibrated Success, and consult with some of the biggest names in the high-performance industry. An aspect that never seems to fail me is that same adherence to the fundamentals in the most complex situations. It's surprising how much of that "useless" theory actually works in the real world when one pays attention. For those of you who saw my name on this title and decided to join me again here, thank you for your continued support. You will see more of the same no-nonsense approach here as I have used in my previous books and live classes.

As I sat down to sketch the outline of this book, I took that same practical approach to the subject of onboard diagnostics (OBD). I have been working with OBD in one form or another since OBD-II appeared in the vehicles we drive.

In this book, I continue my focus on fundamentals that can be applied to most situations and vehicles. The book features a few case studies, but it is simply not possible to specifically cover every single code on every single vehicle in one book. Luckily, this isn't necessary, as I refuse to write just another diagnostic book in a sea of arguably good competition. I aim to deliver the knowledge needed to understand what's going on in the ECU regarding emissions and diagnostics and to show which direction one might go to dig deeper and ultimately find a solution. In today's digital age, terabytes of information are just a click away on a laptop or phone. What is brought here is the first step in a journey of understanding. The best students I've had over the years are those who take these basics and use them to narrow the focus and identify the real issue in any situation.

OBD and repair are closely linked to the practice of engine calibration and emissions. You will see overlapping information in this book to some of my earlier content because much of my personal experience with OBD stems from my work as an OEM calibration engineer. I spent years working with the ECU for both engine controls and diagnostics. Once again, my approach here is to clearly spell out some of the things that one doesn't usually learn from the existing texts or classrooms. When properly applied, this information will speed up your learning curve for diagnostics, repair, and even engine calibration.

Introduction

This book is about OBD, and it focuses on the operation and strategies employed in US OBD-II-equipped vehicles and engine controllers. To the casual consumer, OBD is the magic machine that generates fault codes that can help determine why a vehicle is not performing as expected. At an even more basic level, the malfunction indicator lamp (MIL) or check engine light (CEL) should be illuminated on the dash in the event of any failure to alert the operator of the need for repair.

We will dig deep into the diagnosis and probable repairs associated with fault codes. We also cover emissions in terms of causes, testing, and regulations.

OBD and emissions regulations are inextricably linked. The whole reason that these diagnostics exist within the electronic control unit (ECU) of the vehicle's engine is to make sure that the engine and its associated emissions hardware are working as intended. Regulatory agencies, such as the United States Environmental Protection Agency (EPA), California Air Resources Board (CARB), California Bureau of Automotive Repair (BAR), and countless other state and county level organizations, use OBD-II data to monitor the emissions compliance of the automotive fleet. On a wider scale, European, Australian, Asian, and even United Nations groups also keep an eye on automotive emissions.

The seriousness with which meeting the various regulations are taken by those who work in the transportation industry cannot be understated. This includes both original equipment manufacturers (OEMs) as well as aftermarket corporations, manufacturers, installers, shops, tuners, and enthusiasts.

Regulations have been set for a wide range of conditions that can be tested both in and out of a laboratory environment. Since our focus here is the US domestic regulatory market, we will mostly show examples and information related to both OBD and emissions in the USA.

Today's engines are capable of making impressive amounts of power while emitting less than 10 percent of the emissions compared to their predecessors from a few decades ago.

In 1970, Congress passed the original version of the Clean Air Act (CAA), which became the primary structure for all emissions and diagnostics regulations that followed. The CAA allowed the EPA to establish limits for various pollutants from a vehicle as measured under specific conditions. The CAA also clearly outlined that there are penalties for tampering with the emissions control system of a vehicle. "Tampering" is defined by the EPA as follows:

"Tampering: CAA § 203(a)(3)(A), 42 U.S.C. § 7522(a)(3)(A), 40 C.F.R. § 1068.101(b)(1): [The following acts and the causing thereof are prohibited] for any person to remove or render inoperative any device or element of design installed on or in a motor vehicle or motor vehicle engine in compliance with regulations under this subchapter prior to its sale and delivery to the ultimate purchaser, or for any person knowingly to remove or render inoperative any such device or element of design after such sale and delivery to the ultimate purchaser[.]"

Over time, the limits have become significantly lower, and automotive emissions have been reduced by several orders of magnitude. Modern cars have astonishingly low tailpipe emissions numbers, and the OBD system ensures proper operation of the symphony of features and logic that delivers on the promise of clean air. The side benefit to consumers is that vehicles operate much the same way that they did when they were brand new as long as the OBD system is satisfied that there are no significant errors. This means that torque is available on demand, and fuel economy is in line with expectations.

Emissions testing has not changed too much over the years.

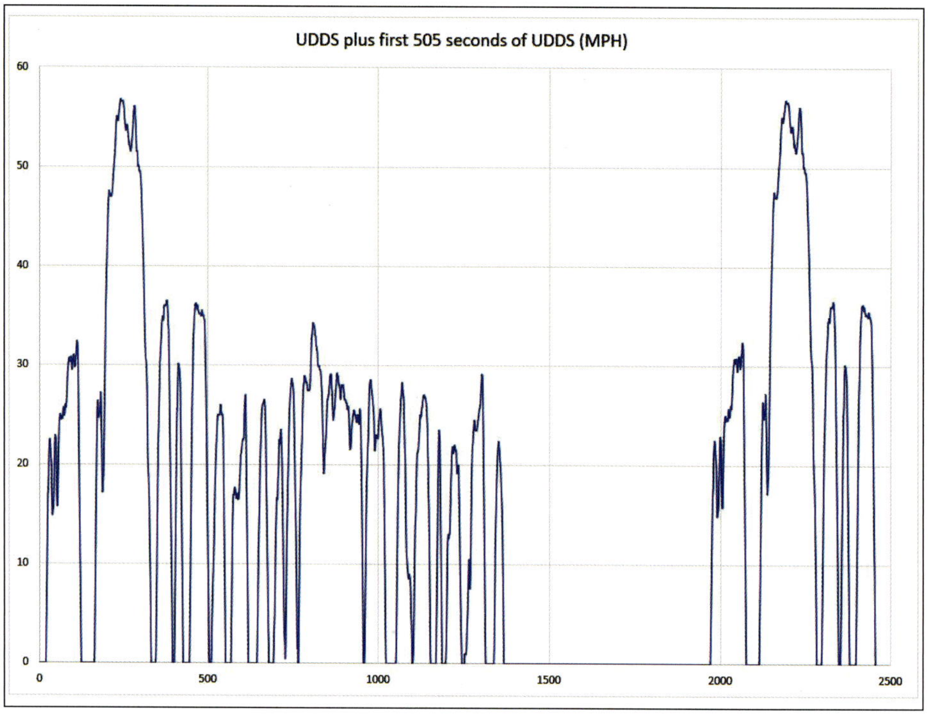

The most common emissions test is the FTP-75 that simulates city traffic driving with 18 events or "hills" after a cold start. There is a 10-minute soak followed by a hot restart and a repeat of the first five hills. These graph titles all call out "MPH," which is the traditional way to display emissions traces.

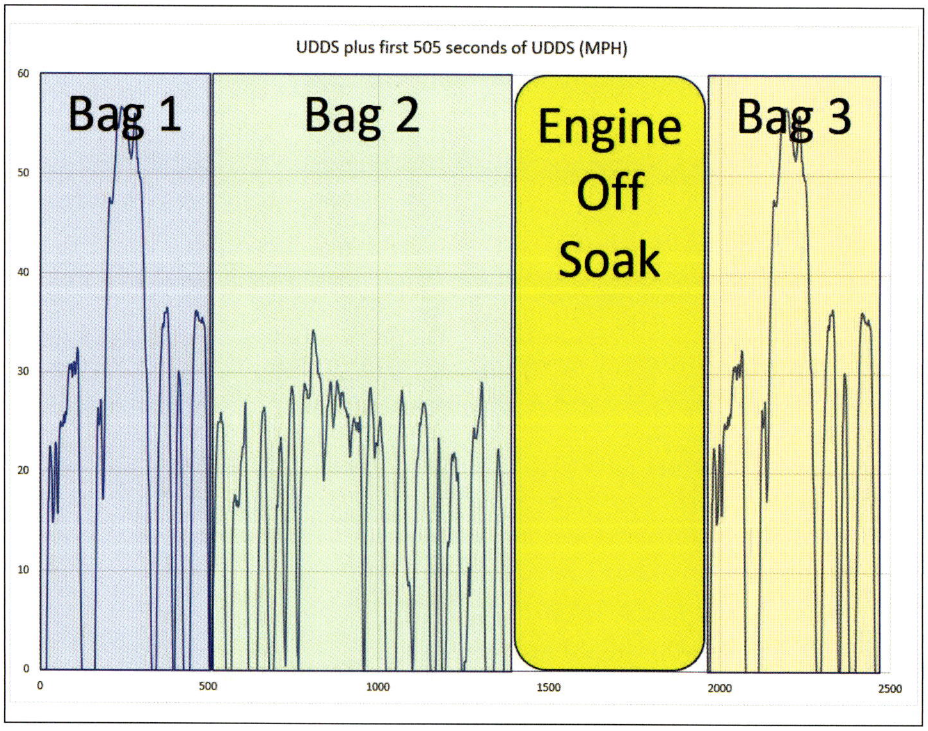

Engineers like to break down the FTP into three separate phases. Each has its emissions sealed into a different bag for analysis by the test bench. This allows for better analysis of the cold or hot start versus normal operation.

Sure, additional checks have come up along the way, but the primary set of tests remain in play today. These federal test procedure (FTP) drive cycles are a series of speed-time profiles that mimic what was seen in real time as a vehicle drove a particular route.

Eventually, the EPA settled on a handful of drive cycles and agreed that all vehicles should drive the same route/speed for comparison. This can be done in a laboratory setting on a stationary test rig known as a chassis dynamometer, where the vehicle itself does not move but the wheels turn a drum that is connected to computer-controller resistance that simulates the same forces seen by that vehicle on a real road.

Since most driving is done in an urban stop-and-go environment, a city cycle known as FTP-75 was developed. It includes a cold start at an ambient temperature of approximately 67°F (22°C), drive off, repeated stop-and-go events, shutoff, a hot restart, and more stop-and-go driving.

The test itself is separated into three phases that allow easier investigation into the cold start, warm phase, and hot restart. Because so much of a vehicle's emissions are created immediately after the cold start, the first 505 seconds of Phase 1 are often used on their own as a "cold 505" by engineers looking to make improvements here.

The test itself is anything but steady. Speed is continuously changing throughout the cycle, so the driver must really pay attention to avoid failing the test by missing part of the cycle. The driver is allowed a window of error of plus-or-minus 2 mph or plus-or-minus 0.5 seconds centered around the target speed and time trace. When driving through this window, the driver can actually have a large impact on test results.

Some drivers are much smoother than others, clipping peaks and valleys slightly to reduce the number of transients the engine must perform. Other drivers may have a more nervous foot that causes the vehicle to perform more small accelerations or decelerations within the window than were originally intended. These additional tip-in and tip-out events often all come with their own small deviations in the delivered air-fuel ratio that can add up to a significant amount of added emissions over the length of the test.

Even without a blatant violation, each test performed is given a driver rating at the end of the cycle. A value between -3 and +3 is assigned based on how closely the driver followed the trace, with "0" being an ideal run right on trace and "-3" being on the "smooth" side.

It takes some practice to repeatably drive these emissions cycles correctly while looking for the target trace out the window, managing the accelerator or brake, and having no sensation of acceleration forces while you do it because the vehicle itself is

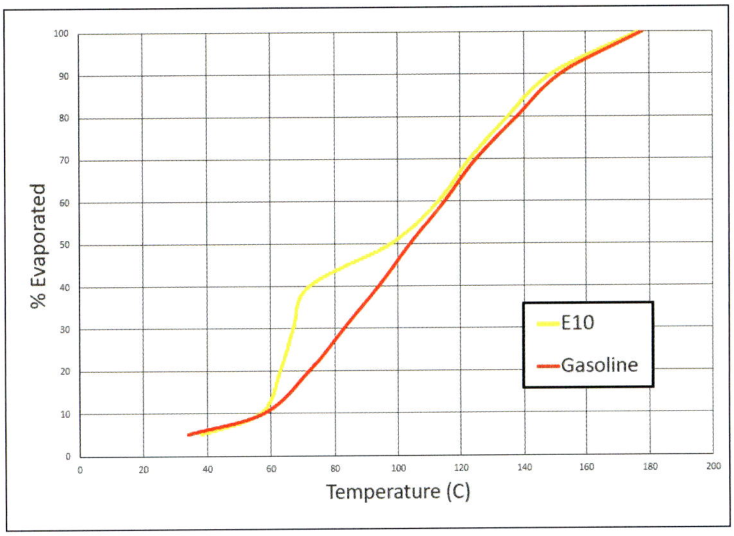

The distillation curve of a fuel tells us how much of it evaporates as temperatures increase. Alcohol fuels actually have a slight advantage at moderate temperatures over pure gasoline.

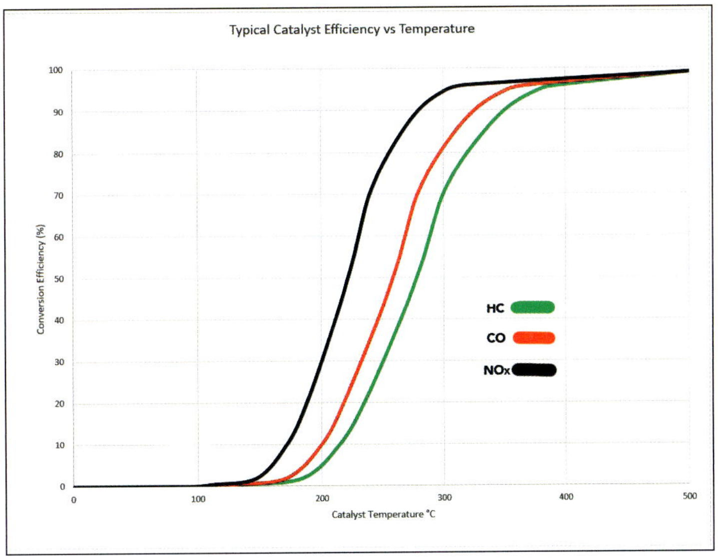

The catalytic convertor needs to reach a minimum temperature before it becomes effective at reducing emissions.

not actually moving.

A good driver can repeatably deliver a "-1" driver rating from test to test, which would make the calibration engineer's job a little easier, as the human element does not override any controls changes that may have been made to the ECU between tests. We have seen plenty of cases where making ECU changes should have made an improvement, but our results got worse due to a driver rating on that cycle of +2 compared to our earlier -1 rating. By simply repeating the test (often with a different driver), we had useful data for comparison.

For the emissions calibration engineer, the first minute or so of the FTP-75 test is by far the trickiest part. Both the engine and catalyst start the test at room temperature. This means that injected fuel does not evaporate as well as it would on an engine operating around 200°F/93°C. The distillation curve of the fuel shows a large improvement in evaporation as temperatures rise.

Because liquid fuel does not burn easily, it leads to large amounts of unburned hydrocarbon being passed out the exhaust. Worse yet, the catalytic convertor does not promote the secondary reactions that help oxidize these excess hydrocarbons and reduce emissions until its temperature is increased as well. Calibration engineers spend most of their time attempting to shorten the time required to get the catalyst up to an effective temperature while simultaneously trying to avoid dumping too much unburned fuel out the exhaust before the engine is up to a normal temperature.

It is entirely possible for these early emissions in the first minute of testing to exceed the total allowable amount for the entire test if the balance is not right. Looking at a graph of the total accumulated emissions for a test, it's easy to see that most of the emissions were collected very early in the test. Add to this the added complexity of spark advance and the formation of oxides of nitrogen (NO_x), and one begins to understand what keeps emissions calibrators busy for a year or more before every vehicle is released for certification and ultimately sale to the public.

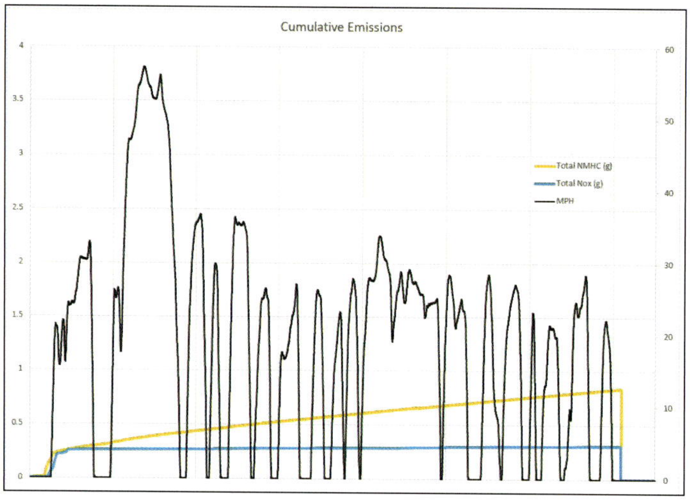

Emissions laboratories have the ability to capture a second-by-second analysis of tailpipe emissions that is known as "modal data." Here we can see that a large part of the total emissions for the whole drive cycle happens just after startup.

The first highway test was largely aimed at fuel-economy measurements and was accordingly named the highway fuel economy (HWYFE) test. This test begins with an engine

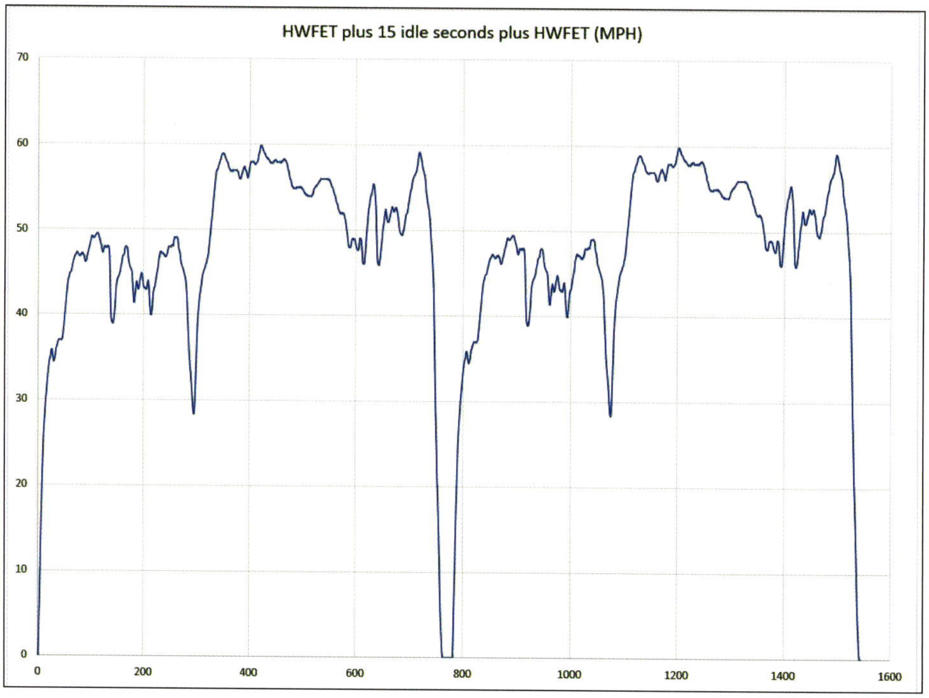

The highway fuel economy test begins with an engine already at operating temperature and follows a speed trace that used to represent highway driving speeds in the 1970s. There are now newer tests that cover actual highway speeds commonly seen today.

Canister Loading

During an emissions test, the intent is to measure the tailpipe emissions of the vehicle. The source of these emissions is usually thought to just be the fuel coming into the engine from the injectors, but this ignores one of the major emissions systems. The evaporative system is so important that it gets its own monitor on the Mode $06 data stream.

The key component of the evaporative emissions system is the charcoal canister that is able to temporarily store gaseous hydrocarbons. These hydrocarbons are displaced from the fuel tank during a filling event as well as those that form over time when fuel is present in the tank.

The evaporative diagnostic system checks for leaks as small as 0.020 inch, but we must remember what should be happening when a normal system (with no leaks) is functioning. The vapors in the system are directed toward the charcoal canister, and a solenoid on the vapor line to the engine's intake allows these gases to be drawn into the running engine and burned just like liquid fuel from the injectors. Think of the purge solenoid as an extra fuel injector that sprays a perfectly evaporated fuel charge into the intake.

To make sure this system is working properly during an emissions certification test, the charcoal canister is removed from the vehicle and weighed when empty. Then, while still on a scale, a mix of butane and nitrogen gas is added proportional to the capacity of the canister. Depending on which test is being run, the canister is filled to either 150 percent of its rated capacity or until 2 grams of the mixture breaks through.

Butane is used as a simple representation of the many "light end" hydrocarbons present in a vehicle's fuel system. The butane is absorbed by the charcoal and will be drawn out during vehicle testing on the dynamometer. With the canister loaded, it is reconnected to the vehicle's evaporative system prior to the soak time and cold start of the emissions test.

During the test, the vehicle must demonstrate that it is able to draw this stored hydrocarbon through the engine to reduce the chance of evaporative losses as well as delivering a clean tailpipe emissions measurement from the combination of fuel sources. The point of this is to demonstrate that any vapors captured by the evaporative control system can be effectively stored and burned cleanly through the engine and catalyst rather than escape directly to the atmosphere. A side benefit to this is that these gases are fuel just the same as liquid gasoline, so burning them displaces a small amount of liquid fuel that would otherwise be required to drive. ■

On this mustang, the charcoal canister is located under the spare-tire well. It stores fuel vapors from the fuel tank until they can be drawn in for clean combustion later.

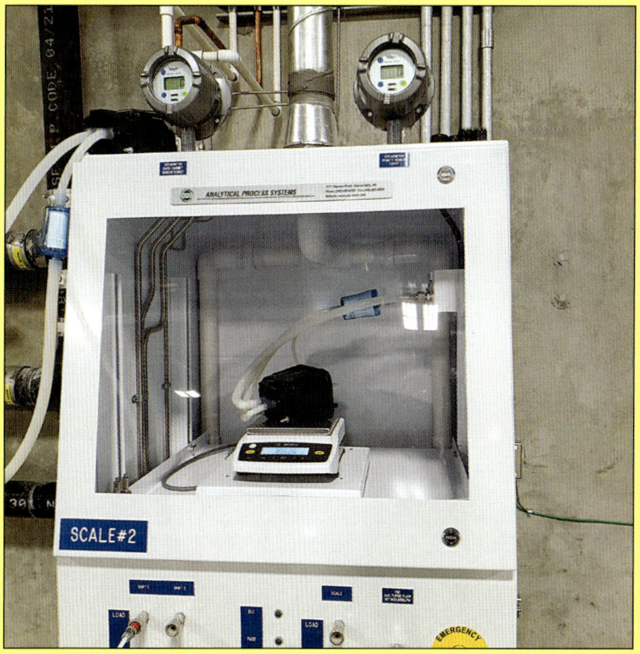

A charcoal vapor canister is carefully loaded and weighed prior to vehicle emissions testing. Because of the small masses in question, the scale must not only be precise but also free of outside influences while taking its measurement.

that is already warmed up, so initial emissions are not nearly as much of a concern when compared to the FTP-75. It follows a mildly wandering speed profile centered around 45 mph for the first half and 55 mph for the second half.

Because this test begins with an engine and catalyst that are already up to their ideal operating temperatures, it is typically not much of an emissions challenge to the engineer as long as the engine is kept relatively close to the stoichiometric air-fuel ratio throughout the test. The combination of balanced, raw engine-out emissions and a fully functioning catalyst are a recipe for low tailpipe emissions numbers.

Acknowledging that vehicles are often driven at temperatures colder than the controlled laboratory conditions, a cold version of the city drive cycle was created with its own scaled emissions limits. It is run in a lab environment where everything is chilled to an ambient temperature of approximately -20°F (-7°C). A cold start is still done at this lower temperature, and the drive cycle follows the exact same speed profile as the FTP-75 but for only the first two phases.

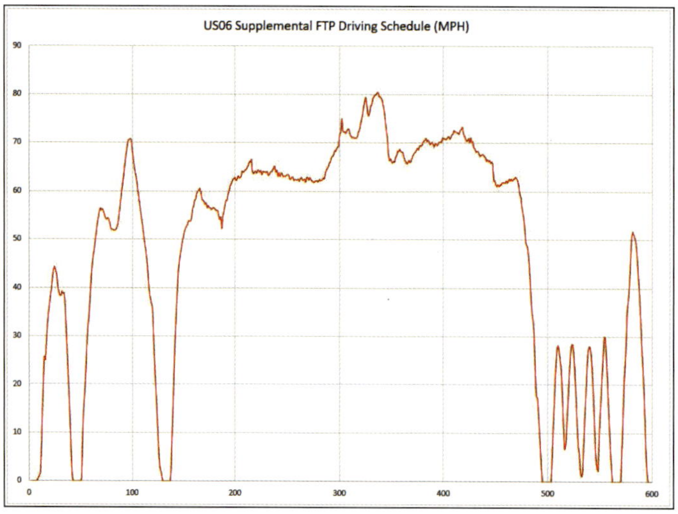

The US06 is a supplemental test that includes the faster acceleration and higher speeds seen by drivers today. Since it does not include a cold start, the primary challenge is avoiding excess enrichment during the more aggressive events.

Collectively, these first three tests are known as the three-cycle test sequence. However, it was eventually recognized that this does not adequately cover how most vehicles are driven. Consumers spend more time at higher speeds, accelerate quicker, and sometimes use the air-conditioning system, which puts additional load on the engine while driving. As such, new supplemental federal test procedures (SFTPs) were added to cover these conditions.

The US06 test includes more rapid-acceleration events as well as higher speeds, whereas the SC03 test added operation at elevated speeds in a heated environment (95°F/35°C), where the vehicle's climate control would be activated for the whole test. When these two tests are added to the original three, we get what is known as five-cycle testing, which is now used for both emissions and fuel economy measurements.

While these five cycles make up the majority of testing, more tests must be passed to certify a new vehicle from the manufacturer. In addition to the FTP-75 and Cold 505, the same cycle is used for a test run at 50°F/20°C. This test was created to bridge the gap between the two temperatures that were so far apart that it left questions about potential pollution as the ECU strategy shifted from "cold" to "hot." The EPA is essentially looking for a smooth transition between the two rather than a step change so that the engine continuously adapts across all operating temperatures without polluting.

TECH TIP

Stoichiometric

Scientists and engineers use the term "stoichiometric" to refer to a condition where there are equal quantities of molecules in a chemical reaction, leaving no leftover or unreacted molecules.

For the combustion of non-ethanol pump gasoline, this is an air-to-fuel ratio of approximately 14.7:1 and 9.85:1 for E85. Theoretically, running at this stoichiometric ratio for the fuel should leave a minimum of leftover carbon, hydrogen, oxygen, and nitrogen molecules to form pollutants after the primary reactions.

Another unit commonly used to express the air-fuel ratio relative to this stoichiometric point is the excess air ratio, lambda (λ), which is just the current ratio divided by the stoichiometric ratio. A value of 1.0 indicates that the current condition is equal to the stoichiometric mixture. Values less than 1.0 indicate a richer condition and those greater than 1.0 indicate a leaner condition. This unit is very handy to engineers because it immediately reveals how rich or lean the ratio is relative to the balance point regardless of fuel composition. ■

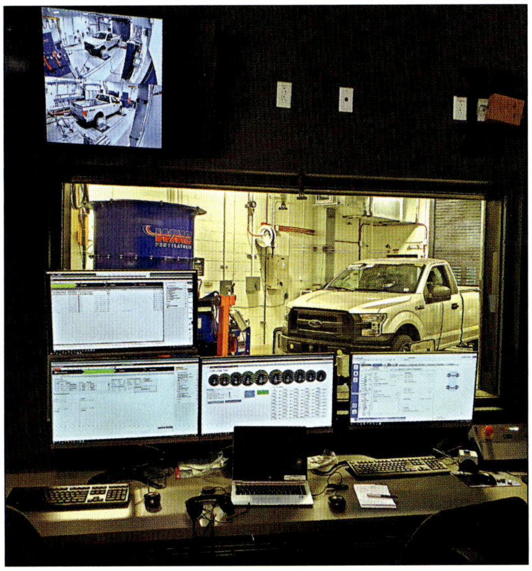

Emissions certification tests are run in the tightly controlled environment of a laboratory test cell. The chemistry of the air in the cell is closely monitored, and temperature is controlled to meet the needs of each test specification.

A special climate-controlled cell with hundreds of radiant heat bulbs hanging from the ceiling provides solar load to the test vehicle during an official SC03 test. Emissions are collected using an identical CVS column as the other FTP variants.

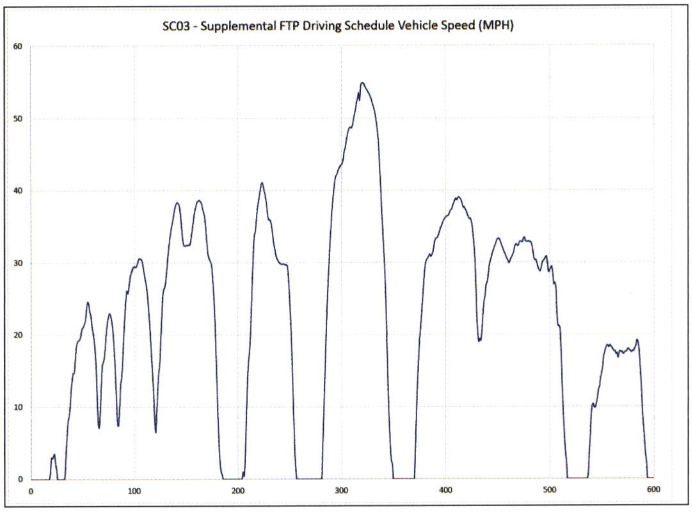

The SCO3 profile has similar aggressiveness to the US06. The test itself is run in a heated cell where the vehicle air conditioning must also be run for the duration of the test, adding load to the engine and cooling system.

Urban Dynamometer Driving Schedule

Some vehicles, including hybrids, run the urban dynamometer driving schedule (UDDS, LA-4, or the "city test"). This again is a variant of the FTP-75, but it only includes the first two emissions phases, spanning 7.5 miles from a cold start at nominal temperature when run once. The UDDS includes a "fourth bag" where the rest of the drive cycle is completed after the Hot 505 when it is run back to back.

During the development of the original Chevy Volt, the UDDS was the prime test that I used when performing battery charge to gasoline power balance control calibration for charge-sustaining mode. We had to ensure that the vehicle would finish this test within 1 percent of the fuel energy equivalent battery charge compared to the starting condition to qualify as a test where it was truly charge sustaining rather than depleting the battery for fuel economy calculations. By the way, the tailpipe has to remain cleaner than the standard while balancing the battery energy in a hybrid too.

Aftermarket Emissions Testing

Per a November 2020 official memorandum, "The EPA reaffirms its longstanding practice of using enforcement discretion not to pursue conduct that could potentially constitute a violation of the Clean Air Act if the person engaging in that conduct has a documented, reasonable basis to conclude that the conduct does not adversely affect emissions."

For aftermarket companies looking to demonstrate that their products have clean enough emissions to

PCV System

Many are familiar with the positive crankcase ventilation (PCV) system's existence. The primary purpose of this system is to draw evaporated hydrocarbons and water vapor from the internals of the engine.

Over time, the engine oil is diluted by fuel that sneaks past the rings as well as condensation from atmospheric air that has made its way in. Worse, the condensed water in the crankcase is exposed to combustion gases that leak past the rings, forming acids that can etch into the metal of the bearings and friction surfaces. Since the crankcase is not perfectly sealed, these vapors need to be actively drawn out. This is done to avoid degradation of the oil that could affect friction and shorten engine life.

The PCV system works by connecting a tube directly from the crankcase to the air-inlet path of the engine through the PCV. This acts like a check valve too. Ideally, this is at a point where there is some natural depression from atmospheric pressure. Because gases seek the point of lowest pressure, they are drawn from the crankcase into the intake and can be burned in the cylinder with the normal air-and-fuel charge. Any resulting emissions can then be further reduced by the catalyst rather than risking evaporative loss to the atmosphere from the crankcase.

To avoid drawing too much vacuum that may damage seals, there is often a make-up air line. This allows the crankcase to draw clean filtered air from behind the airbox into the crankcase when the PCV valve is allowing crankcase vapors to enter the intake. The latest emissions regulations now include the PCV system on the list of "comprehensive components" that must be diagnosed to ensure compliance.

New diagnostics have recently been phased in by OEMs to detect cases where there is an outside leak in the PCV system or if the crankcase has been ventilated to atmosphere. This implementation was another round of headaches for diagnostic-calibration engineers, all in the name of closing one more potential emissions loophole on the vehicle. ■

The positive crankcase ventilation system was one of the first emissions devices added to cars. Here, you can see the large bore line connected between the valve cover and the intake manifold with a check valve and sensor right on the valve cover as well.

be allowed to be used on any public road, CARB created a process for exemption. By running through a series of tests approved by CARB for a specific application (and of course passing the same emissions limits met by the OEM for the unmodified vehicle), a company can be granted an executive order (EO) that declares it to be legal for highway use. Because the California emissions standards are the strictest in the US, the EPA also recognizes that an EO awarded by CARB is sufficient proof that a product does not violate the Clean Air Act.

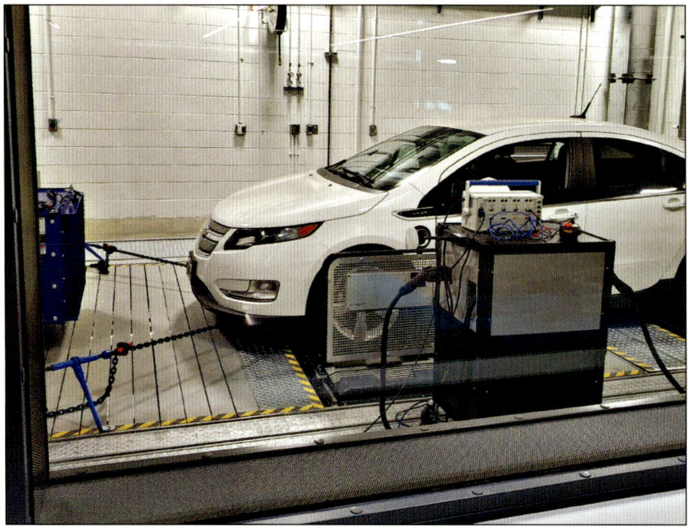

Even hybrid vehicles are required to pass all federal emissions tests. Doing so is sometimes more difficult with the increased number of engine start-and-stop events, which can make it more difficult to control the air-fuel ratio of the catalyst.

To obtain an executive order from CARB, the submitting company must provide some information about the modification. This begins with a description of the product, a listing of the parts included or modified, and operating parameters (such as the boost level on a supercharged or turbocharged application). In addition, changes made to the ECU must be declared if reprogramming is part of the kit.

CARB is particularly interested in things that affect emissions, so it focuses on changes such as fuel delivery, target air-fuel ratios, oxygen sensor controls, and spark timing. Any change that may affect emissions must be demonstrated on the emissions test cycle or be subject to additional scrutiny.

For example, it is allowable to add fuel enrichment to control exhaust gas and component temperatures—but only the amount that is required to prevent immediate thermal failure. Any excess fueling (which would increase carbon monoxide emissions) is not allowed. At full power, additional fueling is limited to lean best torque (LBT) fueling, which is the minimum amount of extra fuel required to increase torque to its potential maximum. Further increasing fueling may increase knock resistance, but it does not satisfy the definition of LBT and is thus excluded unless it is proven to be needed for temperature control.

Once satisfied with the paperwork submission, CARB may issue a test letter that states which emissions information it would like to review to confirm that a product does not negatively impact vehicle emissions. In recent years, this has usually been the same test regimen: FTP-75, US06, and SC03. The highway fuel economy test is often dropped because vehicles that can pass the more-stringent US06 and SC03 cycles typically do not fail on the easier HWYFE test. Cold carbon monoxide is also eliminated because it requires a very specialized test facility that has tremendous cold climatic control in addition to normal emissions-measurement equipment.

CARB recently completed construction of a state-of-the-art emissions test facility in Riverside, California. This cell not only includes an emissions dynamometer and exhaust sampling equipment but also has all of that inside of an evaporative emissions test chamber that can be sealed as well.

The test facility must be recognized as meeting the current standards for internal environmental control, road load simulation, exhaust-gas collection, dilution, measurement, reporting, and repeatability. A modern emissions test cell costs about $3 million and must undergo constant calibration and recertification tests. This cost is obviously prohibitive for most companies, so independent laboratories (such as the SEMA Garage, Automotive Testing and Development Services (ATDS), Roush, Transportation Research Center (TRC), Mahle, and others) offer options at reasonable pricing on a per-test basis. SEMA went a step further by working directly with CARB on behalf of its testing customers to ensure that all submission paperwork is in order because this is the single largest issue seen by CARB reviewers that often delays the approval process even with passing tailpipe measurements.

Once a suitable test facility has been selected, the vehicle is drained of any existing fuel. It is then refilled with a partial tank of a specific fuel for testing, and all adaptive learns within the ECU are reset. The chemical makeup of pump gas is a random mixture of many different hydrocarbons along with alcohol, stabilizers, cleaners, and other additives. To level the playing field, a known mixture of a specific blend is used (at roughly triple the price of pump gas).

The vehicle is driven on the chassis dynamometer in the lab through the first two phases of the FTP-75 test as a "prep cycle" to allow the closed-loop fuel trims to adjust to the new fuel. The vehicle is then parked for 12 to 36 hours in a controlled environment where all parts of the engine and emissions system are allowed to reach the same temperature. The charcoal canister is also filled with a charge of butane to sim-

SEMA answered the call for additional testing resource needs by building a new state-of-the-art lab outside of Detroit. The all-wheel-drive emissions dyno makes it easier to test almost any vehicle without the need to worry about differential wheel speeds or "dyno modes," as all four wheels move together the same as if the vehicle were on the road.

LEV III / Tier 3 FTP Emissions Standards

Program			Tier 3 Hi - Altitude	
LEV III	Tier 3	NMOG + NOx	NMOG + NOx	CO
		mg/mi	mg/mi	gm/mi
LEV160	Bin 160	160	160	4.2
ULEV125	Bin 125	125	160	2.1
	Bin 110*	110	110	2.1
	Bin 85*	85	85	2.1
ULEV70	Bin 70	70	105	1.7
ULEV50	Bin 50	50	70	1.7
SULEV30	Bin 30	30	50	1.0
SULEV20	Bin 20	20	30	1.0
ZEV	Bin 0	0	0	0

* Tier 3 Transitional Bins – expire after 2019MY

Formaldehyde = 4 mg/mi for all categories.

The current Tier 3 emissions standard are separated into bins of increasing cleanliness for each test. Aftermarket testing must clear these values after a deterioration factor has been applied to the raw measurement if taken before the full useful life mileage.

ulate the light ends collected during a typical refueling event.

Finally, it's testing time after the soak. All tailpipes are fitted with an airtight collector hose that routes 100 percent of exhaust gases from the vehicle into a sampling system that dilutes and measures the exact amount of each component in the exhaust.

These results are tallied and compared to an allowable standard. Since the vehicles tested are often new and current emissions standards are written a maximum allowed during the full useful life (FUL) of the vehicle, a deterioration factor (DF) is applied to simulate the anticipated decay in performance over time due to catalyst aging. To pass such a tailpipe-emissions test, the measured results plus the deterioration factor must be a lower number combined than the standard to which the vehicle was originally certified.

The only exception here is that if a baseline emissions test was performed on the vehicle prior to modification that did not pass. Then, the modified version can be no worse than 10 percent greater emissions over the original results when both are taken in a certified laboratory setting. While this second option sounds like it opens up the window for compliance, it also adds further scrutiny compared to an independently clean passing result and is not recommended.

Finally, after passing the necessary tailpipe-emissions tests in the lab, a check is made to see if all the OBD monitors that should be active for the vehicle have been executed and passed since testing began. In an ideal case, all of the OBD-II monitors will have executed somewhere during the emissions test procedures.

In the event that one or more of these monitors has not yet completed, the vehicle can be driven on the road to provide an opportunity to complete the missing monitors. The evaporative system monitor in particular is often tricky to pass, as it requires a specific set of conditions to execute. Failure to execute more than one of the monitors or the presence of an MIL at any point in the test will result in an overall failure. In that case, new testing must be done from the beginning.

For high-performance applications, a check is made of delivered horsepower at wide-open throttle (WOT). Delivered power must be at least 85 percent of the stated number in the original application to ensure that the tested vehicle matches the performance expected to be seen by consumers on the road.

With all testing complete, it is a paperwork exercise to obtain the final executive order number for the product that must be displayed in the vehicle's engine compartment next to the OEM vehicle emissions control information (VECI) label. The VECI label includes emissions certification, engine family or test group, displacement, OBD, model year, fuel type, and catalyst information.

Since the modified parts can affect the vehicle's emissions, it's important that the EO label be clearly presented next to the OEM VECI to show that the vehicle still conforms to allowable standards. Local inspectors are trained

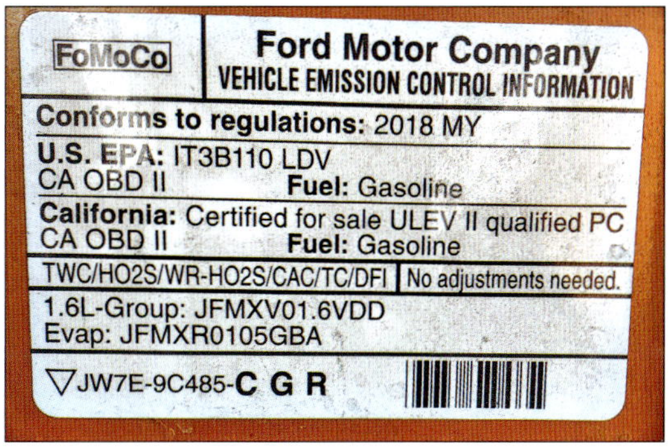

The vehicle emissions control information label is clearly posted on the underside of the hood of this Ford Fiesta ST. The T3B110 means that the vehicle emits less than 110 mg/mile of combined NMOG + NO$_x$ emissions on the FTP-75 test.

to look for the EO sticker as a part of normal compliance checks in regions where such testing is a part of the vehicle registration process.

The current requirements from CARB include a second backup set of passing confirmation tests for approval. At today's prices of approximately $5,000 for each round of testing, one can see how the cost of testing makes the idea of obtaining a CARB EO somewhat challenging to smaller companies. Throw in the cost of initial development, vehicle transportation, travel, lodging, meals, new CARB filing fees, and time away from running the business, and it becomes easier to understand why more companies don't go through the process.

However, the costs associated with emissions violations (which includes selling or installing products that have no emissions exemption) can easily be more than 10 times the cost of certification, just for the first offense. Unfortunately, the new reality is that more and more companies need to do emissions development work right alongside their normal product development to stick around in today's environmentally conscious climate.

Another bright spot for parts manufacturers is that CARB often issues EOs that cover a family of products or vehicles. For example, a supercharger system that may fit a range of SUVs and pickup trucks will often only need to be tested on the worst case for emissions. The worst case is defined as the vehicle in the lowest emissions bin with the highest curb weight. A passing result on a Chevrolet Suburban would cover the same product used on a Silverado pickup of the same family. Because emissions development and testing can be very costly, this saves companies a large amount of time and money during certification. CARB then would issue a blanket EO covering a range of vehicles under the same number.

For the consumer, there is some good news hidden among this emissions-certification talk. If a product is offered for sale on a vehicle where it has passed this rigorous emissions certification, this means that all of the diagnostics and active monitors should be working just the same as they did on the vehicle when it drove off the dealership lot. All too often, I see discussions about repair on modified vehicles where the conversation quickly turns to "that new thing you installed must be the problem." But if a product has been through the CARB EO inspection and certification process, then there is a high likelihood that one should be able to believe the normal vehicle diagnostics.

Even in cases where a supercharger has been added, the ECU should still be able to detect a failing sensor, trip the correct fault code, and illuminate the MIL on the dash. Having the supercharger in place should not affect the ECU's ability to see a fault in the coolant-temperature sensor, coil pack, or catalyst.

When dealing with a modified vehicle but the modifications have a CARB EO, I recommend treating them just like any other stock vehicle when it comes time to diagnose and repair most issues. Granted, the new parts often carry more potential failure points (such as potential vacuum leaks or fuel-delivery concerns), but one should still follow the standard procedure first. As they say in the medical community: "When you hear hoofbeats, think horse not zebra." The obvious answer is usually the right the answer.

TECH TIP

They All Don't Pass

I worked on a supercharger program for a popular pickup truck, where our baseline vehicle with only 2,000 miles on it failed the first emissions test for high carbon monoxide. This occasionally happens due to the stack up of possible tolerances and conditions in production vehicles and the real world.

While we could have simply pointed at this initial failure in the event of a near miss on the final product emissions testing, it was an easier and safer route for me to simply clean up the final emissions to a better result and pass without questions from the regulatory body.

In this case, the culprit was excessive cold-start fuel that was added to protect for low-quality fuels in some markets. Since the product was a supercharger that would use a required premium fuel all the time, I safely removed some of the excess fueling that was causing high carbon monoxide emissions on startup. The final product not only made more than 150 hp over stock but the emissions were also cleaner. ■

CHAPTER 1

Background and Origins

Onboard diagnostics (OBD) have actually been around for a long time. Many of the earliest electronic engine control systems had the ability to detect basic faults and alert the user. The only trouble was that each manufacturer had its own way of storing and retrieving these fault codes, often with differences even among models of the same manufacturer.

Early electronic control units (ECUs) performed simple checks, such as open-circuit (sensor unplugged) faults. A slightly more advanced version of this check also detected if the circuit was shorted to either the battery voltage supply or the ground, which dragged the signal to one extreme or the other regardless of what the sensor actually showed on the engine.

Retrieving these fault codes was a bit of black magic for end users and general repair shops. Sure, the dealership had a fancy tool designed by the OEM that plugged into a proprietary connector under either the hood or dashboard. However, these tools were uncommon outside of a dealership repair bay. A backup method of retrieving the error codes was usually available.

Diagnosing carbureted engine issues historically required a skilled technician. Even with an update to a more modern standalone EFI system, this Porsche 912 only has very limited diagnostic capability compared to anything in a new vehicle showroom.

The most obvious of faults is the open circuit from a missing connection. If a sensor is left unplugged, OBD should catch it immediately.

Before OBD-II, technicians needed a unique way to read each manufacturer's ECU faults and data. This meant having a variety of scan tools, which was a great expense to cover each unique connector and communication protocol.

In 1984, ECUs themselves were just becoming normal on vehicles, and the available diagnostics were crude at best. While some faults could be stored, retrieving them was a challenge for consumers.

Typically, the backup method involved some trickery, such as shorting two pins on a connector with a wire (or paperclip) to get a light on the dash to flash. One would count the number of flashes and refer to a chart to see the potential source of the error. Again, these codes were anything but standardized across the industry, but at least they gave the technician or owner a place to start looking for problems under the hood.

These basic circuit integrity checks eventually became known as "OBD-I" faults within the industry. The Society of Automotive Engineers (SAE) worked with the various manufacturers to create a standardized list of these faults and corresponding codes. This list was later integrated into what we know today as "OBD-II."

Reader's Tip

Acronyms in this book are spelled out on first reference. However, subsequent references use only the acronym. Due to the large number of acronyms in this book, you can check the glossary in the back of this book for the acronyms and their meanings. ■

Over time, the diagnostics became more involved (and useful for repairs) with some added complexity. The question began to be asked, "How do I know this sensor is working properly?" So, new checks were born that are known as rationality checks.

These new tests look for a specific range of output from a sensor under known conditions. For example, both the intake air temperature (IAT) and engine coolant temperature (ECT) sensors should start at similar values after the engine has been off for a long time. Additionally, the ECT sensor should increase its signal steadily toward the thermostatic control temperature of the coolant over time. Failure to meet these conditions indicates a potentially bad ECT sensor because the output signal is not rational as to the expected behavior.

Similarly, an engine that is operating at an idle condition should have a throttle position sensor (TPS) signal that falls within a specific range. Many traditional single-track TPS sensors have a 0 to 5V circuit range with functional readings falling between 0.5 and 4.5V if measured directly with a meter. Since the throttle is not completely closed, we expect to see some slightly elevated voltage signal at idle, usually just under 1.0V. The ECU checks the circuit voltage when the vehicle speed is 0, engine speed is near the target idle speed (typically 800 rpm or less), and total airflow is also low enough to be in the idle range. If the TPS circuit shows 1.5V here, it would be a mismatch with regard to rationality.

Every sensor has some sort of rationality check in OBD-II. This

Name	Value
Engine RPM (SAE)	580 rpm
Vehicle Speed (SAE)	0 mph
Throttle Position (SAE)	18.8 %
Timing Advance (SAE)	14.0 °
Knock Retard	0.0 °
Mass Airflow Sensor	2,178 Hz
Mass Airflow (SAE)	7.5 g/s
Intake Manifold Absolute Pressur...	42 kPa
Engine Coolant Temp (SAE)	142 °F
Intake Air Temp (SAE)	55 °F
IAT Advance	0.0 °
Equivalence Ratio Commanded (SAE)	1.000 λ
O2 Voltage B1S1	0.877 V
O2 Voltage B2S1	0.859 V
Injector Pulse Width Avg. Bank 1	1.0 ms
Injector Pulse Width Avg. Bank 2	1.0 ms
Short Term Fuel Trim Bank 1 (SAE)	-1.6 %
Short Term Fuel Trim Bank 2 (SAE)	2.3 %
Long Term Fuel Trim Bank 1 (SAE)	7.8 %
Long Term Fuel Trim Bank 2 (SAE)	1.6 %
Cylinder Airmass	0.19 g

A look at the data from an engine warming up at idle reveals a relatively low throttle position and corresponding airflow. This electronic throttle control (ETC)-equipped vehicle resolves the raw throttle position sensor voltages into a percentage that can be seen in a scan tool.

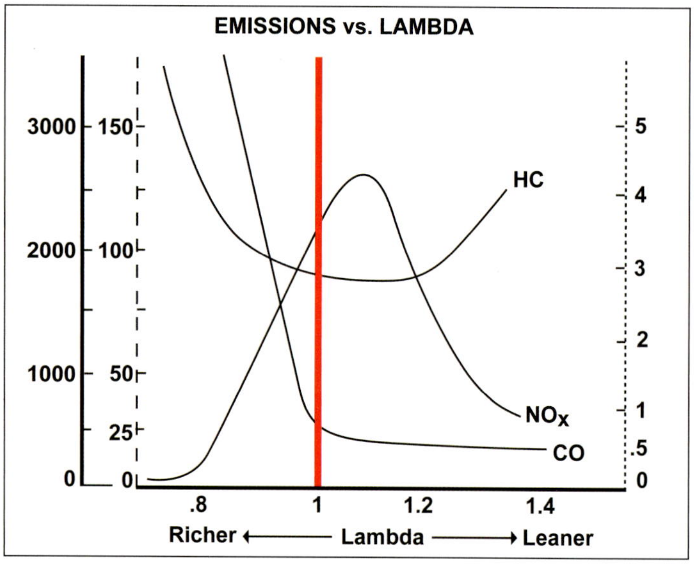

The ratio of air and fuel being burned has a pronounced effect on emissions. ECUs attempt to maintain control close to the stoichiometric balance for the best tradeoff between the various resulting emissions.

The malfunction indicator lamp (MIL), also commonly referred to as the check engine light, is tested at every startup to make sure it is working. After that, it is used to alert the driver to a condition that needs to be addressed to keep the engine running properly.

is part of what makes OBD-II an improvement over the basic early diagnostics. But let's get to the real reason OBD-II exists: emissions.

Emissions

With the implementation of stricter emissions standards in the 1996 model year, further requirements were placed on manufacturers. They had to ensure that their vehicles were not only clean when tested for certification but also that they tracked the operation of the vehicle throughout its life to help keep the emissions clean. The logic is simple: broken cars pollute more.

Anything that changes the combustion behavior of the engine by affecting the air-fuel ratio, spark timing, exhaust gas recirculation function, or throttle control usually has a measurably negative impact on tailpipe emissions. The OEMs spend countless engineering hours dialing in the engine controls to keep operation close to a stoichiometric air-fuel ratio with optimized spark timing. A single bad sensor input can throw a virtual wrench into these controls.

Although the actual tailpipe emissions are not measured directly on modern cars as they drive down the road, the ECU can recognize conditions that lead to increased emissions. Anything that makes the engine run rich of the stoichiometric air-fuel balance will drive up carbon monoxide and unburned hydrocarbon emissions. Likewise, a lean condition can increase production of oxides of nitrogen (NO_x). Improper dosing of exhaust gas recirculation

Preparing Diagnostic Monitors for Testing

We often need to make sure that the vehicle is ready for testing, whether that's at a state inspection site or elsewhere. This may be needed after disconnecting the battery or if the ECU has been reflashed with a calibration or software update. Both of these actions usually reset the monitor statuses in the vehicle, so it's important to make sure we give the vehicle a chance to run the tests (and pass) before having it checked for that all-important inspection. Your ability to get new tabs for your license plate may depend on this procedure.

The question often comes up as to how best to make sure that all the monitors have run. There are multiple routines or "drive cycles" that should allow all of the monitors to run, but they all have much in common. The common theme is that these drive cycles all mimic events seen in the FTP-75 emissions certification test, during which the OEMs are supposed to be able to execute all of their monitors when tested by the EPA or CARB. The cold start is similar to the beginning of the FTP-75, but it gives the vehicle more idle time, allowing for better warmup on the oxygen sensors and catalyst before jumping into driving conditions. After that, a mix of low-speed and light-load conditions are used to gently exercise all the sensors and monitors. Pausing at various vehicle speeds allows some other monitors that require steady-state conditions to execute at various points as well.

Following this procedure should be enough in most cases to get a properly running vehicle to execute and pass all the emissions monitors. The evaporative emissions monitor in particular can be rather tricky because this is the one that depends most on those steady-state parts of the procedure.

Any speed change can make the fuel in the tank slosh around and void that attempt at checking tank pressure sensor readings. It's also the reason why fuel tank levels need to be between 15 and 85 percent to run in the first place. Actually, getting the evaporative monitor to run may take multiple attempts, so focus on avoiding fuel-tank slosh while driving to help give it a better chance at success.

If the vehicle has been modified, all bets are off as to whether it will pass—even if the right test conditions have been presented and the test is actually run. Aftermarket exhaust systems in particular are notorious for not passing the catalyst monitor. Any leaks in the system can skew the oxygen sensor readings enough to fail. Non-OEM catalytic converters usually do not include as much precious metal content, so the downstream monitor may not be happy with their lower conversion ratio.

When a vehicle goes to an inspection station with an incomplete downstream O_2 or catalyst monitor, it usually triggers a visual inspection where the non-OEM parts are identified. If the aftermarket parts are not clearly marked with a CARB EO number, they will likely be rejected. Unfortunately, the fix for this is replacing the hardware with something that can pass the monitors (and has a CARB EO number stamped on it) rather than just re-running and hoping for the best.

Procedure to Pass Emissions Monitors

- Prerequisites: cold start, fuel level between 15 percent and 85 percent; all accessories off.
- Start the vehicle and idle for 4 minutes.
- Idle the vehicle in Drive for 1 minute.
- Drive toward an empty street or highway and accelerate to 45 mph slowly. Stay in second gear for 5 seconds during this acceleration. Get to fifth gear.
- Maintain a speed of 45 mph for 30 seconds.
- Stop the vehicle.
- Idle the vehicle in Drive for 1 minute.
- Drive at 25 mph, and then drive for 15 minutes at speeds between 15 and 35 mph. Within this time, stop at least 5 times, and have at least 3 periods of steady speed for 90-second durations.
- Drive the vehicle between 45 and 60 mph for 8 minutes.
- Maintain a steady speed between 45 and 60 mph for 5 minutes.
- Drive the vehicle between 45 and 60 mph for 8 minutes.
- Stop the vehicle and idle for 40 seconds.

Confirmed Emissions DTC's: 0   MIL Is On: False

Misfire	Complete	Catalyst	Complete
Fuel System	Complete	Heated Catalyst	Not Supported
Components	Complete	Evaporative System	Complete
		Secondary Air System	Not Supported
		A/C Refrigerant	Not Supported
		Oxygen Sensor	Complete
		Oxygen Sensor Heater	Complete
		EGR System	Not Supported

Passing the emissions inspection in many locations now requires that your vehicle report a completed status for the required monitors. The tests necessary to run these monitors should be under normal driving conditions.

(EGR) or camshaft position control can also lead to similar increases in emissions constituents.

The ECU continuously monitors all of its sensors and actuators to ensure that they are performing as intended. It is assumed that improper operation has a negative impact on emissions. Conversely, if everything checks out properly, it is very likely that tailpipe emissions are in line with those that were originally certified by the OEM during development.

The next question is: "How far is too far?" Any single sensor or actuator on the engine can be off a little bit and the vehicle may still pass a random emissions test. In fact, the US Environmental Protection Agency (EPA) routinely pulls random samples of road-driven vehicles into its lab in Ann Arbor, Michigan, for testing. It does not need permission from the manufacturer since in-use monitoring has long been part of its charter under the Clean Air Act.

The rule for manufacturers is that they must illuminate the malfunction indicator lamp (MIL, or CEL) under any condition that causes the tailpipe emissions to exceed 150 percent of the standard for which the vehicle is certified.

In plain English, this is what it means: if something, such as the manifold absolute pressure (MAP) sensor, should fault and cause the engine to begin running rich enough to make the hydrocarbon emissions 50-percent worse than the allowable standard on one of the federal test cycles, the MIL must be illuminated, and a code must be stored in the ECU.

Diagnostic calibration engineers at the OEMs spend a lot of time running repeated emissions cycle tests with induced failures to make sure that each one is caught before the limit of tailpipe emissions has been reached on the test cycle. A summary report of each of these diagnostic failure demonstrations must be included with the manufacturer's federal certification submission and may be audited at any time by the EPA.

Among OEM diagnostic calibrators, dark humor still exists: "You can pollute all you want, as long as the MIL is on!" While this is true, the presence of a current fault code is an automatic failure on any emissions test. So, while "it's okay to pollute," the test certainly did not pass, and more work is required before the program can proceed.

Defeat Devices

Anywhere there is competition, cheating is sure to follow in some form. Make no mistake, there is always competition in the automotive industry, as there are billions of dollars at stake in sales. Manufacturers are constantly challenged to meet incredibly strict emissions targets, which requires almost Herculean engineering efforts, time, and budgets. With so much at stake, it is not surprising that some look for an easier path.

Unfortunately, this is not NASCAR, where cheating is met with a slap on the hand and an updated rule book for everyone else on Monday morning. Attempting to outsmart the rule book makes one more of an Al Capone than Smokey Yunick, and the Feds always seem to get their man in this game. Cheating at emissions testing is actually a violation of federal law under the Clean Air Act of 1970. This means that there are real criminal penalties for those who willfully break these laws.

The EPA defines a "defeat device" as "any motor vehicle hardware, software, or design that interferes with or disables emissions controls under real-world driving conditions, even if the vehicle passes formal emissions testing." This definition is plain and obvious to most engineers and automotive executives. Enforcement is also possible in cases where the device in question violates the "spirit of the law."

The feds really have no sense of humor here. There are plenty of cases in recent history where companies and individuals faced criminal prosecution related to the implementation of defeat devices into production vehicles. As an experienced calibration engineer, I can assure you that regular training on the matter was quite common at every automotive company for which I worked. It really isn't possible to be working at the OEM and claim that one wasn't aware of the rules here.

Defeat devices are not limited to manufacturers. Countless examples are in the repair and aftermarket world as well. As mentioned, any device that renders part of the emissions-control system inoperative is deemed a defeat device under the law.

This means that items such as "test pipes" or "off-road" exhaust systems that remove the catalytic convertor fit this description because the catalytic convertor plays such a huge role in maintaining clean emissions from the vehicle. Even most "high-flow" catalysts sold in the performance aftermarket could be argued as defeat devices by regulatory agencies because their conversion efficiency is less than that of the OEM part they replace. EGR delete

Although popular for the immediate performance increase, kits like this are illegal in the United States and other countries. Removing the DPF or EGR system dramatically increases emissions even on a modern engine.

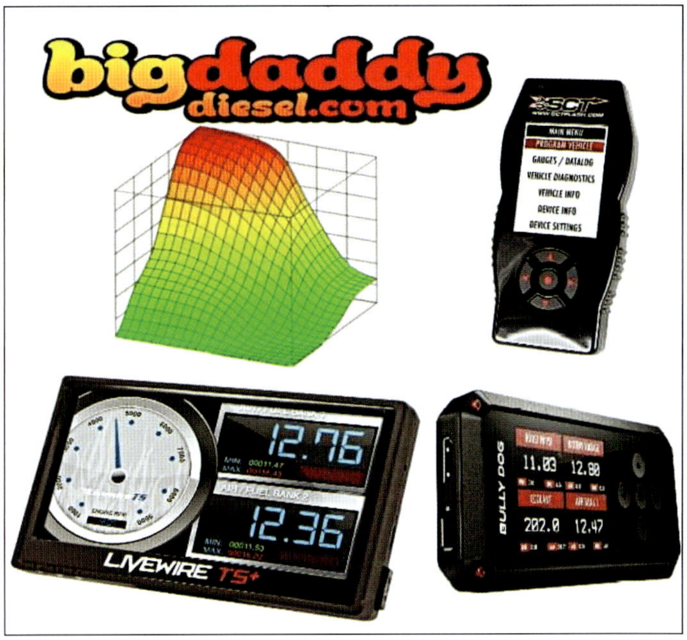

Defeat devices are not limited to hardware. A handheld programmer like this that changes the stored ECU calibration also meets the definition and can bring serious legal issues to sellers and installers.

or bypass kits, PCV vents or open catch cans, colder thermostats, diesel particulate filter (DPF) delete kits, selective catalyst reduction or diesel exhaust fluid dosing (SCR/DEF) delete kits, handheld ECU reflashing tools, and computer software or piggyback control modules all fall in this category.

The only way changes like these can be approved is by demonstrating that their installation does not negatively impact the vehicle's emissions. This means that the company offering them usually has to (at their own expense) send a vehicle to a certified emissions laboratory to run the same tests that the OEM did before releasing the vehicle to the public. The emissions of the modified vehicle are measured and compared to the allowable standard to which the vehicle was certified originally.

Obviously, attempting to reproduce clean emissions in the absence of something critical, such as the catalytic convertor, is just not going to pass, which is why they are not allowed to be installed on street-driven vehicles. Manufacturers and resellers of these "delete" kits have been the target of many EPA and CARB enforcement actions over the years. This trend is not likely to change with the continued push to keep our environment clean. The dollar amounts at stake from fines makes this enforcement no joke within the industry.

Even a local corner muffler shop will often refuse to remove the original equipment catalyst on a vehicle unless it is being replaced with a certified direct replacement piece. The fine for getting caught doing so as an installer can be as much as $4,500 per tampering offense. This amount is sure to give pause to the owner of almost any small business such as the typical exhaust, repair, or high-performance shop.

The final amount of some of these fines is often so great for parts manufacturers or installers that have multiple violations that it is adjusted "based on the offender's ability to pay." In other words, the wrong violation can absolutely bankrupt a company. These fines are usually not dismissible in a bankruptcy, either. In 2020, CARB issued more than $2.5

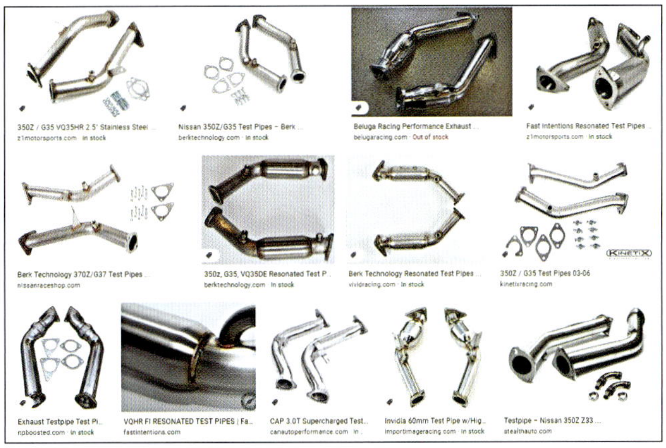

Replacing the factory catalytic convertor with a test pipe is a direct violation of the Clean Air Act as a defeat device. Using an empty resonator may help with noise a little, but it does not do anything to clean up the tailpipe emissions.

1995 Cadillac Defeat Device Settlement

This is an example of one violation, showing the EPA consent decree that ultimately resulted from the violation.

For Immediate Release
Thursday, November 30, 1995

U.S. Announces $45 Million Clean Air Settlement with GM

First Judicial Environmental Recall—470,000 Cadillacs

WASHINGTON, D.C.—General Motors Corporation will spend approximately $45 million to settle government charges that it put illegal devices to defeat pollution controls inside nearly a half-million Cadillacs since 1991 that resulted in carbon monoxide emissions of up to three times the legal limit. The case is the largest ever brought under the Clean Air Act rules for car and truck emissions by the Justice Department on behalf of the Environmental Protection Agency, and the first judicial auto recall aimed at curbing damage to the environment.

GM will pay an $11 million fine, more than $25 million to recall and retrofit the polluting vehicles, and up to $8.75 million on projects to offset emissions from these vehicles. These projects may include buying back older vehicles or purchasing new school buses that burn cleaner fuels.

The case grew out of EPA's investigation that showed that the Cadillac "defeat devices" resulted in the illegal release of approximately 100,000 tons of excess carbon monoxide pollution.

"Carbon monoxide can cause cardiopulmonary problems and can lead to headaches, impaired vision, and a reduced ability to work and learn," said Attorney General Janet Reno. "These so-called defeat devices are not just paper violations but result in real increases in emissions that affect real people."

The agreement, filed in federal District Court in Washington, D.C., resolved government allegations that GM sold vehicles that did not conform with the Clean Air Act, made and sold vehicles equipped with illegal defeat devices, tampered with certain 1991 and 1992 model-year Cadillacs, and failed to describe the use of emissions-control devices to the EPA. GM agreed to recall and to repair the 470,000 Cadillacs.

"These devices sacrificed public health and defied the laws that are in place precisely to prevent the long-term health effects that carbon monoxide air pollution causes. These illegal devices caused enough additional air pollution to blanket a major U.S. city, such as Washington, D.C. with a 10-foot layer of carbon monoxide," said EPA Administrator Carol Browner. "Today's action demonstrates the very real need for (and the Clinton Administration's commitment to) strong enforcement of the law that protects public health and the environment for the American people."

The government's allegations centered on GM's 1991–1995 model-year Cadillacs, including Seville and DeVille models, equipped with GM's 4.9L engine. An additional claim involved GM's failure to notify EPA about certain emissions control strategies for light-duty vehicles sold in model years 1991–1995.

Lois Schiffer, the Assistant Attorney General for the Environment and Natural Resources Division, said: "At a time when many consumers are being asked to use oxygenated fuels to reduce carbon monoxide, GM has engaged in practices that improperly increase the carbon monoxide emissions from these cars. That's not right, and it's unfair to the American people."

During routine testing in the fall of 1993, the EPA discovered that the Cadillacs failed to comply with federal emissions requirements. EPA tests showed that the engines emitted up to 10 grams of carbon monoxide per mile with the climate control on (well above the 3.4 grams/mile limit).

"GM's actions constituted a serious violation of the Clean Air Act and undermined the EPA's efforts to improve air quality," said Steven Herman, Assistant Administrator of the EPA's Office of Enforcement and Compliance Assurance. "Since the vehicle-certification program depends on complete and accurate information supplied by automobile manufacturers, GM's conduct jeopardized the integrity of the program."

"This action today sends a signal that violations of the Clean Air Act will not be tolerated," said Eric Holder, United States Attorney for the District of Columbia. "The act's requirements protect the health and welfare of our citizens, and we will vigorously enforce it."

In 1991, GM designed a new engine-control computer chip to respond to customer complaints of stalling and other drive problems in the 1991 Cadillacs. The device nearly tripled the output of carbon monoxide when the car's climate control system (for heating or cooling) is on. The instructions on the computer chip enriched the fuel (increased the amount of fuel relative to air), which overrode the emissions-control system and resulted in multiplying the carbon monoxide emissions. For the 1993–1995 model years, GM again failed to disclose the use of the device or its adverse emissions effects. ■

million in fines to the aftermarket parts category alone. The EPA numbers dwarf these with 2020 single violations of $12 million (Harley-Davidson), $850,000 (Punch It Performance), and $875,000 (Daimler-Benz), for just three cases.

Having the ECU sense and perform differently when the hood is open is a big red flag for investigators now. The vehicle must run the same in the emissions lab as it does for customers on the road.

Notable Defeat Infractions

Among the hours of training that I received regarding defeat devices as an OEM calibration engineer, several legends were passed along as examples of companies getting caught with defeat devices. The following are some of the most notable infractions.

GM Hood Latch Switch

The formal procedure for the FTP-75 test includes running the vehicle on a stationary chassis dynamometer where only the driven wheels are moving. To cool the vehicle, a specific fan is used to blow across the front of the vehicle while the hood is allowed to remain open to aid cooling. On the road, one cannot drive with the hood up like this, so this condition clearly indicates that the vehicle is being tested rather than driven normally. In this case, it was found that the ECU was connected to a hood switch that triggered a different fuel map that affected tailpipe emissions (allowing it to pass).

As a result of this infraction, the EPA is now on the lookout for hood-switch connections to (or logic within) the ECU. When I worked on the Chevrolet Volt Hybrid, I had to insert a dummy hood anchor into the latch at the top of the radiator to make the hood switch close when testing, even if the physical hood was up.

Cadillac Air-Conditioning Switch

Activation of the climate control system triggered an enrichment of the air-fuel mixture that increased torque to offset the losses associated with driving the air-conditioning compressor. This added richness significantly increased carbon monoxide emissions, but it only occurred when the air conditioner was active, which does not happen on the FTP-75.

This infraction ultimately led to the creation of new federal test cycles that all manufacturers (and now aftermarket performance companies looking to obtain a CARB exemption) must pass. These new Supplemental FTP (SFTP) cycles became known as US06 and SC03. SC03 specifically is run in a heated chamber with the climate-control system set to keep the interior at a cool temperature while still monitoring tailpipe emissions.

Ford Lean Cruise Mode

At one point in the mid-1990s, Ford Motor Company was found to have implemented logic into its ECU that would change the target air-fuel ratio of some vehicles when operated at a steady highway speed. It recognized these smooth-throttle, constant-speed conditions and shifted the target ratio to one that was slightly lean of stoichiometric.

While this does indeed have a modest improvement in thermal efficiency of combustion and a slight improvement in fuel economy, a leaner burn is hot enough at the flame's tip to significantly increase formation of oxides of nitrogen (NO_x), which falls under the current emissions-monitoring rules. Because the federal test procedures do not have a truly steady-state operation, this feature would not be active during certification and therefore evaded the rules until caught.

This particular violation earned Ford a $7.9 million consent decree from the EPA and eventually led to a new series of tests for automakers. Now, all programs must pass a series of steady-state on-road tests known as "9-bag." This is when the vehicle is driven on a freeway with the cruise control set at a series of constant speeds between 30 mph and 85 mph and emissions are checked with a portable emissions monitoring system (PEMS).

Each speed breakpoint (30, 50, 60, 65, 70, 75, 80, then 85 mph) is held for approximately 600 seconds, which ensures that any rich or lean imbalance would eventually saturate the catalyst and show up in tailpipe emissions as checked by the PEMS. OEM calibration engineers must ensure that not only are their closed-loop control switch points centered on the stoichiometric mixture but also that the excursions to the rich and lean sides are balanced over time to pass this test.

Critically, this also means that large vehicles that are tested this way cannot use catalyst-cooling fuel enrichment when delivering the power required to match their road loads (rolling losses and wind drag) at 85 mph if they want to pass. While this sounds easy in concept, getting a real vehicle to do this with a tight balance in real-world driving conditions can keep a single engineer busy for months. It has also driven hardware design changes on several programs I have seen over the years to make sure that catalyst cooling did not become an issue at constant 85-mph speeds.

"Dieselgate"

In 2014, a group of researchers at West Virginia University were among a group commissioned by CARB to study emissions discrepancies between US and European models of vehicles. During their testing, it was found that some Volkswagen diesel-powered cars would get significantly better emissions results when run in a stationary laboratory setting compared to what was seen when the vehicle was equipped with a portable emissions monitoring system (PEMS, see sidebar).

Upon further investigation, it was discovered that logic existed inside the ECU that detected motion from the vehicle's stability-control accelerometer. Based on this measured acceleration, or lack thereof, engine operating conditions were changed that significantly degraded tailpipe emissions when the vehicle was tested in a laboratory as opposed to actually moving on the road. Effectively, they had created a hidden test detection algorithm that would force the vehicle to run clean when following the published test procedure but allowed customers a different driving experience with more harmful emissions.

Clearly, the regulators were not amused by this obvious attempt to skirt the rules across so many vehicles. Once proven, the violation garnered fierce repercussions. Volkswagen leadership was questioned before Congress, and resignations and firings quickly followed as the facts became public.

In April 2017, a US federal judge ordered Volkswagen to pay a $2.8 billion fine for "rigging diesel-powered vehicles to cheat on government emissions tests." The total cost of the scandal likely topped more than $33 billion in fines, penalties, and financial settlements, and it forced vehicle buybacks. This doesn't account for the damage done in the eyes of the public to the reputation of all modern diesel passenger cars that were once adored for their fuel efficiency and quiet operation.

The Volkswagen scandal also put immediate extra scrutiny on all other manufacturers of diesel passenger cars and light trucks. The effects of which were felt shortly thereafter with similar accusations at Fiat Chrysler Automobiles (FCA) (now Stellantis) with their own investigations and subsequent settlements.

Beyond that, future emissions certification routines now include more real-world driving measurements (using a PEMS) rather than just laboratory dynamometer-based testing. This forces the engineering teams to explore many more possible failure points during the development process, which adds costs to the program and ultimately to the vehicle's price tag for the consumer.

While these examples of defeat devices got the manufacturers in hot water with regulatory agencies, cases remain where controls or elements of design are allowed that may impact emissions. These are known within the industry as auxiliary emissions control devices (AECDs).

The logic states that while all defeat devices are AECDs, not all AECDs are defeat devices. The trick is that they must be disclosed ahead of time to the regulatory agencies, and their operation must not cause the vehicle to pollute excessively.

Features that add fuel to control exhaust-component temperatures increase the output of carbon monoxide, so they fall under this category. What makes them allowable is that they are only adding the minimum amount necessary to affect protection and that they are a part of the normal operation of the vehicle outside the emissions-cycle testing. There are also exemptions for emergency and military vehicles due to their high priority for response time and public safety.

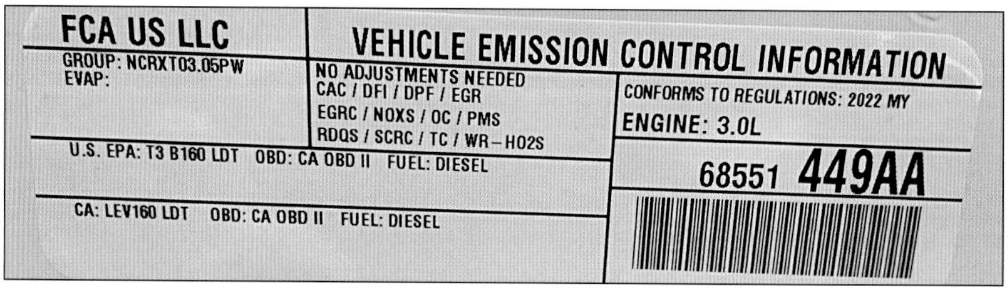

FCA was forced to implement a series of software updates in the controls of the 3.0L diesel engine to ensure compliance with emissions regulations in the wake of the "Dieselgate" scandals.

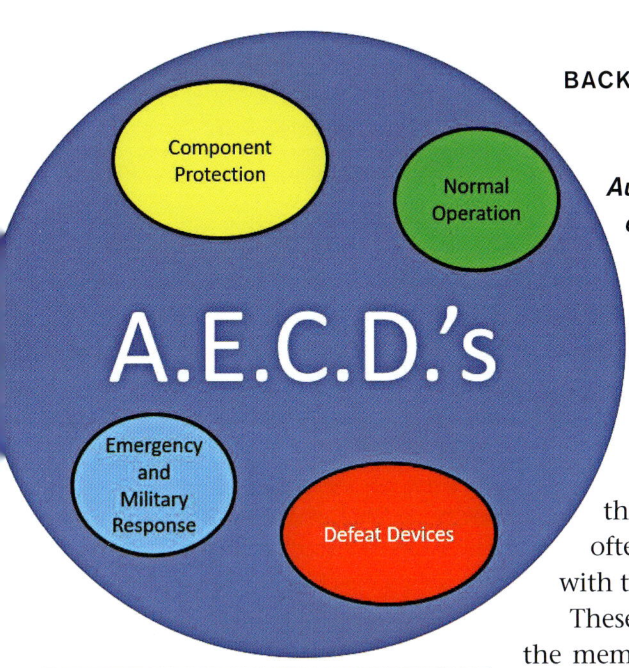

Auxiliary emissions control devices (AECDs) include many different functions that are allowed for safety. Engineers must be careful to make sure that their new functions do not also qualify as defeat devices.

Controls for actuators, such as these muffler bypass valves, would be deemed an auxiliary emissions control device (AECD). In their open state, volumetric efficiency changes, which may impact emissions.

What Is OBD-III?

For years, rumors have swirled in the automotive industry regarding what emissions and diagnostic requirements will be in the future. We saw the shift from basic monitoring (OBD) to the inclusion of plausibility checks and onboard stored information with OBD-II. Modern ECUs now not only run their diagnostic monitors and store the pass/fail results but they also keep track of how often this has happened along with the passing percentage.

These results are written into the memory of the ECU and can be retrieved under OBD-II-mandated protocols with a proper service-tool interface as long as the request follows the established procedure. Many state vehicle inspections are performed in this exact manner.

In parallel to these developments, other areas of the vehicle have marched forward with their own technological advances. Consumers have enjoyed an incredible amount of integration between their vehicle and other aspects of their daily life. Radio displays shifted from single-line LCD displays to screens large enough to display maps and help drivers navigate to their destinations. GPS location capability was quickly integrated to these maps to allow for real-time updates to the vehicle's position. Cell phones now connect to the radio to allow for hands-free calling, dialing, and even navigation through their own GPS connection. Emergency contact services were added, where the vehicle is able to reach out in the event of a collision and request help on its own.

This emergency connection is the vehicle's independent connection to the outside world that can be expanded to include other data. In fact, the emergency contact is triggered outside of the radio from a signal generated in the airbag or stability control modules elsewhere on the vehicle's internal communication bus. These modules already share a high-speed network connection with the ECU, as "black box" data is stored in the event of a crash that includes things such as engine speed and throttle position.

Today's vehicles offer the option of being their own Wi-Fi hub as well, now that they are connected to the internet. It is a short leap to a situation where this large amount of previously onboard-only information about diagnostics can be broadcast over the internet to another destination for monitoring. This is essentially what OBD-III is.

These advances have the possibility to eliminate the need for the vehicle to physically appear at a state inspection station to transmit its diagnostic status and history. The vehicle can now "phone home" to report any anomalies or a clean status on demand.

The uses for this live connection to vehicles extend beyond monitoring. The OEMs can now also use this same connection to deliver live updates to any module in the vehicle on demand. This means that flash-over-the-air (FOTA) technology can be used to send updates that would have otherwise required a visit to the dealership to resolve emissions, drivability, or quality issues for customers. The signal is simply sent to the network, and each vehicle can download, store, and then execute the update when parked.

While this is great news for some, it comes as an annoyance to others. The high-performance industry in particular faces challenges with FOTA updates. Many engine performance upgrades require that the ECU be reflashed with a new calibration

PEMS

The portable emissions monitoring system (PEMS) is a term used to describe an apparatus that can be easily added to almost any vehicle to measure its emissions when driven outside of the laboratory environment. The device is small enough to be carried by one person, is self-powered, and can be set up in a short amount of time. It is primarily used to measure real-world on-road emissions performance in situations that are not easily replicated in the tightly controlled environment of a multimillion-dollar Part 1066 compliant emissions test cell. The PEMS is small enough to allow the vehicle to operate as it would normally in traffic. Typically, it is either fitted in the trunk area of the vehicle or attached to a bracket that hangs off the back bumper near the trailer hitch.

PEMS may employ several methods of data collection, depending on what measurements are desired and with what degree of accuracy. Flame ionization detection (FID, or "Fast FID"), Fourier transform infrared detection (FTIR), and non-dispersive infrared detection (NDIR) all offer a high degree of accuracy in identifying individual species of molecules in a sample. Essentially, they find the chemical "fingerprint" of a molecule.

The FID combines the exhaust sample with a controlled hydrogen flame and measures the ions generated with two electrodes. The chemical makeup of the substance is based on the charge generated between the two electrodes.

The FTIR passes infrared radiation (light outside of the visible spectrum) through the sample. As some of this radiation is absorbed, the resulting signal can be analyzed to determine the species of chemicals present.

NDIR also passes a light through the sample, but it uses a light filter on the detector element to select specific wavelengths. By focusing on a single element at a time, the amount of signal caused by the sample absorbing light in that wavelength correlates to the concentration present in the sample. Unlike FTIR, which measures a broad spectrum of wavelengths simultaneously, the NDIR attempts to measure them one at a time.

These broadband measurement systems come at a price. Most are well over $100,000, with reference units from AVL and Horiba currently costing just under $500,000 each. There has been relatively good correlation between these portable units and the CVS column in a 1065-compliant laboratory. This allows both regulatory agencies and private companies to quickly test vehicles under a wide range of operating conditions in the real world without tying up scarce laboratory resources.

Mini PEMS

In addition to the highly specific chemical species measurements available from FID, FTIR, and NDIR systems, there is also work being done with simpler setups to catch more obvious emissions faults. The "mini PEMS" system combines a series of more affordable and compact sensors together with thermocouples, OBD ECU data, and GPS tracking to paint a picture of current vehicle emissions.

Rather than an exact measurement of each chemical,

A gasoline engine with another portable emissions monitoring system is tested to quickly assess cold-start emissions performance. These instruments can save a great deal of expensive laboratory time during development.

The ECM mini PEMS system is installed on a diesel pickup truck for a demonstration at the University of California, Riverside. This system can be installed in minutes to quickly generate a signature of the vehicle's emissions performance.

PEMS *continued*

the system tracks excursions of air-fuel ratio and NO_x with one sensor, particulates with another, and uses known vehicle parameters combined with GPS-based speed and acceleration to determine horsepower and exhaust flow rates. Thermocouplers are used to detect when the catalyst has activated by showing the sharp increase in temperature across it once the conversion efficiency increases and it begins reacting to leftover exhaust constituents.

The mini PEMS is accurate enough to quickly catch gross polluters where the catalyst is not functioning; the engine is consistently running too rich or lean; or NO_x is high due to combustion, EGR, or camshaft control issues. As more data is collected with these systems, models are being built to compare to FID, FTIR, NDIR, and constant volume sampling (CVS) column laboratory data.

The cost for mini PEMS systems is a fraction of the cost of reference PEMS systems. This has the potential to make them a practical widespread solution for validation of in-use emissions, provided that the governing bodies can agree on a standard and reporting format.

While neither of these matches the final precision of the CVS column seen in a 1065-certified emissions laboratory, they are accurate enough to make an assessment of compliance for on-road testing. The EPA and CARB continue to investigate the feasibility of such on-vehicle measurements as they look toward the next generation of emissions regulations. ■

EV Emissions

I spent years as part of the development team for the first Chevrolet Volt plug-in Hybrid. During testing, the team looked closely at the tradeoff between gasoline and electric power under all conditions.

If you think electric vehicles (EVs) are zero emissions, think again. The whole concept of EVs being zero emissions comes with a giant asterisk where the fine print reads "at the back of the vehicle." The cold, hard truth is that the tailpipe for electric vehicles is miles away if not scattered around the world.

Let's start with a obvious question: "Where does the power come from?" To the simplest consumer, the answer is an electrical connection at their home or favorite charging station. The electricity that is available at that charging connection came from somewhere.

In the United States, the vast majority (more than 60 percent) of electrical generation comes from fossil fuels. Roughly two thirds of this from natural gas (which is mostly methane), and most of the remainder is from coal. Luckily, the United States is extremely rich in coal deposits, so as long as we can keep mining it and feeding it to our powerplants, the lights stay on and EVs can zip around quietly. But both of these fuels require combustion in the burner of a powerplant to boil steam and drive a mechanical turbine.

One of the key lessons in engineering school is that any time energy changes state, the process is always less than 100-percent efficient. Stick with me here as we walk from the stored chemical energy in the fossil fuels to miles driven in an EV.

First, the mined fuel must be freed from the earth, refined, and transported for use at the powerplant. This is roughly a wash when compared to our use of oil to make gasoline that is available at stations around the world. Both networks are rather efficient for transporting their respective fuels, but both consume a fair amount of energy on their own just to make the fuel available. Those mining rigs, transport trucks, trains, ships, and support vehicles are all thirsty as well.

Getting back to the powerplant, fossil fuel with stored chemical energy is burned and converted into thermal energy that boils water into steam. Again, if you have ever boiled a pot of water on your stove, you have a small appreciation for the losses here, as much of that heat escapes. The thermal energy converts into fluid work as steam travels through pipes with non-zero losses until it drives a mechanical turbine to perform mechanical shaft work at a generator. The efficiency of modern power generation plants varies, but the losses can be shocking to those who have never seen them. Natural gas–fired plants can be relatively good, losing only about 55 percent of the

EV Emissions *continued*

energy before creating electricity. Other types of powerplants are closer to 65-percent losses.

We now have high-voltage electricity, but it must be transferred long distances over wires, which again have their own losses. The high voltage must then go through a transformer to reduce it to a safer household level and then through yet another transformer to step it back up above EV battery voltage for charging. "Charging" is just a fancy way of hiding yet another energy conversion from electrical back into chemical energy within the battery pack.

Finally, the onboard stored chemical energy must be converted back to electrical energy that is fed to a drive motor that can convert it to mechanical torque that drives the vehicle. Conservatively, we have about 10 exchanges here compared to the internal combustion–powered vehicle's 3. High-voltage system losses are typically around 4 percent in transmission and another 4 percent in distribution.

Even if every other step in the EVs energy conversions was 96 percent efficient, we would have lost about 70 percent of the "well to wheel" energy in the many processes of conversion. In a grid like the United States, where 60 percent of the power comes from such combustion, it cannot be ignored when talking about emissions and the efficiency of electric vehicles.

But what about the other 40 percent of power generation? Wind, solar, hydroelectric, and nuclear power all seem attractive, especially when talking about charging an "Earth-saving" EV. Even though these sources eliminate the combustion problem, they still come with their own maintenance and relative efficiencies in addition to the transmission and distribution losses mentioned earlier. The manufacturing of wind turbines today consumes almost as much energy as the finished turbine will eventually generate. Add to that the troubling reality that used wind turbine blades find their way to landfills at the end of a fixed life, as they are not currently recycled. Nuclear powerplants operate at efficiencies close to coal-fired powerplants, unfortunately. The trick here is that nuclear plants trade production of CO_2 and carbon monoxide for nuclear waste that must still be stored safely.

All of this and we still haven't addressed the elephant in the room. The battery itself represents an extremely large impact to the Earth, using today's manufacturing methods and technology. Lithium-ion packs require large amounts of the Earth to be strip mined and processed to get the raw lithium, a process largely done by large diesel-powered equipment with almost no emissions aftertreatment compared to light-duty passenger vehicles.

Other associated battery chemicals, such as cobalt, are acquired in a similar manner. Many of these deposits are far away in remote regions, so not only must they be mined but also transported to a port where they are loaded onto ships that burn low-grade fuels. Bunker fuel in giant marine diesel engines have next to zero emissions controls, and they travel halfway around the globe to a battery-manufacturing plant. The resulting heavy batteries must then be shipped to a vehicle-manufacturing facility, just like engines—only heavier.

All of these mining, manufacturing, transmission, distribution, storage, and conversion losses mean that every mile driven by an EV requires slightly more energy to be generated in the first place. It is anything but pollution free. Now that we're back to driving miles with the EV, we recognize that the greater weight of most EVs when compared to their internal combustion or hybrid counterparts requires more energy to get up to speed and produces greater rolling losses once moving too. Yes, a portion of this is recovered during regenerative braking, where the EV motor turns kinetic energy into a charge for the battery, but there's two more conversion losses there when the energy goes from kinetic to electrical to chemical again.

Once we consider the losses associated in electrical power generation, distribution, and propulsion, we have a relatively close efficiency of around 30 percent for both internal-combustion and electric vehicles. There is no free lunch. The internal-combustion vehicles must still be accountable for their tailpipe emissions. As a result, the automotive industry has gotten quite good at reducing the emissions per mile driven to incredibly low numbers. The same cannot always be said for the support network behind EVs today. Hopefully, time will show the EV industry advancing in a similar manner as more demands are placed on the electrical grid. ■

to properly work with the new hardware, such as a supercharger or other induction package change. Many of these packages have been certified through the CARB EO process as clean and legal with respect to emissions, so the ECU calibration change is an integral part of the package that must not be changed. An unexpected FOTA update to one of these vehicles is an inconvenience at best and potentially dangerous in other cases. As such, the vehicle's ability to receive these over-the-air updates must either be disabled or the vehicle must be re-flashed with an updated program after each FOTA instance before it is driven.

ADAS

The SEMA Garage in Detroit has recognized the importance of the advanced driver assistance system (ADAS) operation in modified vehicles. To help members better test these new systems, it installed an ADAS calibration room at its new facility.

In recent years, as vehicles have become progressively more connected, they have also brought new safety features and driver aids. The amount of electronics in a modern vehicle is absolutely staggering compared to those just a few decades ago.

There was a time when computer-controlled anti-lock braking systems were state of the art with regard to helping bring the vehicle safely to a stop in an emergency. Today's vehicles now use a suite of sensors, cameras, logic, and controls to detect a possible collision and automatically apply the maximum possible braking effort if needed to avoid the collision. This automated emergency braking (AEB) system was the first step toward driverless function.

However, it wasn't just emergency braking that appeared. Those same cameras could now be trained to recognize lane lines and alert the driver if they drift from their current lane. Alerts were eventually tied to actual steering correction once hydraulic power-steering systems were replaced with electronic-assist hardware. In addition to freeing up some otherwise-lost parasitic power on the crankshaft from the power-steering pump, these systems opened a gateway to allow both stability control and safety systems that could make meaningful course corrections at the request of another computer on the vehicle's network.

Blending all of these driver aids together, we now have what is known as an advanced driver assistance system (ADAS). Through the combination of sensors and actuators, the ADAS can now also perform pedestrian detection/avoidance, traffic-sign recognition, and blind-spot detection along with the basic functions of stability control and stopping mentioned above.

ADAS allows for "smart" cruise control, where the vehicle recognizes changes in the posted speed limit and has the authority to change the setpoint for vehicle speed control accordingly. This means that a camera detecting a change in the numbers on a speed-limit sign can lead to a change in electronic throttle-control position through the use of the network already in place.

There are also diagnostics that check to make sure these changes were made appropriately, and errors are stored when present. Clearly, the stakes get elevated quite a bit when automated computers have authority over what have been traditionally very driver-regulated features, such as steering, throttle, and braking. Diagnosing any faults in this system becomes critical for occupant safety in addition to emissions.

The aftermarket must also be aware of these complex interactions. Because these ADASs are so carefully designed at the OEM, they can be rendered inoperable by modifications that were previously not much of a concern.

Lowering a sports car or sedan in the name of handling and appearance or raising a truck for more off-road ground clearance can change the view of the cameras enough to upset their readings and force the control system to make improper adjustments. Ultrasonic or radar-based systems, such as blind-spot detection or park assist, may also no longer be aimed correctly, missing cues when it's time to alert the driver before a collision.

In today's litigious society, no one wants to cause accidents or disable a safety system that may have prevented one. As such, both aftermarket parts manufacturers and the Specialty Equipment Market Association (SEMA) have stepped up testing capabilities for ADAS-equipped vehicles to help make sure that new products aimed at these modern vehicles are able to perform as safely as possible on the road. So important is this new line of testing that SEMA has dedicated almost half the space in its new SEMA Garage in Detroit to testing ADAS alongside its already very capable emissions testing laboratory to support the aftermarket industry.

Uses of OBD

Understanding what OBD-II is leads to the next step of how it is used. The integration of individual component diagnostics, requirements to be precise enough to capture potential emissions issues, execution of specific monitors, data collection, and read/write capability all open the door for many uses of the OBD system. While many of these are intertwined, we will look at them independently for now.

At this point, let's review what is meant by "modes." By definition, any system that adheres to the structures set forth by the SAE in standard J1979 must return a response to specific requests. Each of these requests is grouped into "modes" that are numbered and have their own uses.

It is important to note that these are presented in numbered order based on their labels, not necessarily in the order in which one might encounter or wish to use them in practice. While this may be a bit confusing at first, they are being presented here in that order for clean reference. We will dive deeper into how they are used later.

Mode	Description
Mode $01	Live data
Mode $02	Freeze-frame data
Mode $03	Current faults
Mode $04	Clear faults
Mode $05	Oxygen sensor monitoring
Mode $06	Specific monitor results
Mode $07	Pending faults, monitors
Mode $08	Special controls
Mode $09	Vehicle information
Mode $0A	Permanent faults

Mode $01

You're not reading that wrong. Yes, there is a dollar sign in the official

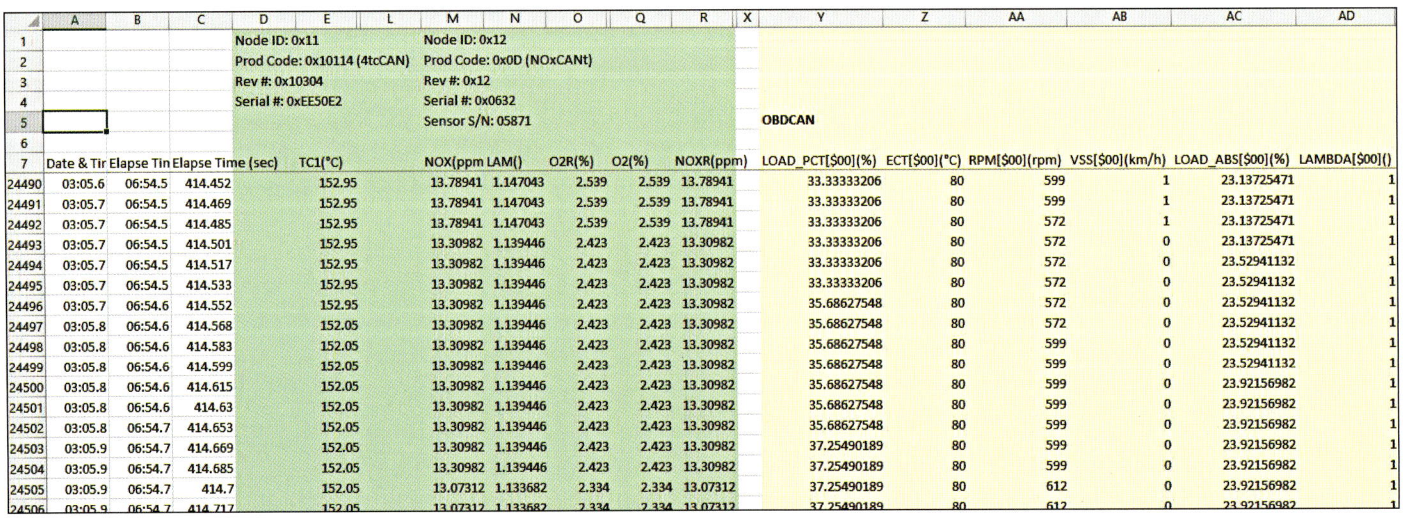

	A	B	C	D	E	L	M	N	O	Q	R	X	Y	Z	AA	AB	AC	AD
1				Node ID: 0x11			Node ID: 0x12											
2				Prod Code: 0x10114 (4tcCAN)			Prod Code: 0x0D (NOxCANt)											
3				Rev #: 0x10304			Rev #: 0x12											
4				Serial #: 0xEE50E2			Serial #: 0x0632											
5							Sensor S/N: 05871						OBDCAN					
6																		
7	Date & Tir	Elapse Tin	Elapse Time (sec)		TC1(°C)		NOX(ppm	LAM()	O2R(%)	O2(%)	NOXR(ppm)		LOAD_PCT[$00](%)	ECT[$00](°C)	RPM[$00](rpm)	VSS[$00](km/h)	LOAD_ABS[$00](%)	LAMBDA[$00]()
24490	03:05.6	06:54.5	414.452		152.95		13.78941	1.147043	2.539	2.539	13.78941		33.33333206	80	599	1	23.13725471	1
24491	03:05.7	06:54.5	414.469		152.95		13.78941	1.147043	2.539	2.539	13.78941		33.33333206	80	599	1	23.13725471	1
24492	03:05.7	06:54.5	414.485		152.95		13.78941	1.147043	2.539	2.539	13.78941		33.33333206	80	572	1	23.13725471	1
24493	03:05.7	06:54.5	414.501		152.95		13.30982	1.139446	2.423	2.423	13.30982		33.33333206	80	572	0	23.13725471	1
24494	03:05.7	06:54.5	414.517		152.95		13.30982	1.139446	2.423	2.423	13.30982		33.33333206	80	572	0	23.52941132	1
24495	03:05.7	06:54.5	414.533		152.95		13.30982	1.139446	2.423	2.423	13.30982		33.33333206	80	572	0	23.52941132	1
24496	03:05.7	06:54.6	414.552		152.95		13.30982	1.139446	2.423	2.423	13.30982		35.68627548	80	572	0	23.52941132	1
24497	03:05.8	06:54.6	414.568		152.05		13.30982	1.139446	2.423	2.423	13.30982		35.68627548	80	572	0	23.52941132	1
24498	03:05.8	06:54.6	414.583		152.05		13.30982	1.139446	2.423	2.423	13.30982		35.68627548	80	599	0	23.52941132	1
24499	03:05.8	06:54.6	414.599		152.05		13.30982	1.139446	2.423	2.423	13.30982		35.68627548	80	599	0	23.52941132	1
24500	03:05.8	06:54.6	414.615		152.05		13.30982	1.139446	2.423	2.423	13.30982		35.68627548	80	599	0	23.92156982	1
24501	03:05.8	06:54.6	414.63		152.05		13.30982	1.139446	2.423	2.423	13.30982		35.68627548	80	599	0	23.92156982	1
24502	03:05.8	06:54.7	414.653		152.05		13.30982	1.139446	2.423	2.423	13.30982		35.68627548	80	599	0	23.92156982	1
24503	03:05.9	06:54.7	414.669		152.05		13.30982	1.139446	2.423	2.423	13.30982		37.25490189	80	599	0	23.92156982	1
24504	03:05.9	06:54.7	414.685		152.05		13.30982	1.139446	2.423	2.423	13.30982		37.25490189	80	599	0	23.92156982	1
24505	03:05.9	06:54.7	414.7		152.05		13.07312	1.133682	2.334	2.334	13.07312		37.25490189	80	612	0	23.92156982	1
24506	03:05.9	06:54.7	414.717		152.05		13.07312	1.133682	2.334	2.334	13.07312		37.25490189	80	612	0	23.92156982	1

Any tool that can access the communication bus and request data has the ability to poll at least generic ECU data from Mode $01. This tool from the ECM actually integrates ECM data (yellow region, right) with emissions sensors (green region, left) into a single file for engineers to review.

name of each of the OBD-II data modes. It is not pronounced in normal discussion, but that's how it's written. The first of these would simply be called "Mode 1" in conversation. Mode $01 is actually quite specialized, and it opens the door for access to a tremendous amount of data. It is not usually the first stop when investigating a potential issue in a malfunctioning vehicle, but it remains incredibly useful nonetheless.

Mode $01 allows access to specific data values in real time by requesting the values of individual parameter identifiers (PIDs). SAE J1979 set forth a list of universal values that must be accessible that return the values currently seen by most common engine sensors, calculated or estimated values, and commanded values for various systems. All of these are displayed in their native engineering units rather than a cryptic hexadecimal value that must be later decoded. Status bits for a wide range of monitors are also included in Mode $01.

PID	Description	Mandatory or Optional
0	PIDs supported (01–20)	Mandatory
1	Monitor status since DTCs cleared	Mandatory
2	DTC that caused required freeze-frame data storage	Mandatory
4	Calculated load value	Mandatory
5	Engine coolant temperature	Mandatory
OC	Engine RPM	Mandatory
OD	Vehicle speed sensor	Mandatory
1C	OBD requirements to which vehicle or engine is certified	Mandatory
20	PIDs supported (21–40)	Mandatory
21	Distance traveled while MIL is activated	Mandatory
30	Number of warmups since DTCs cleared	Mandatory
31	Distance since DTCs cleared	Mandatory
OB	Intake manifold absolute pressure	Optional
OF	Intake air temperature	Optional
10	Airflow rate from mass airflow sensor	Optional
1F	Time since engine start	Optional
42	Control module voltage	Optional

The SAE has specified a minimum amount of information that must be reported by the ECU under all conditions. Manufacturers have the option to add even more data to the bus as well, which is available by specific request using Mode $01.

Many basic code scanners do not query or display the Mode $01 data even though they are on the bus already and are collecting fault codes from another mode. Other universal tools will grab only these generic SAE values specified here and nothing else. While this can be entertaining (and even useful) to technicians and end users, those looking to do more, involving ECU recalibration or tuning work, eventually require more than just the generic SAE PIDs.

The SAE specification states a data rate and resolution at which these PIDs are to be returned when requested. For basic diagnosis and repairs, this is usually just fine. More advanced scan tools, and many computer-based logging programs, use Mode $01 requests to gather large amounts of data over time to display as either strip charts or histograms that make it easier to see specific events or correlate measurements with each other. By requesting manufacturer-specific PIDs or direct-memory reads (DMRs), the logging software can access even high levels of resolution and data rates that can now support engineering-level analysis.

Mode $02

This mode is often the second stop when checking for a current issue on a vehicle. Mode $02 stores the conditions that were present when an MIL was triggered (and stored in Mode $03). Referred to as the "freeze-frame data," this information helps paint a picture of what was happening when a fault occurred. This can steer the technician toward possible causes as well as provide a way to check the robustness of any repair that is made by replicating these conditions afterward.

Data here includes calculated engine load, coolant temperature, open/closed-loop fueling status, fuel trims, fuel pressure, MAP, engine speed, vehicle speed, and the fault code that triggered the recording. In the event that multiple failures and fault codes have been registered, Mode $02 should have multiple instances of stored freeze-frame data with one set for each fault code that is present.

PID	Description	Value	Units
0x02	DTC that caused required freeze-frame data shortage	P0112	—
0x04	Calculated load value	0	percent
0x05	Engine coolant temperature	23	°C
0x0B	Intake manifold absolute pressure	97	kPa
0x0C	Engine RPM	0	RPM
0x0D	Vehicle speed	0	km/h
0x10	Airflow rate from mass flow sensor	0	gm/sec

Whenever a fault code is stored, the ECU also takes a snapshot of the conditions present at the time of the fault. These can be handy if the technician has trouble easily replicating the fault.

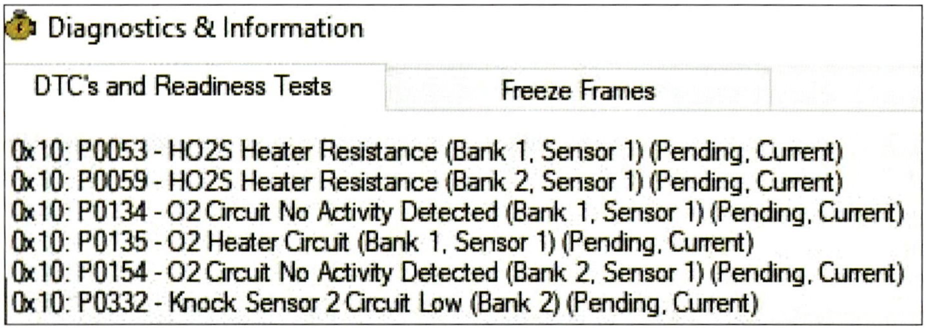

When querying the ECU for faults, tools usually include data from Modes $03 and $07 together (as seen here). This particular vehicle appears to need inspection of the oxygen sensors.

Mode $03

This request asks the ECU for a list of current fault codes. Mode $03 is usually the first stop for anyone entering into OBD data looking for an explanation as to why a vehicle is not running properly. This includes the current reason the MIL is on, but it may return more than one fault code at a time. Often, codes that are grouped together give the technician more information.

Just because there is no fault code stored here in Mode $03 does not mean that the vehicle is running perfectly. It just means that whatever may be wrong is not so bad that it has tripped the fault in the diagnostic to illuminate the MIL. It often takes multiple trips to set a stored fault, so the first occurrence may not be enough to leave a telltale sign here—even if the fault is severe enough to fail the diagnostic. Pending codes are stored in Mode $07 rather than here in Mode $03 in cases where the diagnostic may have failed once, which isn't enough to set the MIL just yet.

Mode $04

Used to clear stored and current trouble codes, Mode $04 is probably the favorite among readers. This

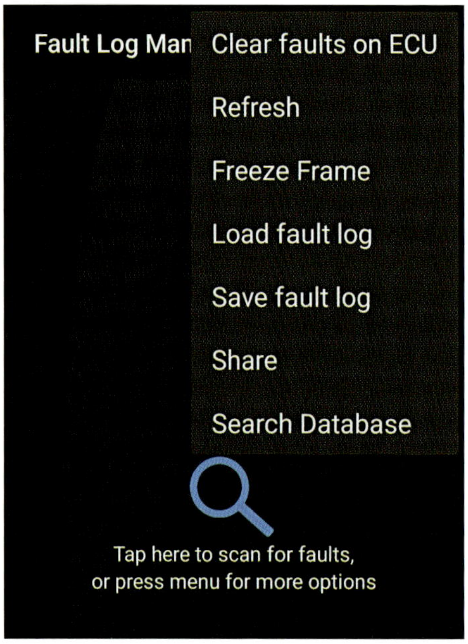

Sending the Mode $04 request to clear faults can be as simple as tapping the screen on your phone with a connected smartphone application, such as TorquePro and a bluetooth OBD dongle.

mode allows the user to clear the faults and reset the MIL, but it does nothing to prevent it from coming right back on if the problem persists.

Yes, it is a critical part of the repair process, but only the laziest of repairs will consider this to be "the fix" without other actions. It should also be noted that some manufacturers store "permanent" faults that cannot be reset with generic scan tools and the SAE Mode $04 request. These are stored in Mode $0A and require more specific messaging laid out by the OEM so that a dealership technician can see important history of faults that may lead to a certain investigation path.

One example of this is a crank sensor fault on a GM vehicle. Because this sensor is so critical to the operation of so many other functions in the ECU, any fault here is worth noting. Only the OEM-approved tool can send the right request to erase it unless the vehicle is repaired and it passes the associated diagnostic monitor again on its own a prescribed number of times.

Mode $05

One of the lesser used modes, Mode $05 supports the oxygen sensors, their status, and monitor results. This mode is rarely used since most technicians will look to Mode $01 for data that includes not only the oxygen sensors but also supporting information on fuel delivery, airflow, and learned trims at the same time. Mode $05 is also not available on newer vehicles that have a controller area network (CAN) communication system to link the various modules on board. For those vehicles, one would go directly to Mode $06 to get the oxygen sensor monitoring results.

Mode $06

Mode $06 provides an advanced diagnostic mode where one can access specific test results. These are the individual tests that make up the monitors reported out in Mode $07 and $09. Along with the latest test results, Mode $06 also has the ability to display the working limits for each test. This allows for comparison of the current value to the limit to help detect components that have not yet failed but are approaching the limits. This may prove to be useful in cases where the issue is more elusive, such as misfires or evaporative system issues. Originally, this mode was never intended for use by technicians, and access to it requires a very specific interface tool configuration to match the vehicle application.

Most generic scan tools do not support this more complex communication, so they simply leave it out of their options on the display in the first place. Worse yet, even if accessed, the data can be very confusing or misleading if one does not have the right "decoder ring" that matches the exact vehicle being tested. This is one area where OBD-II standards do not apply, so it's not uncommon to see different manufacturers configure their Mode $06 data in a unique fashion.

Some applications may even return data for tests that the vehicle is not even capable of running, such as misfires on cylinders 7 and 8 of a V-6 engine or for sensors that do not exist on the vehicle. As they say, "Bad data can be worse than no data," so proceed with caution if attempting to use this during diagnosis because it's easy to get steered down the wrong path if the data is translated incorrectly.

If a tool is configured to properly read Mode $06 data, the tester may find data sorted by test identification (TID) and component identification (CID). In CAN–equipped vehicles, TID is replaced by monitor identification (MID).

The TID or MID indicates the monitor group to which the test belongs. The CID describes the individual component test within each monitor group. Both are often listed in hexadecimal similar to the mode numbers, appearing as something like MID$31 and CID$85, respectively, for a late-model Ford EGR monitor and its delta pressure EGR flow test.

Mode $06 Monitors for a Late-Model CAN-Equipped Ford	
MID$01	Oxygen sensor
MID$02	Oxygen sensor
MID$03	Oxygen sensor
MID$05	Oxygen sensor
MID$06	Oxygen sensor
MID$07	Oxygen sensor
MID$21	Catalyst monitor
MID$22	Catalyst monitor
MID$31	EGR monitor
MID$32	EGR monitor
MID$33	EGR stepper motor
MID$3A	EVAP monitor
MID$3B	EVAP monitor
MID$3C	EVAP monitor
MID$71	Air injection monitor
MID$A1	Misfire monitor
MID$A2 through MID$AB	Misfire monitors for each cylinder

Mode $07

The request for onboard monitor results is handled in Mode $07. SAE J1979 has specified system readiness separately for spark-ignited and compression-ignition (diesel) engines. The first in both cases is the misfire monitor, which runs continuously on all ECUs.

The misfire monitor takes up quite a bit of the ECU's processor power because it must closely monitor the crank signal in real time at a rate fast enough to catch any single-cylinder-misfire event, all the way up to and including maximum-rated engine speed. Subsequent monitor groups include fuel

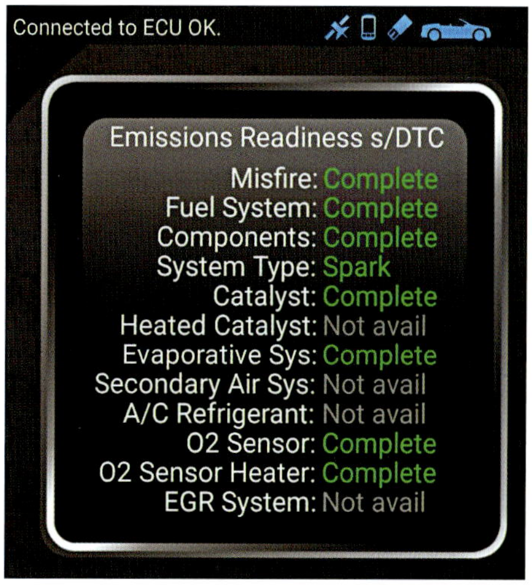

Supported monitors can be viewed with most OBD-II tools. Those labeled as complete have run and passed their diagnostic tests, indicating good operation of the vehicle.

systems, catalysts, oxygen sensors, EGR, and other emissions-related components.

If the vehicle has completed a valid drive cycle similar to what was discussed in the previous chapter, all of the monitors that are enabled for the vehicle should run and pass on that trip if the system is working properly. The ECU keeps track of how many times each monitor has passed when it ran and stores that ratio in Mode $09. Ideally, this should be a very high percentage for a properly running vehicle.

Mode $07 Monitors for Gas and Diesel	
Gasoline engine monitors	Misfire, fuel system, comprehensive components, catalyst, heated catalyst, evaporative (EVAP) system, secondary air system, oxygen (O_2) sensor, oxygen sensor heater, exhaust gas recirculation (EGR), and/or VVT system
Diesel engine monitors	Misfire, fuel system, comprehensive components, NMHC catalyst, NOx/SCR aftertreatment, boost pressure, exhaust gas sensor, PM filter, and EGR and/or VVT system

Some trouble codes are stored here as "Pending" in Mode $07 when the fault has not occurred enough times yet to register as a current trouble code in Mode $03. In many cases, this starts with a monitor that ran but did not pass on this drive cycle, which explains the grouping here in Mode $07.

If the vehicle is experiencing an intermittent issue, this mode may return more useful information than one could get from the generic scan tool alone in Mode $03. Taking it a step further, a skilled technician may look at the history of completions for a specific monitor system stored in Mode $09 data. This compares the number of times each monitor passed to how many times it was run. In a perfect world, these would be the same number, but you also wouldn't be reading this book if vehicles never had faults.

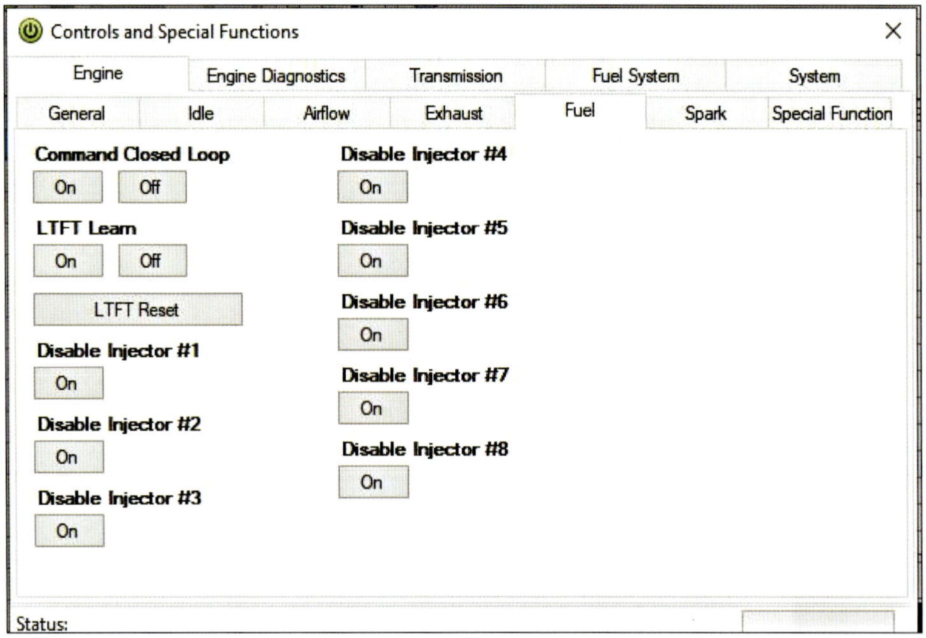

Two-way controls available in some diagnostic tools are actually sending commands to the ECU under OBD-II Mode $08 protocol. Fuel trims or even individual injectors can be temporarily disabled to help narrow down an issue on an engine.

Mode $08

Not all of the OBD-II system is focused on running internal tests within the ECU and reporting the results. Mode $08 allows for external testing to be performed through the use of advanced scan tools or computer software. These tests can actively take over the ECU outputs to individual actuators to allow the technician to check if a part is working or to perform other tests.

At the most basic level is illumination of the MIL to verify that the circuit and light are actually working. However, that is just the tip of the iceberg. Fuel pumps, intercooler pumps, the AC clutch, alternator field, EGR valves, AIR pumps, purge solenoids, and more can be activated on command to test both their circuits and their component functionality.

Before replacing any one of these items, it's always handy to see if they can be forced into operation manually before opening the toolbox and getting dirty. It may be that some other condition is preventing them from working, which may send the technician in a completely different direction for the repair and save some money that would otherwise be wasted on unnecessary replacement parts and labor.

Mode $08 Real-Time Adjustments

The two-way communication and control link doesn't end with simple on-off requests. Mode $08 also provides for some really cool adjustments that can be made in real time. Learned fuel trims can be reset to 0 and held off. This comes in really handy when attempting to diagnose a fuel-delivery issue on one bank.

It is also helpful when diagnosing a specific oxygen sensor fault that may be hard to recognize if the ECU is in normal closed-loop fuel-control mode. This is when the ECU is constantly making adjustments to center fuel delivery around a stoichiometric ratio. Mode $08 is also important for aftermarket calibrators because we don't always have access to the correct closed-loop disabling bits in the ECU calibration. Using Mode $08 to force open-loop fueling (with no corrections being applied) allows the calibrator to see the current fueling error when attempting to correct the airflow model with wideband O_2 sensor data.

These bi-directional controls also allow for some freedom on delivered spark-advance timing, within limits prescribed by the ECU calibration. Used properly, they can slew the delivered spark timing in real time while operating in controlled conditions. One such use would be to find maximum brake torque

EVAP Diagnostics Using Mode $08

The evaporative control system can be one of the trickiest parts of the vehicle to properly diagnose and service. The monitors are calibrated to detect leaks as small as 0.020 inch in diameter, which is impressive considering the size and volume of the fuel tank, the vapor canister, and all associated plumbing.

Should such a small leak be detected by the monitor, actually locating it is still easier said than done. The prevailing instructions for locating these leaks usually revolve around either smoke or pressure testing the system to find the leak. The problem is that the large system volume is also attached to the intake manifold, which also has a path to some cylinders, depending on which valves remain open at the engine's stopped position, as well as the throttle body that does not form an airtight seal.

By accessing the Mode $08 controls, the purge valve near the engine's intake manifold can be forced closed along with the vent solenoid, which is usually closer to the charcoal canister or fuel tank. This combination should effectively seal the evaporative system in most vehicles. Now, a small amount of pressure (or smoke) can be applied through the service port that is usually near the purge solenoid under the hood. This is the same port used by OEM diagnostic calibrators to test the system against the small fixed leaks during development, so it's a solid location to work from when doing your own tests.

If doing a pressure test, don't apply too much pressure since the system is not designed to hold too much. It's possible to apply too much pressure and create yet another leak, as seals can be blown or lines may pop off even as the original failure point remains. After that, it's on to the usual scavenger hunt for the hissing or smoke to locate the leak. ■

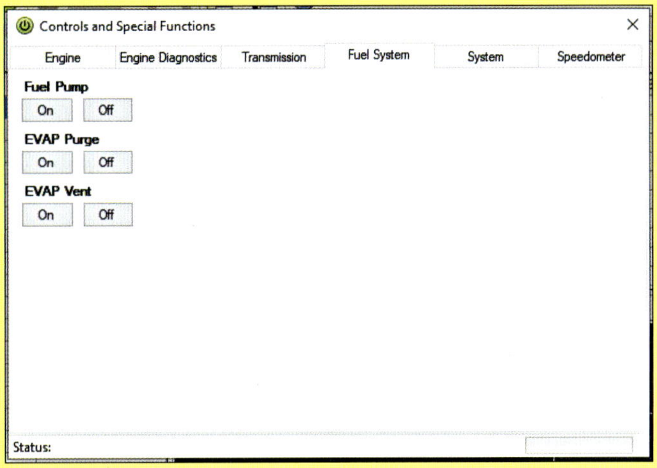

Using the Mode $08 controls to override the evaporative control system status can be useful to identify a stuck valve or a leaking system. Closing the valve and vent makes pressure testing easier.

(MBT) timing on a modified engine by holding a constant engine speed and airflow while on a load-bearing dynamometer. Then, timing changes can be correlated to measured torque on the dyno to identify MBT at various points. Stitching the necessary adjustments together allows a skilled calibrator to quickly make changes to large areas of a spark table to improve combustion quality and efficiency.

It's important to note that I said "while operating in controlled conditions" here. Adding too much spark advance at higher engine loads can lead to knock that can damage the engine. But again, where there is risk lies opportunity as well. Most engines can tolerate modest amounts of spark knock at light loads where the total cylinder pressure isn't as likely to cause component failures. This can be useful to test the knock-sensor circuit.

By adding timing at part load, response from the knock sensor can be seen in real time and confirm that everything is working there. This is essentially the same way the ECU probes the knock sensor during its normal diagnostic with the exception

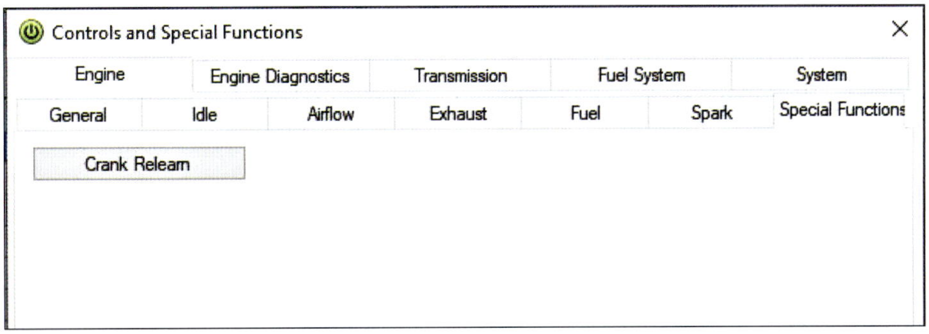

The "crank relearn" function is required on many vehicles after servicing the clutch or the torque convertor. Small deviations in the balance can affect the misfire monitor and engine position determination.

that a human is much slower than the ECU at recognizing knock, so tread with caution here when trying such a test.

Mode $09

A large amount of vehicle information related to the emissions and diagnostic system is stored in Mode $09. This starts with the most basic description, including the vehicle identification number (VIN) stored in both the ECU and the body module. These should match.

Beyond that, the ECU type and a calibration part number or calibration ID (CAL ID) is also logged here that is unique to the calibration values stored in the ECU. Any change to the calibration data stored in the ECU should result in a revised CAL ID being issued by the OEM, which typically happens when the OEM issues a field update.

Many aftermarket reflash tools do not overwrite this CAL ID when flashing in new values, so another watchdog was created for verification. This watchdog, known as the calibration verification number (CVN), is a checksum of the values in the calibration segment of the ECU memory. Any change results in a new number being calculated by the ECU here in the CVN, which can be accessed by OBD-II tools in Mode $09 data. Many state inspection stations now look for these CVN values to match published lists of known good values to pass.

Earlier, we saw that Mode $07 data keeps track of whether the vehicle has passed its appropriate monitors in service. Mode $09 takes this a step further by continually logging the pass/fail results of each of these monitors and comparing them to the number of valid drive cycles performed where the monitors would have been expected to pass. This comparison is known as the in-use monitor performance ratio (IUMPR). This ratio gives an easy way to spot monitors that have trouble passing on a consistent basis and can direct the technician toward a particular system when faults may be difficult to reproduce.

Mode $0A

This name is tricky unless you recognize the ECU's work in hexadecimal numbers, where 0A immediately follows 09. The number "10" in hexadecimal is actually the 17th number, which would come later if needed.

Tune Overview | Controllers

Hardware	P01, ECM, GM Gen3 V8, 4.3L V6		ID	CVN
VIN	2GCEK19T411105892	Operating System	12208322	D839
Serial	0EB00ALE0139	Engine	9358694	37DE
Operating System	12208322	Engine Diagnostic	9359043	AD39
		Transmission	16264213	3648
Security Key	0x4AE3 (Unlocked)	Transmission Diagnostic	16264334	E269
	<Double Click to Change Lock>	Fuel System	16264629	86E5
		System	9373478	B218
		Speedometer	9359167	2DE3

Mode $09 reveals the calibration identification and part numbers used in the vehicle controllers. Regulatory agencies have a large database that can be used to check for tampering.

As mentioned, Mode $0A is the home for a history of trouble codes, regardless of what may have been cleared from Mode $03 for current errors or Mode $07 for pending errors. Mode $0A holds these error codes until they have passed their associated diagnostic monitor or a specialized dealership-level tool is used to clear them. They cannot be cleared with generic scan tools.

Sure, spouting chapter and verse Mode and PID numbers can have you strutting around the workshop (or internet) like a proud peacock as you impress everyone with your intimate knowledge of OBD-II structure. It's even a great hit at parties or as a pickup line at your local bar. If you believe that, I have a bridge for sale as well. While it's nice to know some of this, the trick will be to apply this knowledge to actually work on a vehicle. Let's move forward with that, instead.

Emissions and MIL Connection

Starting with the most fundamental aspect of the diagnostic system, the primary job is to detect vehicle problems that would lead to an increase in emissions and point the technician in the right direction for a proper repair. This may mean a skilled dealership employee using the latest service diagnostic tool or the do-it-yourself owner who may not have more than a simple handheld OBD code reader.

The design of the diagnostic system is such that once a problem is significant enough to be detected, it triggers a stored code related to the issue in the Mode $03 data. While this may not pinpoint the exact repair required, it still does a great

Some auto-parts stores allow you to connect a scan tool to your vehicle for free while you're there in hopes that you will also purchase the parts necessary to repair the vehicle on the same visit. Of course, they also sell several versions of these tools.

job identifying major symptoms that will be used to make a repair. As we discuss later, a good diagnosis often requires a little more digging to confirm. Luckily, OBD-II provides an excellent framework in which to collect the additional data needed.

Because OBD has various modes of data to choose from (if the communication tool is capable of making the right request to the ECU), a skilled technician can bounce between these modes or data streams to effectively build his or her case for specific component repairs.

The journey may begin with the dreaded CEL on the dash that is confirmed with a scan tool that accesses the Mode $03 data to get the P-code responsible for the MIL. After that, things get more specialized in a hurry unless you're standing in the parking lot of your favorite auto-parts store. Where the parts-store tool may simply recommend replacing a few sensors based on the P-code present, that's kind of like remodeling the kitchen to fix what may only be a leaky faucet.

The other modes of OBD-II data can be used to get a better picture of what is really going on with the engine. Mode $02 can be used to see the conditions that existed at the moment the failure occurred. This helps if one wants to replicate the conditions later to see if the repair was effective as well.

We went over various emissions tests that modern vehicles are subject to during their certification phase before sale. Part of the agreement between automakers and the EPA (among other regulatory agencies) is that the diagnostics be calibrated tightly enough to catch conditions that would lead to a vehicle not being within 50-percent variation of the allowable emissions standards.

In a new vehicle emissions certification submission, they must include data that proves that a certain failure was induced in the vehicle before an emissions test and the ECU detected the failure and set the appropriate trouble code to indicate it during the emissions test. As long as the MIL is set, the measured increase in pollution is allowed, but a repair is required to fix both issues.

This required testing process is quite time consuming and expensive for manufacturers, adding millions to the cost of every program. The logic is that if the diagnostics have been proven to catch conditions associated with vehicles that pollute, then the absence of faults when such a diagnostic system is fully active would lead to a reasonable belief that the vehicle's emissions must also be sufficiently clean. Since the vehicle itself is not a rolling emissions laboratory, the best we can do here is circumstantial evidence that the tailpipe emissions should be in range of normal.

The key here is that not only must the MIL not be currently illuminated but also the ECU has demonstrated that it has been actively looking for faults. Various monitors are periodically run on the fuel system, oxygen sensors, evaporative system, catalysts, ignition system, and air path to make sure that the values being returned pass the plausibility checks that correlate with a properly functioning system for that vehicle. Simply showing no errors when no test or not enough tests have been applied to the various systems is not reason alone to say that they are working properly.

State Inspections

All new vehicles must have an emissions certification granted to their manufacturer before being legal

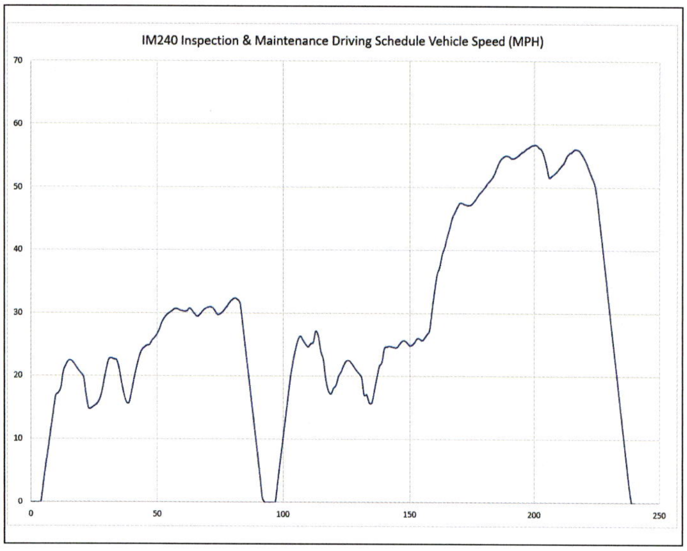

The IM240 was used (instead of the more-involved FTP-75 cycle) before states switched to OBD-based testing. The moderate speeds and loads could be run on a light-duty dynamometer at the inspection station.

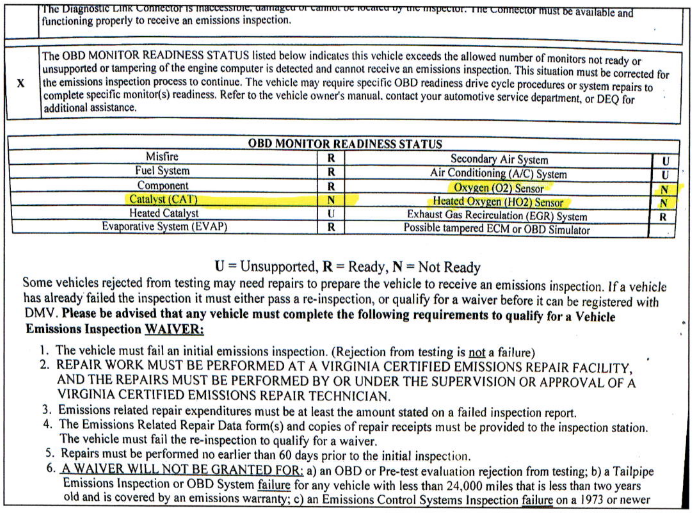

	The Diagnostic Link Connector is inaccessible, damaged or cannot be located by the inspector. The Connector must be available and functioning properly to receive an emissions inspection.
X	The OBD MONITOR READINESS STATUS listed below indicates this vehicle exceeds the allowed number of monitors not ready or unsupported or tampering of the engine computer is detected and cannot receive an emissions inspection. This situation must be corrected for the emissions inspection process to continue. The vehicle may require specific OBD readiness drive cycle procedures or system repairs to complete specific monitor(s) readiness. Refer to the vehicle owner's manual, contact your automotive service department, or DEQ for additional assistance.

OBD MONITOR READINESS STATUS			
Misfire	R	Secondary Air System	U
Fuel System	R	Air Conditioning (A/C) System	U
Component	R	Oxygen (O2) Sensor	N
Catalyst (CAT)	N	Heated Oxygen (HO2) Sensor	N
Heated Catalyst	U	Exhaust Gas Recirculation (EGR) System	R
Evaporative System (EVAP)	R	Possible tampered ECM or OBD Simulator	

U = Unsupported, **R** = Ready, **N** = Not Ready

Some vehicles rejected from testing may need repairs to prepare the vehicle to receive an emissions inspection. *If* a vehicle has already failed the inspection it must either pass a re-inspection, or qualify for a waiver before it can be registered with DMV. **Please be advised that any vehicle must complete the following requirements to qualify for a Vehicle Emissions Inspection WAIVER:**

1. The vehicle must fail an initial emissions inspection. (Rejection from testing is not a failure)
2. REPAIR WORK MUST BE PERFORMED AT A VIRGINIA CERTIFIED EMISSIONS REPAIR FACILITY, AND THE REPAIRS MUST BE PERFORMED BY OR UNDER THE SUPERVISION OR APPROVAL OF A VIRGINIA CERTIFIED EMISSIONS REPAIR TECHNICIAN.
3. Emissions related repair expenditures must be at least the amount stated on a failed inspection report.
4. The Emissions Related Repair Data form(s) and copies of repair receipts must be provided to the inspection station. The vehicle must fail the re-inspection to qualify for a waiver.
5. Repairs must be performed no earlier than 60 days prior to the initial inspection.
6. A WAIVER WILL NOT BE GRANTED FOR: a) an OBD or Pre-test evaluation rejection from testing; b) a Tailpipe Emissions Inspection or OBD System failure for any vehicle with less than 24,000 miles that is less than two years old and is covered by an emissions warranty; c) an Emissions Control Systems Inspection failure on a 1973 or newer

Getting the annual license-plate renewal now includes a stop at a state emissions-inspection station for many Americans. In just a few minutes, the inspector has enough information to determine if all of the emissions components are working properly—or, in this case, not.

for sale. This may come from the EPA, CARB, or another regulatory agency (if outside the United States). The VECI label under the hood clearly states which specific emissions certification the new vehicle has at the time of sale.

Once the vehicle drives off the lot, the manufacturer is not off the hook. Manufacturers are obligated to ensure that as long as their vehicles are properly maintained, tailpipe emissions will remain acceptable as designated by the full useful life standards discussed earlier.

Some states require that vehicles be monitored for emissions compliance to remain eligible for use on their roads. Previously, this meant a costly and time-consuming process of running the vehicle in either a stationary idle and high-idle check or dynamometer-based test, such as the IM240.

Over time, states recognized that this testing not only created a bottleneck in their annual registration process but also didn't necessarily catch vehicles that were polluting. Since the tests usually did not include any cold-start events, they missed the single largest contributor to tailpipe emissions. There were also several mechanic tricks that could be employed to squeak past testing for a single day only to quickly return to a polluting condition minutes later. Modern testing has closed these loopholes.

Some states completely abandoned the cumbersome emissions-testing routines and others adapted more streamlined solutions. Today, most state emissions testing is done without ever checking the actual tailpipe. Instead, they simply plug into the diagnostic port and query data. In seconds, enough information is transferred to see if the vehicle is and has been operating in good condition.

Using standard logic here, the combination of no current or pending P-codes, completed system monitors, and some correlating identifier data, a customer can be quickly approved for registration. We'll discuss more of the details of what information gets polled from the ECU during this testing later. For now, we simply recognize that it provides a quick snapshot of vehicle health and emissions tendencies. When enough of the vehicle fleet in any location all passes these same data-based emissions verifications, a measurable improvement can also often be seen in local air quality.

Another question often comes up in the discussion of state certification: "Can I pass with a standalone engine controller instead of my OEM ECU?" The short answer is no. As of this writing, I have yet to see an aftermarket ECU capable of performing all the necessary OBD-II tasks and communications.

Most aftermarket standalone ECUs have their own diagnostics to detect bad sensors and open circuits, but this only equates to what the OEMs had in OBD but without conforming to a universal standard. All of the OBD-II-level diagnostics, such as plausibility checks, emissions codes, active monitors, and required reporting modes, are absent in pretty much every aftermarket ECU out there today. Even if they had a plug that looked like the OBD-II SAE J1962 connector, the communications and data behind it just isn't there. This means an almost immediate failure at the inspection station.

But what about running a standalone along with the factory ECU with a split wire harness? This is unlikely to pass as well. I have seen several installations where the original ECU was left in a vehicle to retain communication with the dash, gauges, body control module, and other things, but a new ECU was used to control fuel and spark.

While this may let the user successfully run his new high-power engine hardware without damage, it effectively eliminates the OEM ECU's ability to run intrusive diagnostic monitors that are often executed through control of fuel and spark delivery. Without running these monitors, there is no way to store successful completion data in Mode $07. This, in turn, also means that the IUMPR stored in Mode $09 is also invalid. Current state-level inspection tools are checking both of these.

Manufacturer Audit/Tracking

Manufacturers work closely with their dealership networks to pass information both ways. Just as much as the dealers need the OEM to send them the latest vehicle data for repairs, the OEMs themselves are constantly looking at what comes through the service bays.

Every time a vehicle comes in for service, it is usually checked for OBD-II data. Any current or history of faults can be logged into a central database that gets forwarded to the engineering team for investigation. The object is to make sure that customers have fewer occasions to bring a vehicle into the dealership (under warranty) for an MIL and to proactively look for opportunities to improve the quality of vehicles being delivered to future customers.

Whenever a significant number of vehicles with a common engine and transmission package experience the same fault, it starts the conversation at quality meetings that usually get passed on to the calibration teams who drive the development vehicles every day. These calibration engineers quickly try to replicate the conditions to see if they can identify the root cause of the issue. Once the cause and an appropriate fix has been identified, a new calibration or hardware solution can be rolled out to the fleet. OBD-II requires that there be a method to perform in-field updates of customer-owned vehicles after they have left the assembly plant.

A Useful Access Point

It's these updates or repairs that once again show us one of the really cool features of OBD-II. The protocol for OBD-II requires that there be a way to update the ECU in the field. Because the actual calibration is just a computer file buried deep inside the ECU, it can be rewritten by a newer version as long as the proper procedure is followed to access and overwrite it.

Manufacturers have various levels of security that must be cleared to access this stored data and change it. The layers of security are there to prevent accidental overwrites as well as perform some level of gatekeeping against those who would wish to tamper with the good work of the engineering team that built those files originally. Any change to the ECU could potentially damage the engine, endanger the driver or public, increase the emissions, or all of the above. Some manufacturers are more risk adverse than others when it comes to potential tampering and

Enthusiasts have widely embraced the GM LS engine family as a popular swap for their classic vehicles. Using the ECU that came with this modern engine allows for a massive amount of control through the OBD-II data stream for both reprogramming and data logging.

their liability. As a result, they may have more sophisticated methods of preventing access by unauthorized people.

What used to be a simple security-lock method to limit access between the ECU and a programming tool can now rival bank or credit-card levels of security that effectively lock out any unauthorized access. Because dealerships are factory authorized, their programming tools are equipped with the matching key to whatever security is needed. The only catch here is that the technician at the dealer has no way of actually seeing what changes are being made. The technician must trust that the network connection has downloaded a known good file from the OEM calibration engineering team each time there is a rewrite for an ECU file.

Whenever there's a door, someone will try to find a way to pick the lock. The performance aftermarket is sufficiently motivated to gain access to this OBD-II door into the ECU so that it can apply its own changes to fuel, spark, torque, and more.

What used to take a wrench and a screwdriver with a carburetor and a distributor is now done with a laptop. However, going from a laptop table to a working vehicle ECU definitely takes a few extra steps. Luckily, these steps happen almost seamlessly in the background of many aftermarket ECU programming tools. The makers of these tools have reverse engineered not only the security routines necessary to unlock access to an otherwise encrypted ECU but also converted the raw binary stored files into easily readable engineering units shown in clearly labeled tables in a Windows program on a common laptop.

This is where things get really interesting for the performance enthusiast. These aftermarket tools turn hexadecimal gibberish into things that make sense even at a high-school science level. Instead of "0x19C3h" at an address within the file, we can see something more intuitive like 23.5° BTDC in a particular cell of a spark advance table with axes of RPM and engine load.

As a mechanical engineer and not a computer science guy, I am thankful for tools like this. They also make it easy for me to teach the underlying concepts of engine operation to classrooms of students without violating confidentiality of any OEM. In decades of teaching proper electronic fuel injection (EFI) calibration techniques, I have never needed to mention hexadecimal values in class because the commercially available tuning software has already translated the confusing computer language into something that more closely matches what our human brains can understand.

If I want to add two degrees of timing, I merely do so in the engineering units in the table, save my file, and connect to the vehicle to perform the flash routine with my aftermarket tool. This can all happen in less time than it would take to get the distributor wrench from the toolbox.

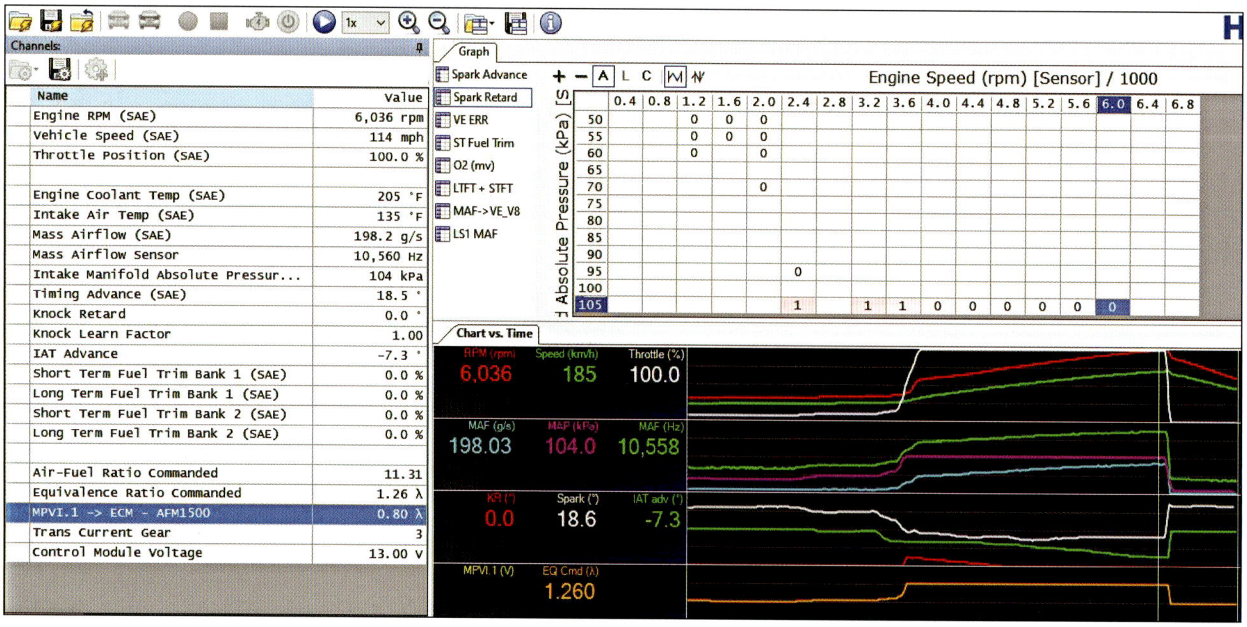

Programs, such as those from HP Tuners, take a lot of the guesswork out of interfacing with an OBD-II ECU. These tools display vehicle information in normal engineering units rather than confusing raw hexadecimal values.

CHAPTER 3

CAN and Other Networks

Vehicle networks come in many shapes and sizes today. The earliest networks were very simple and often limited to just the engine and transmission control modules. All OBD-II-equipped vehicles have some sort of network connecting various modules to a standardized connector under the dash. From here, things can get a bit messy, depending on the vehicle.

At the beginning of OBD-II, manufacturers began to standardize what they broadcast, just not how they broadcast it. There were several protocols in play simultaneously for many years, all delivering very similar data in different formats. This kept diagnostic toolmakers on their toes as they scrambled to keep up with the changes.

The serial data buses (as they came to be known) allowed various modules to send messages directly to one another, often passing through another module or node along the way. As the name implies, messages run in series can stack up for efficient transfer. However, adding too many of them with sufficient length begins to clog the system at a given baud rate. As processing power increased in the modules, baud rates and message lengths were able to increase. Longer messages meant that more information could be bundled together or that more precision could be assigned to specific data values.

While we dive into a history lesson here, this book by no means covers the complete specifications of each protocol. There are already countless textbooks on each that go far deeper into detail than any casual repair specialist needs to understand. The important points here are the major differences and the underlying theme that each can be read with commonly available tools on the market today.

Although the SAE J1850 protocol had become the standard at the origin of OBD-II, manufacturers could implement it in either variable pulse width (VPW) or pulse width modulated (PWM) schemes. General Motors opted for the former, and Ford took the latter. These unique schemes each came with their own data pin designations on the datalink connector. Of course, they are not interchangeable. Luckily, the diagnostic toolmakers figured this out, and their tools do a good job of detecting what type of vehicle they are connected to and configuring their communications appropriately. This is not a task that I would recommend for the casual DIY enthusiast. It's absolutely worth it to just buy a

This Innova handheld diagnostic tool has the ability to connect to a wide range of vehicles using a variety of communication protocols. The user does not need to know whether they are using serial or CAN bus; the user just wants the information.

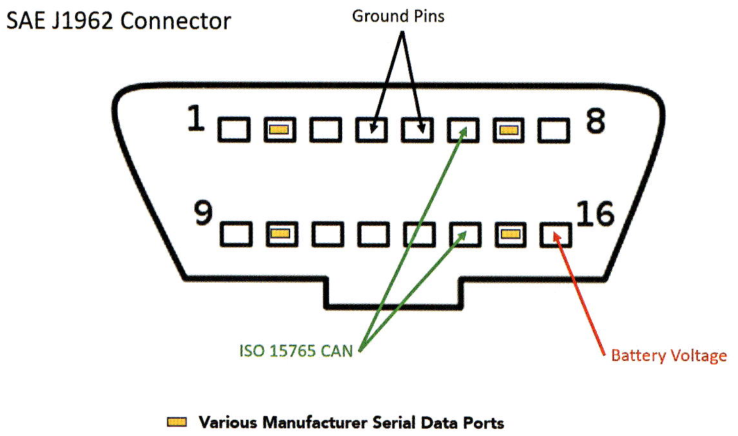

The introduction of SAE J1962 brought a common connection point to all vehicles along with common power and ground locations within that connector. Early data pins varied, but eventually became standardized with the introduction of CAN.

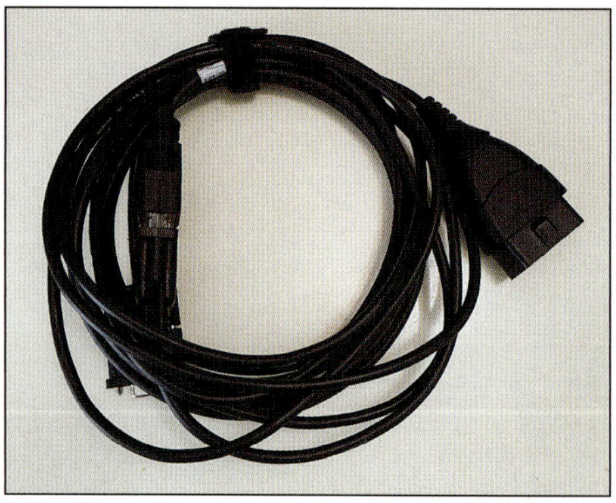

SAE J2534 brought a standard for pass-thru communications and reprogramming. Simple cables like these could be attached between the vehicle's J1962 port and an outside computer program to reflash the ECU or access the data stream with the right commands and security access.

working tool already developed by someone else, considering their relative affordability these days.

Not to be outdone, Chrysler and some Asian OEMs opted for the ISO 9141-2 protocol on their early OBD-II vehicles. ISO 9141-2 is often referred to as "K-Line." This comes with its own unique data pin designations on the connector and a unique communication scheme as well. Luckily, the pins used do not overlap with SAE J1850, so scan tools can easily identify and communicate with these vehicles as well.

By this point, one would hope we're done. We're not. Many European and Asian OEMs used yet another protocol: ISO 14320. This is similar to but not interchangeable with ISO 9141-2. ISO 14320 employs a longer message-length capacity. Again, aftermarket scan tool manufacturers come to the rescue of the repair bay with tools that can speak this protocol as well.

SAE J2534 and ISO 15765 CAN

In 2002, the SAE adopted J2534. This standard brought with it a new "pass-thru device" along with the means for controlling it.

The device gave service technicians a common device for multiple applications instead of buying new, expensive hardware to support various vehicles. Over time, SAE J2534 evolved through many similarly named variants that all prove to be quite confusing to anyone who doesn't write code for OBD tools for a living. See if you can keep up with the confusion:

- SAE J2534-1 2002
- SAE J2534-1 2004
- SAE J2534-2 2006
- SAE J2534-2 2010
- SAE J2534-1 2015
- SAE J2534-2 2019

As of 2008, US auto manufacturers finally joined other manufacturers around the world that had implemented a new communication standard. ISO 15765 brought us the controller area network (CAN) protocol. Now, with everyone agreeing on voltage, pin location, message length, baud rate, and general operation, sending and receiving data became much easier.

With a CAN network, many messages can be circulating simultaneously, each of which may be read by multiple modules. The data transfer rate of CAN networks is up to 1 Mbps. Various modules are connected along the CAN bus in parallel, and each is assigned its own address. Specific requests can be made of individual modules as well as generate a general broadcast to all modules on the bus. Common data values (such as vehicle speed, engine speed, and temperatures) may be used by multiple electronic modules, so a single message placed on the bus has the ability to satisfy the needs of all consumers at once.

The CAN network itself is actually rather simple. Just two wires carry the data among all modules on the bus. New modules can be added to tap into the "CAN Hi" and "CAN Lo" lines at any point. The two lines form a long string between points in the vehicle. At each end of the string is a termination resistor that is shunted between the two. The termination resistor effectively absorbs the data flow, preventing a reflection that would render all messages unreadable.

The agreed standard is to use a 120-ohm resistor at each end of the

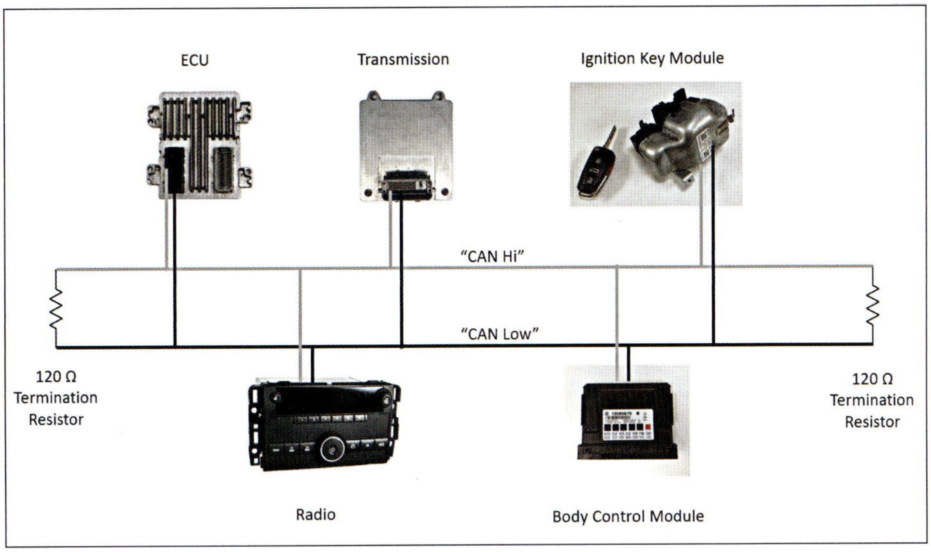

The CAN bus is fundamentally an information superhighway with access points at each module. Termination resistors at each end keep the traffic organized.

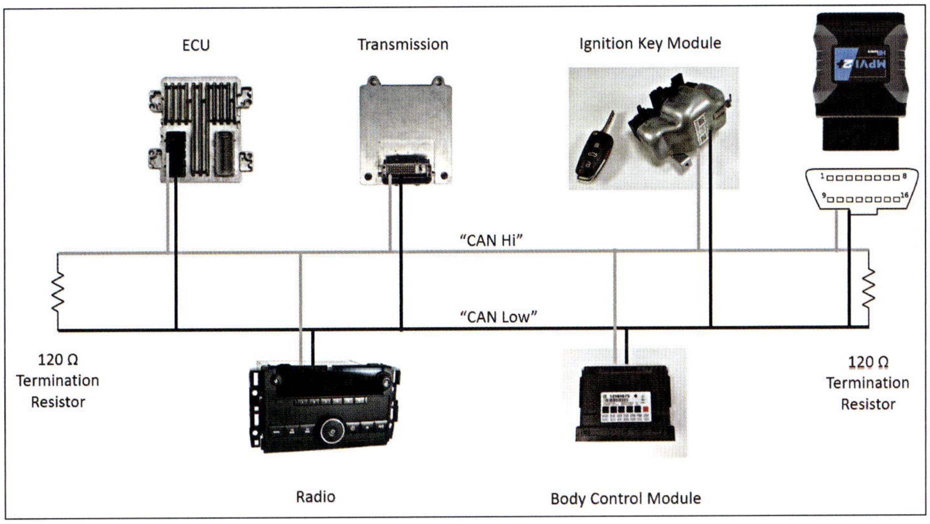

Tapping into the data already floating around on the CAN bus can be as simple as plugging a tool into the openings at the J1962 connector under the dash. Once on the bus, the tool may either monitor existing data or send its own commands.

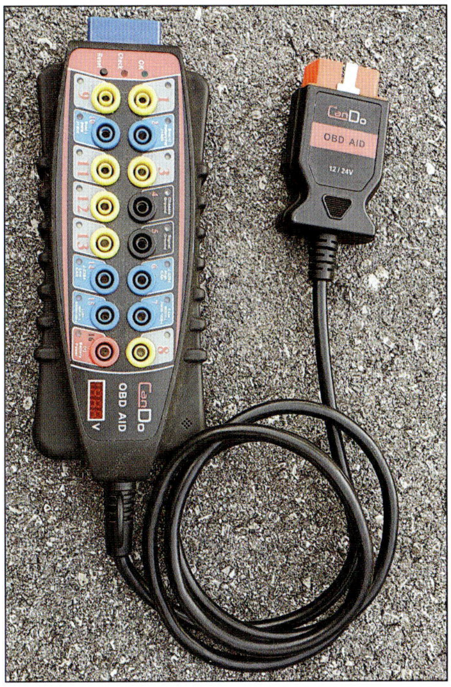

This breakout box not only doubles as a convenient extension cord for the BOD connector but it also lets the user confirm the communication status via LEDs. Further CAN or serial bus investigation is made easier with banana-plug connections available at each labeled pin number.

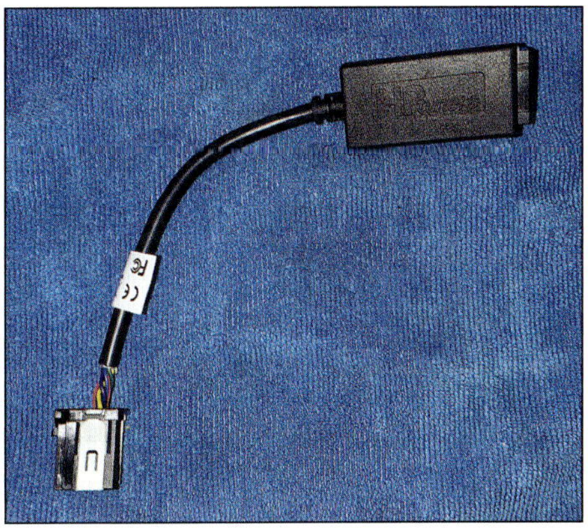

This adapter cable is required when attempting to connect to a late-model Chrysler vehicle with a secure network. It bypasses the security module and allows scan tools to connect to the ECU's CAN bus directly.

network string. A properly isolated CAN network should show a DC impedance of 60 ohms across the two wires as a result of the two parallel resistors. In OBD-II applications, this can be checked by measuring across Pins 6 and 14 on the J1962 connector under the dash. In automotive applications, the termination resistors are sometimes built into one of the modules when it is at the far end of the string.

Although accessing the CAN network on many vehicles is as simple as tapping into the two wires anywhere along the chain, it's not always that simple. In reaction to security concerns, automakers began to hide the powertrain CAN bus behind a firewall of sorts. They added security gateway modules that maintain a "clean side" and a "dirty side" to the data streams to reduce risk exposure.

Most of the good ECU data that we want to see is over on the "clean side." This often requires that our tools be able to access that as well. In some cases, the aftermarket has responded with bypass harnesses that

The hardest part about using a security bypass module can be finding the right place to plug it in. On this Ram, the module is tucked high under the driver's side of the dash. Some vehicles have it hidden behind the radio in the center console or other less intuitive places.

can be installed to allow a normal connection between tools or gauges that plug into the J1962 connector and the clean ECU data stream.

CAN Flexible Data

To add to the word salad that is CAN protocol naming conventions, SAE J2534-2 2019 added something called CAN FD. The "FD" stands for "flexible data," a rate based on ISO 11898-1, which overcomes the classical limitations of a traditional CAN bus data transfer. This new architecture is able to achieve data transfer speeds up to eight times faster than traditional CAN networks.

Not interchangeable with previous CAN networks, CAN FD added ISO-TP FD along with a discovery mechanism. This mechanism allows user applications to query the dynamic link library (DLL) to find which protocols it supports or how many channels a device has. This standard is actually based on the older J2534-1 2004 version, and not the intermediate J2534-1 2015.

FlexRay

Some automakers have added another variant known as FlexRay. Although similar to CAN, FlexRay allows for more nodes or modules on the same bus. Each is capable of sending or receiving requests and data. The data transfer rate is 10 times higher than standard CAN rates, at 10 Mbps. FlexRay may be transmitted over either a dual wire similar to CAN, or it may use a fiber-optic connection.

LIN

Local interconnect network (LIN) is newer to the automotive industry. It is typically used to connect one master module, such as the ECU, to an array of sensors. The master module itself is usually attached to another network, such as CAN. A single LIN wire can be used to relay MAF, MAP, or temperature sensors to the ECU digitally. This replaces the need for individual single-wire runs in the harness, saving cost and weight.

Moving analog sensors to a digital output also makes them less sensitive to ground or voltage offsets with regard to the quality of data seen by the ECU. LIN networks transmit data at a rate of 20 Kbps, which is more than sufficient resolution for most engine sensors. It is important to note that the sensors themselves may appear identical to older analog (or digital) output sensors, but they are not interchangeable during repairs or upgrades.

SENT

Another method now used to connect some sensors is the single edge nibble transmission (SENT) protocol. It is more completely defined in SAE J2716.

SENT provides for one-way communication, where a sensor is only transmitting a signal to a controller. It supports a high resolution at a low cost with a transmission rate of up to 30 Kbps. The sensors themselves are powered by a regulated 5V circuit rather than vehicle 12V (variable) power. The sensors also have a ground and signal wire that switches between <0.5V and >4.1V.

The signal is not easily decoded by hand. Some oscilloscope companies, such as Tektronix, assist in setting up their tools to analyze these signals, but it is not as simple as traditional PWM signals by any means. Tektronix has a great writeup on their

LIN-enabled sensors look exactly like their predecessors from the outside. Probing their signal output quickly reveals that it is no longer a simple analog voltage or frequency output, though.

CAN Bus Diagnosis

If a CAN-equipped vehicle does not show 60 ohms across the two CAN-bus wires, more investigation is needed before attempting to diagnose any actual powertrain faults. There may be an issue with the wiring of the bus itself, with one of the modules, or even with the scan tool. The following procedure should help quickly identify the root cause.

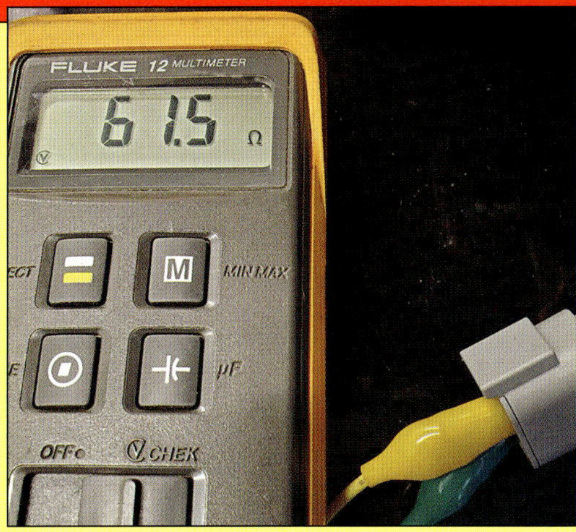

A properly working CAN bus should have approximately 60 ohms of impedance across each pair of wires. If this is not the case, use an oscilloscope and the procedure here to diagnose it further.

1) Without any communication active on the bus, check impedance between CAN Hi and ground along with CAN Hi to the power supply. There should be 10,000 ohms of impedance with proper isolation here in both directions. Repeat for the CAN Lo. Any short circuits should be identified and remedied.
2) Next, connect an oscilloscope to the CAN Hi line. It should read 2.5V during the idle phase and increase to 4.0V in a clean square wave as message bits pass the probe. There should be no ringing on either rising or falling edges.
   a. Voltage offsets can shift the idle voltage level. This is often caused by a bad ground.
   b. If CAN Hi does not move, there may be a short to another circuit that is obscuring the message bits display.
   c. Ground noise may make these measurements impossible, see Step 4. CAN networks are actually surprisingly tolerant to ground noise, as the two channels move in opposition to each other.
   d. Ringing of the signal is a result of impedance issues, usually with a specific module or the wires connecting it to the main CAN bus. Individual modules typically have an input impedance of 100,000 ohms to ensure the complete reflection of all signals back onto the bus without any phase shift.
3) Repeat Step 2 on the CAN Lo line. It should read 2.5V during the idle phase and decrease to 1.0V in a clean square wave as message bits pass the probe. There should be no ringing on either rising or falling edges.
   a. Diagnosis and repair is the same as for the CAN Hi in Step 2.
4) If there is a lot of ground noise on both CAN Hi and CAN Lo, connect a differential probe between the two CAN wires. This test should show 0.0V during the idle phase and an increase to 1.0V in a nice clean square wave as message bits pass the probe. If either wire is shorted, there will be a lower signal as the message bits pass the probe. ■

website about the structure and recording of SENT messages, but that quickly goes beyond the scope of this book.

Again, SENT-enabled sensors are not interchangeable with traditional analog sensors. Remember to check carefully when attempting to swap modern components, such as electronic throttle bodies and MAP or MAF sensors that may be configured for SENT communication. Both VAG Car Coding and Ford have already adopted numerous applications.

Ford moved several sensors from a direct analog ECU connection to SENT protocol on this GT500 engine. Your choices when investigating a throttle-position fault on this car are now between a scan tool with the proper definitions or an oscilloscope and a lot of research to decode the digital signal yourself.

Basic Engine Controls

To all of the performance tuners who jumped right to this page, welcome to my third book. I hope you take some time to review the preceding chapters to gain some context. Since I have already published two other books focused on engine operation and calibration procedures, this is an abbreviated review aimed at the repair technician or DIY enthusiast.

This is by no means intended to be an exhaustive explanation of how an engine controller works, since the details vary significantly among manufacturers and even different models of the same make. The key here is to understand the basic mechanisms in place that allow an ECU to optimize engine operation. These same features are what must be constantly checked by the OBD system to make sure emissions are acceptable and the vehicle is operating correctly.

Airflow Models

Whenever I teach my "Secrets of EFI Calibration" live class through Calibrated Success, I begin by explaining what I call the most important calculation going on inside the ECU. Put simply, I describe it as "how much stuff is in the cylinder" at any given moment. Technically speaking, engineers refer to this as air charge or cylinder filling, and it is usually expressed in a units of mass per cylinder event.

The reason that it's so important is that most of the physics behind engine operation is tied to this value. When this number is low, molecules are loosely bouncing around inside the cylinder leading up to and during combustion. When this number is

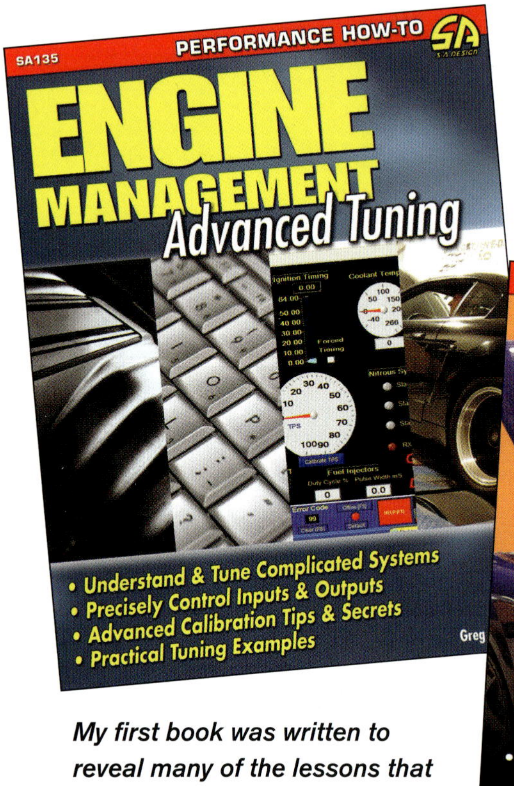

My first book was written to reveal many of the lessons that no one seemed to teach the beginning tuner. Today, it is used in the classrooms of many trade schools as an instructional text.

My second book took aim mostly at speed density control systems seen in both aftermarket and OEM controllers. With timeless math examples, many of my students enjoy taking home their own copy for future reference.

higher, we have tightly packed molecules with much more potential for heat release during combustion that are also more likely to react at a faster rate under those conditions. Further, making a calculation as to how much fuel is needed for a clean combustion event is directly tied to the amount of fresh air present inside the cylinder on that cycle.

Over the years, vehicle manufacturers and the aftermarket alike have employed several methods of quantifying both total airflow through the engine and per-cylinder filling. Luckily, these two are basically the same set of calculations, since one can be derived from the other as long as the number of cylinders and engine speed is known.

$$\text{Air per Cylinder (g/cyl)} = \frac{\text{Mass Airflow (g/s)} \times 120}{\text{(\# of Cylinders)} \times \text{Engine Speed (RPM)}}$$

$$\text{Mass Airflow (g/s)} = \frac{\dfrac{\text{Air per Cylinder (g/cyl)} \times}{\text{(number of cylinders)} \times \text{RPM}}}{120}$$

There are now basically two types of ECU systems for determining engine airflow and, hence, cylinder filling: mass airflow (MAF) and speed density (SD). Both have their advantages and disadvantages from a technical and cost standpoint. In truth, either is perfectly capable with today's high-speed processors and data acquisition. This is evidenced by OEMs using either method (or in some cases both simultaneously) and having vehicles that run clean enough to pass very strict emissions standards and deliver precise torque-based controls.

Mass Air

The first type of ECU system is known as a mass-air-based system, where a physical sensor is present in the intake tract. The sensor directly measures total airflow through the engine. The design of these sensors is now almost exclusively of the hot-film element type, where a small portion of the incoming air comes into direct contact with a heated element that is kept at a specified temperature relative to the incoming air charge. The amount of energy required to maintain this temperature gradient is directly related to the number of incoming air molecules hitting the element (and attempting to cool it).

There is a fixed geometric relationship in the design of the sensor that allows the ECU to accurately measure total airflow based on the smaller amount of molecules actually touching the heated element. The amount of heating to the total air charge in this case is negligible, and it works regardless of ambient air temperature and pressure in the sensor. As long as the sensor and inlet tract are not modified from the original design supplied by the OEM, it is a relatively safe assumption that the reported total airflow from the sensor is within 2 percent of reality under almost all steady-state conditions.

That last sentence is key when speaking to the performance crowd. One of their favorite things to do seems to be modifying the airbox, tubes, or MAF sensor itself. If any of these are changed from stock, it is up to the installer or tuner to supply a new representative sensor calibration into the ECU if they wish to have accurate airflow readings going forward.

One can be off quite a bit on this, as closed-loop fuel control often does a good job of learning the shift. The ideal situation is to not need to rely on the O_2 sensors to fix what is actually an airflow measurement error. In extreme cases, this can also lead to either MAF sensor rationality faults or electronic throttle-control faults. The latter often presents as a case where the drive-by-wire safety system sees a big enough mismatch to trigger a safe default mode that is anything but pleasing to the driver with its limited engine power availability.

Speed Density

The second airflow model is known as a speed density system, where airflow itself is not directly measured. Instead, it is calculated based on engine speed, the temperature, and the pressure of incoming airflow to the cylinder.

A MAP sensor is connected to the

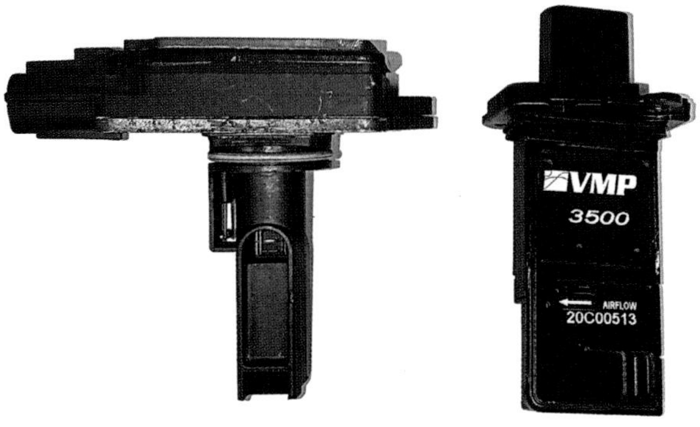

Two different MAF sensors are seen here that both employ a hot wire element and an ambient temperature probe. When fitted to a fixed pipe size, there is a consistent relationship between airflow across the wire and total airflow entering the engine.

MAF Tuning

Cars equipped with mass airflow sensors enjoy the advantage of being able to instantly have a direct measurement of airflow at any moment. This is really handy as long as the measurement is valid. To make sure the measurement is a real number, OEMs specify the construction of the MAF. This includes its geometry relative to the airbox or any bends and electrical circuit to be within about 2 percent of a reference standard. By consistently building and installing exactly the same hardware and electronics each time, they can move forward knowing that the reference values can be used for each vehicle coming off the assembly line at the factory.

The OEM reference values that correlate raw MAF sensor signal output to actual airflow are not determined on a running engine. Instead, a precision flowbench is used where the entire inlet system is attached as one piece. All airflow through the filter and inlet system is measured and logged against the raw sensor output. This data is then curve fit with high precision to generate values that will be passed along to the engine calibration team for population in the ECU tables.

Without a doubt, this is the most precise method available to calibrate a MAF sensor. It removes some of the noise factors associated with the pulsations and variation of a running engine, and it focuses strictly on the MAF element. Any other variations in airflow estimation on the running engine later can then be put into other calibration tables for transients, manifold filling, or other fudge factors used by the calibration engineer.

In the aftermarket, it's quite popular to replace inlet plumbing or even the MAF sensor itself to support higher airflow and power levels with minimal pressure drop. Any time a part of the inlet system is modified in a way that may impact the MAF sensor output relative to actual flow, a new calibration curve must be developed for the ECU. In a perfect world, this data would again come from a calibrated flowbench.

Since most enthusiasts, tuners, shop owners, and even high-performance parts manufacturers don't have MAF flowbenches handy, another solution is often needed. Luckily, there is still another valid option. The engine itself is a large air pump. Using the engine's airflow, we can solve for the actual mass airflow in real time as long as we have a couple other key pieces of information. These calculations all revolve around the basic air-to-fuel ratio of the engine. If we know the desired air-fuel ratio (AFR), the current fuel flow rate, and the current actual air-fuel ratio, then we can solve for the current airflow rate. This is best done when the engine is attempting to run at the stoichiometric air-fuel ratio because it makes the math much easier to use units of lambda (λ, excess air ratio) rather than raw AFR.

In a lab environment, we would install a precision fuel flow meter on the line supplying the engine. Return fuel systems with a mechanically regulated rail pressure would also need another meter on the return line. This line determines the actual fuel delivered through the injectors, not counting the amount returned to the tank. Since most people don't work in this laboratory environment with lots of expensive flow meters sitting around, we have to get fuel flow another way.

If we are using fuel injectors that have known characteristics entered into the ECU-fuel-flow model, then we can assume that the desired fuel flow and actual fuel flow are the same. This is a potentially dangerous assumption, though. Any error in the physical behavior of the injectors will be directly transferred into an offsetting error in the resulting

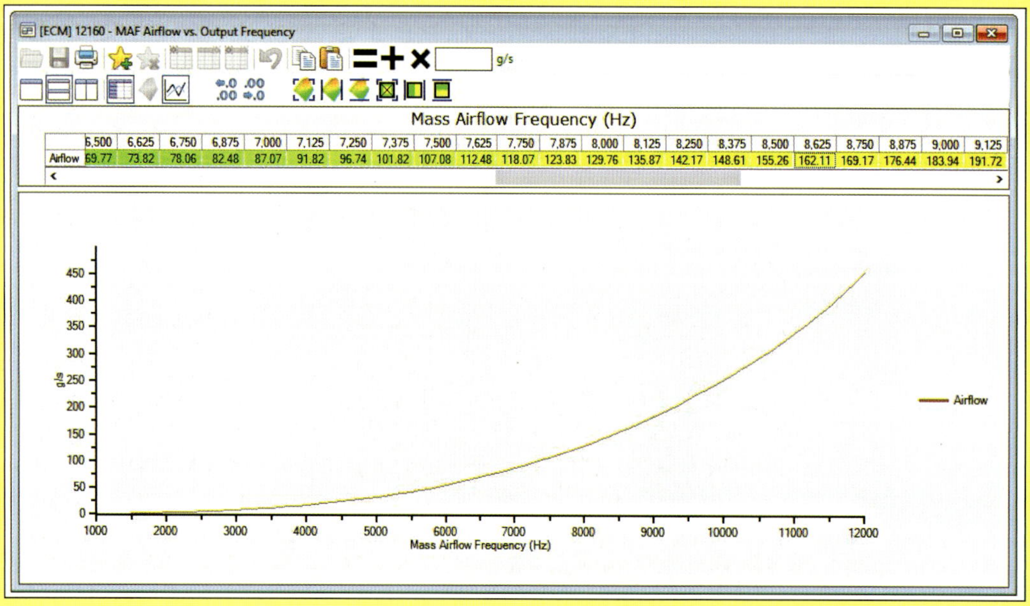

Inside the ECU, there is a table that translates the raw MAF sensor signal into a physical airflow number. The physics of how a MAF sensor works demands that this table always has a smooth, progressive curve.

With aftermarket intake plumbing like this ProCharged Camaro, a new MAF curve must be found for the ECU to deliver accurate fueling. A load-bearing dyno makes the data-collection process much easier, as a series of steady-state error measurements can be collected along the curve.

airflow model later. This can result in a condition where the fueling is precise in one set of conditions during testing but inaccurate with any changes in weather, temperature, boost level, or a number of other factors. It is absolutely imperative that accurate fuel injector characterization data be used for this process to avoid headaches later.

Once we confirm that the fuel injector characterization data is accurate, we install a similarly accurate wideband oxygen sensor into the exhaust (upstream of the catalyst) to measure the actual air-fuel ratio of the engine at the moment.

There is much room for debate about the accuracy of various wideband O_2 sensors, and I have a history of leaning toward my own laboratory-grade equipment for this task. The good news is that we perform the majority of the necessary MAF testing centered around the stoichiometric (λ=1.00) mixture in the engine where wideband O_2 sensors generally have the lowest amount of error around zero pump current. Attempting this at more rich or lean ratios introduces the opportunity for more wideband error on cheaper consumer-targeted units, which is why we try to do as much of this near λ=1.0 as possible without hurting anything else. Getting to higher airflow numbers will eventually require additional fuel for cooling, though.

Mass Airflow Frequency (Hz) [Sensor]

3900	3972	4050	4122	4200	4350	4430	4500	4583	4650	4715	4800	4872	4950
1.013	1.013	1.018	1.016	1.024	1.045	1.060	1.091	1.115	1.125	1.116	1.111	1.092	1.118

Logging calculated lambda error into a histogram against the same points of the MAF curve from the ECU makes precise adjustments much easier. Remember that these errors should be taken from a large number of samples and should result in a smooth MAF curve without jagged steps.

MAF Tuning *continued*

Getting the actual calculations, we have a surprisingly simple process once we trust the data. Even if we work from the original MAF curve in the ECU software, we at least have a starting point for an airflow estimate. The ECU will see the raw MAF signal and look up an airflow value from the stock table to determine the right amount of fuel to be delivered by the injectors. As long as the injectors' fuel delivery is close enough to trust (as discussed earlier), we can then assume that any error between the desired and actual measured AFR is caused by the error in the MAF table. We use the ratio of this error to correct the MAF values.

$$\text{Correction Factor} = \frac{\text{Measured AFR}}{\text{Target AFR}}$$

Or, using units of lambda, the math gets even easier when targeting stoichiometry where λ=1.00:

$$\text{Correction Factor} = \frac{\text{Measured } \lambda}{\text{Target } \lambda}$$

As I often joke with my live classes, dividing by 1.00 is so easy that an engineer like me can do it in his head. In these cases, the current-delivered lambda is the correction factor that needs to be applied to the airflow numbers in the ECU (MAF table).

The only thing to worry about here is making sure to work with steady-state airflow numbers and not transients where manifold filling or fuel-to-wall factors come into play. These can greatly skew what would otherwise be good correction data in a hurry. Having the patience to test in the right conditions makes a huge difference.

Modern ECU data-logging software makes this even easier by being able to record a calculated lambda error (actual/target) in a histogram of averages laid out against the same breakpoints of the ECU MAF table. These histograms can be populated relatively quickly. It's just up to the tuner at this point to not go too quickly and pollute nice steady-state measurements with transient values that should be dealt with later in the calibration process.

When properly done, this process yields a new MAF curve for the ECU that is within about 3-percent error at all points. Just remember that any errors in the fuel-injector data, wideband accuracy, or transients have a direct reduction in accuracy here. It also means that all normal MAF diagnostics should still work on completion. If the vehicle throws an airflow-related error code or MIL later, the same diagnostic process could be used on a modified car as one would use for a factory vehicle. ■

intake plenum. The sensor measures pressure below atmospheric during throttled conditions and above atmospheric if a turbo or supercharger is present. Combined with a temperature reading, the density of the incoming air is calculated and multiplied by the volume of the cylinder.

While this sounds straightforward, there remains a twist. We are not guaranteed complete filling of the cylinders under all speeds and loads.

The engine operates much like a musical instrument. The various pipe lengths, areas, and chamber volumes all combine to form resonances within the engine's air path. These resonances change how much air

Speed density systems do not require a mass airflow sensor in the intake path. Instead, they may only have a two-wire intake air temperature sensor near the airbox or throttle body, as seen on this Hemi engine.

actually makes it past an open intake valve to fill the cylinder.

To account for this changing effect, a variable called volumetric efficiency (VE) is used to adjust the basic equation used to calculate cylinder filling. VE is basically a fudge factor that combines all resonances, restrictions, and pumping effects into one number that allows Boyle's gas law to be applied to the running engine.

$$\text{Air per Cylinder (g/cyl)} = \frac{\text{Cylinder Volume (L)} \times \text{VE} \times \text{MAP (kPa)}}{(0.28705) \times \text{IAT (°K)}}$$

$$\text{Mass Airflow (g/s)} = \frac{\text{V Cylinder (L)} \times \text{VE} \times \text{(Number of Cylinders)} \times \text{RPM} \times \text{MAP (kPa)}}{34.446 \times \text{Air Temperature (°K)}}$$

VE can change quite a bit depending on what conditions are present. Taking a slice through a typical VE table at a constant manifold pressure, we can see that the values for volumetric efficiency rise and then lower with RPM. This clearly shows where some engine speeds develop harmonic waves that are more helpful to filling the cylinder in the mid- to high-RPM range compared to lower engine speeds.

Not coincidentally, this effect usually peaks around the same place the engine torque peaks when measured on a dyno. As I pointed out in my previous book, the shape of the VE curve generally matches the shape of the torque curve for the engine. There is more on this later when we discuss torque modeling and control.

Fundamentally, we see a strong relationship between VE and airflow

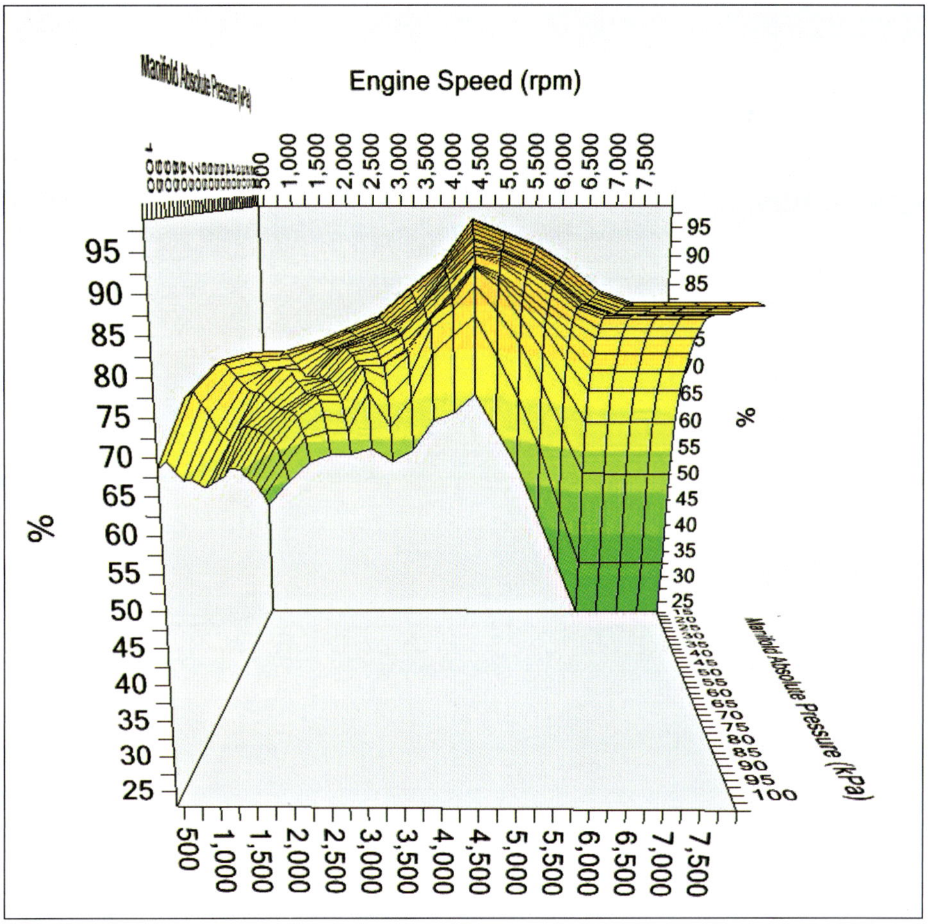

Looking at slices of VE against RPM shows us that the cylinder filling changes with RPM. The peak cylinder filling is usually close to the engine's torque peak because cylinder charge has a large impact on delivered torque.

as intake manifold increases. Most engines have a fairly linear relationship here through much of the pressure range above 50 kPa and even into moderate amounts of boost. It does tail off down at low manifold pressures, but Ford went so far as to skip the VE table altogether and just describe this relationship between MAF and MAP with a straight line in their code for a long time. There was no VE table, only a series of slopes and offsets that varied by RPM. Don't laugh—customers never noticed, and it was accurate enough to pass emissions.

These two forces of engine speed and manifold pressure alone are enough to provide a relatively complex VE surface when viewed in three dimensions. But wait, there's more! Since we already pointed out that the engine behaves much like a musical instrument, what happens if the player selects different keys?

With the advent of variable cam timing (often per cam and potentially different across banks of the same engine), variable intake manifold runner tuning, closed-loop wastegate control, and variable intake-plenum valves, we have many extra degrees of freedom that can all independently affect the final volumetric efficiency.

Accounting for all of these in

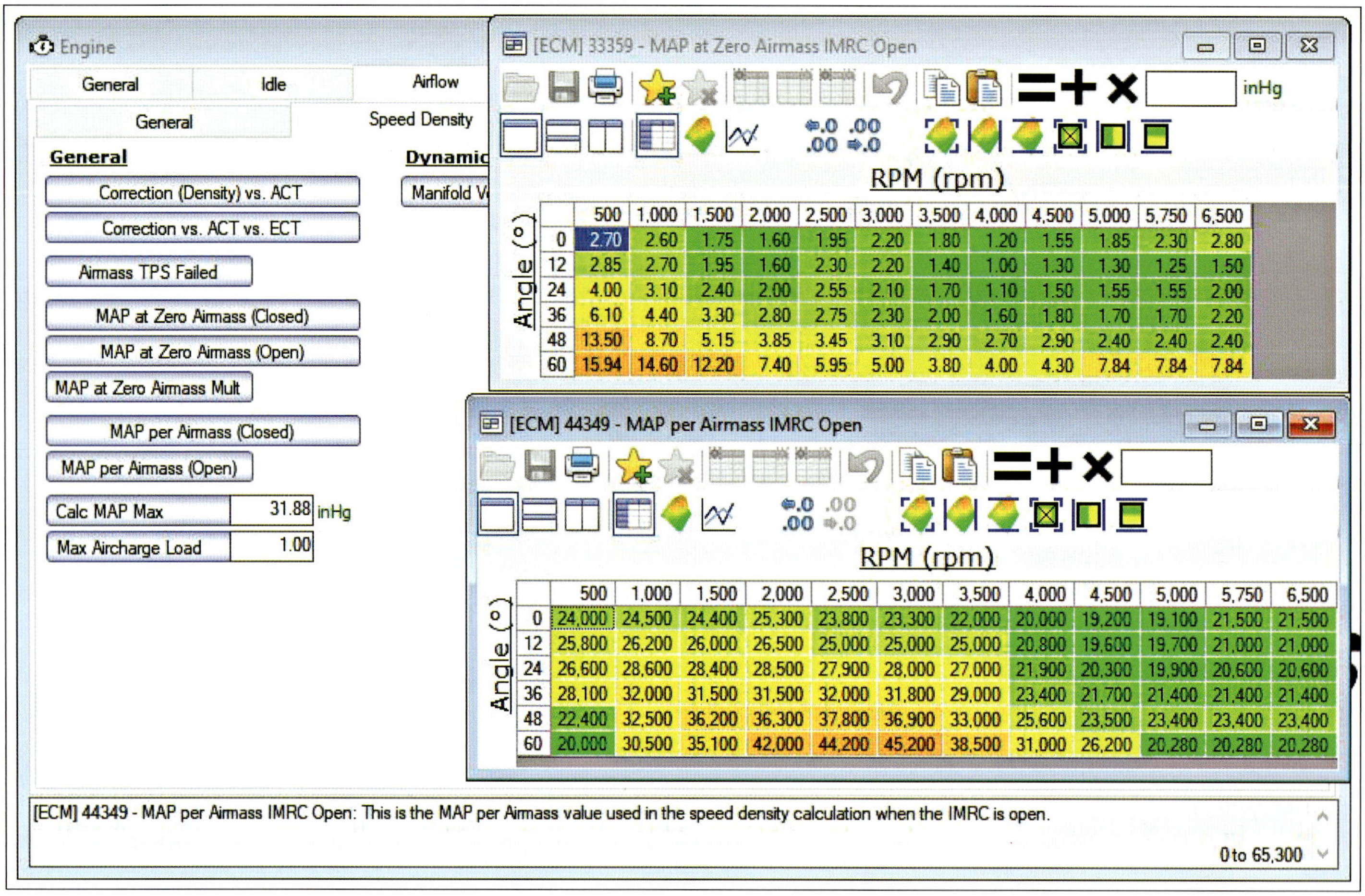

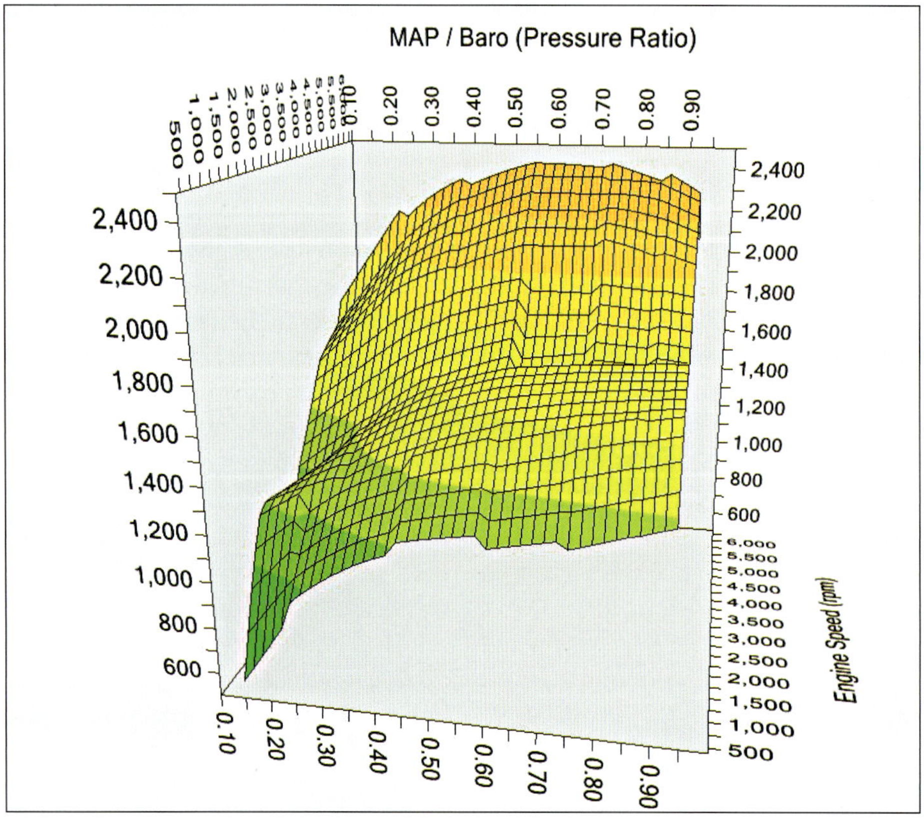

The Ford speed density model uses straight lines with a slope and offset to describe the relationship between manifold pressure and cylinder air charge. For the 3V single variable cam engines, they needed rows of these values at various cam angles as well to account for the tuning difference from phasing.

An accurate speed density model should result in a smooth surface, but remember that this is only true for a single set of valve events. Phasing the cams fundamentally changes the shape of this table, so tools like this one must allow the user to see the effects of moving the cam by updating the three-dimensional surface accordingly.

Speed Density Tuning

Speed density airflow models often require updating whenever new engine parts are installed. The VE table was the original catch-all for fudge factors that make the gas-law model work correctly for the engine. That means anything that changes pumping efficiency, port resonance, cylinder scavenging, valve events, or pressure ratios is likely to require updates to this reference surface to bring everything back in line regarding air-fuel ratio control.

Factory engineers do much of this work empirically in an engine dynamometer test cell. Much of the process is automated to save time and effort, but they essentially run the engine through a thorough combination of working conditions to figure out what VE number is needed at each point to make the cylinder air mass estimate reasonably accurate.

In an engineering environment, the VE is solved for by carefully measuring the fuel flow (typically with an expensive but highly accurate fuel flow meter) and either a wideband oxygen sensor or an exhaust gas chemical analysis to determine the current airflow. Errors in the estimated VE are corrected by the same method described previously for the live MAF testing on a running engine. Using an accurate fuel flow meter takes the question of injector flow accuracy away, so that remains the preferred method for OEMs.

In practice, it's still reasonable to use the fuel injectors as our flow meter with the assumption that their flow matches the characterization data stored in the ECU. Again, any errors here between actual injector fuel delivery and modeled behavior results in an offsetting error that will get baked into the VE calculations. It is imperative that accurate and complete fuel-injector data be used when performing this method of VE correction.

With a running engine, the same air-fuel ratio or lambda error can be determined during steady-state testing as described for MAF tuning. The only difference is that this correction factor is applied to the VE model rather than a MAF table.

Just like with the MAF testing, it's important that this lambda error data be collected in steady-state conditions. Transient effects can easily lead an inexperienced tuner (or even calibration engineer) to build a VE model that has "blisters" of raised VE calculations right around the same areas where throttle tip-in often occurs.

It is not uncommon for modern engines to have actual volumetric efficiencies over 100 percent near peak torque where manifold tuning effects align to help really pack the cylinder with fresh incoming air. However, a calculated value of more than 130 percent would be a flag that closer examination may be needed to find out what's really happening. Often, these large numbers lead to exposing errors in the fuel-injector characterization, fuel system performance, air-temperature measurement, or other hardware faults. Having the discipline to stick to steady-state data collection helps avoid this trap and saves a lot of grief later as conditions change. ■

Graph

Spark Advance
Spark Retard
LT Fuel Trim
ST Fuel Trim
O2 (mv)
LTFT + STFT
e92 VVE lambda err
MAF Err

Engine Speed (rpm) [

Pressure Ratio () [Math]

	400	600	800	1000	1200	1400	1600	1800	2000
0.60			0.790	0.799	0.831	0.877	0.937	0.938	0.965
0.62			0.790	0.813	0.856	0.876	0.947	0.953	0.968
0.64		0.789	0.789	0.815	0.870	0.872	0.956	0.954	0.976
0.66		0.788	0.838	0.826	0.884	0.880	0.963	0.957	0.979
0.68		0.847		0.870	0.893	0.890	0.965	0.960	0.981
0.70		0.859	0.879	0.880	0.906	0.899	0.970	0.972	0.985
0.72		0.817	0.879	0.885	0.911	0.919	0.978	0.979	0.991
0.74		0.818	0.874	0.905	0.926	0.925	0.984	0.989	0.995
0.76	0.856	0.837	0.867	0.927	0.935	0.938	0.990	0.995	1.011
0.78		0.846	0.878	0.917	0.940	0.957	1.006	1.009	1.038
0.80		0.857	0.874	0.954	0.957	0.968	1.018	1.012	1.049
0.82		0.838	0.907	0.955	0.968	0.982	1.039	1.030	1.062
0.84		0.850	0.934	0.976	0.992	1.004	1.066	1.046	1.066
0.86	0.831	0.859	0.923	0.996	1.001	1.034	1.082	1.063	1.077
0.88		0.871	0.916	1.005	1.026	1.049	1.092	1.075	1.082
0.90		0.867	0.968	1.035	1.042	1.075	1.098	1.083	1.096
0.92		0.850	0.990	1.049	1.063	1.105	1.108	1.081	1.091
0.94		0.836	1.034	1.084	1.083	1.124	1.123		
0.96		0.837	1.063	1.085	1.097	1.136	1.141		

Plotting calculated lambda error into a histogram of the VE model inputs allows the calibrator to quickly assess which areas of the table need adjustment and in which direction. With changes to the heads, cam, and intake, it's not unusual to see some areas require an increase in VE calculation while others a decrease to correct the error.

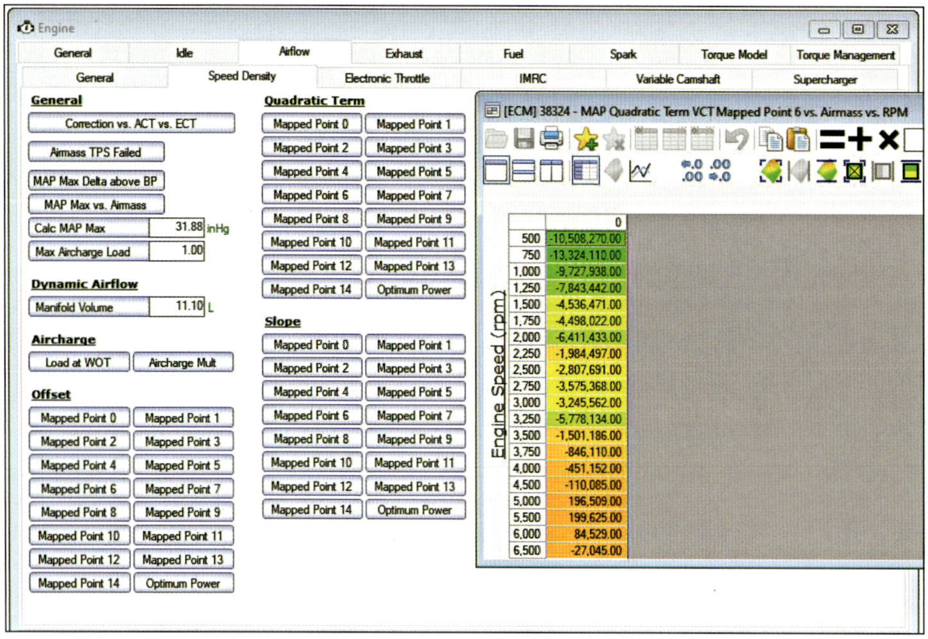

Ford addressed the influence of camshaft phasing on the MAF-MAP relationship by adding a quadratic term to its ECU equation linking the two. Each cam angle results in a unique quadratic term at each engine speed, resulting in a model that more closely follows the complex engine pumping behavior.

real time drove the industry to some creative solutions in speed density airflow modeling. What used to be a single three-dimensional surface stored in the volumetric efficiency table now requires layers of control to accurately describe all of these effects on the same fudge factor that must be applied to the basic gas-law calculations to produce the right number.

Phasing the cams earlier tends to push peaks in volumetric efficiency toward lower engine speeds. Likewise, retarding the camshaft and valve closing events shifts the peak toward higher speeds. Moving the intake cam position enough can actually bend what used to be a linear relationship between MAF and MAP. In the equation-based Ford speed density model, this was acknowledged by adding a quadratic term to what used to be a slope- and offset-only model for each engine speed.

Bringing the valve-event centerlines closer together can result in overlap where the intake valve is beginning to open while the exhaust valve has yet to close. The same can happen on a single-variable-cam application where only the inlet valve timing is adjusted or the two move together to have the intake valve opening before top dead center (TDC) as the piston is still pushing spent gases out of the chamber.

This opens the door for exhaust to travel up the intake runner during the early part of the intake-valve event, increasing exhaust gas recirculation (EGR). This can be so effective that variable camshaft control can often replace the need for an EGR valve on the engine entirely. Diluting the fresh incoming air charge with a portion of the previous cycle's spent gases has a very measurable effect on cylinder filling of the following cycle since we only want to add the appro-

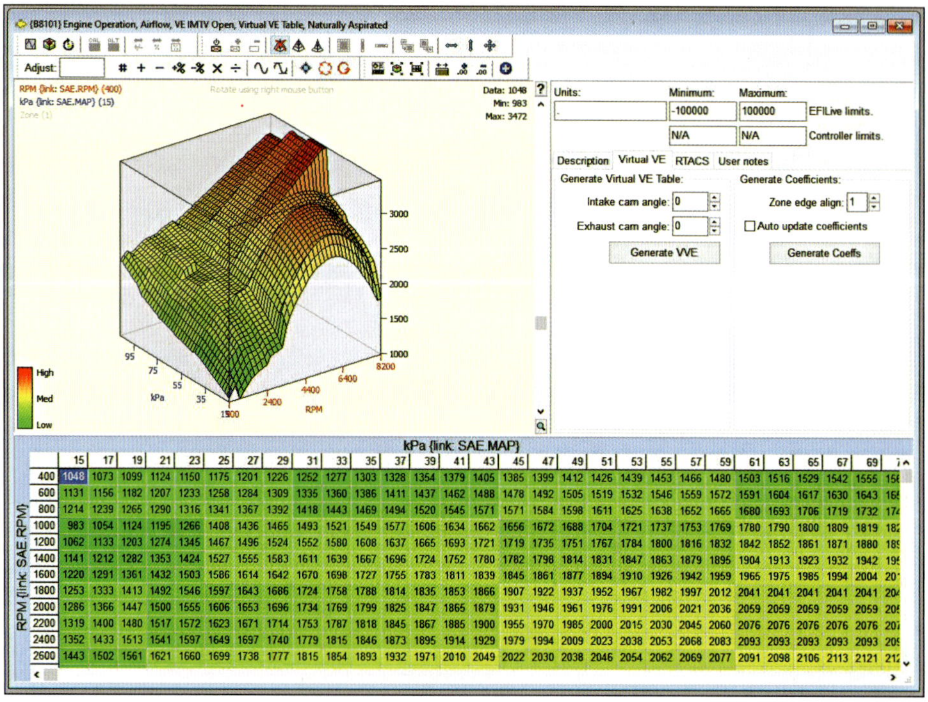

EFILive was the first aftermarket company to include a tool in its software that allowed users to easily visualize, modify, and rewrite the GM coefficient-based VE model. Other companies have since added the capability as well, giving aftermarket tuners several good options.

priate amount of fuel for the fresh air entering the cylinder to burn clean.

The math required to simulate this effect requires very advanced computer programming, such as the GT-Power software suite. It also requires a lot of training and of course accurate input models. In practice, the final VE is normally found by running an engine in a controlled environment and solving for the airflow and cylinder filling based on known fuel flow rates and resulting lambda measurements.

Virtual VE

As more and more features were added to engines, each with their own degree of freedom affecting the final VE, OEMs had to get progressively more creative with how they modeled cylinder filling in speed density systems. At first, there were base VE surfaces with adders for cam angle. Then, multiple adders for intake and exhaust angles.

Eventually, these many layers had increased the possible combinations of testing and operating conditions exponentially. This burdened the ECU's processor with many calculations that must be done on the fly. CPU processing power is not unlimited in automotive ECUs, and these same processors are required by law to be running both basic engine functions and a large number of diagnostics simultaneously, even at the maximum rated engine speed. This leaves precious little time to sample sensors, look up values in tables, interpolate, and come up with the right number before it's too late. Simplification was needed and found in the form of math.

General Motors answered the challenge by replacing the basic VE surface with what came to be known by tuners as virtual VE (VVE). With VVE, a large polynomial equation could be used to solve for the instantaneous VE value based on inputs for RPM, MAP, intake cam position, exhaust cam position, and manifold tuning valve position.

Each noise factor was given its own piece of the polynomial equation, and they were simply added together to find the final value. If a vehicle was not equipped with a variable exhaust cam position for example, then the coefficients for that part of the equation would be set to zero and the same calculation was done with the zeros added in but not affecting the final output.

This proved to be easier on CPU loads by only requiring a single calculation at any moment rather than each component being looked up and interpolated from within its own reference table. The result was a much quicker calculation of cylinder filling that remained accurate as a large number of inputs were changing.

The only downside to this was that some form of math-based tool was now required to turn a series of coefficients into surfaces that a human calibration engineer could check and modify if necessary. Luckily for the high-performance aftermarket, this format has largely been decoded, and math-based tools are now available as part of several popular tuning software suites.

Meanwhile, other manufacturers, such as Chrysler, went with a different approach to addressing the problem. Machine-learning principles were applied and an

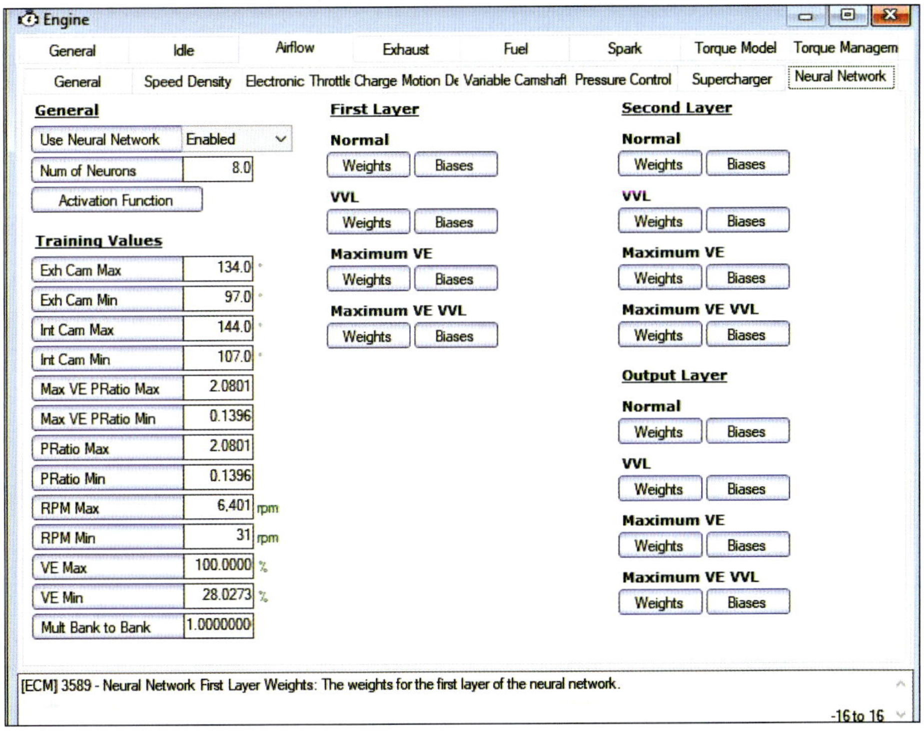

Neural networks and machine learning are a great way to process large amounts of complex data, but weight and bias coefficients do not give humans an intuitive way to adjust them. If a neural network is to be adjusted, it requires another software tool to help visualize the resulting output and solve for new coefficients if a change is desired.

Adding boost to a vehicle with a neural network SD model requires the calibrator to completely retrain the network to include data points beyond atmospheric pressure. The factory calibration on this Challenger does not have any way of coping with pressures above 100 kPa accurately.

artificial neural network (ANN) was developed. It could handle the many inputs and determine an appropriate output.

The ANN is a bit of a black box to those on the outside. Lots of things go in, something happens, and an output is delivered. The internal math is anything but simple. The ANN must be "trained" by running many sample cases through its own math-based tool that ultimately solves for the weight and bias values used by the calculator.

Given enough input examples that cover all possible combinations of input variables, the ANN is trained to recognize these combinations and deliver the desired output. The execution of this logic again takes much less processing power than layers of traditional lookup tables, freeing up valuable CPU load at high engine speeds. Over time, other OEMs, including General Motors, adopted this same approach to complex modeling of airflow to account for a wide range of input variables.

Neural networks and VVE still have a few limitations of concern to the performance calibrator. They both require some additional tools in the tuning software to visualize the model, even at the basic fixed-cam position. There is no VE surface in the actual ECU, so these tools are critical to those looking to develop their own calibrations for engines with revised airflow capabilities.

One cannot simply add 10 percent of some value in the ECU and expect a 10-percent change in estimated airflow and delivered fueling. All changes must be done in the math tool, and new coefficients or weights and biases must be calculated that can then be written into the ECU calibration. While this sounds much more challenging, experienced calibrators can jump in and out of these tools quickly while making changes. It just takes a few extra clicks along the way, as we demonstrate in our Calibrated Success training videos and live classes.

Finally, for the gearheads who enjoy pushing the envelope, there is another concern with neural networks. When they are trained, they are exposed to a wide range of operating conditions and inputs. However, if one goes outside of these bounds, the machine learning has no way to extrapolate.

The biggest concern here is adding boost from a supercharger to what used to be a naturally aspirated engine. When calibrated at the factory, the ECU was given values that work with manifold pressures equivalent to sea-level barometric pressure and below. The neural network was never exposed to boosted conditions much above 100 kPa, so that is completely uncharted territory for the ANN.

Even if the 1-bar MAP sensor is replaced with a 2- or 3-bar unit and the sensor transfer function is fixed in the calibration, the SD calculation done in the ANN has no clue what to do with an input value of 110 kPa or greater. It is a random guess at best what air-charge calculation comes out of the box at this point, and the fate of the engine's pistons may weigh in the balance.

Properly recalibrating modern ECUs that employ a neural network requires commitment to completely retraining it across all operating ranges. This moves the edges of its learning envelope beyond where it is intended to operate. Keep in mind that airflow, throttle body, and torque diagnostics are all relying on this most important basic calculation as well. There is no shortcut here.

Fuel Delivery

Once the ECU knows how much air is expected to be in the cylinder on a particular intake event, it is much easier to determine the right amount of fuel to add for a clean combustion event. The starting point for this is the stoichiometric air-to-fuel ratio for the fuel being used.

For years, we have been told that the magic number for pump gas is 14.7:1, meaning that for every 14.7 grams of air entering the engine, we needed to supply 1 gram of fuel to have the right balance of oxygen, hydrogen, and carbon during combustion so that there are theoretically no leftover parts. If we did everything right, the only thing leaving the engine would be carbon dioxide (CO_2) and water (H_20).

The reality is that gasoline is not made of pure iso-octane (2-2-4 trimethyl pentane, C8H18) but rather a cocktail of ingredients, all with their own chemical structures. On any given day, this number varies with what the delivery truck dumped in the tank at the local gas station. Before we pick an average ratio, we must take into consideration a new issue: ethanol content.

Today's pump gas contains 8- to 10-percent ethanol (C_2H_5OH) that carries with it a significant amount of oxygen that can contribute to combustion much the same as the atmospheric air that is made up of roughly 20.9-percent oxygen on its own. This pushes the balance point between air and fuel to a slightly richer number to compensate. Most OEMs now use a number around 13.9 to 14.2:1 because there is now a specific fuel used during emissions testing that contains 10-percent ethanol. I use the same values for my road-driven projects today as well.

The next step is taking a desired fuel mass from this ratio and turning it into a feed-forward control signal for the fuel injector. Before any corrections are applied, this first guess is known as "open-loop" fuel calculation. We'll discuss "closed-loop" corrections a little later.

If the cylinder is calculated to have 0.5 gram of air filling it, we would need to deliver 0.035 g (0.5/14.2) of fuel to the same cylinder to hit the magic number. To do this, the ECU must have sufficient information describing the relationship between activation time and actual fuel flow through each injector.

The image below on the left shows a typical injector characterization curve across a wide range of pulse widths (time for which the injector is activated by the ECU). In the simplest of terms, there is a linear relationship through most of the range. This straight line's slope, defined as rise over run, is the flow rate of the injector in milligrams per millisecond (g/s).

The steeper the line, the greater the flow rate of the injector when open and the more total fuel it has the potential to deliver in a fixed window of time. The linear relationship also clearly shows an offset from the 0-0 point, meaning that there is some amount of activation time that must pass before any fuel is delivered.

Using the slope-intercept characterization, most desired fuel masses

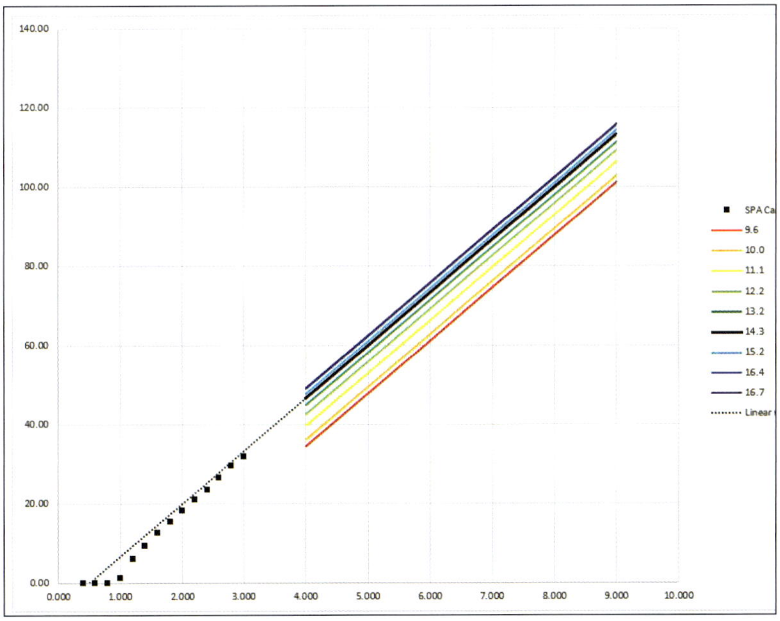

The delivered fuel mass from an injector can be estimated with a linear relationship over most of its range. Smaller pulse widths used at idle and cruising conditions may require additional data for the ECU model to accurately deliver the correct amount each time.

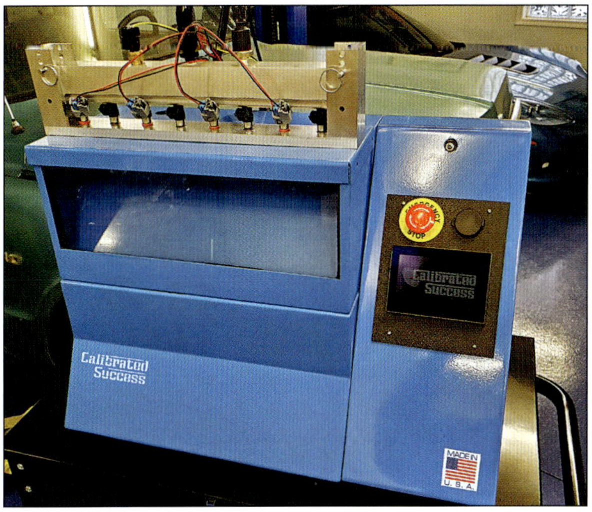

After years of struggling with poor injector data, I created my own test bench capable of running the necessary tests to derive accurate ECU calibration data from any set in just minutes. This bench is now available commercially through Calibrated Success for shop owners who also wish to take the guesswork out of fuel delivery.

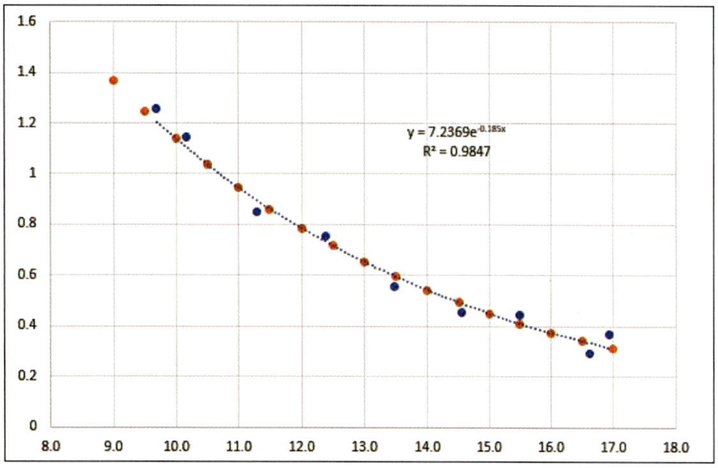

The calculated offset from a series of injector flow tests at various voltages shows how much quicker the injector responds at increased voltage. The Calibrated Success injector bench tool fits this data to a clean curve that closely fits the data.

ulated high voltage supply that stays consistent even if vehicle battery voltage varies. This has a side benefit of making the opening time not only consistent, but usually very short. Voltages often around 70V through low-resistance coils mean that the DI injectors have very fast response.

The large changes in rail pressure possible with many DI systems mean that there is still a need to adjust the closing delay in relation to this pressure. The closing delay forms a small but still significant part of the total injector offset.

can be turned into an appropriate "on" time for the circuit that would result in the desired air-fuel ratio. It is important to note that the value for the injector slope is tied to the working pressure change between the fuel rail and the intake manifold (or rail and combustion chamber in the case of direct injection). Any change in this pressure differential can have a significant impact on how much fuel is delivered, even at short pulse widths.

The offset is also a variable that depends on the voltage applied to the coil inside the fuel injector. Higher voltage means more total energy delivered, and thus allows the coil to overcome its internal spring and the fuel rail pressure quicker before opening. The offset value is unique to each fuel-injector design and varies with both voltage and working pressure. The offset includes the fluid effects of fuel pushing though the solenoid and orifice plate, so if the injector is modified for greater flow, it needs a new offset characterization in the ECU as well, even if the coils did not change.

Direct-Injection Offset

Direct-injection (DI) systems are a little more fortunate in this aspect because they are often run with a regulated high voltage supply that stays consistent even if vehicle battery voltage varies.

Small Pulses

For some OEMs (and most aftermarket standalone ECUs), flow rate and offset get us close enough to an accurate delivered fuel mass. But if we want true accuracy at low flow rates, there is another physical phenomenon to consider. Whenever a fluid valve is opened, the instantaneous flow rate is higher for a short amount of time until we reach continuous flow.

Imagine standing on the driveway with your thumb over the end of the hose as you wash the car. The moment you lift your thumb, water shoots out in a strong stream that eventually settles into a more-predictable and lower flow. The same thing happens every time a fuel injector fires.

If a fuel injector is tested using a process similar to the SAE J1832 standard, we are able to see this phenomenon at work. Zooming in on the lowest fuel masses at the very beginning of flow, we can see that there is a gap between the linear fit that worked so well up top and the reality of what happens down low.

The actual offset is longer than the simple slope-intercept model,

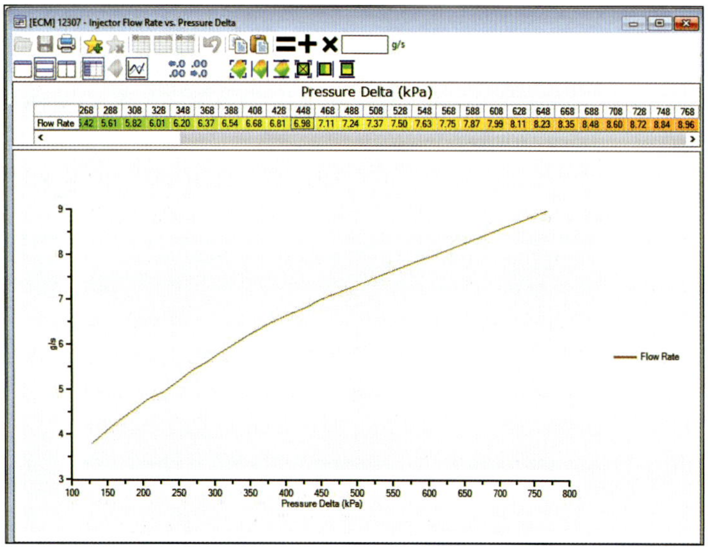

The Bernoulli equation tells us to expect flow rate to change with the square root of the pressure across the injector. This square root function gives us a good fit to the curve, seen here for injector flow versus delta pressure across it.

Calibrated Success
EFI Training - Tuning - Consulting

Chrysler Injector Characterization

Injector Pulse Width vs. Fuel Mass			Fuel Mass vs. Injector Pulse Width	
g	ms		ms	g
0	0		0	0
0.003634003	0.581775435		0.581775435	0.003634
0.0048	0.7818		0.781775435	0.0048033
0.0061	0.9818		0.981775435	0.0061161
0.0071	1.1818		1.181775435	0.0070729
0.0081	1.3818		1.381775435	0.0081491
0.0092	1.5818		1.581775435	0.0091504
0.0102	1.7818		1.781775435	0.0101896
0.0112	1.9818		1.981775435	0.0112181
0.0123	2.1818		2.181775435	0.0122626
0.0133	2.3818		2.381775435	0.0133082
0.0182	3.3818		3.381775435	0.0182176
0.0494	9.3818		9.381775435	0.0493675
0.2570	49.3818		49.38177544	0.2570332

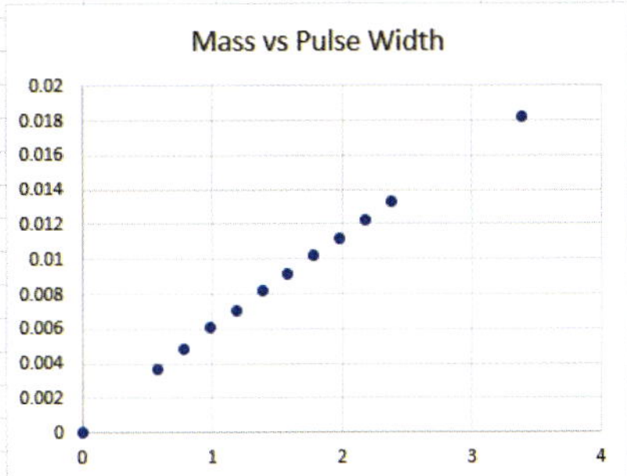

Startup Inj PW Scalar	Inj PW Min
5.236 mg/ms	0.582 ms

Inj PW Offset

kPa	6.0	7.0	8.0	10.0	12.0	14.0	15.8	15.8	15.8 V
0	2.509	2.111	1.775	1.264	0.913	0.669	0.520	0.520	0.520
20	2.565	2.157	1.813	1.290	0.932	0.682	0.529	0.529	0.529
40	2.622	2.205	1.853	1.317	0.951	0.695	0.538	0.538	0.538
80	2.740	2.303	1.934	1.374	0.989	0.722	0.558	0.558	0.558
100	2.801	2.354	1.977	1.403	1.010	0.736	0.568	0.568	0.568

Starting with a complete characterization report like this one in exact plug-and-play format from Calibrated Success makes the engine calibration process much easier.

but it's followed by a steeper slope that quickly catches up to and merges with the basic linear fit. This nonlinear region of injector flow can be modeled in the ECU, and every OEM has its preferred method. The more accurate one can be with the fuel-delivery model at small masses, the more precise one can be with emissions, idle, cruise, and evaporative canister purge control.

For the high-performance tuner, using higher-flow-rate fuel injectors to support additional horsepower and airflow means that you are more likely to operate down in this nonlinear flow region for a given fuel injector. If the ECU being tuned allows updates to these values with accurate data for the injectors, it makes a huge improvement on idle and drive quality as well as emissions.

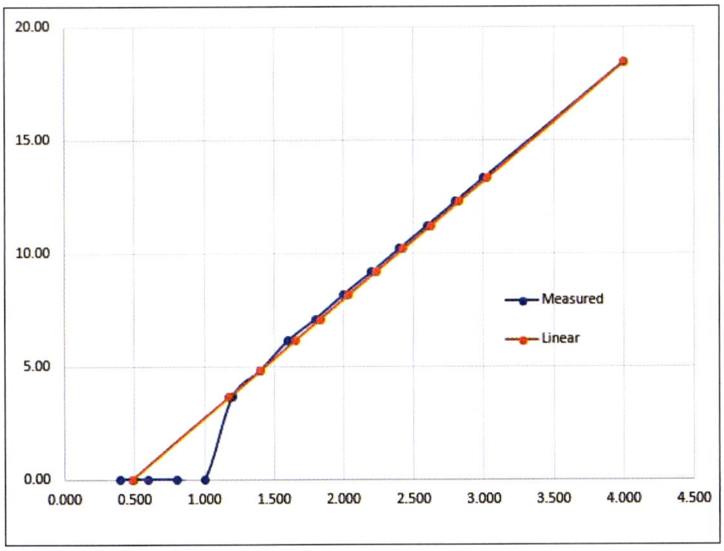

Very small fuel mass requirements can get into the area where the simple linear fit is no longer accurate. Some OEMs have creative solutions to model fuel delivery as the injector just begins to open.

Unfortunately, this is not something that can be determined accurately on a running vehicle. There are multiple variables and just a single equation, so high-school algebra says that we need another solution. The proper way to derive this data is to test the fuel injectors on a dedicated flowbench that is capable of running the right test sequence, collecting accurate data, and post-processing that data into the units needed for ECU calibration.

This is such an important step in the calibration process that I eventually made my own fuel-injector test bench to perform the work. We now sell copies of this test bench through Calibrated Success in addition to performing characterization work for our clients. The time saved by avoiding bad corrections during the airflow tuning process more than pays for the additional injector characterization work, especially on programs that must pass today's emissions standards.

Transient Air-Fuel Control

In a perfect world, we would simply match the incoming airflow with a single shot of fuel flow and have clean combustion. Surprisingly, DI systems come pretty close now. For port-injected systems, we must contend with a few challenges. During steady-state operation, continuous airflow and continuous fuel flow at a certain injector pulse width work out to provide a good balance. The problem that this ignores is that a significant process is happening inside the intake port and even manifold runners themselves.

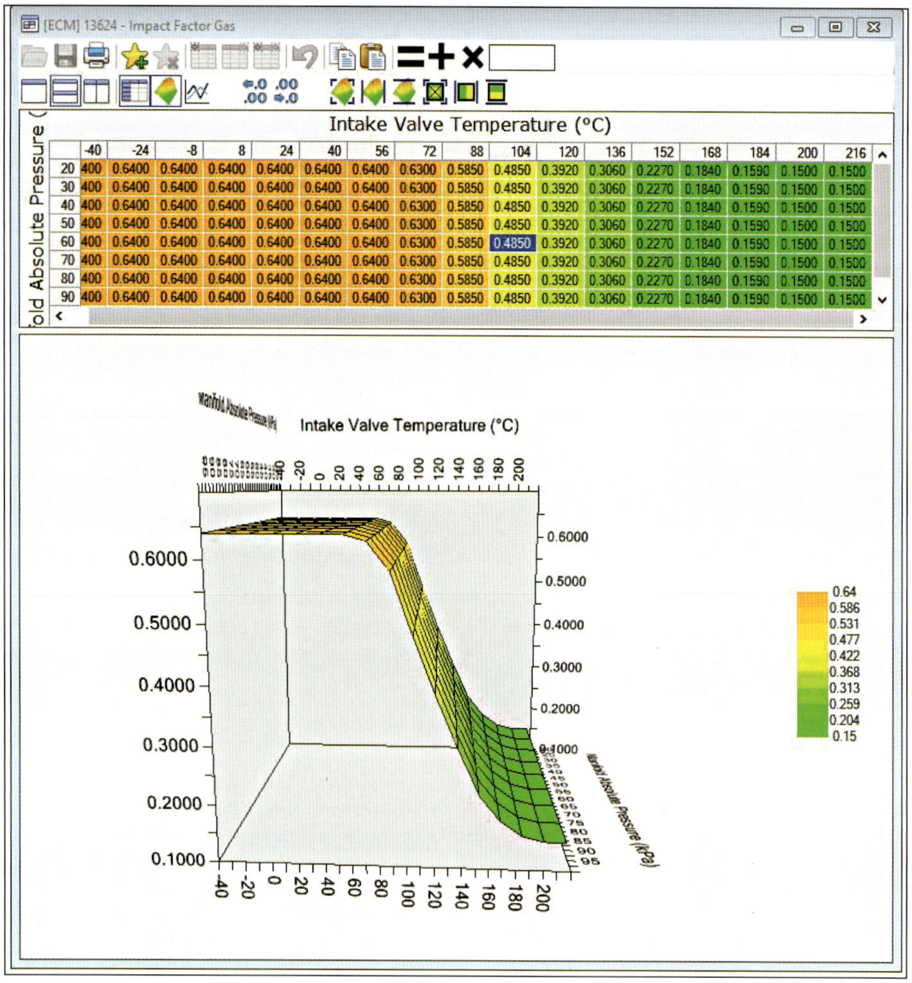

Intake Valve Temperature (°C)

fold Absolute Pressure (	-40	-24	-8	8	24	40	56	72	88	104	120	136	152	168	184	200	216
20	400	0.6400	0.6400	0.6400	0.6400	0.6400	0.6400	0.6300	0.5850	0.4850	0.3920	0.3060	0.2270	0.1840	0.1590	0.1500	0.1500
30	400	0.6400	0.6400	0.6400	0.6400	0.6400	0.6400	0.6300	0.5850	0.4850	0.3920	0.3060	0.2270	0.1840	0.1590	0.1500	0.1500
40	400	0.6400	0.6400	0.6400	0.6400	0.6400	0.6400	0.6300	0.5850	0.4850	0.3920	0.3060	0.2270	0.1840	0.1590	0.1500	0.1500
50	400	0.6400	0.6400	0.6400	0.6400	0.6400	0.6400	0.6300	0.5850	0.4850	0.3920	0.3060	0.2270	0.1840	0.1590	0.1500	0.1500
60	400	0.6400	0.6400	0.6400	0.6400	0.6400	0.6400	0.6300	0.5850	0.4850	0.3920	0.3060	0.2270	0.1840	0.1590	0.1500	0.1500
70	400	0.6400	0.6400	0.6400	0.6400	0.6400	0.6400	0.6300	0.5850	0.4850	0.3920	0.3060	0.2270	0.1840	0.1590	0.1500	0.1500
80	400	0.6400	0.6400	0.6400	0.6400	0.6400	0.6400	0.6300	0.5850	0.4850	0.3920	0.3060	0.2270	0.1840	0.1590	0.1500	0.1500
90	400	0.6400	0.6400	0.6400	0.6400	0.6400	0.6400	0.6300	0.5850	0.4850	0.3920	0.3060	0.2270	0.1840	0.1590	0.1500	0.1500

Transient fuel delivery to the cylinder is heavily dependent on wall film in the intake ports. Even a fully warmed-up PFI engine can have 15 percent or more of its delivered fuel coming from "the puddle" in between the injector and the cylinder.

Even in multi-port injection systems, where each cylinder has its own fuel injector aimed directly toward the inlet valve, a significant portion of the fuel injected will make a detour on the way into the cylinder. A portion of each injection shot sticks to the walls of the intake port to form a thin puddle. Over time, fuel evaporates from this puddle to join the fuel that makes it directly from the injector into the cylinder.

In steady state, the engine can reach equilibrium, where the amount of fuel entering the puddle is equal to the amount of fuel evaporating from the puddle, and its effect is negligible. However, during transient conditions where airflow, throttle position, manifold pressure, cam position, or charge temperature is changing, the equilibrium is disturbed. Then, we have the potential for the cylinder mixture to be either richer or leaner than desired unless some compensation is made to account for the puddle's influence on delivered fuel.

The size of the puddle and its influence varies mostly with temperature and airflow. Cooler intake port walls allow more fuel to condense and take longer for it to evaporate. Sharp increases in airflow can act much like a fan drying up the puddle and reducing the amount of fuel it is able to deliver, leading to a lean condition unless proper compensation is made. The larger the wetted area of the intake tract, the more significant the fuel puddle effect becomes. Carbureted or central-port-injection engines are the extreme cases where almost the entire intake manifold contributes to wall-film effects, requiring significant corrections in the ECU.

Since we do not directly measure or control the puddle, there are no diagnostics for it specifically. However, incorrect estimation of fuel delivery through the puddle can lead to misfire events (P0300). They can also help a skilled technician identify an injector with a bad spray pattern or flow.

Whenever installing parts that are expected to increase the engine's pumping efficiency, one should also expect to make corrections to the ECU tables that cover transient fueling. These are sometimes simply labeled "acceleration enrichment," similar to a carburetor's pump shot. There may be more complex X-Tau models that calculate the percentage of actual fuel hitting the wall on each injection event followed by an estimate of the current evaporation rate.

This can be difficult to calibrate properly, so I always instruct my students to perform steady-state fueling and airflow measurements first before trying to smooth out transients. Even a change to a set of higher-flowing fuel injectors can impact the wall wetting, so it's always a good idea to perform separate steady-state and transient fuel-delivery checks when tuning.

Spark Delivery

We wouldn't have a combustion process in the gas engine if it wasn't initiated by something. That something is a high-voltage discharge across the gap of the spark plug. The voltage is increased above nor-

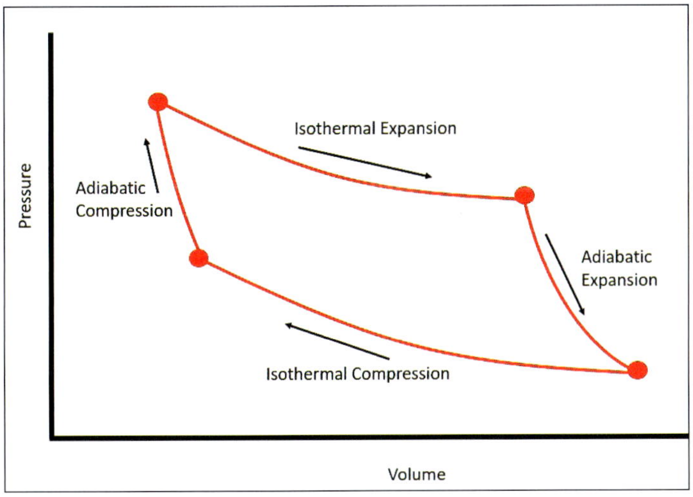

In a perfect world, the Carnot cycle would represent the gasoline combustion process. In reality, we must deal with some additional losses. Combustion must be initiated a little early during the compression process if we are to optimize output.

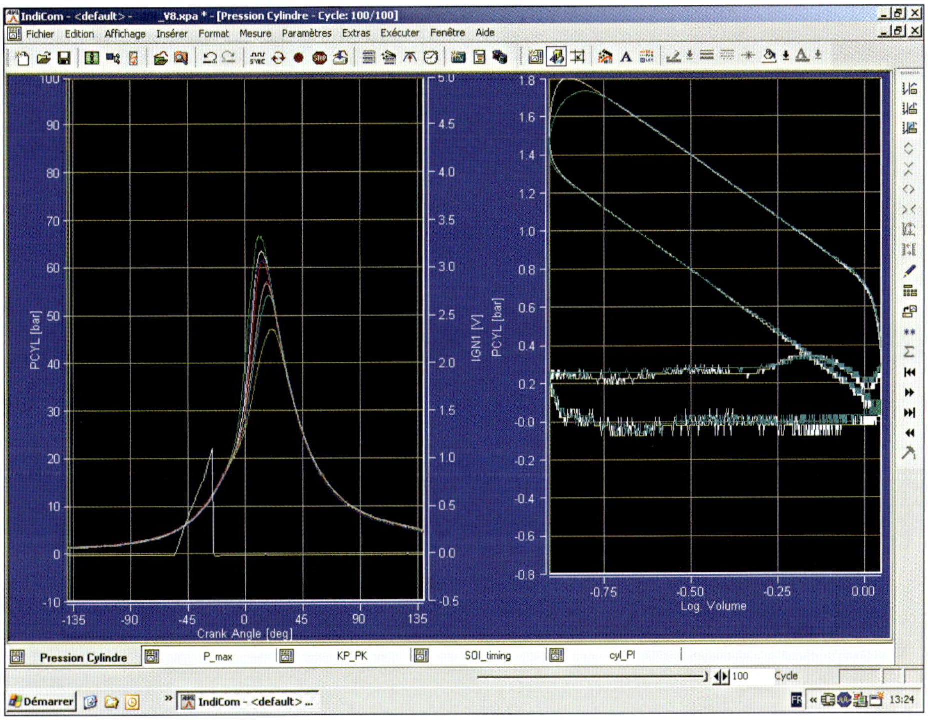

Here's a look at what is really happening inside a spark-ignited engine. The triangular spike of the spark event triggers the start of the combustion process during the last part of the compression stroke.

mal battery voltage in the ignition coil, which is basically an electrical transformer with a varying number of windings on the primary versus secondary circuits to achieve the step up in voltage.

The ECU is able to control how long the primary side is charged by system voltage before an ignition event, a time known as "dwell." It was originally controlled by the contact points in early distributors. Today, the ECU has a table that can vary dwell in relation to system voltage and engine speed to make sure that the right amount of energy is available to fire the spark plug without overheating the coil or transistors in the circuit. The coils and their circuits are subject to diagnostics (P0351–P0358).

Timing of the spark discharge has a profound effect on how the engine runs. For any combination of conditions, there is some ideal time in the operating cycle to initiate combustion that results in the best mechanical efficiency for that combustion event. Gasoline engines mostly follow the Carnot cycle of constant volume heat addition with the key exception that the heat addition isn't always ideal.

The dirty secret here is that fuel does not burn instantly, nor does it always burn at the same rate. Higher loads of air and fuel in the cylinder will burn quicker than light charges, so they require less lead time to get the cylinder pressure to peak at the most useful point.

For piston engines, it has been determined that the best balance of net output power can be found when cylinder pressures peak at approximately 12 to 15 degrees after TDC. The spark timing that lights the charge in time to yield this correctly timed pressure peak is known as MBT timing, measured in degrees before TDC. If the spark event happens later than this, the combustion happens a little later as well.

The result is that more energy is released later in the cycle where the piston is already falling away from TDC, and the combustion does not have as much average pressure on the piston. This, in turn, could help turn the crankshaft effectively through the power stroke of the engine cycle. The result is a reduction in torque that is somewhat proportional to how delayed the actual spark event is from the theoretical MBT point for that cycle. We'll come back to this when we discuss torque controls, as it proves quite useful.

Getting the right spark timing is like skeet shooting. It requires one to aim ahead and account for various speeds to coincide with effect at the right moment. Higher engine speeds mean that the engine covers more degrees of rotation in 1 second, so spark advance is increased at higher speeds to compensate.

As mentioned previously, cylinder load also plays a big part where flame speeds increase for dense charges that are releasing more energy, so less advance is necessary at higher loads. The basic spark-advance tables in the ECU will have engine speed as one axis and some measure of cylinder load (g/cyl, percent load, manifold pressure, etc.) as the other axis. More complex factors (such as cam timing and EGR dilution) also have an effect, so there are tables within the ECU to specifically address these.

Air-charge temperature also plays a large role, since warmer things tend to burn faster than colder things. It may sound obvious, but I've lost count of how many tuners I have seen zero out spark versus air temperature tables in their work because they thought this was robbing them of precious horsepower. As an OEM calibration engineer, I can assure you that we laugh at such practices that ignore basic science.

With pump gas, we have another concern beyond just picking what would be the ideal spark timing for the current conditions. We buy fuels by their octane rating, a number that represents the anti-knocking index of a fuel or its resistance to unintended combustion.

At elevated loads, an engine can develop sufficient pressure in the cylinder to auto-ignite the end gases farther away from the flame front. This creates a second flame front and pressure wave that collides with the first, which can result in significant damage to the engine. This collision is often audible outside of the engine, even over the ambient noise of the road, intake, and exhaust systems. Fuels with a higher octane rating are less likely to experience this but also cost more. The telltale "marbles in a can" noise is not one we expect to hear from a properly running engine.

To avoid all of this mess and potential damage, OEM calibration engineers spend hours in the development dyno cells testing the engine to find the points at which this knock begins with the fuel for which the engine is designed to run. Tables are populated within the ECU to express a limit of spark advance that can be run without encountering damaging knock. The ECU then uses the lower value of MBT to time the spark plugs. While running lower spark advance than MBT is not good for efficiency and horsepower, it still beats breaking parts and a walk-home failure.

Knock Sensors

As a final safety measure, modern engines are fitted with knock sensors.

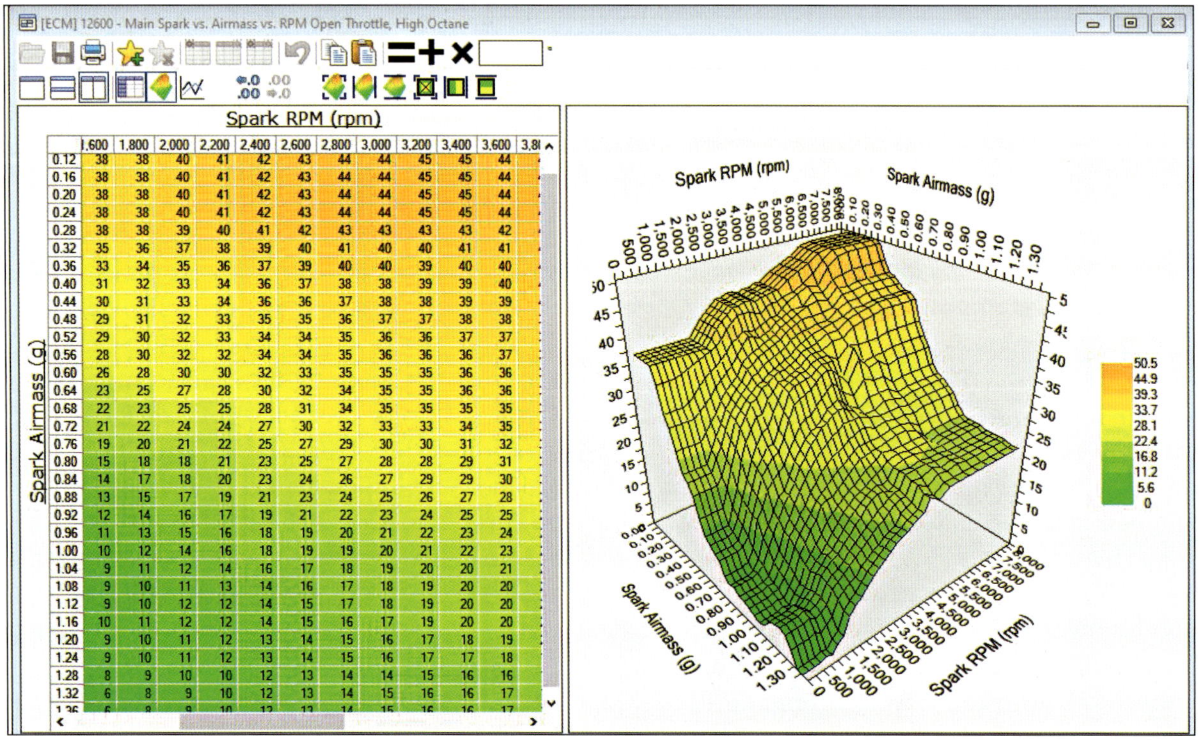

Spark Airmass (g) \ Spark RPM (rpm)	1,600	1,800	2,000	2,200	2,400	2,600	2,800	3,000	3,200	3,400	3,600
0.12	38	38	40	41	42	43	44	44	45	45	44
0.16	38	38	40	41	42	43	44	44	45	45	44
0.20	38	38	40	41	42	43	44	44	45	45	44
0.24	38	38	40	41	42	43	44	44	45	45	44
0.28	38	38	39	40	41	42	43	43	43	43	42
0.32	35	36	37	38	39	40	41	40	40	41	41
0.36	33	34	35	36	37	39	40	40	39	40	40
0.40	31	32	33	34	36	37	38	38	39	39	40
0.44	30	31	33	34	36	36	37	38	38	39	39
0.48	29	31	32	33	35	35	36	37	37	38	38
0.52	29	30	32	33	34	34	35	36	36	37	37
0.56	28	30	32	32	34	34	35	36	36	36	37
0.60	26	28	30	30	32	33	35	35	35	36	36
0.64	23	25	27	28	30	32	34	35	35	36	36
0.68	22	23	25	25	28	31	34	35	35	35	35
0.72	21	22	24	24	27	30	32	33	33	34	35
0.76	19	20	21	22	25	27	29	30	30	31	32
0.80	15	18	18	21	23	25	27	28	28	29	31
0.84	14	17	18	20	23	24	26	27	29	29	30
0.88	13	15	17	19	21	23	24	25	26	27	28
0.92	12	14	16	17	19	21	22	23	24	25	25
0.96	11	13	15	16	18	19	20	21	22	23	24
1.00	10	12	14	16	18	19	19	20	21	22	23
1.04	9	11	12	14	16	17	18	19	20	20	21
1.08	9	10	11	13	14	16	17	18	19	20	20
1.12	9	10	12	12	14	15	17	18	19	20	20
1.16	10	11	12	12	14	15	16	17	19	20	20
1.20	9	10	11	12	13	14	15	16	17	18	19
1.24	9	10	11	12	13	14	15	16	17	17	18
1.28	8	9	10	10	12	13	14	14	15	16	16
1.32	6	8	9	10	12	13	14	15	16	16	17

The base spark table for this C6 ZR1 supercharged Corvette includes cylinder loads of greater than 100-percent filling. Additional adjustments will be added to these values for fueling, charge temperature, and other factors.

Manufacturers have gone from single knock sensors to the most sensitive applications having one almost touching each individual cylinder to better capture the noise at the source. Raw knock-sensor signals are filtered for timing relative to those cylinders' combustion events and the frequency of the expected noise.

These are basically microphones attached to the block or cylinder head that listen for the signature sounds of knock. The ECU constantly reads the signal from the knock sensor and must do some creative filtering to discern genuine knock from other background noises generated by the many moving metal parts in an engine.

The first filter is frequency based because spark knock occurs in a specific range based on the bore size and speed of sound within the cylinder. Next, the sensor is sampled during specific time windows that align with combustion events for each cylinder near TDC. There is no reason to listen for knock at other times, so this takes some load off the processor.

Finally, a calibration engineer must go through a wide range of test conditions and determine what knock sensor output matches the normal noise floor of the running engine so that the knock mitigation routine does not become active when it is not needed. This is a time-consuming process for the OEM calibrator and has a significant impact on quality, fuel economy, and rated power.

If the knock sensor does recognize what it believes to be real knock while the engine is running, the ECU has the ability to execute several potential remedies. The first response is to retard the spark advance, which will also reduce cylinder pressure and torque. How fast this response is and how long the reduction remains in place are adjustable by the calibrator to ensure the safety of the engine.

Some ECUs have the ability to also add fuel, close the throttle, or reduce the desired boost of a turbo or supercharger system when knock is detected. Once the knock is gone, the ECU follows a prescribed recovery pattern in an attempt to return to normal operation and spark advance.

If repeated knock events happen, the ECU may learn a global shift to protect for what it thinks is a bad tank of gas or other engine condition that will not tolerate full spark advance at high loads. The value of this learned shift is often stored in the ECU as some variant of a "knock learn factor" that can be accessed or reset with the right OBD scan-tool request.

Torque Control

Modern ECUs have what is known as torque-based controls. This means that throttle position, camshaft phasing, spark, and fueling are often adjusted based on what the resulting torque would be at the flywheel. The first fly-by-wire throttle controls picked throttle position mostly as a function of accelerator-pedal

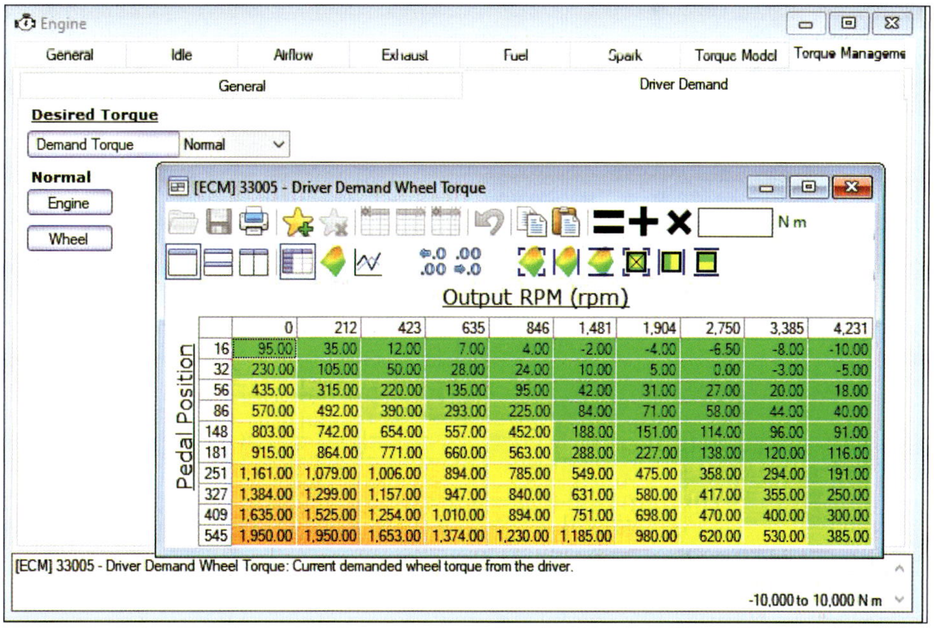

Pedal Position \ Output RPM (rpm)	0	212	423	635	846	1,481	1,904	2,750	3,385	4,231
16	95.00	35.00	12.00	7.00	4.00	-2.00	-4.00	-6.50	-8.00	-10.00
32	230.00	105.00	50.00	28.00	24.00	10.00	5.00	0.00	-3.00	-5.00
56	435.00	315.00	220.00	135.00	95.00	42.00	31.00	27.00	20.00	18.00
86	570.00	492.00	390.00	293.00	225.00	84.00	71.00	58.00	44.00	40.00
148	803.00	742.00	654.00	557.00	452.00	188.00	151.00	114.00	96.00	91.00
181	915.00	864.00	771.00	660.00	563.00	288.00	227.00	138.00	120.00	116.00
251	1,161.00	1,079.00	1,006.00	894.00	785.00	549.00	475.00	358.00	294.00	191.00
327	1,384.00	1,299.00	1,157.00	947.00	840.00	631.00	580.00	417.00	355.00	250.00
409	1,635.00	1,525.00	1,254.00	1,010.00	894.00	751.00	698.00	470.00	400.00	300.00
545	1,950.00	1,950.00	1,653.00	1,374.00	1,230.00	1,185.00	980.00	620.00	530.00	385.00

Driver input from the accelerator pedal is translated into a torque request at the axle in this table. This ECU calculates the desired engine torque based on transmission and axle ratios where some ECUs request flywheel torque directly from accelerator-pedal inputs.

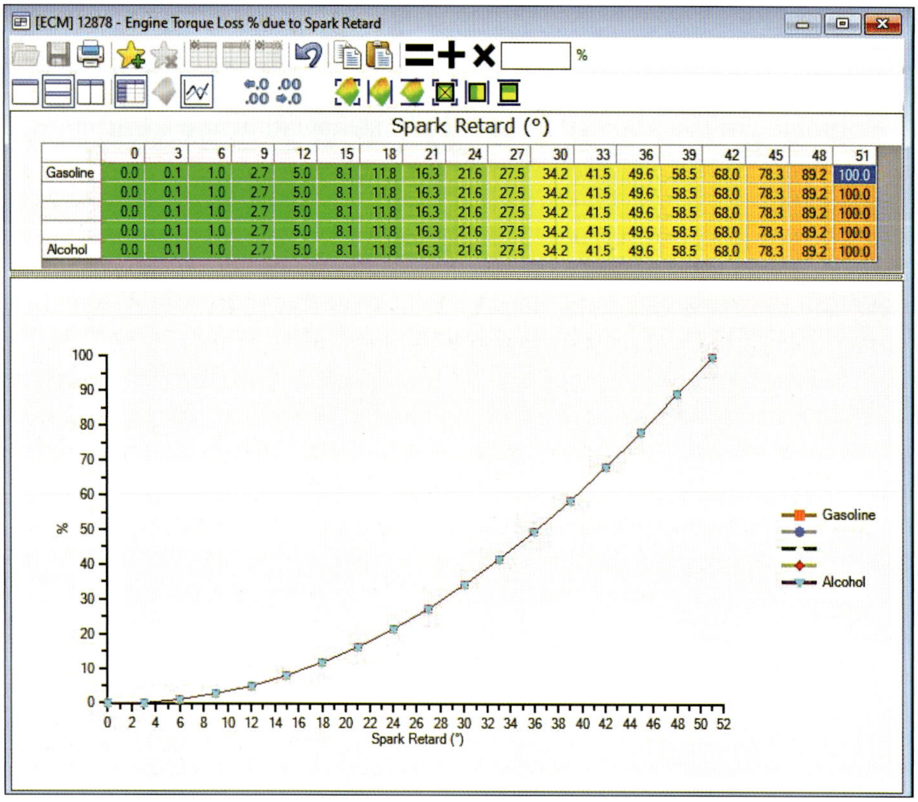

	0	3	6	9	12	15	18	21	24	27	30	33	36	39	42	45	48	51
Gasoline	0.0	0.1	1.0	2.7	5.0	8.1	11.8	16.3	21.6	27.5	34.2	41.5	49.6	58.5	68.0	78.3	89.2	100.0
	0.0	0.1	1.0	2.7	5.0	8.1	11.8	16.3	21.6	27.5	34.2	41.5	49.6	58.5	68.0	78.3	89.2	100.0
	0.0	0.1	1.0	2.7	5.0	8.1	11.8	16.3	21.6	27.5	34.2	41.5	49.6	58.5	68.0	78.3	89.2	100.0
	0.0	0.1	1.0	2.7	5.0	8.1	11.8	16.3	21.6	27.5	34.2	41.5	49.6	58.5	68.0	78.3	89.2	100.0
Alcohol	0.0	0.1	1.0	2.7	5.0	8.1	11.8	16.3	21.6	27.5	34.2	41.5	49.6	58.5	68.0	78.3	89.2	100.0

By modeling the amount of torque reduction versus retard from MBT, the ECU gains the ability to make rapid adjustments to delivered torque with changes in delivered ignition timing. These values are relative to MBT, regardless of whether the engine is already retarded from MBT to respect the knock limit. In those cases, it would simply slide farther along the torque curve as timing shifts.

position. While this worked well, it had limitations when the OEMs attempted to integrate behavior of the engine and transmission together or add hybrid electronic propulsion aids.

Torque-based controls recognize accelerator-pedal position as a driver request to speed up, slow down, or hold the current vehicle speed. This translates to adding, reducing, or holding the current torque being applied to the drive wheels.

In a torque-based control system, a driver request to speed up can be satisfied by adding torque by some means other than just opening the throttle. This may be phasing the camshaft, changing the transmission ratio, or adding electrical power from a hybrid device, all of which would feel the same to the driver. The system then decides how much of that torque needs to come from the engine, and how best to make the engine deliver. A request is then made for a specific engine torque, which can be compared to a modeled estimate of the torque currently being produced. There is no actual torque sensor in the system.

Earlier, we discovered that the torque curve of an engine looks a lot like the VE curve. This is not an accident. Torque and cylinder filling are so closely tied that almost all OEM torque models begin with the cylinder filling to create their initial estimate. This gives the ECU a reference number for flywheel torque that may be modified based on how far the current spark advance is from an MBT reference table, actual air-fuel ratio, accessory drive losses, friction losses, or other factors.

Assuming that these other factors are stable, the ECU has a fairly accurate method of scaling engine torque output simply by controlling airflow and cylinder filling. While this is effective and has a great deal of authority, it moves relatively slow compared to the expected engine response in some cases. It takes time to physically move the throttle blade and allow more air to fill the intake manifold plenum before any increase actually hits the cylinders. Because of this, airflow control is referred to as "slow path" torque control by OEM engineers.

To provide a quicker torque response, another method of adjusting torque must be used. Requests from traction control, stability control, transmission shifting, or even idle control require that the engine make adjustments faster than what can be done by adjusting airflow alone. Here is where we come back to the relationship between spark advance and torque that was previously mentioned.

Any time spark timing is intentionally retarded from MBT, there is a predictable reduction in torque generated from that combustion event. Because spark timing can be changed as rapidly as the next cylinder's TDC event in the firing order, this change in delivered torque is almost immediate and referred to as "fast path" torque control. The trick here is that it really only works in one direction, with torque being reduced as timing is retarded away from the MBT reference point.

Torque is not added when timing is advanced beyond MBT. To get any fast-path increase in torque, the ECU must be starting from a point that is already intentionally retarded from

MBT to recover the untapped reserve of torque set aside by the original retard from MBT. This is exactly how modern ECUs control idle.

A "torque reserve" amount is picked that leaves the fast path control with room to either increase or decrease torque on demand. This is done by adjusting spark advance, allowing the ECU the ability to make rapid compensations for things such as accessory or transmission shift loads at idle.

This fast path is indeed very quick, but the total authority range is limited by how far the spark can be retarded from MBT before combustion becomes unstable. So, larger corrections must be transferred to the slow-path airflow control over time to make sure that fast-path spark control still has enough range to react at any moment.

Retarding spark for an immediate torque reduction at high engine speeds and loads can dump a substantial amount of heat into the exhaust, catalyst, or turbocharger. As such, a limit for spark retard and torque control usually exists in the ECU to prevent heat damage based on modeled exhaust temperature and component temperature limits.

While this sounds like a lot of extra complexity, it actually allows the OEM engineers to perform some really neat tricks. For example, a torque-based control system can carefully balance engine torque, speed, and inertia during a transmission shift so closely that the driver never feels the gear change. They do this by using just the right amount of engine torque adjustment to offset the change in inertia due to engine speed changes in a shift.

Speaking of transmissions, it also allows for much-improved clutch-pressure controls, where the transmission control module (TCM) can now apply only as much pressure to a clutch pack as is needed to hold the input torque without slipping, saving fuel and clutch life.

Most aftermarket transmission calibration issues I see on torque-based systems can be traced back to inaccurate engine torque modeling that feeds a bogus number to the TCM. The TCM cannot help but react to whatever torque is being relayed to it from the ECU, so it picks a line pressure and clutch activation based on this number.

The adaptive learns in the TCM can only go so far to attempt to fix these errors. It's even more difficult if the errors are not consistently in the same direction. So, a torque model that is higher than reality in some areas and lower in others can thoroughly confuse the TCM. The solution here is usually to go back to the fundamentals and properly map the ECU airflow models first, then polish the torque models and watch the TCM almost fix itself once fed accurate numbers for torque. Modern clutch-to-clutch automatic transmissions are surprisingly robust, but not so if they are forced to constantly deal with torque discrepancies.

Additional Features

Many engines today use boosting systems that employ either a supercharger or turbocharger to increase their output. These extra pumps force more air into the same size of cylinder than it would normally consume in naturally aspirated form. Today's ECUs treat these devices as an extension of the throttle control logic because they determine how much airflow will enter the engine at any moment.

In an effort to reduce pumping losses and increase fuel economy, boosted engines now have logic that attempts to quickly drive them to an open-throttle condition at low-pedal requests from the driver. This works because the engine's lower compression ratio doesn't necessarily make a lot of torque at atmospheric-pressure levels in the intake manifold. The engine only makes full power when the boosting system is fully active, so

Electronically controlled wastegates can act as a second airflow control device on turbocharged vehicles. The ECU just drives the primary throttle open as soon as possible to reduce pumping losses. Then, it varies the signal to the wastegate to control torque.

Compressor bypass valves used to only be passively vacuum actuated. Now, with more advanced ECU control, they can be used to prevent compressor surge or control load to avoid low-speed preignition.

Running a GM e67 ECU, this restomod now has active control over alternator-output voltage and the supercharger bypass valve. Drive-by-wire throttle control also allows for more predictable response from this 900-hp engine at parking-lot speeds.

wide-open throttle without boost on these engines is similar to part throttle on a larger naturally aspirated engine—as far as delivered torque is concerned.

A key benefit here is that by running with an open throttle, less energy is wasted, creating a vacuum in the intake path. This improves fuel economy at medium loads. If more torque is requested, then the boosting system is progressively dialed up with either closure of a supercharger bypass or turbocharger wastegate until the desired airflow and engine torque is reached. It's all harmonious logic for slow-path torque control in modern ECUs.

The ECU may also have control over several other actuators on the vehicle. Tunable exhaust valves that alter the noise level are now ECU controlled. They close at light loads and cruising speeds to reduce drive-by noise as mandated by government standards, but they can open up to an enthusiastic roar at full load. There is now a market for devices that plug into this circuit to force the valves open on command so that the driver can get whatever exhaust note is desired regardless of the ECU commanded position.

The good news is that the backpressure change for most OEM exhaust valves is not as dramatic as a traditional set of cutouts. So, even though the noise level changes, engine volumetric pumping efficiency is not affected enough to force errors in airflow estimation. The majority of backpressure that the engine sees results from the catalytic converters or turbocharger housing. Most modern catback exhaust systems are fairly low restriction, making aftermarket mufflers and pipes mostly a choice of sound and appearance, rather than performance.

Drag-reducing grille shutters may also be fitted in front of the radiator. These can close at highway speeds, where there is more than enough airflow to cool the radiator. Closing the shutters forces air to go out around the outside of the vehicle rather than through the restrictive path inside the engine bay, thus drag is reduced and fuel economy improved. Because these active grille shutters can impact emissions performance, their actuators and function have their own diagnostics as well.

Let's not forget that some engines have additional ECU-controlled components as well. Modern alternators often have their target output voltage controlled by the ECU. This lets the controls quickly recharge the battery after starts with elevated voltage but settle into a lower voltage as the vehicle continues to drive, saving fuel. Electric water pumps and variable-displacement oil pumps are now reality on some vehicles. If any of these components has the potential to change emissions, they too must have their own diagnostics.

CHAPTER 5

FAULT CODE FUNDAMENTALS

Over the last 30 years or so, the automotive industry has become spoiled with an easy-to-use system to determine what's wrong with most cars. It used to be that the local service station mechanic who had a knack for listening to an engine and determining just what was wrong was the best option for most vehicle owners. Often, he was right too. After all, there's not much that can go wrong with a carbureted flathead Ford with a distributor. Today's engines are different and a lot more complicated.

A rough-running engine today rarely does so without leaving some rather obvious signs as to why. The first of which is the MIL, or CEL. This is the first flag that leads us on the path to repair and happiness. We've all seen TV commercials from auto-parts stores offering to read codes and help fix a vehicle.

The process is now so simple that even a retail parts store clerk can do what used to require a skilled mechanic with years of experience. All vehicles newer than 1996 now support OBD-II functions that include illuminating the MIL and storing codes whenever a significant fault is present. Now, we just need to get to the next step after seeing the light on the dash.

If this light is on, there is work to be done. If it's blinking, stop driving, as this indicates a more serious problem that could cost a lot more if you keep going.

Once alerted by the telltale MIL, the next step is to use some form of interface tool to plug into the vehicle and get a little more information. At this point, there are a lot of options. Because the SAE protocols for OBD-II data are so well known and relatively easy to implement by tool manufacturers, it's a crowded market.

Auto-parts stores offer handheld code-reading tools that are entirely self-contained and powered by the vehicle's OBD-II data port. Many auto-parts stores go a step further and walk outside to the vehicle, plug their tool in for free, and read the codes. They're going to make the money from purchases of whatever parts are needed to fix what they find, so it's usually in their best interest to help get a customer a step further down that path.

For some, attaching the tool may be a challenge. "Where do I plug it in?" is the most common question from those who have never done much modern vehicle work. Our proverbial skilled mechanic knows to look under the driver-side dash and steering-wheel area to find the uniquely shaped OBD-II connector.

The connector may be in plain sight, cleverly hidden among other connectors and wires, or behind an appearance cover. SAE rules state that the connector should be accessible without any tools, so if it is hidden, look for the panel that will pop open with minimal effort from a finger

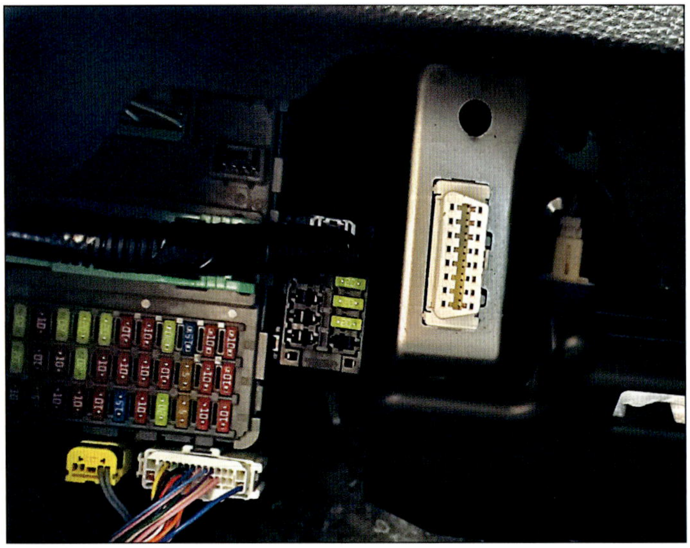

All OBD-II-equipped vehicles have a trapezoidal connector like this one (usually under the driver-side dash). While the color and orientation may vary, manufacturers are required to put it within 3 feet of the driver and make it accessible without any tools.

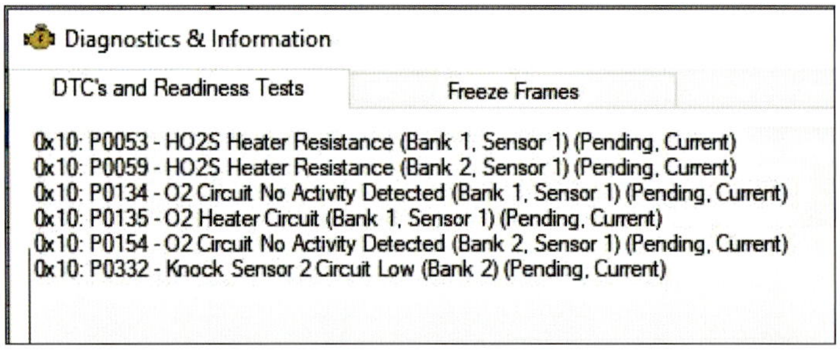

Whenever the MIL is illuminated or the diagnostics have detected a failure, fault codes will be stored in the ECU that can be retrieved by a scan tool. It's not uncommon to have multiple codes for the same general problem, such as an unplugged oxygen sensor harness connection (shown here).

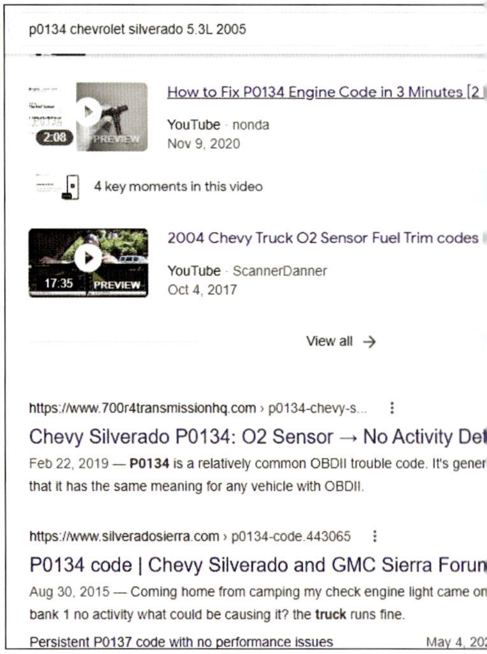

Being specific in search terms helps narrow down the thousands of potential links to those that are most likely to help you. Most searches return a combination of web pages, videos, and discussion forums tailored to the exact vehicle and failure in question since you're probably not the first person to experience this.

to reveal our target. The connector is trapezoidal, so it only plugs in one way—unless you're really determined to break something.

Simply plug in the OBD reader, wait for it to boot, and follow the prompts to discover the potential cause of the vehicle's troubles. These tools are actually accessing Mode $03 and $07 data, but to the casual consumer, it's as good as talking to that old service-station mechanic. In a perfect world, this would be all that's needed to figure out exactly what is needed to fix the vehicle. About 80 percent of the time, this is true.

At this point, our repair adventure is just beginning. Before rushing to get a screwdriver, wrench, or hammer, write down all current and pending fault codes that the handheld tool has revealed to you. Don't erase any of the codes at this point. There is always a chance of losing that piece of paper and not all of them may reappear quickly if you have to re-poll the vehicle.

If using a generic tool, it will only read the basic (P0xxx range) SAE codes. If the tool is able to access the more-advanced manufacturer-specific (P1xxx range) codes, it may get additional similar codes that help point toward a particular failure mode rather than just a sensor or circuit that the basic tool would reveal. Again, write them all down. Then, go to a laptop or desktop computer and work smarter, not harder.

Using a search engine, enter the P-code(s) found along with the make, model, engine, and year of the vehicle. The object here is to use the mind-hive of the internet to quickly access years of knowledge, case studies, and fixes in less than a second. A good example would be something such as "P0300 Chevrolet Silverado 5.3 2005." This narrows the scope to avoid the millions of other discussions about P0300 codes on Honda Accords, Toyota Tundras, Ford Tauruses, or even other Chevrolet Silverados with the V-6 engine that have a completely different wire harness than your current subject of frustration.

Many times, the answer is

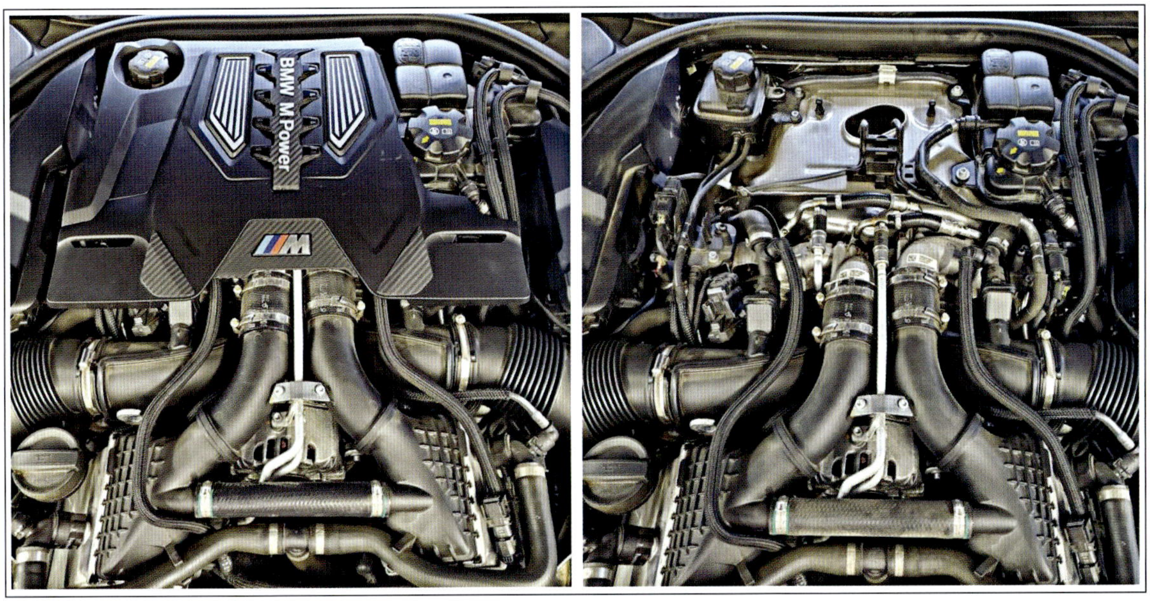

Opening the hood on many vehicles only reveals a beauty or noise cover that must then also be removed to get at almost anything useful in the repair process. Where to go from here is dictated by what codes have been recorded and some of your following online research.

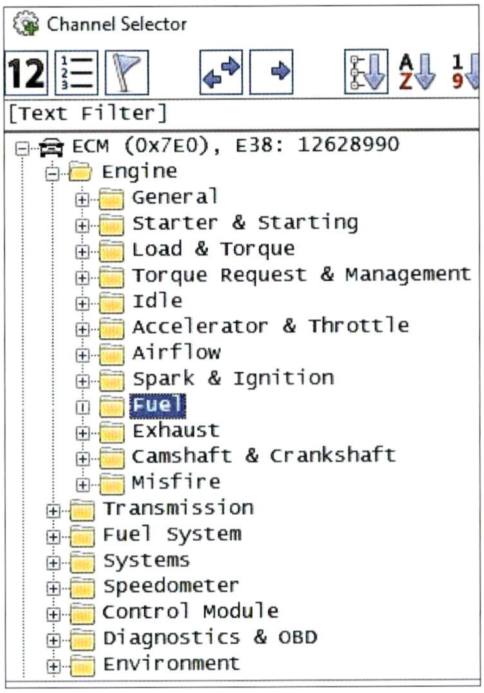

Set up the data-logging tool to display the same Mode $01 values shown in the Mode $02 freeze-frame data at the time of the fault to make it easier to replicate the condition. Add more channels as necessary until there is a good picture of what's really happening.

Vehicle engine compartments are a hostile environment for electrical connections and components. Although the connections are designed to be sealed, they are still exposed to heat, vibration, dirt, water, and sometimes engine fluids that can compromise their integrity.

obvious, and a faulty sensor simply needs to be replaced. Other times, a combination of failures or stack up of conditions leads to a repair that we would not have originally imagined based solely on one P-code. There are countless occasions where a particular vehicle is known for a certain failure (such as a particular connector, coil pack, plug wire, or spark plug) that may lead to the P0300 code.

It is rare to be the first one to talk about a code online. When two or three people mention the same failure and the same fix, you know you are on the right track. I have found that the best sources often end up being enthusiast message boards or groups populated by other DIYers who have walked your exact path before.

If still uncertain about what caused the failure at this point, it may be time to join one of the online conversations. Here's where we can go a step further by accessing the Mode $02 freeze-frame data. As discussed before, this data represents the conditions present at the time of the failure. This may be helpful if the problem is harder to reproduce.

Things like misfire or evaporative diagnostics may be elusive, requiring a little more help to identify just what was going on when they failed. The Mode $02 freeze-frame data helps a skilled technician (and internet mind-hive) receive a better idea of what the root cause of the failure may really be. Knowing that a code was tripped at idle right after a cold start versus on a fully warmed up engine driving down the road at 40 mph may push us in very different directions for the repair of a P013A O_2 Sensor Slow Response B1S2 or P0420 catalyst diagnostic failure. If the tool also grabs the manufacturer-specific (P1xxx range) codes, these will also help technicians zero in quicker on the cause.

If you are fortunate enough to be working with a more sophisticated tool like the ones dealerships usually have, you may be able to look at Mode $01 data in real time or plot it over time. Many aftermarket tuning software packages include scan tools that access this data through a laptop computer and OBD-II connector interface. Compared to old-fashioned methods of probing the harness to check voltages, this is a video-game cheat-code level of improved effectiveness.

As an experienced calibrator, most of my diagnostic work is done through this type of interface rather than simple plug-in code readers. The aftermarket scan tools usually have Mode $01 data logging right alongside Mode $03 and $07 code lists, and a Mode $04 code clear or reset button.

If we have a stored P0102 MAF Low fault stored in Mode $03, one would expect to see a very low or zero value for MAF readings in Mode $01. This simple check confirms that the stored code was not a fluke and that the problem is persisting right now.

Looking at the real-time data also lets you check the connections or wiggle wires to look for issues other than a faulty sensor before spending money on replacement hardware. If unplugging and reinstalling the connector on the sensor suddenly results in a valid signal in Mode $01 data, the fix may be to clean the connectors of any corrosion and ensure a good seat and lock upon connection rather than buying a new sensor.

This problem is not unique to MAF sensors, as it can happen to almost any connector under the hood. Remember that the engine lives in a hot environment that shakes a lot with the car and gets drenched with water every time it rains.

Even with the hood closed, a significant amount of water is blown through the radiator at speed. These droplets settle everywhere, including on connectors that can corrode or leak over time. Other droplets hit hot components that turn them into steam vapor that can later condense in the strangest of places. Almost nothing is immune to this process on the car, so one of the first stops with any sensor failure is to check the connection integrity before throwing new parts at it. Mode $01 real-time data is a great way to visualize and speed up this process if you are able to access it.

If Mode $02 freeze-frame data from when a failure occurred is available, the ability to see the same conditions live in the Mode $01 data stream will help replicate the same conditions. This becomes very helpful when trying to find misfire, cam phasing, boost control, transmission events, or other events that may not be visible at idle.

Single or Multiple Failures

Once you have the fault code from the tool, it's easy to assume that you are looking for a single point of failure in the system. Experienced technicians read this and chuckle, while neophytes think I'm joking. Do repairs long enough and you will end up seeing all kinds of head-scratchers and hilariously improbable failures.

Here is a case in point: A vehicle has a fastener come loose that allows a sensor or actuator to come off its normal mounting point on the engine. While the component is loose, it bounces around under the hood and occasionally hits other things. There's lots of sharp and hot stuff under the hood that can cut, melt, or short circuit to ground given the right conditions.

If this is the case, there may not only be a loose fastener but also a damaged component. We may also

This damaged catalytic convertor didn't get that way on its own. Simply replacing it with a new cat is likely to result in another similar failure if the root cause of poor fuel control or misfire is not found and corrected.

have some secondary impact on the wiring or ECU circuit that drove it. It's quite possible that shorting one of the component wires directly to ground could either spike the current from the ECU or allow it to run (unfused) directly to ground with almost no resistance, smoking the driver circuit in the ECU. Simply changing the component with a fresh, undamaged unit and tightening the fastener is a rookie "parts changer" move.

The questions that I would ask are: Why did it come loose in the first place? Is that the right fastener for the component? Are all fasteners there? Were they torqued properly? Is there supposed to be thread locker on the fastener? Missing any one of these just resets the slow-burning fuse before another failure.

Getting back to the failure and electrical impact, we know that the banged-up component needs to be replaced. But what else could be going on here? If the electrical circuit driving that component was overloaded, we may find additional damage within the ECU or the wiring.

The worst case here is damage within the ECU itself, which is often a rather expensive fix by means of replacement at dealer parts-counter pricing. In a less extreme case, the wire harness was tensile tested, and one or more pins may need to be re-seated or a frayed wire may need to be soldered back together. This will require careful inspection of the wire harness, connectors, and each pin before blindly plugging everything back together with the new component. Missing a bad pin connection at this point will cost hours of diagnosis and frustration later.

If able to actuate the component using Mode $08 active testing controls on your tool, now would be a good time to probe the ECU output while commanding a change. This may be done with either a digital multimeter or even a simple test light. Both of these have their own impedance that makes further damaging the ECU circuit unlikely.

There should be a positive indication of ECU function when the Mode $08 control is actuated. This is proof that the failure was limited to the component itself or the wiring harness. If we don't see any positive indication from the ECU output, we can at least be honest about the need for a more expensive repair of the ECU along with the component. Admittedly, this is a bit of a corner case, but it happens.

Decoding the Codes

By this point, the tool has displayed at least an alphanumeric code that helps explain why the MIL is illuminated on the dash. Most tools follow that code with the SAE or manufacturer's definition of the code to provide a better idea of what it means. Some don't. Luckily, there's a standard that every manufacturer has agreed to use for these codes, and it follows a straightforward pattern regardless of what vehicle you're looking at. They are all five-digit codes starting with a letter followed by at least two numbers.

The first letter designates whether the code is from the powertrain (P), body control (B), chassis control (C), or other vehicle network (U). The majority of cases are powertrain related, which is why calibration engineers often just refer to them all as "P-codes" when talking about errors. All engine, fuel system, emissions, and transmission related codes will start with a P.

We will occasionally experience issues where the ECU has trouble communicating with outside modules

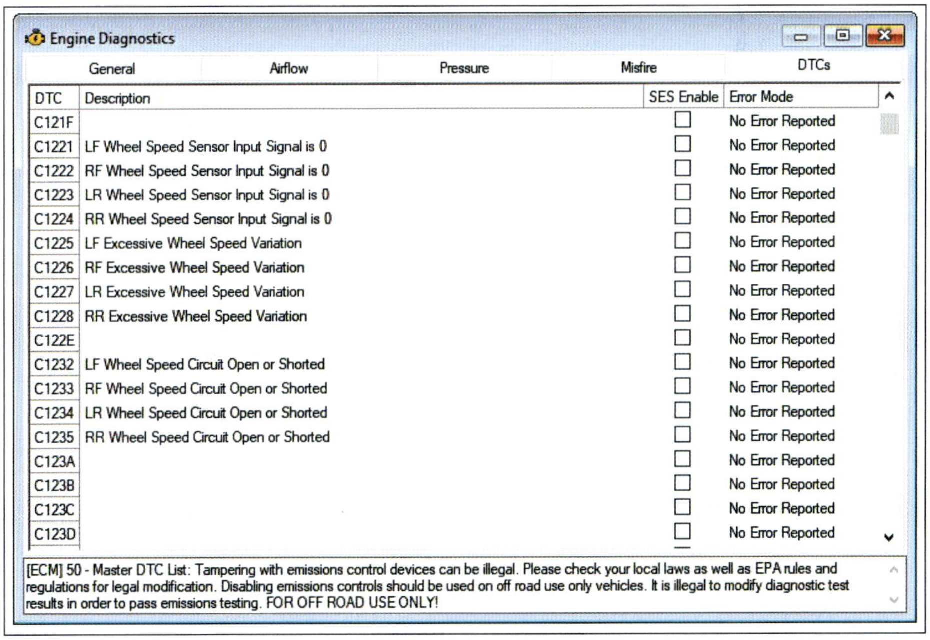

Chassis-control faults, such as wheel-speed sensor errors, can also be transmitted over CAN to the ECU and diagnostic tools. These faults may in turn cause other issues with vehicle speed-based controls.

If a wheel-speed sensor is unplugged or failing, it should show up as a C code on the scan tool. This may have a direct impact on powertrain behavior because so many engine and transmission controls are tied to vehicle speed inputs.

and it will generate a U code related to the network connection (or lack thereof). U, C, and B codes often originate outside of the ECU, but they are transmitted via network connection. For example, a problem with the airbags or safety restraint system would show up as a B code but typically have nothing to do with the operation of the engine controls.

An issue with the wheel-speed sensors may generate a C code from the chassis side, which may in turn impact the engine or transmission controls, as some of these rely on the outside modules for a valid vehicle speed number. For most scan tools, the ECU is the gateway to the rest of the vehicle communication bus, so these codes show up in OBD-II data.

The second digit, a number, designates whether it is a generic SAE or manufacturer-specific fault code. SAE generic codes will all have a zero, thus appearing as "P0xxx." Manufacturer-specific codes have a one as their second digit, thus appearing at "P1xxx."

Keep in mind that the SAE J2012 specification does not require all manufacturers to retain the same numbering system for their specific codes in the "P1xxx" range as they do in the generic "P0xxx" range. A P1380 points to "Misfire detected – Rough Road" on a GM vehicle, but the same code points to "Variable Cam Timing Solenoid A" on a Ford. Obviously, those are two very different issues and fixes. This is precisely why I recommend writing down all codes seen on the tool and individually searching each one with terms that link it to the vehicle in question.

The manufacturer-specific codes can change over time, so attempting to have a single enduring reference in this book would not be possible. SAE has also added more range for generic fault codes to address new technologies that many manufacturers are now using. These are grouped in the "P2xxx" and "P3xxx" ranges. These new groups cover things such as variable intakes, electronic throttles, and auxiliary emissions-control devices.

Many "P2xxx" codes appear redundant to those in the "P0xxx" range at a glance, but their descriptions often lead to a much more clearly identified root cause of the failure. For the technician or DIY enthusiast, these are actually quite a neat improvement and time-saver for newer vehicle repairs.

The third digit breaks down the codes into various monitoring groups. Codes for various failures within a common engine system are grouped together to make life a little easier for the diagnostic calibration engineers working behind the scenes. Numbered 1 through 8, they

Code	Description		MIL
P2101	Throttle Actuator Control Motor Circuit Range/Performance	☑	MIL on First Error
P2119	Throttle Actuator Control Throttle Body Range/Performance	☐	No MIL Light
P2120	Throttle/Pedal Position Sensor/Switch D Circuit	☑	MIL on First Error
P2122	Throttle/Pedal Position Sensor/Switch D Circuit Low Input	☑	MIL on First Error
P2123	Throttle/Pedal Position Sensor/Switch D Circuit High Input	☑	MIL on First Error
P2125	Throttle/Pedal Position Sensor/Switch E Circuit	☑	MIL on First Error
P2127	Throttle/Pedal Position Sensor/Switch E Circuit Low Input	☑	MIL on First Error
P2128	Throttle/Pedal Position Sensor/Switch E Circuit High Input	☑	MIL on First Error
P2135	Throttle/Pedal Position Sensor/Switch A/B Voltage Correlation	☑	MIL on First Error
P2138	Throttle/Pedal Position Sensor/Switch D/E Voltage Correlation	☑	MIL on First Error
P2176	Throttle Actuator Control System - Idle Position Not Learned	☑	MIL on First Error

Codes in the P2xxx range are still SAE codes. They were added long after the original implementation of OBD-II and are tied to newer technologies, such as electronic throttle controls and cam phasers that were not as common back in 1996.

represent fuel and air metering, injector circuit, ignition and misfire, auxiliary emissions controls, vehicle speed and idle, computer circuit, and finally two groups for transmission controls, respectively.

Starting from the fourth digit, the remaining numbers (or letters) dial in on specific failures within various monitoring groups. Here, code groups are broken down into individual failures that are numbered from 00 to FF because they are actually hexadecimal numbers, giving manufacturers a little more room for additional codes than standard decimal numbers would allow.

For example, a P012D is a powertrain generic SAE fault within the air-metering group with a specific failure of "2D," representing "Turbocharger/Supercharger Inlet Pressure Sensor Circuit High." As written, this provides a rather specific thing to go look at on a specific circuit. In this case, we would begin by checking the instantaneous value if it's maxed out in Mode $01 real time or Mode $02 freeze-frame data when it happened. Failures like this are often traced to either a short circuit that pulls the signal voltage high or a failed sensor itself. The former is an easy check before spending money on a new sensor.

Clearing Codes

Ah, the payoff—right? Not quite, but clearing the stored codes after a cause has been identified and a repair has been made is probably the biggest moment of triumph in the process. The same scan tool that told the code (or list of codes) accompanied the MIL on the dash and whatever foul behavior the vehicle was experiencing should also be capable of clearing those same codes. Mode $04 communication allows the tool to send a message to the ECU that clears this stored list of both current and pending trouble codes.

The key here is to be confident that a root cause has indeed been found that would sufficiently explain the fault code before clearing it. If not, chances are good that it will just come back. Maybe it won't come back immediately, but eventually missed or incomplete repairs come back to haunt us. Worse, some codes are a bit elusive and take longer for the ECU to detect the fault. Some faults must also happen more than once before they trip the MIL, so the driver may not know the failure exists until the car has been driven long enough to meet the conditions for a valid drive cycle twice and get another MIL on the dash. When it does, get on the phone with a technician quickly. If you're in a DIY situation, you'll just be mad at yourself here.

There is also the case where the

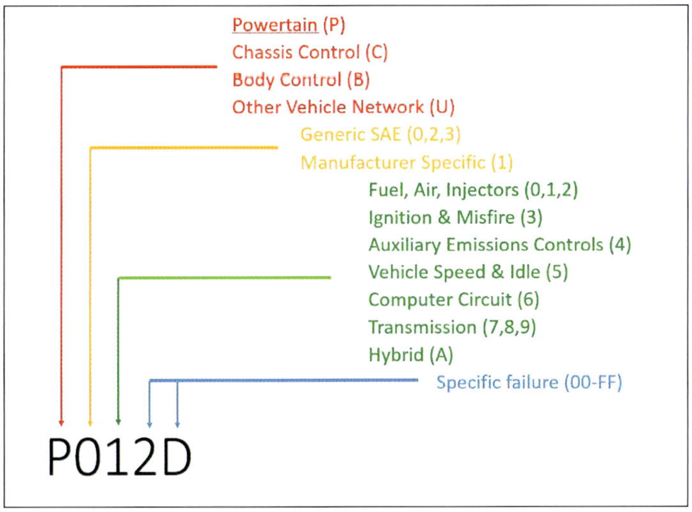

All fault codes follow a pattern mandated by SAE for their structure that sorts them by origin.

Clearing the fault code immediately in the auto-parts store parking lot before you have completed the repair is not a great idea. It's best to verify proper operation first, as there may be more than one cause or the fault may take longer to trip again if it is intermittent.

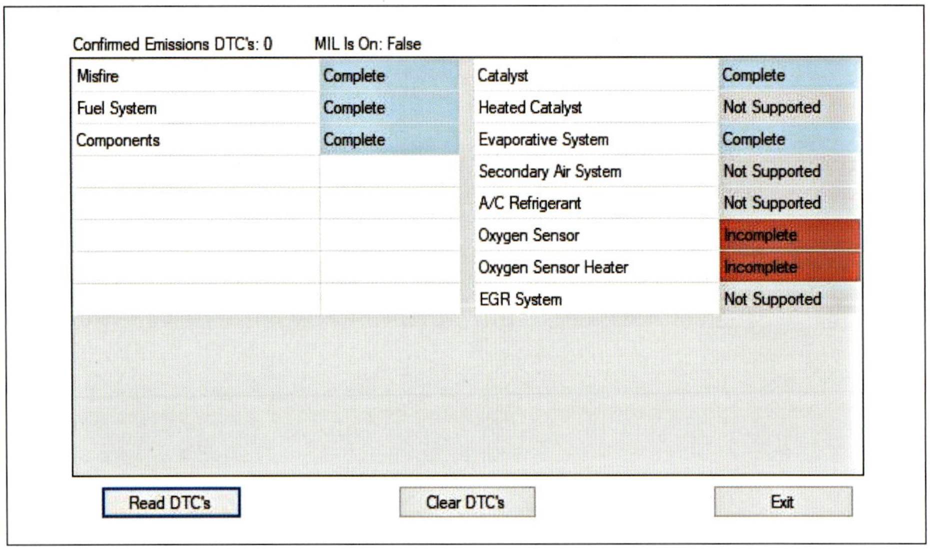

Although the MIL is not illuminated on this vehicle, it has yet to run and pass the oxygen sensor monitors after a repair. Another drive cycle may be required to let the ECU run and pass the diagnostics again before declaring it fixed.

repair may have fixed one code but not another. This is why I recommended writing down all stored codes in the first steps. Again, no one likes an incomplete repair. Forgetting that there were a couple things to look at because you got distracted halfway through the process is no fun, either. Check all the original codes and ask yourself "Did the repair address the probable root cause for this one too?" before clearing them. If so, press that clear button with pride.

But it's still not done. If fighting an electrical-circuit integrity issue, such as a short or an open circuit, these OBD-I checks happen very quickly after key on and startup, so the answer will appear almost immediately. If addressing one of many OBD-II plausibility codes, it may require one or more valid drive cycles for the ECU to run the correct diagnostic test in the correct conditions. The object here is to allow the ECU to see the same situation that was present when the failure was noted and have the vehicle working correctly, such that it passes this time.

If the Mode $02 freeze-frame data earlier was noted, this would be a good time to review it and try to replicate that same condition after the repair. Chances are very good that if the repair was successful and complete, it will pass the diagnostic without drama.

Another good check is to look at the Mode $07 data that includes the status of the various system monitors. The act of resetting stored fault codes via Mode $04 messaging also clears the status of monitor completion in Modes $07 and $09.

The final step in these repairs is to let the ECU run its normal diagnostics and pass so that these monitors can change their reporting status to "complete." If all reported systems indicate that their monitor has passed, you are in good shape and probably ready to show up for your state inspection as well. If one or more of the supported monitors reports as "not ready," "incomplete," or "failed," you obviously still have work to do.

As a working example, if addressing a P0442 (Evaporative System Small Leak Detected) code, final checks are very important. Sure, pressure or smoke testing the evaporative fuel lines found a bad connection that was re-seated. This does not guarantee that there were no other cracked lines or loose fittings elsewhere in the system.

Since they can be quite difficult to find, it's understandable that we may miss something here. Letting the vehicle rerun its internal diagnostic check is a great way to see if we truly did fix the issue before the vehicle leaves the shop or garage. This requires clearing the codes, a process that also resets the monitor status to "incomplete."

The evaporative diagnostics require a particular set of conditions that can only be executed while driving the vehicle on a smooth, level surface at constant speed. If there was an additional leak that wasn't found in the initial inspection, chances are good that the first time the monitor runs, it may store another pending P0442 in the Mode $07 data or in Mode $03 as a current fault code, depending on whether the manufacturer calibrated it after one or two faults, respectively. It may take some patience, but seeing that "complete" indicator in the Mode $07 data for Evaporative System Monitor gives us the confidence that the repair was successful.

Another sometimes-unfortunate condition is that some codes are stored as "permanent," meaning that they cannot be reset with a generic SAE tool using a Mode $04 command. As previously mentioned, it will take a specific OEM tool to send the proper message to clear this permanent code stored in Mode $0A. The good news here is that if a proper fix is made, the ECU is also likely to clear the code itself after the successful completion of a valid drive cycle and passing diagnostic check.

It just takes a little more time than pushing a button to get rid of the MIL in these cases. One should still perform the normal post-repair check to ensure proper operation even when it can't be cleared with the scan tool. This routine post-fix checkup just might be enough to clear the code through normal ECU operation too.

Generic SAE Fault Codes

Let's look at the most common OBD codes: the generic SAE fault codes. These are a large group of common codes agreed on by the industry and published as part of the SAE standard J2012.

In this standard, a list of the most common faults that engines will have is spelled out, assigning each one its own number called a diagnostic trouble code (DTC). All manufacturers have agreed to use this same format for a set of numbers for the same fault conditions. Although, there may be additional information available (often covered under manufacturer specific codes of a different number) as well. For now, let's focus on these common codes in groups that make them easier to understand.

These fault codes are grouped based on what they have most in common as far as function and root causes. In each group, we will discuss basic definitions and some theoretical background. This allows us to move on to common causes, typical repair methods, and how to validate that the repair was successful.

Input Sensors

The most fundamental group of OBD codes is tied to the diagnosis of individual input sensors. These are most critical because they are the

The crankshaft position sensor is accessible from outside the engine, but its sensing element must be very close to the target inside the crankcase. Because of the highly critical nature of this signal, wires are often shielded from noise and closely tied to reduce vibration.

Crankshaft target wheels have evenly spaced teeth with a gap or missing teeth at a specific angle relative to cylinder number-1 TDC. This "60-2" wheel has 58 actual teeth that give the crankshaft position sensor a rising edge signal every 6 degrees of rotation for high resolution.

There will be a lower resolution target wheel on the slower-moving camshaft that is used by the ECU to determine the difference between the engine cycles that take two crankshaft revolutions to complete. Should the crankshaft position sensor fail, this can also be used for a limp mode engine speed signal at low resolution.

This GM LS3 engine employs both MAF and SD airflow models simultaneously. Even in modified trim, this vehicle still employs both sensors and all of their diagnostics.

"eyes and ears" of the ECU. If any of these sensors are missing, it should come as no surprise that the ECU would have trouble determining the outputs needed to run the engine properly and pass emissions.

Without the crankshaft (P0335/P0336 and P0315) and camshaft (P0340–P0346) position sensors, it would be impossible to know the most basic engine parameter of speed in RPM to which almost everything else is referenced. Further, the relative position of the camshafts relative to the crankshaft (P0010–P0024) is also critical to allow the ECU to verify that valve events are indeed happening at the expected time.

Know when to expect airflow and exhaust flow by anticipating valve events. This allows the ECU to determine when to sample things such as the manifold absolute pressure (MAP) sensor or exhaust gas oxygen sensors as well as anticipate power delivery on the combustion stroke of a particular cylinder versus an intake event.

When teaching basic calibration classes, I always point out to my students that the number-one job of the ECU is to determine "how much stuff" goes into the cylinder on the intake stroke. The calculation for this is typically done one of two ways: mass airflow measurement or speed density estimation. Both exploit the same set of equations. One is just worked backward relative to the other, as I pointed out in Chapter 4 of CarTech's *Designing and Tuning High-Performance Fuel Injection Systems*.

Sparing a repeat of that math, let's just agree that the sensors used

Most automotive temperature sensors are almost identical in design. They are essentially resistors that vary with temperature, so they only require one signal wire and one reference wire.

This vehicle has been updated with an ethanol content sensor on the fuel feed line. By enabling the flex-fuel logic and diagnostics in the ECU, the vehicle can now cleanly burn any blend of gasoline and ethanol.

This turbocharged 4-cylinder engine employs a multifunction MAF sensor that also includes measurements for inlet pressure, temperature, and humidity. The pressure reading doubles as both barometric and compressor inlet pressures here.

for those equation inputs are critical to the accuracy of the calculation. In a mass airflow measurement system, this means that the MAF sensor (P0101–P0103) itself must be present. To calculate the SD-based version, the ECU needs the intake air temperature (P0096–P0098), MAP sensor (P0106–P0108), and/or throttle position sensors (P0120–P0123) at a minimum to work the equation.

Engine temperature is usually monitored with a coolant-temperature sensor (P0116–P0118) installed in the water jacket of either the cylinder head or block. Some newer vehicles replace this sensor with a cylinder-head temperature sensor that more closely follows the temperature needed to control startup emissions. Then, they can synthesize a number for coolant temperature based on the metal temperature reading if needed for other systems. Oil temperature (P0196–P0198) and oil pressure (P0520–P0523) may also be directly monitored in some cases. Transmission-fluid temperature (P0218) may also be monitored directly by the ECU in some cases.

Additional monitors, such as the charge air-cooler pump (P023A) circuit, flex-fuel composition sensor (P0178–P0179), and knock sensors (P0324–P0333), are also used when the vehicle is so equipped. Each of

The throttle inlet air pressure (TIAP) sensor installed on the shiny S-shaped pipe leading from the front intercooler to the rubber coupler on the throttle body is functionally identical to a MAP sensor. Its output is used by the ECU to fine-tune the wastegate controls to deliver the correct pressure and flow to the throttle body, which may not be at wide-open throttle, where the MAP sensor would have a good reading of turbocharger pressure.

these can have a profound impact on combustion quality for the engine. The knock sensor in particular tends to be of interest to the repair crowd owing to the sometimes-fragile nature of the design.

Turbocharger or supercharger inlet pressure (P012B–P012D) is also often measured. This gives the ECU a different number than MAP (which may be elevated during high load) as a draw-through throttle body or airbox upstream of the compressor changes pressure relative to the current barometric condition. Monitoring this additional pressure point is often critical to the software models used on drive-by-wire or closed-loop boost-control systems.

We have intentionally omitted the oxygen sensors and evaporative emissions system components for now, as those will be covered separately in another segment.

Some of these input sensors have inter-related behaviors. This means that for a given signal from one sensor, an expected range of input should be seen from a different sensor under certain conditions. This correlation is part of what makes OBD-II more robust than the simple OBD-I faults that cover open circuits, shorts, or missing connections.

P0068 is one such correlation that looks at the relationship between the MAF and MAP sensors. It can be used to diagnose things like an improperly controlled drive-by-wire system, vacuum leak, or impeded flow somewhere. Coolant temperature is often monitored to detect potential impacts to emissions with P0125/P0128, where the sensor does not see an expected increase in temperature over time, as the engine should normally be warming up.

Input Sensor Faults: Common Causes and Repairs

With all of these basic faults related to input sensors, the most common causes are either an open circuit or a faulty sensor. The good news is that the OBD code points right toward the sensor or circuit in question, saving time from having to check all the sensors or engine wiring circuits.

Don't initially jump to looking for some complex problem or solution with these basic fault codes right away. The open circuit may be the result of something as simple as a loose connector (or one that was forgotten during reassembly from some other repair). This self-inflicted error is often easy to spot when looking at the sensor itself and seeing the connector laying inches away.

Beyond that, wiring integrity is another common cause. In these cases, the connector is plugged in but there is no connection to the ECU. This can be checked with a standard voltmeter. Many sensors have a power, ground, and signal wire as indicated in the service manual (or a quick internet search). If the connector is tested and found to be missing both power and ground, the repair is almost certainly focused on the wiring harness rather than the sensor itself. When in doubt, use the voltmeter to perform a continuity check between the sensor connector and the ECU connection on the wire harness.

If the integrity of the wire harness has been verified, then the next-most-common cause for these failures is the sensor itself. These sensors are usually very affordable and readily available. One does not typically "fix" any of these sensors. Rather, a replacement sensor is simply swapped into the same location and the harness connector plugged back into it.

One word of caution here: make sure that the replacement sensor is indeed the right one for the application. Some OEMs have been known to spec completely different sensors

Replacing the factory 1-bar MAP sensor with a 2.5-bar sensor from a different GM application was a direct plug-in solution for this turbocharged LS3. After adjusting the MAP sensor calibration values in the ECU, the MAP diagnostics worked like normal again.

Common Circuit Tips

Many sensors and actuators in the engine wiring harness share common leads. Battery voltage or controlled 5V reference circuits may have only one output pin at the ECU that feeds a chain of sensors or actuators. The same holds true for both ground- or sensor-specific reference grounds known as "signal return" loops. This is great for efficiency and cost control when designing ECU and harness hardware, but it opens up some interesting potential failure points.

Part of the basic OBD-I circuit integrity check looks at a sensor's returned value to determine if there is an open circuit, a short to ground, or a short to battery. The trouble comes when multiple sensors share a common lead, such as a 5V reference power supply. If one point in the electrical circuit is shorted, we may see an indicated fault on one or all of the sensors that share the circuit. This means that an OBD-I fault for a shorted wire on the ECT sensor may actually be on the lead to the IAT or MAP sensor if they share part of the same wire connections. This will confuse those who rush to check a P-code and just replace a sensor only to find that the problem persists.

The correct diagnosis should involve checking continuity on the circuit for all sensors involved. This means breaking out a wiring diagram to verify and then grabbing a trusty digital multimeter (DMM) to localize the fault in the harness and avoid replacing what may be perfectly good sensors.

More savvy technicians have been known to probe the harness right at the ECU connector to check resistance all the way through the harness between a power supply and ground or between a signal wire and its reference ground or "signal return." This method tests two wires leading to and from the sensor simultaneously along with the sensor itself. If a sensor is found to be in range for this test, it's safe to say that both the sensor and the harness between the sensor and ECU are in good working order. This can save a lot of time checking multiple individual wire runs between the ECU and sensor. ■

in various models using almost identical wiring connections. Don't get caught putting a 2-bar MAP sensor into an application with a 1-bar OEM sensor unless that's part of the performance upgrade plan.

With that said, some "upgraded" sensors such as higher-range MAP and MAF sensors may require a different pinout at the sensor connection than the OEM piece. Re-pinning these correctly is key to having the engine run upon startup. Of course, the ECU calibration data is needed to change the sensor's characteristics to match the new hardware before starting the engine.

With the physical repair completed, always validate proper operation afterward. The simplest way is to clear the original P-code using a scan tool and operate the vehicle to see if it returns. Granted, that's a little less than ideal for today's skilled technical or even DIY repair.

If the scan tool provides access to live OBD data, it's best to select that particular sensor's output for display while running the engine. Do the new reported values show up and make sense? If checking a MAP sensor, does it show barometric pressure with the key on and engine off? Does the throttle position or mass airflow sensor signal increase when pressing the gas pedal? If the previous sensor (or wiring) failed, resulting in a lack of signal, the repair's success should now be obvious.

Output Circuits

Fuel-injector circuits (P0201–P0208) are monitored to make sure that the injectors are actually plugged in and hopefully delivering fuel. Likewise, if the fuel-pump circuit (P0230–P0232) has a fault, it doesn't matter if the injectors are opening or not. Even slightly reduced fuel pressure from an intermittent pump circuit fault can lead to a lean condition or poor atomization that results in poor combustion quality and increased emissions.

Ignition coils (P0351–P0358) are checked for circuit integrity. Clearly, any disconnect here would result in not only a loss of power but also a considerable increase in vehicle emissions. There are few ways to create less favorable combustion than to not have it happen in the chamber at all in the first place.

Exhaust gas recirculation (P0401–P0406) systems are checked for circuit integrity as well as flow when activated. Since EGR is used to control combustion temperature inside the cylinder, it is of critical importance that this system be operational to achieve emissions compliance if the system was designed to use it from the factory.

Although many aftermarket solutions exist for EGR deletes, all would

Ignition coils can usually be found right on top of each bank of cylinders near the spark plugs. A beauty or noise cover may have to be removed to see them.

The EGR valve on this supercharged 5.4L Ford GT engine can be seen attached directly behind the throttle body at the compressor inlet with an integrated differential pressure feedback (DPFE) sensor on top of it. Gases are routed from a port on the exhaust manifold to the valve through the insulated pipe threaded into the lower side of the valve.

fail one or more of these diagnostics unless the ECU was reprogrammed to accommodate the change. Now is a good time to remind you that turning off this diagnostic to avoid having an annoying MIL on the dash is still a violation of federal emissions laws for road-going vehicles.

Boost control valves (P0033–P0035) are used by the ECU to regulate the amount of pressure or vacuum being applied to a diaphragm that opens or closes either a turbocharger wastegate or a boost bypass valve on a supercharged system. Many of these are regulated in a rapid on-off sequence known as pulse width modulation, where the on versus off time is adjusted at a constant frequency.

The resulting on percentage is known as duty cycle. It correlates to how much of the boost or vacuum signal is actually being passed to the actuator. The ECU sometimes intentionally holds this valve all the way open or closed to limit how much boost is available to the intake manifold when other faults are present to protect the engine.

Output-Circuit Faults: Common Causes and Repairs

Much like the input circuit faults, these output-circuit faults are usually pretty straightforward in their cause and repair. Starting with the obvious again, use the code to point toward a specific actuator or connector under the hood. Look for loose connections first, before chasing a more complex wiring problem. As with the input sensors, if it has been confirmed that the wiring is indeed correct and working, then it's time to consider replacing the offending component.

As with the input sensors, there are often many different output actuators that may be able to plug into a vehicle's harness. This doesn't mean that they are a workable replacement. Fuel injectors in particular are easily mistaken when finding replacement parts in the aftermarket. Worse yet, many aftermarket sources offer fuel injectors that are outwardly identical but have wildly different flow characteristics. Just because they fit the fuel rail and plug into the harness is no guarantee that the engine won't run worse after the "repair." Make absolutely certain what you are getting when purchasing replacement fuel injectors.

For a performance application, higher-flow-rate injectors may have been intentionally installed. These can still fail and require service or replacement. If installing non-OEM fuel injectors, it is absolutely critical to also get a complete set of

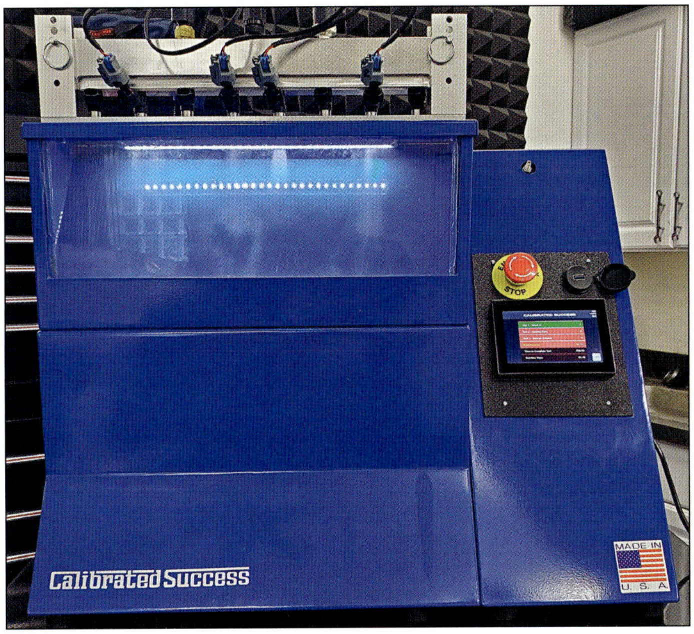

Injectors are run through the characterization routine on the Calibrated Success test bench. The resulting data can be directly input to the ECU using aftermarket tuning software.

characterization data to input to the ECU at the same time.

This complete data should include more than just the flow rate. Specifically, it should include values for flow rate, offsets at all voltages (and working pressure), and some values that adjust the injector behavior at small pulse widths. Getting this complete data right is one of the first steps that I always coach my performance calibration students on before spending time mapping the rest of the engine parameters.

This data is developed off the engine in a laboratory environment, where the injector can be run consistently across a wide range of conditions and the data later post-processed to create the calibration values needed to exchange one working fuel injector for a different design or flow rate in an application.

At Calibrated Success, we made a fuel injector test bench specifically to perform this task on performance applications. The result has been a huge improvement in the accuracy of data used in the ECU to control the injectors and greatly reduced calibration time in the vehicle to get the engine running clean under all conditions.

The ignition coils have a distinguished history of headaches for modern automotive technicians—and for good reason. They are often installed in the worst of locations, and they are subject to heat, vibration, water, and oil immersion while being tasked with delivering a critical high-voltage supply to the spark plugs or wires.

Fortunately, many modern engines are equipped with more than just one ignition coil, so any failure does not render the entire engine a boat anchor. Still, having just one ignition coil malfunction causes a noticeable loss of power, fuel economy, and smoothness, and it will drive emissions up significantly. It is this last point of emissions increase that mandates the need for OBD-II monitoring status for each coil present.

The boost-control valves may have electrical and valve hardware faults, as discussed with other circuits. They may also register as faulted when one of the vacuum lines going either to or from the actuator comes loose, is broken, is cracked, or has a small leak in it. When inspecting a boost-control circuit, pressure test the pneumatic circuit in addition to checking the electrical circuit and actuator condition. The proper fix may be as simple as a few cents worth of vacuum hose instead of a trip to the parts counter.

When all else fails here, check the actual wastegate or bypass valve

Factory supercharged engines have a valve capable of rapidly dumping boost pressure. If either the vacuum line or solenoid fails, the engine may not be able to make manifold boost and full power.

too. It may be that the solenoid is working fine and the diaphragm is not moving or the shaft is seized on the bypass valve. When the ECU does not see a pressure change resulting from its request to the solenoid, it may be that the electrical circuit, solenoid, and pneumatic connections were all fine and there really is a mechanical hardware issue due to corrosion, carbon buildup, or other contamination.

Catalyst Group

The catalytic convertors and oxygen sensors are lumped into a single group here. The reason is that the main purpose of oxygen sensors is to improve and monitor the function of the catalytic convertors. In a spark-ignited engine, we generally attempt to maintain a stoichiometric balance of air and fuel going through the engine. This provides clean combustion with a minimum of leftover "parts" leaving the exhaust port. In fact, if we had perfect combustion inside the engine, the hydrocarbons in the fuel and oxygen in the air would react in harmony, and we would only have carbon dioxide and water in the exhaust. Since we live in an imperfect world, combustion is not always perfectly clean. Modern engine controls get us surprisingly close, but even so some leftover components are inevitable.

Think of the catalytic convertor as a sort of "cleanup crew" for the engine when it comes to reacting leftover hydrocarbons, oxides of nitrogen, carbon monoxide, and a few other chemical players. The catalytic convertor is essentially a glowing hot oven with lots of surface area where these leftover parts can park temporarily until the right matching molecule comes along to make the reaction to reduce or oxidize these molecules down to higher concentrations of carbon dioxide and water, rather than leaving the tailpipe as harmful emissions.

The catalyst has no moving parts of its own and is powered by

Pushing the catalytic convertor closer to the exhaust valve during design shortens the time required to bring it up to operating temperature and reduces emissions. Cylinder heads with integrated exhaust manifolds have become more popular with automakers looking to reduce their part count and improve emissions.

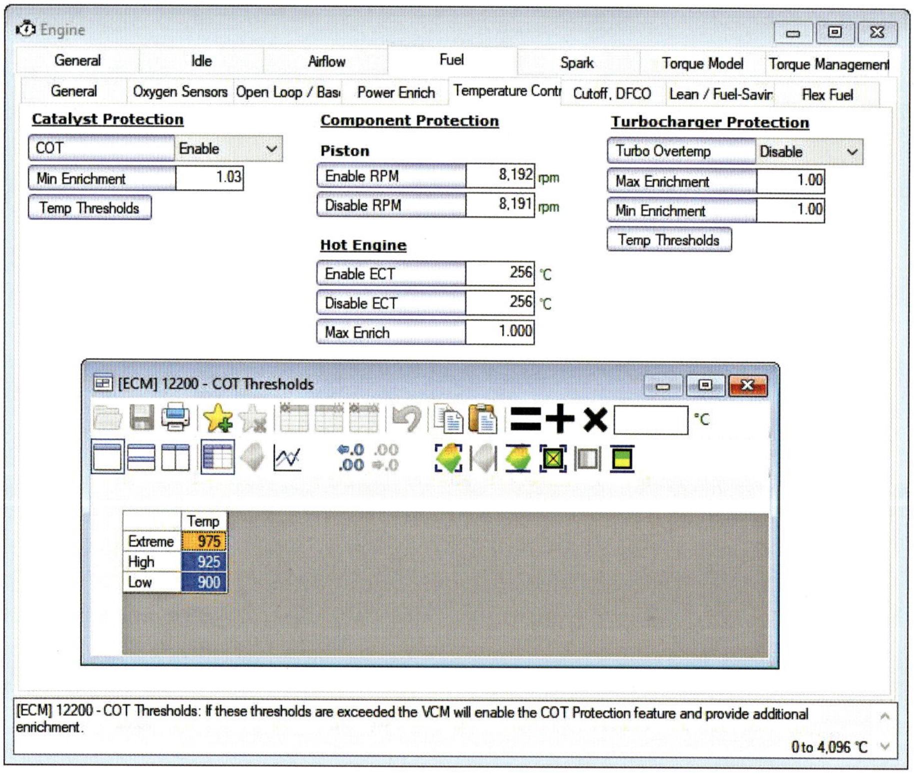

Whenever the catalyst temperature gets beyond 900°C, this ECU begins progressively adding fuel to protect the catalyst from damage. The input temperature to this function comes from a math model elsewhere in the calibration.

Pin Testing Tip

There is an old saying in the scientific community: "The act of observation can change the system."

In the world of diagnostics, we often find ourselves with our trusty digital multimeter (DMM) in hand, looking for circuit problems or voltage measurements that are out of the desired range. In doing so, I often see technicians and DIY guys alike simply jam the DMM probes into the connector on a harness or ECU. This usually works, as far as getting a measurement is concerned.

The problem arises when attempting to put everything back together and run the engine again. If during measurement, the pins become distorted, they may not seat properly when the connector is reinstalled. Male pins may become bent or even fold when they no longer align with the incoming connector. The inside of female pins may get distorted to the point that a properly inserted male pin no longer makes reliable contact. Even more infuriating is the case where this damage leads to an intermittent contact that is only seen when agitated by real-world driving conditions and vibrations but tests fine when parked in the garage.

Modern electronics have smaller pins and lighter-gauge wires, which are both prone to damage when not handled with care. Even if the larger DMM probes are not directly used, some connectors can still be damaged by shadetree inspections. The paperclip or safety pin is a leading culprit here. While significantly smaller than the DMM probes, they can still be much larger than anything the connector was designed to accommodate. Pushing a pin or a paperclip into the connector can give a solid feel and reliable electrical connection for testing, but the deformation to the interior walls or spring tab inside some pins may not be seen by eye.

Once the pin is removed after testing, one is left with a loose connection at best when the harness is reassembled. Before jamming whatever conductor one may have on hand into the connector, it's a good idea to look at both the gauge and the geometry of the mating pin. Pins may be round, square, or flattened. All require appropriate selection of test probes to avoid damage.

There are a number of test lead kits sold under both automotive diagnostic tool brands as well as electronics repair brands that are just an internet search away. If you are going to work on a modern harness and connectors, these can be a lifesaver. ■

the energy present in the exhaust stream itself. When the engine is cold started, the catalyst is often at the same temperature as the environment around the vehicle. It is not until the catalyst reaches a temperature of roughly 400°C that it begins to have high efficiency at converting emissions components into CO_2 and H_2O.

Luckily, the exhaust coming out of the engine is typically hotter than this, so it's only a matter of time until these reactions start occurring at impressive rates inside the catalyst. These reactions are essentially combustion, so once lit off, the catalyst makes its own heat to some extent as well. It is cooled by the air around the outside of the shell or in cases where this internal reaction can no longer happen.

If the catalyst is flushed with raw air and no fuel (such as during a long deceleration event), all of the storage sites on the surface of the catalyst are depleted of hydrocarbons and CO. There is no longer any fuel for the

Wideband oxygen sensors can be quickly identified by their increased wire count. These sensors have five or six wires instead of the four or fewer that are seen on traditional narrow-band oxygen sensors.

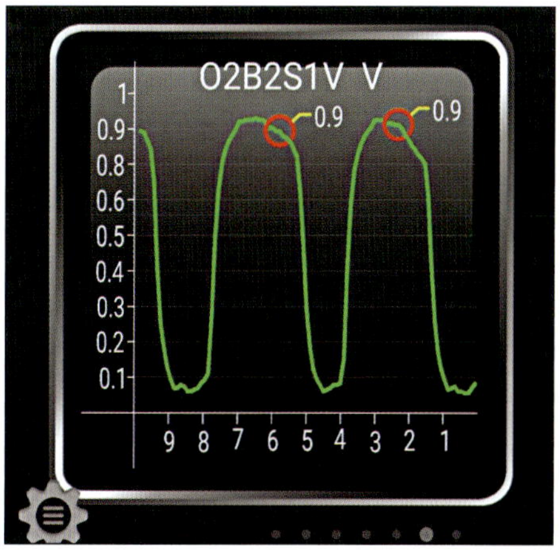

The rich-lean swings of engine fueling can be seen in a trace of oxygen-sensor output over time. With today's software, an impressive level of detail is available even on a smartphone application.

The oxygen sensor on the right is downstream of the catalyst on this vehicle. While I applaud this user for keeping some form of cats on his high-performance vehicle, it is unlikely that the emissions are anywhere near as clean as they were originally with the new long-tube headers and lower effectiveness catalysts.

fire, and temperatures will drop until engine fueling is resumed. Likewise, when the engine is run rich of stoichiometry (such as at full power or after operating at high load for long enough for the ECU estimate that exhaust temperatures are becoming unsafe), all the oxygen is eventually depleted inside the catalyst and reactions can no longer occur.

Adding more fuel at this point can also be an effective method of reducing exhaust and catalyst temperatures and is common practice for ECU calibration engineers. Great care is taken with the calibration of the ECU to make sure that exhaust components, especially the catalyst (which is arguably the most important emissions device), do not get so hot that they are damaged. Typically, temperatures are kept to a limit of around 950°C to avoid such damage.

Now it becomes easier to see how the oxygen sensors integrate with the function of the catalytic convertor. Since the catalyst must stay close to stoichiometric chemical balance to function, it is important that the engine must also be kept at a similar operating chemistry. By using oxygen sensors in the exhaust, a measurement can be taken to give the ECU an indication of the actual exhaust chemistry. A closed-loop feedback logic inside the ECU can then use this sensor reading to adjust the engine's fueling in real time to keep the exhaust roughly on the stoichiometric ratio that reduces raw emissions and leaves the minimum amount of work for the catalyst "cleanup crew" on the way out.

Depending on the application, the upstream oxygen sensor (P0131–P0134, P0151–P0154) may be either of the classic "narrowband" or "switching" design or the newer "wideband" or "universal" design. The former has a steep change in output voltage signal based on which side of the stoichiometric balance is sensed at the tip. The latter uses a different sensor topology that slews a pump current either positive or negative to the ECU proportional to the amount of excess oxygen present in the gases.

Both types have heating-element circuits (P0030–P0060) inside them to speed warmup and allow the ECU to get readings for closed-loop fueling operation quicker. In addition to basic functionality of the sensor, they also enable a diagnostic of bank lean and bank rich (P0171–P0175) conditions when fuel trim based on feedback from the sensor is not able to bring the engine to stoichiometry. Even a slow responding (P0133/0153) or inactive (P0134/0154) sensor can be detected when shifts in delivered injector pulse width do not show a matching response from the corresponding oxygen sensor in a reasonable amount of time.

Since the catalyst works by actively trading rich and lean exhaust constituents to create a continuous stream of cleaner emissions, it's actually desirable to drive engine chemistry that periodically shifts between slightly rich and slightly lean conditions centered close to stoichiometry. This can actually be seen by observing the "short-term fuel trim" values in a scanner, as they continuously toggle back and forth to make sure they keep the catalyst working optimally. Using the feedback from the upstream oxygen sensors is an easy way to keep track of this process.

The downstream sensor's primary purpose is to monitor the

operation of the catalytic convertor. If the upstream sensors are effectively helping the engine toggle closely around the stoichiometric mixture, then the catalyst should be very effective at converting all the leftover parts. As such, it acts much like a sponge under a faucet that is being periodically turned on and off.

Done right, water flow from the sponge is much more continuous than the intermittent flow from the faucet above. Now replace water with oxygen, and that is how the catalyst monitor works. The downstream oxygen sensor signal will still move but at a much slower rate than that of the upstream sensor when the catalytic convertor is functioning correctly. Fundamentally, catalyst monitor diagnostics just compare the upstream and downstream signals to each other, looking for a significant change between the two. If the downstream signal too closely resembles that of the upstream sensor, it's a good indicator that the catalytic convertor is not converting (or even there at all).

Catalyst Group Faults: Common Causes and Repairs

Whenever an oxygen sensor code appears, the most common issue is the sensor itself. Oxygen sensors do not live forever, even on healthy engines. Over time, they are slowly poisoned, and ceramic tips accumulate damage from heat, vibration, and chemical exposure.

Much like other basic diagnostics, the first step is always to make sure the offending sensor is actually plugged in. Their location in tight confines under the vehicle make them prime targets for absent-minded technicians to fail to ensure proper seating of the connectors. If the circuit integrity has been verified, then we are back to the sensor itself.

Savvy repair technicians may swap the physical sensor location side to side on a two-bank system to see if the failure follows a particular sensor before recommending the customer purchase a new sensor. When working on high-performance engines, it was common practice for us to replace aging oxygen sensors as a part of normal routine. Cam swaps, turbocharger kit installs, and intricate exhaust systems often received this preventative maintenance in our shop.

Notice that in the causes and repair segment, no distinction has been made between circuit, sensing, and heater failures. That's because they all lead the repair in the same direction. Either there is a disconnect in the wiring or the sensor assembly is bad. We do not replace the sensor independent from the heater element, threads, or plug, so one replacement addresses all of these simultaneously.

One area where we take some extra time before simply replacing the sensor is a bank lean/rich (P0170–P0175) fault, particularly if it is present only on one side of an engine. While these sometimes are the fault of a failing sensor, there are other engine-related issues that lead us here too on occasion. True, a failing sensor element will not return the proper voltage to the ECU. The ECU adds fuel in an attempt to elicit an increased voltage signal from the oxygen sensor. If the sensor itself is failing, this richer mixture may not register with the sensing element and the ECU continues the closed-loop fuel addition until the fuel trims are high enough (usually 30 percent or so) on that bank to trigger the "bank lean" code.

However, we have a few more things that can lead us here as well. A vacuum leak can allow additional unmetered air into the combustion chamber, leading to a genuinely lean oxygen sensor signal. In this case, we should take the usual steps of checking for a vacuum leak. Spraying a can of carb cleaner or brake cleaner on all areas around the airbox discharge, zip tube, throttle body, intake manifold, and cylinder head mating surfaces

Name	Value
Vehicle Speed (SAE)	0 mph
Engine RPM (SAE)	797 rpm
Cylinder Airmass	0.09 g
Engine Coolant Temp (SAE)	205 °F
Intake Air Temp (SAE)	147 °F
Intake Manifold Absolute Pressur...	72 kPa
Throttle Position (SAE)	2.0 %
Short Term Fuel Trim Bank 1 (SAE)	13.3 %
Short Term Fuel Trim Bank 2 (SAE)	18.0 %
Long Term Fuel Trim Bank 1 (SAE)	25.0 %
Long Term Fuel Trim Bank 2 (SAE)	25.0 %
Mass Airflow	4.3 g/s
Mass Airflow Sensor	2,033 Hz
Timing Advance (SAE)	20.5 °

Looking at Mode $01 data shows both banks of this engine maxed out with 2-percent positive fuel trims and still more positive adjustment happening in the short-term trims. This is normal for a case where the P0171/P0174 faults have been set for "Bank 1/Bank 2 Lean" as the ECU tries to correct the error.

If the fuel injectors are removed from the engine and checked for spray pattern differences, we may quickly discover why one cylinder was not running as well as the others. If cleaning the injector in an ultrasonic bath while cycling it does not clear this up, it will probably need to be replaced.

should expose a leak with an audible change in engine performance as the fluid is drawn in through the leak. There would also be a momentary increase in the oxygen sensor signal if you were watching real-time data on a scan tool while doing this. If a leak is found and repaired, it's important to reset the fuel trims immediately to allow the ECU's closed-loop fuel trims to go back to normal and not foul the plugs while you wait.

The fuel injectors themselves are also suspect here. Injectors that are clogged, stuck open, or otherwise not flowing as intended often manifest as oxygen sensor or bank rich/lean codes rather than a fuel-injector code if their electrical circuit is not interrupted. The easiest way to test this on a running engine is to momentarily disconnect one fuel injector at a time. Sure, the engine will stumble a little, but it will likely keep running.

With the injector disconnected, there should be a sharp decrease in that bank's oxygen sensor raw output coupled with a quick rise in positive fuel trim. This is because the closed-loop fueling of the ECU tries to compensate for the large volume of oxygen being passed through the affected cylinder. If no such change is detected, then we can zero in on that fuel injector for further inspection.

Again, swapping between cylinders/banks should have the problem follow the injector, just like with oxygen sensor. If you are fortunate enough to have a fuel-injector test bench, pulling all the injectors and checking them against each other for variation in flow is great at this point. An engine with one bad injector has several others that were borderline.

Check the filter basket at the top of the injector for debris to see if the rest of the fuel system is suspect for contamination. Clean the injectors in a heated ultrasonic bath of water/methanol (windshield washer solution actually works well here on a budget) along with a surfactant like Dawn dish soap. After 20 minutes or so of cleaning and a good rinse with brake cleaner, recheck the injector flow. If it does not resurrect the injectors' performance, complete replacement is usually the best option going forward.

Finally, for those doing high-performance work, we have the special case of ECU calibration and its effect on oxygen sensor diagnostics. I have seen countless cases where bank lean/rich codes (often presenting on both banks simultaneously) can be traced to poor engine calibration accuracy. This means that either the fuel-injector characterization data does not match the new injectors that were installed, or the airflow model (MAF curve or VE estimate) is not matching what's actually happening in the engine.

The whole point of most engine

I've been preaching it for years: proper calibration requires a fair amount of steady-state measurement on a load-bearing dyno to build the base maps. Thus, a Mustang dynamometer with an eddy current absorber lets the user hold the engine at a constant RPM while the driver controls engine load with the accelerator pedal to get the necessary measurements.

performance upgrades is to increase the airflow of the engine. If this change in airflow is not properly modeled in the ECU, then the closed-loop fuel trim will attempt to fix it after the fact once the vehicle is driving. Sloppy work on the calibration side is a great way to have inconsistent fuel trims and often leads to oxygen sensor–related fault codes.

If the process that we teach in our Calibrated Success EFI training materials is followed faithfully, this rarely happens. Our approach to calibration is based on getting the physics of engine fuel and airflow correct. By mapping the fuel-injector delivery correctly and solving for airflow in either MAF or VE based on good steady-state open-loop lambda error measurements, we usually find that closed-loop fuel trims are very small once corrections are re-enabled after base mapping of the ECU. In these cases, if we find a bank rich/lean code, we continue to diagnose the vehicle level problem much the same as a technician would at a dealership for a stock vehicle.

With the base engine functions and oxygen sensors themselves validated, we are left with the catalysts themselves for the remaining issues. Over the course of the vehicle's life, the effectiveness of the catalytic convertor slowly erodes. Knowing this, the emissions standards are written such that a vehicle at the end of its "full useful life" (FUL) still passes the tailpipe measurement standard on the dynamometer test even with the reduced effectiveness of an aged catalyst.

Automakers actually age catalysts for these specific tests by heating them with large amounts of hot exhaust gases and intentional poisoning to simulate the life of the vehicle. For the LEV III US federal emissions standard for light-duty vehicles, this FUL is defined as 150,000 miles of mixed vehicle usage. The aging process is designed to pack a similar amount of accumulated damage into a procedure that can be done in a few weeks, resulting in a catalyst of sufficiently reduced conversion efficiency for the engineers to use for emissions development to make sure vehicles in the fleet are compliant at all stages of life.

Criteria Pollutant Assigned DFs

Tier 3 Bin	Useful Life	CO (g/mi)	HCHO (g/mi)	NMOG (g/mi)	NO_x (g/mi)	NMOG + NO_x (g/mi)	PM (g/mi)
0	150,000	0.00	0.0000	0.0000	0.0000	0.0000	0
20	150,000	0.06	0.0001	0.0025	0.0019	0.0043	0
30	150,000	0.11	0.0001	0.0034	0.0024	0.0058	0
50	150,000	0.16	0.0002	0.0062	0.0047	0.0109	0
70	150,000	0.24	0.0003	0.0098	0.0070	0.0168	0
125	150,000	0.38	0.0005	0.0149	0.1150	0.0264	0
160	150,000	0.50	0.0006	0.0198	0.0149	0.0347	0

GHG Assigned DFs

Tier 3 Bin	Useful Life	N_2O (g/mi)	CH_4 (g/mi)
0	120,000	0.0000	0.0000
20	120,000	0.0004	0.0010
30	120,000	0.0007	0.0020
50	120,000	0.0011	0.0026
70	120,000	0.0012	0.0027
125	120,000	0.0028	0.0069
160	120,000	0.0034	0.0083

The emissions standards for LEV3 are written for a full useful life (FUL) of 150,000 miles for light-duty vehicles. Certification testing by OEMs is done with specially aged catalysts that have been heated and poisoned a bit to represent the same wear they would have in a vehicle over this amount of time prior to testing. These assigned deterioration factors (DFs) may be applied in lieu of using aged catalysts for aftermarket testing.

So how does this work? The catalyst is manufactured with a relatively even coating of precious metals deposited on a substrate that has lots of surface area exposed to the exhaust gases passing through it. Inside, the platinum, palladium, and rhodium (no wonder they get stolen so often!) promote reactions between carbon monoxide, oxides of nitrogen (NO_x), and unburned hydrocarbons, giving them a second chance at burning clean before exiting the tailpipe.

During a cold start, the exhaust gases warm the leading edge of the catalyst first, getting the washcoat of precious metals up to reaction temperature first. This creates its own exothermic reaction further heating the catalyst brick and allowing the rest of the sites downstream to assist in cleanup. Over time, the leading edge of washcoat burns off or is poisoned to a non-working state and moves the "burn" farther backward like the top of a candle.

If everything is indeed working as intended, the downstream oxygen sensor should see the result of the reactions inside the catalyst while the upstream sensor continues to see raw engine measurements. The comparison of these two signals, even on an aged catalyst, is the fundamental way in which modern ECUs determine the health of the catalytic convertor.

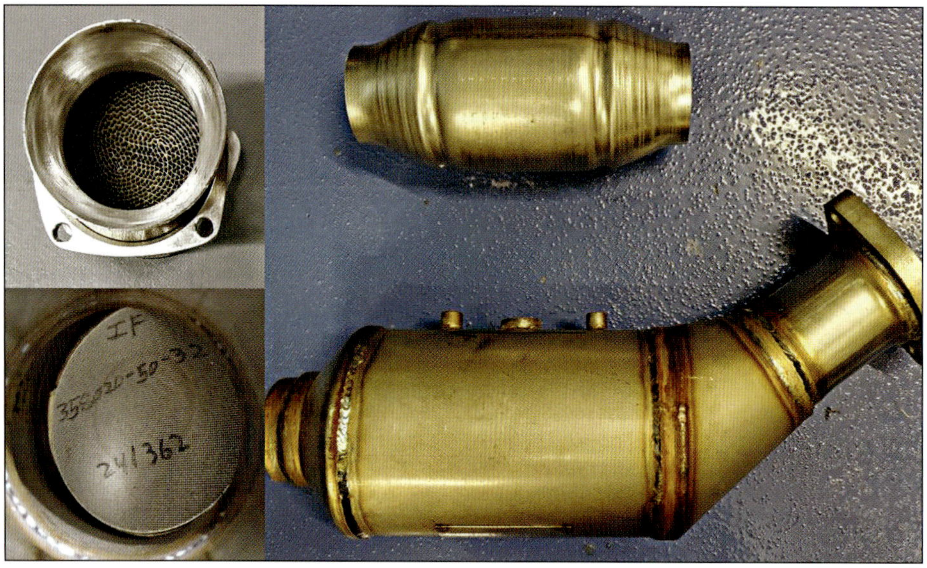

Looking at an aftermarket "high-flow" 100-cell-per-inch convertor (top) next to a 600-cell-per-inch OEM convertor, it's easy to see why there is such a difference in emissions performance. The larger volume along with denser packing of coated cells exposes much more of the exhaust gases to the conversion process needed to pass LEV3 standards.

Assuming the sensors themselves are in good working order, a failure here brings bad news, as the only remaining option is to replace what is often a very expensive catalytic convertor assembly.

In the high-performance world, it has been common to see exhaust modifications that negatively impact the catalytic convertor's functionality. The most obvious is a complete removal of the catalyst, often in the form of a "test pipe" or "off-road" exhaust. To be clear, this is a very plain violation of the Clean Air Act, a federal law that has been on the books since the 1970s. Although enforcement has not been strict for end users, manufacturers and installers face stiff fines for the sale or installation of these parts on a road-going vehicle. (I doubt race teams are reading this book on diagnostics for the trailer queens and tube-chassis monsters.)

Should the catalyst be removed, it's common for a modern ECU to quickly set a P0420/P0430 code. Shutting off the code in the ECU is just as big of a violation in the eyes of an EPA/CARB investigator, so it is strongly discouraged as well. Plenty of OEM and aftermarket examples exist, proving that large amounts of power can indeed be made through catalytic convertors. Sawing them off in the name of performance has become a bit of a caveman-level maneuver these days.

Other high-performance applications replace the OEM catalyst with a "high-flow" unit. While some of these do indeed offer good conversion efficiency along with reduced backpressure at high flow rates, there are equally as many out there that simply don't do the fundamental job of cleaning up the exhaust anywhere near as well as the original equipment. In these cases, the loss of conversion efficiency may be evident immediately or appear over time much quicker than one would see with the original equipment. Again, the factory catalyst performance diagnostic is a good indicator here as to whether the new hardware is doing a good job of keeping emissions clean.

Evaporative System

When Ford resurrected the "Boss 302" name for a new Mustang package in 2012, it was for noted monumental efficiency and emissions improvements that had taken place over several decades. So great were these improvements that the new car created less harmful emissions driving on the freeway than its 1970 namesake did while parked. Admittedly, that is a bit of an unfair comparison but true nonetheless.

While the completely new Coyote 5.0L engine family certainly helped with better combustion, the addition of a whole host of modern catalytic convertors and electronic controls all work together to keep tailpipe emissions to a minimum. So, why would this running car still pollute less than one that's parked? The answer lies in the evaporative emissions system.

In classic cars, the fuel tank was vented to atmosphere. This allowed fuel vapors to escape through these vents directly from the fuel tank. Making matters worse, carburetors are little more than a controlled fuel leak themselves, sitting on top of the engine with only a simple paper filter separating them from the atmosphere. Every time fuel was added to the tank, the liquid volume displaced a large amount of gas vapors in the top of the tank that would simply be pushed out into the environment.

As emissions standards were

tightened over time, these evaporative emissions (almost exclusively hydrocarbons or organic gases) were addressed in standards that required the automakers to prevent their unfiltered release to the outside world. Systems were devised that could direct fuel-tank vapors toward a canister filled with activated charcoal that could temporarily absorb and store them until they could be drawn into the running engine later. These systems have their own diagnosis routines and codes (P0440–P0457) to ensure that everything is working as intended.

When properly sealed, this system does a remarkable job of capturing, storing, and later using these fuel vapors. This means that not only would the raw hydrocarbon emissions be greatly reduced but also the vapors themselves would contribute to useful combustion work inside the engine, improving mileage rather than being wasted. (At today's fuel prices, this is not a bad idea at all.)

The good news is that since we are already talking about vaporized fuel, we have something that mixes exceptionally well with the incoming air charge in the intake manifold and burns clean in the cylinders. On the way out, any leftovers go past the catalytic convertor just like liquid fuel sources did. The only trick for the ECU controls engineers (and calibrators) is that this additional fuel must be accounted for in the process and subtracted from the amount of fuel to be delivered to the engine from the injectors. This happens seamlessly in modern ECUs, where we have very precise control of the fuel injector down to minute quantities.

Typically, the ECU has logic that attempts to maintain a small amount of depression in the evaporative system (including the fuel tank) relative to the current barometric conditions. This means that even if there were to be a small leak, outside air would be drawn in, rather than allowing the harmful vapors to escape to the outside world. This is accomplished by placing a control valve (P0443) on or near the intake manifold. When the valve is opened, intake manifold vacuum pulls vapors from the charcoal canister into the engine. This results in a modest downstream vacuum all the way to the fuel tank as well. During a refueling event, the gases that filled the tank are pushed into the charcoal canister as they are displaced by the incoming liquid fuel.

The sealed housing for evaporative determination (SHED) test uses a container large enough to fit the entire vehicle and precisely measure any vapors that come from it. Any leak in the evaporative emissions control system will be easily detected here.

Following the flexible line from the intake manifold back, we find the evaporative emissions control, or "purge," valve. When opened, engine vacuum draws raw fuel vapors into the intake manifold from the charcoal canister.

Because the whole evaporative emissions system is sealed, it is easy to manage the pressure. Any leaks in the system would show up as a loss of the intentional vacuum during operation. Fuel tank pressure is typically monitored directly with a pressure sensor on or near the tank that is very similar in design to a typical MAP sensor. The sensitivity of the system is now so good that even a single leak as small as a 0.020-inch-diameter hole can be accurately detected and trigger a fault code (P0442/456).

As a former OEM diagnostic calibration engineer, it was my job to install a special cap on the service port of the evaporative system with a 0.020-inch hole drilled in it. This helped us to make sure we were robust to detection without false passes or false fails. Yes, they really are that capable and it's not that hard for the engineer to dial in the right values to capture such a condition. I was the guy with this exact job at one time.

Evaporative Group Faults: Common Causes and Repairs

The most common evaporative emissions fault today is far and away one that seems obvious. A loose or uninstalled gas cap will often trigger gross or large leak detection (P0455/457) in seconds. The reason is simple. The system vacuum that we were just talking about cannot be achieved at all if such a large part of the system is open to the atmosphere.

Normally, the fuel tank pressure sensor sees an almost immediate depression the moment the control valve by the engine is opened to manifold vacuum. The ECU is looking for this immediate response downstream, and its absence triggers an immediate failure. More often than not, the solution is to walk to the back of the vehicle and check/replace the gas cap, where the seal is restored to the system and normal operation resumes.

Many modern vehicles have done away with manually removed gas caps for this exact reason. Instead, they have an integral seal on a trap-door mechanism that is opened by inserting the gas pump nozzle into the fuel-filler neck. This makes user error less common, but at an added price to the vehicle. Even these systems are not immune to large leaks, though, as any disconnected line would have the same net effect. In the absence of a filler-cap seal issue, the next thing to look for is a more obvious disconnect in the evaporative system.

Small leaks (P0442/456) are present in a similar manner but take a little longer for the diagnostics to find. In these cases, some degree of tank vacuum is established quickly but it fails to hold that vacuum as long as expected between opening

A loose gas cap is a large leak. It will immediately fail the P0455/P0457 diagnostic. This failure is so common that it's the first thing technicians often tell a customer to check if the MIL came on after a refueling event.

TECH TIP

Conditional Failure

Once upon a time, I saw a set of high-flow catalysts mounted after a pair of long-tube headers on a performance truck that registered only 8 to 11 percent conversion efficiency while driving in cruise control on the highway at 70 mph.

The combination of lower cell density, reduced precious-metal loading, and increased underbody cooling airflow combined to render them almost non-existent in terms of emissions. The funny thing is that at lower speeds, there wasn't as much underbody airflow, so the catalysts remained hot enough in city traffic to allow the diagnostic monitors to execute and pass. It was only when driving for long enough on the freeway that the cooling was enough to drop the temperature of the bricks below a point where conversion efficiency tanked.

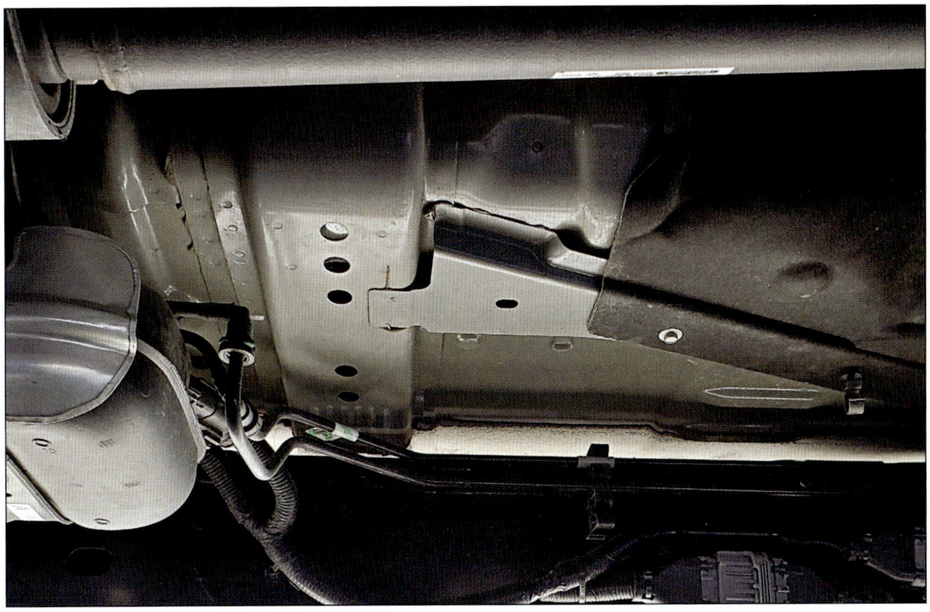

The extra lines connected to the fuel tank of this Ford Ranger direct fuel-tank vapors toward a charcoal canister, where they are temporarily stored before being drawn into the engine. The system is sensitive enough to detect leaks as small as 0.020 inch in size.

events from the control valve. It may also detect these small leaks when the vehicle is shut off, as the system should have a predictable change in pressure over time when it is parked. Deviations from this pressure-time profile flag the fault logic.

Finding a leak as small as 0.020 inch somewhere in a 20-foot-long system can be a daunting task. The culprit can be a single crimped hose connector, a cracked line, a worn O-ring, or a misaligned connector in addition to the possibility of a pinhole anywhere in the system. Once we are down to leaks this small, a smoke machine or handheld hydrocarbon leak detector may be your only hope if there is not an obvious visual issue found. If you are not lucky enough to have either one in your shop, you may also try the shadetree-mechanic solution of pressurizing the fuel system with shop air and spraying the various components with a solution of soapy water to watch for bubbles near the leak.

The aftermarket performance enthusiast should pay special attention here when swapping in that new high-flow in-tank fuel pump. Take an extra minute or two to make sure that the fuel pump hat has sealed properly before putting everything back in place and adding a bunch of fuel.

Failing purge control valves (P0443) are checked much the same way as a fuel injector. The ECU is nice enough to check the circuit integrity, which may lead to a pinched or cut wire. If the wires between the valve and the ECU check out, the valve itself is likely the issue, as these do indeed fail on occasion. Luckily, replacement is usually pretty easy.

Pressure sensor/switch faults (P0451–P0454) follow a path similar to MAP sensor diagnostics. Again, circuit wiring integrity should be checked first between the ECU and the sensor. The placement of these (usually on the top of the fuel tank) can make accessing them a physical challenge, but once it is seen, replacement is relatively easy. Unfortunately, this often means dropping the fuel tank from the chassis, so plan ahead on fuel level (or draining) if the tank needs to drop.

Scan this QR code with your smartphone to view a list of SAE fault codes.

www.cartechbooks.com/sa532-qr1

Manufacturer-Specific Diagnostic Codes

The amount of standardization present in generic SAE fault codes is amazing. The vast majority of engine and powertrain failures are covered by these generic codes, and skilled technicians can usually complete their diagnosis and repair based on the clues contained in them. However, the service bays of dealerships around the world and manufacturers realize that time is money. In an effort to more quickly drive the technician to the correct repair on a specific family of vehicles, control systems, or hardware, manufacturers have decided to include some of their own more specific diagnostics that work in parallel with the generic SAE requirements.

Ferrari follows standard OBD-II guidelines for all generic fault codes, but like many other manufacturers, it is free to add its own specific diagnostics as well. Ferrari's unique method of turbocharger speed and throttle controls require matching unique diagnostics.

Complex systems such as torque-based drive-by-wire controls, turbocharger boost control, active intake manifolds, variable valve timing, and other technologies may all be used simultaneously. Because of the complex interactions among these systems, finding the true root cause of a particular issue may prove to be difficult using only the generic SAE faults available through standard OBD-II protocols.

Most manufacturers have elected to add more diagnostics and assign them their own P-codes in the ECU to call out more specific failures. Some of these may correlate with generic fault codes already in use in the P0xxx range, but these enhanced trouble codes offer a more specific definition of what has been found by the ECU.

Part of the OBD-I requirement was to detect a constantly open or shorted circuit, but a manufacturer may also opt to add a separate diagnostic that detects an intermittent failure of this sort. These intermittent failures can be especially frustrating because the technician must be looking at the exact circuit in question as the fault occurs. If the fault does not persist long enough for a counter to pass a predetermined threshold of failure for the OBD-I fault for

[ECM] 14040 - Calculated Airmass vs. TPS vs. RPM - P1514 Error

Engine Speed (rpm) \ Throttle Position (%)	0.0	6.3	12.5	18.8	25.0	31.3	37.5	43.8	50.0	56.3	62.5	68.8	75.0	81.3	87.5	93.8	100.0
0	0.60	0.60	0.60	0.60	0.60	0.60	0.60	0.60	0.60	0.60	0.60	0.60	0.60	0.60	0.60	0.60	0.60
500	0.11	0.22	0.38	0.47	0.50	0.52	0.53	0.53	0.53	0.53	0.53	0.53	0.53	0.53	0.53	0.53	0.53
1,000	0.06	0.12	0.25	0.38	0.48	0.52	0.54	0.54	0.54	0.54	0.54	0.54	0.54	0.54	0.54	0.54	0.54
1,500	0.05	0.08	0.16	0.29	0.45	0.53	0.56	0.57	0.57	0.57	0.57	0.57	0.57	0.57	0.57	0.57	0.57
2,000	0.04	0.06	0.12	0.24	0.40	0.50	0.55	0.57	0.58	0.59	0.59	0.59	0.59	0.59	0.59	0.59	0.59
2,500	0.03	0.05	0.08	0.18	0.34	0.45	0.52	0.57	0.58	0.60	0.60	0.61	0.61	0.61	0.61	0.61	0.61
3,000	0.03	0.05	0.08	0.15	0.31	0.41	0.52	0.58	0.60	0.62	0.63	0.63	0.63	0.63	0.63	0.63	0.63
3,500	0.03	0.05	0.07	0.12	0.25	0.38	0.48	0.56	0.61	0.65	0.66	0.67	0.67	0.68	0.68	0.68	0.68
4,000	0.03	0.05	0.06	0.10	0.21	0.35	0.45	0.56	0.61	0.64	0.66	0.68	0.69	0.69	0.69	0.69	0.69
4,500	0.03	0.05	0.05	0.09	0.15	0.28	0.43	0.54	0.58	0.62	0.67	0.69	0.69	0.69	0.71	0.71	0.71
5,000	0.03	0.05	0.05	0.09	0.15	0.27	0.41	0.52	0.56	0.61	0.65	0.69	0.70	0.71	0.71	0.72	0.72
5,500	0.03	0.05	0.05	0.09	0.15	0.26	0.42	0.51	0.55	0.60	0.62	0.64	0.67	0.68	0.69	0.69	0.69
6,000	0.03	0.05	0.05	0.09	0.15	0.26	0.42	0.50	0.54	0.58	0.59	0.60	0.61	0.62	0.63	0.63	0.63
6,500	0.03	0.05	0.05	0.09	0.15	0.26	0.40	0.48	0.52	0.55	0.56	0.57	0.57	0.58	0.58	0.58	0.58
7,000	0.03	0.05	0.05	0.09	0.15	0.26	0.38	0.46	0.48	0.50	0.51	0.52	0.53	0.53	0.54	0.54	0.54
7,500	0.03	0.05	0.05	0.09	0.15	0.26	0.37	0.44	0.46	0.47	0.49	0.49	0.50	0.50	0.50	0.51	0.51
8,000	0.03	0.05	0.05	0.09	0.15	0.26	0.36	0.41	0.44	0.45	0.45	0.46	0.46	0.47	0.47	0.47	0.47

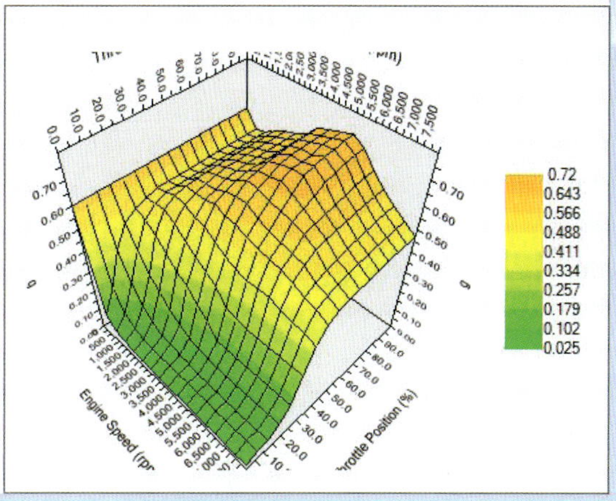

The GM-specific logic used to detect excessive electronic airflow is tied to the P1514 code. This table is used to trigger a failsafe mode if airflow is unexpectedly high, indicating a run-away event.

Engine Diagnostics

General | Airflow | Misfire | Exhaust | DTCs

DTC	Description	SES Enable	Error Mode
P1251	Throttle Position	☐	No Error Reported
P1252	Pedal Correlation PDS1 and LPDS High	☐	No Error Reported
P1253	Pedal Correlation PDS1 and LPDS Low	☐	No Error Reported
P1254	Pedal Correlation PDS2 and LPDS High	☐	No Error Reported
P1258	Engine Coolant Overtemperature - Protection Mode Active	☑	MIL on First Error
P1380	Misfire Detected - Rough Road Data Not Available	☐	No MIL Light
P1381	Misfire Detected - No Communication with Brake Control Module	☐	No MIL Light
P1400	Differential Pressure Feedback EGR Circuit Low Input	☑	MIL on First Error
P1482	Catalyst Temp Sensor Low	☑	MIL on Second Error
P1513	Intake Manifold Runner Control Stuck Closed (Bank 2)	☐	No Error Reported
P1516	Throttle Actuator Control (TAC) Module Throttle Actuator Position Performance	☑	MIL on First Error
P1553	Adaptive Cruise Control Signal Circuit	☐	No Error Reported
P1574	Stoplamp Switch Circuit	☐	No Error Reported
P1575	Extended Travel Brake Switch Circuit	☐	No Error Reported
P1598	A/C Pressure Sensor High	☐	No Error Reported
P1629	Theft Deterrent System - Cranking Signal	☐	No Error Reported
P1630	Theft Deterrent Learn Mode Active	☐	No MIL Light
P1631	Theft Deterrent Start Enable Signal Not Correct	☐	No MIL Light

P1516 is another one of the drive-by-wire watchdogs used by General Motors. It is triggered when the throttle actuator control module does not agree with the ECU.

something like a P0106 (MAP circuit high voltage), the technician may be stumped. But a modern GM vehicle that can store a P1106 (MAP circuit intermittent high voltage), the technician now has a solid starting point for investigation under the hood.

Access to these unique codes requires a tool smart enough to decode them. The most basic of generic scan tools may not display these correctly or at all. However, many newer scan tools have updated software that will also access and display these codes along with their generic SAE counterparts. Ultimately, it is up to the tool and software companies to decode this for the user. Getting a device with the most recent updates is always a good idea, as these codes can change over time as well.

Drive-by-wire control systems have a necessary level of complexity not only for their general operation but also for safety redundancy as well. A simple diagnosis of "throttle position" or "pedal position" error does not tell the whole story. These systems have multiple tracks within the sensors that each generate a different output voltage response curve. These curves must then be checked against each other to confirm that the ECU has a valid reading of either pedal or throttle-blade angle.

The independent assessment of airflow, allowable manifold pressure, torque estimation, and their correlation to each other often falls under the authority of these manufacturer-specific diagnostics. The SAE does not require a single universal method of diagnosis here, but rest assured that each manufacturer's legal team is satisfied with their liability coverage.

P1XXX Range

Since each manufacturer is free to define its own codes here, things could potentially get really messy really fast when one thinks about how many possible combinations there are. The same number could mean two very different things to two different vehicle manufacturers.

To avoid confusion, these manufacturer-specific codes are assigned numbers in the P1XXX range. Making matters worse, a manufacturer could update these codes over time, resulting in different meanings for the same number depending on the year and application. Printing an exhaustive list of all

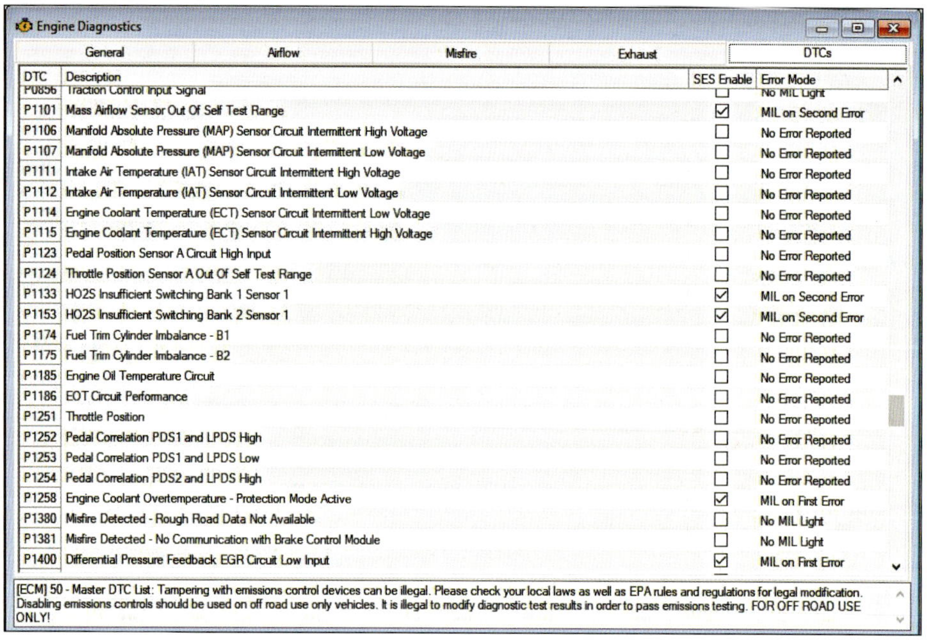

Here we see a segment of the P1xxx code range on a GM vehicle. These codes are unique to General Motors, so don't expect to see the same listing on another make.

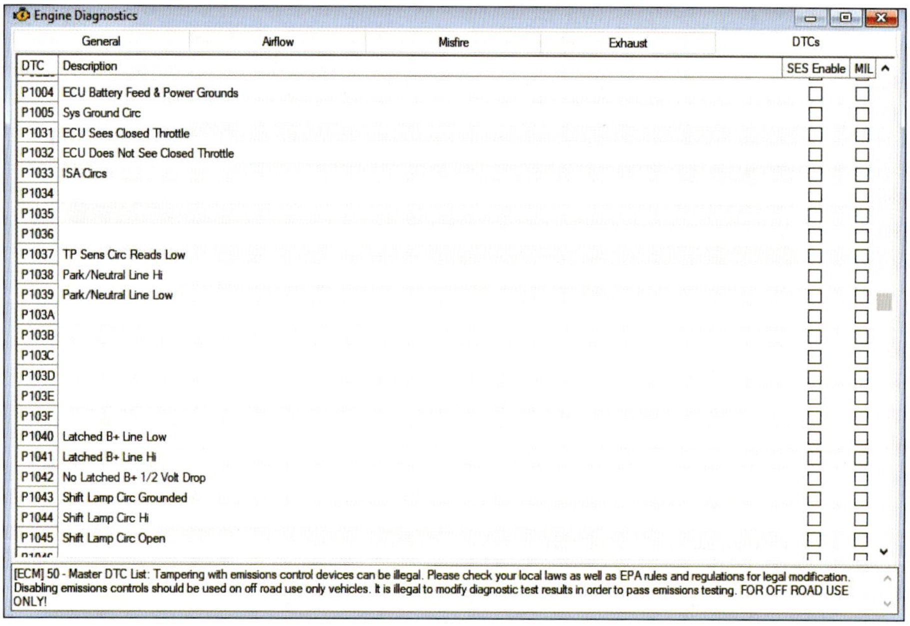

The Chrysler P1xxx codes are different than those seen on the GM vehicle. Manufacturers are free to populate this range of faults however they see fit.

manufacturer-specific codes in this range is an almost impossible task. The list would already be out of date by the time this book was published.

Instead of attempting to be a sole printed source of all possible P-codes, let's instead remember what we learned in Chapter 5 about how best to use the massive resources of the internet to find what you're really looking for anyway. Chances are good that not only will you turn up a proper definition but someone out there may also already have a step-by-step guide to fixing the most common root cause as well.

As previously mentioned, the manufacturer-specific code number itself may be unique to your application, so don't just run off to fix the first item that comes up on a simple search for something like "P1380." This can have you operating on the wrong end of the patient altogether. Instead, be sure to include more detail in your search terms.

Read the linked articles, forum posts, or guides that come up to make sure they are common to your vehicle. This can be the difference between a quick fix and hours of wasted time and cash. I can't repeat this enough: there's no way to publish a book that can keep up with the ever-changing world of manufacturer updates. Think critically while evaluating the information from an internet search if you are to be successful in working with these codes.

Example: Code P1380 Differences for Various Automakers

Description	Automaker
Misfire Detected – Rough Road	General Motors, Ford, Honda, Acura, Citroen/Peugot
Detonation Detected	Porsche
VCT Solenoid Circuit	Volkswagen, Audi, Toyota, Jaguar, Lincoln, Oldsmobile
Inlet Valve Not Operated at Cylinder Cutoff	Mercedes
Glow Plug Relay Circuit	Subaru
Many generic OBD websites steer you in the completely wrong direction for repair if you are not specific enough when entering your search criteria.	

One bright point here is that many scan-tool makers include a brief description of the fault codes along with reporting the number. If these tools are routinely updated with an online connection, then chances are better that they may indeed give you the correct answer from this first step. It's still worth a minute or two to search based on the number and description provided to verify, though.

CHAPTER 8

OBD Monitors

Earlier, we looked at various fault codes within the ECU and mentioned that the individual tests also contribute to a larger group called "monitors." OBD-II calls out a series of specific monitors that must be reported if the vehicle is equipped with the accompanying hardware. Here, we will look a little closer at each monitor's background and the conditions under which they are typically run.

Much like the content of my Calibrated Success classes and training videos, the object here is to equip you with a thought process that helps solve today's unique problem rather than attempting to spoon feed a list of answers based on historical findings. If you understand what the monitor is looking for and how it is executed, it becomes much clearer as to how to go about finding and fixing the root cause of a failure.

There's no way I could give every possible failure mode in this one book, but I can set you on a path that helps you think about the "why" and "how" the ECU works. This will give a better overall understanding as you approach each case.

The monitors themselves now play a pivotal role in emissions certification for many end users. More and more state inspections are requiring a "plug-in" emissions inspection, part of which has their computer looking at the MIL and monitor statuses. If a vehicle is unable to set more than one monitor, the vehicle is often denied the ability to renew its registration for road use until it is fixed. Understandably, this upsets some owners whether it was originally their own doing or not. Let's take a look at the individual monitors to know a little more about each one.

The first three monitors are known as "continuous" monitors for the obvious reason that the ECU is always looking at them while the engine is running. This group includes misfire, fuel system, and comprehensive components. They cover critical systems that would lead to a significant increase in emissions the moment any issue should occur, so they are always being reviewed by the ECU. The remaining monitors are consequently known as "non-continuous," as they only need to be run once per valid drive cycle to keep the ECU happy.

Misfire Monitor

In a normal-running four-stroke engine, rotational speed is never truly constant. We have acceleration events every single time a cylinder enters the power stroke and

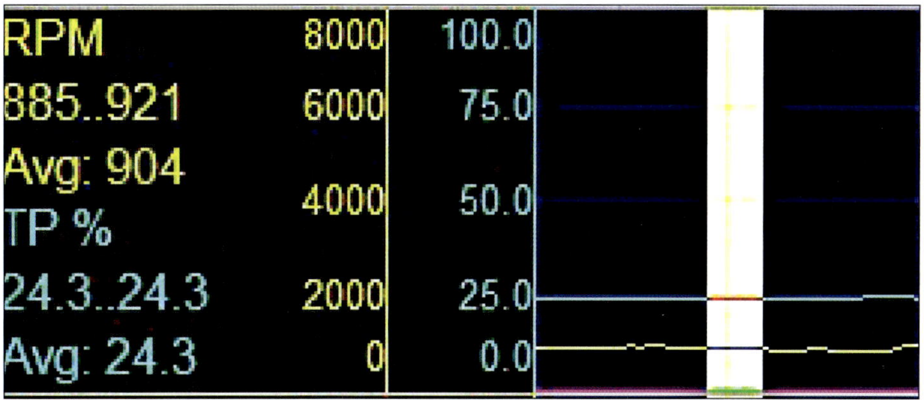

Zooming in on what looks like a very stable idle speed trace shows variations of 36 rpm (peak to peak) caught by the ECU recording while throttle position was constant. This is the result of each cylinder's acceleration after ignition followed by slowing due to friction.

fuel releases energy into the piston, connecting rod, and crankshaft. At the same time, we have friction and compression work in other cylinders attempting to slow the engine down. Between the two, the running engine develops a rhythmic cycle of accelerations and decelerations that looks a lot like a sine wave when RPM is plotted against time. Zoom in enough and we see the wave firsthand, but zoom out and see a slightly noisy line representing the current average engine speed.

Next, we need to understand how the ECU determines rotational speed. The primary input for this is the crankshaft position sensor, which is pointed at a ring on the crankshaft itself that has a number of teeth around its circumference. As each tooth passes the sensor, a signal change is observed at both the rising and falling edges.

Knowing the total number of teeth on the ring, the ECU can count how long it takes for all of them to pass in the completion of one revolution, giving us RPM when normalized to minutes instead of milliseconds. Even better, the ECU can also calculate the tooth-to-tooth time on the fly. Knowing that each tooth represents a certain number of crankshaft degrees of rotation, it gets a much faster calculation of instantaneous engine speed.

The location of the "gap" or missing tooth/teeth on the crankshaft lets it know where it is in relation to top dead center of cylinder number-1. Combined with the camshaft position sensor, it knows the difference between the two revolutions that make up one complete engine cycle of all cylinders and which cylinder in the firing order should be up next.

Knowing which cylinder should be accelerating next (just after its spark plug has fired), the ECU expects to see a slight acceleration in engine speed. It witnesses the shortening of tooth-to-tooth times as the combustion process pushes down on the piston.

In this cutaway of a GM 6.0L V-8, both crankshaft and cam sensor target wheels are visible. The ECU is programmed to look for each edge on the target wheel a certain rotation angle past TDC number-1 to identify the current position and speed.

The misfire monitor simply follows this process in real time for every expected combustion event to make sure that all cylinders are contributing to engine operation. The absence of acceleration or too long of a measured tooth-to-tooth time in a given target window of time indicates that the combustion event was not effective. There may be many causes of this missed combustion event, but our focus for the moment is on detection.

Within the ECU, there are calibratable tables that define the size of the time window during which the ECU expects to see these acceleration events. These tables separate the various operating cases of idle, light load, and full load, but federal law requires that manufacturers operate the misfire diagnostic continuously under all conditions. This includes wide-open throttle and all engine speeds from idle to redline.

Since there can be 60 teeth per revolution (58, with two "missing teeth"), this means that the ECU must register the passing of one tooth at the crankshaft position sensor every 0.166 millisecond on average. Beyond that, it must further detect the subtle increases and decreases in instantaneous speed that show the accelerations from each cylinder's power stroke to pass.

This calculation may not be skipped, so it becomes a high-priority task for the processor that eats up a lot of the available resources at high speed. It is one of the main drivers that forced OEMs to use faster and faster ECU processor chips over the years.

Turning off this calculation would be a direct violation of the Clean Air Act because engine misfires lead to a significant increase in emissions

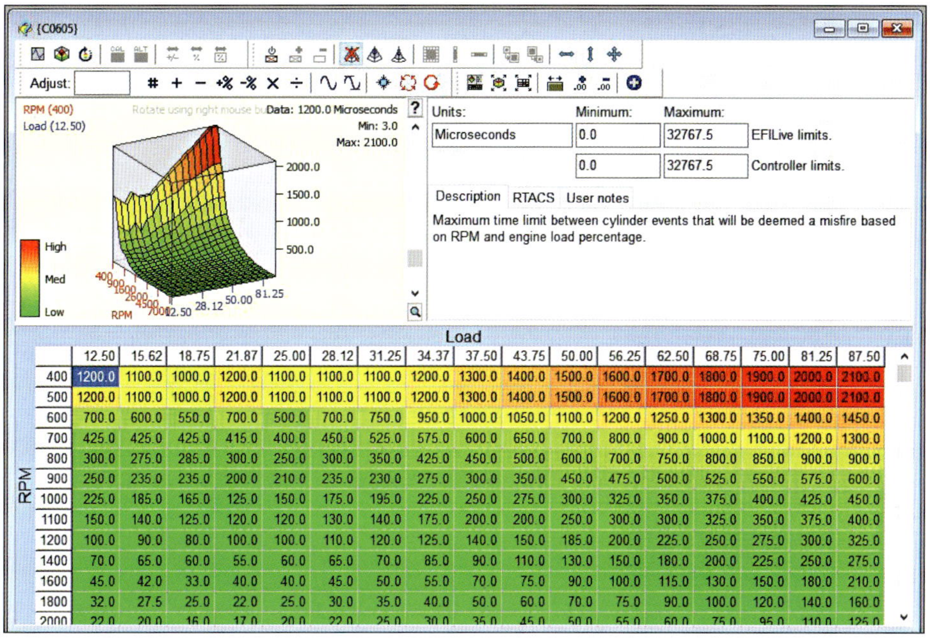

RPM	12.50	15.62	18.75	21.87	25.00	28.12	31.25	34.37	37.50	43.75	50.00	56.25	62.50	68.75	75.00	81.25	87.50
400	1200.0	1100.0	1000.0	1200.0	1100.0	1100.0	1100.0	1200.0	1300.0	1400.0	1500.0	1600.0	1700.0	1800.0	1900.0	2000.0	2100.0
500	1200.0	1100.0	1000.0	1200.0	1100.0	1100.0	1100.0	1200.0	1300.0	1400.0	1500.0	1600.0	1700.0	1800.0	1900.0	2000.0	2100.0
600	700.0	600.0	550.0	700.0	500.0	700.0	750.0	950.0	1000.0	1050.0	1100.0	1200.0	1250.0	1300.0	1350.0	1400.0	1450.0
700	425.0	425.0	425.0	415.0	400.0	450.0	525.0	575.0	600.0	650.0	700.0	800.0	900.0	1000.0	1100.0	1200.0	1300.0
800	300.0	275.0	285.0	300.0	250.0	300.0	350.0	425.0	450.0	500.0	600.0	700.0	750.0	800.0	850.0	900.0	900.0
900	250.0	235.0	235.0	200.0	210.0	235.0	230.0	275.0	300.0	350.0	450.0	475.0	500.0	525.0	550.0	575.0	600.0
1000	225.0	185.0	165.0	125.0	150.0	175.0	195.0	225.0	250.0	275.0	300.0	325.0	350.0	375.0	400.0	425.0	450.0
1100	150.0	140.0	125.0	120.0	120.0	130.0	140.0	175.0	200.0	200.0	250.0	300.0	300.0	325.0	350.0	375.0	400.0
1200	100.0	90.0	80.0	100.0	100.0	110.0	120.0	125.0	140.0	150.0	185.0	200.0	225.0	250.0	275.0	300.0	325.0
1400	70.0	65.0	60.0	55.0	60.0	65.0	70.0	85.0	90.0	110.0	130.0	150.0	180.0	200.0	225.0	250.0	275.0
1600	45.0	42.0	33.0	40.0	40.0	45.0	50.0	55.0	70.0	75.0	90.0	100.0	115.0	130.0	150.0	180.0	210.0
1800	32.0	27.5	25.0	22.0	25.0	30.0	35.0	40.0	50.0	60.0	70.0	75.0	90.0	100.0	120.0	140.0	160.0
2000	22.0	20.0	16.0	17.0	20.0	22.0	25.0	30.0	35.0	45.0	50.0	55.0	60.0	75.0	95.0	110.0	125.0

This ECU table defines the limits for allowable variation between cylinder events to declare a misfire. Values decrease at higher RPM because there is physically less time between events as engine speed rises.

The ignition coils on this Hemi engine each feed two spark plugs per cylinder. It only takes one cracked or fouled plug to ruin their coordinated output and engine operation.

as the raw fuel exits the engine. Worse, the raw fuel and unburned oxygen have the potential to light off in the exhaust. The result is combustion outside of the water-cooled cylinders of the engine block.

Misfire events send raw fuel and oxygen down the pipe where they easily burn in the catalyst and can melt the thin metal substrate. If the tightly spaced metal grid melts just a little bit with these clearances, it can quickly begin blocking flow.

This is a process that very effectively melts the washcoat and substrate of the catalytic convertor, damages turbine blades, and cracks oxygen sensor elements. It is to be avoided at all costs, and the presence of misfires is so important that the ECU will immediately display a flashing MIL on the dash if the ECU currently detects them. This is to alert the driver that they need to let off the gas and possibly even stop driving the vehicle completely right now to avoid such expensive damage to the exhaust components.

Ignition Failures

The most common causes for engine misfires are the ignition and fuel delivery system, with ignition usually being the first stop for most technicians. Any fire needs fuel, oxygen, and an ignition source. The automotive ignition system can be quite complex when one considers the operation of modern smart coils on a distributed network working in a hot environment that shakes a lot. Any link in the chain between the ECU, wire harness, coil pack, plug wire, and spark plug itself can lead to a failed ignition event.

Fortunately, the P0301 cylinder-1 misfire code is often accompanied by another diagnostic code in this case, such as P0351 ignition coil a primary/secondary circuit. The combination of these two together give us a solid reason why the failure is present and where to begin looking for a fix. It might be something as simple as a loose plug or coil connection wire. But a cracked spark plug or wire boot may be offering the spark energy an easier path to ground than the plug gap inside the cylinder.

Careful inspection of each hardware component is needed here. Barring that failure, the next step would be to test the coil itself for impedance across both the primary (low-voltage input) and secondary (high-voltage output) windings. The primary should have relatively low impedance of a few ohms or less, where the secondary circuit should be much higher in the range of kilohms, depending on the design. Even brand-new coils should be checked to avoid losing time chasing other less likely sources. Finding every possible ignition-related issue has the potential to fill hours of live class time. There are some great diagnostic trainers out there who have proven methods of finding these with an oscilloscope, a DMM, or a test light if you need more ideas.

This 5.4L supercharged Ford GT has twice the opportunity for fuel delivery failure with two injectors per cylinder. The newer version keeps the tradition alive with one port and one direct injector per cylinder too.

Fuel System Failures

Fuel delivery is another common cause of misfires. Check the obvious to see if there is enough gas in the tank. You laugh, but it happens. Next, look at delivered fuel pressure to confirm that the pump and regulator are working. If a single fuel injector fails, that cylinder can run lean enough to misfire.

Checking the injector circuit of a port-injected engine is easy with a DMM before taking anything else apart. There should be battery voltage on one wire and a pulsing ground from the ECU on the other when the engine is running. Most modern port fuel injectors are "high impedance," with 12 to 16 ohms across their terminals.

If all of that checks out, it may be time to pull the injectors and have them flow tested to see if they are all behaving similarly to each other and within the expected flow range for the application. This is done offline on a specific injector flow test stand. For direct injected (DI) engines, the operating voltage going to the injectors is much higher, often around 60 to 80 volts from a regulated circuit on the ECU.

DI injectors are also "low impedance" with around 1 to 6 ohms at the coil. If the DI injectors need to be removed for testing, plan to replace their seals where they insert into the cylinder head each time. Some of the high-pressure hard lines or fittings may also need to be replaced, which are one-time crush to fit between the high-pressure pump and rail.

Airflow Failures

The third leg of the combustion triangle is oxygen, which comes from intake air. Although less common, we have seen plenty of cases where a misfire was traced to the valvetrain. If either the intake or exhaust valve is not opening or sealing completely, the cylinder will not exchange exhaust and fresh air as well as the other cylinders.

I have seen cases that ranged from loose rockers, bent pushrods, or broken valve springs to damaged seats that gave us a misfire, but these were certainly not our first guess as to what went wrong. Since this investigation is much more invasive, we prefer to check all other options first before going down this path.

Fuel System Monitor

The second continuous monitor looks at the fuel system. Specifically, it's looking at the ECU's ability to accurately control fuel delivery close to the stoichiometric ratio during closed-loop operation. As was discussed in Chapter 4, the ECU is constantly estimating the amount of cylinder fresh-air charge and attempting to deliver an appropriate amount of fuel with that fresh air.

If everything works right, we get clean combustion with a minimum of leftover emissions for the catalyst to clean up on the way out. Sometimes, the first guess isn't as close as we would like, so some correction is necessary to get things back in line. The legitimate reasons that the

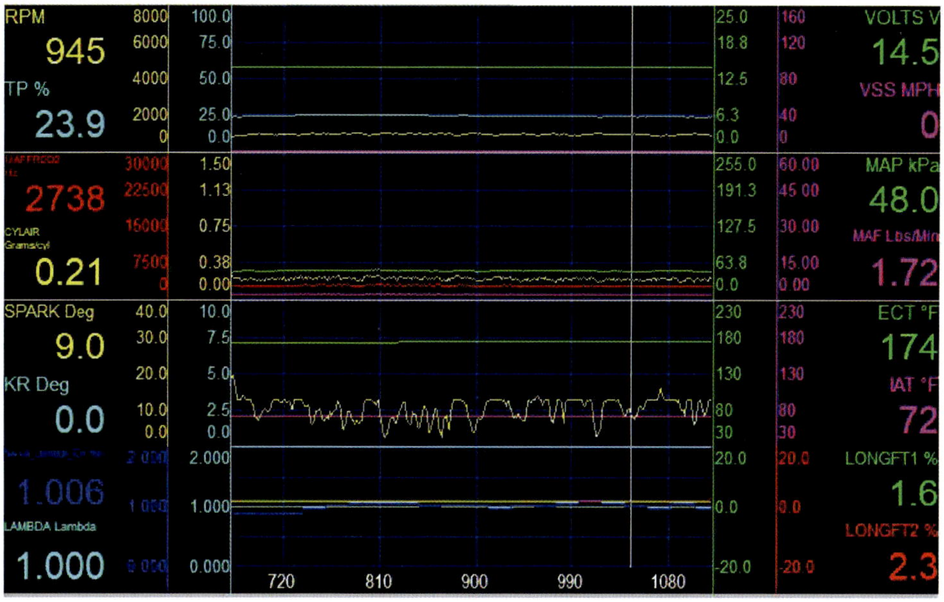

An example of a properly calibrated engine is shown here where the long-term fuel trims (bottom right) are almost zero. This means that both the airflow and fuel delivery models are properly calibrated to the engine hardware.

correction is necessary may range from fuel chemistry, slight variations in evaporative system fuel contribution, engine or sensor aging, buildup in the injectors, or environmental changes.

On the other hand, closed-loop corrections may also become larger for bad reasons, such as vacuum leaks, stuck injectors, improper fuel rail pressure, failed oxygen sensors, evaporative system issues, ignition system issues, stuck EGR, or a number of other concerns.

An engine produces the least amount of overall emissions when it is operated close to the stoichiometric ratio for whatever fuel is in the tank. Manufacturers attempt to get to this condition as quickly as they can after startup to avoid sending too much excess fuel to the catalyst or out the tailpipe.

Since the majority of automotive emissions happen during this critical startup phase, they are motivated to get out of it and into controlled closed-loop operation as quickly as the hardware will allow. Once the engine is operating in closed loop with active feedback from the oxygen sensors, the emissions drop to a small fraction of what was seen in startup.

Closed-Loop Fueling

All of this assumes that the feedback from the oxygen sensors is correct, which is where the fuel system monitor comes into play. By watching the fuel trims, the ECU gets an early warning that something else may be happening.

Failing oxygen sensors often begin doing so by slowly losing their ability to show a rich condition. As the sensor falsely reports a leaner-than-actual condition in the exhaust, the ECU responds by increasing the fuel trim to compensate. If the value for these fuel trims gets too big, it will eventually set a code, such as P0172 (bank 1 rich).

The exact point at which an excessive amount of long-term fuel trim will set the MIL is again tied to the fundamental requirement that a failure that results in tailpipe emissions being 150 percent of the standard to which the vehicle was certified must set the MIL (with a matching P-code). Depending on how tight the standard was or how clean the engine runs, this could mean anything from 20 to 40 percent fuel trims setting a bank rich/lean code. Most calibration engineers are not worried if fuel trims are in the single digits, but anything higher than about 25 percent is usually a strong indicator that something is wrong here.

Modified vehicles can also struggle to pass their fuel system monitor if the oxygen sensor has been moved to a new location. The timing between fuel injection at the engine, combustion, and travel through the exhaust down to the oxygen sensor is carefully calibrated into the vehicle's closed-loop control system.

Moving the sensor farther downstream after the installation of something such as long-tube headers can disrupt the carefully timed dance between the commanded rich/lean swings at the engine. When they are reported by the oxygen sensor, that puts them out of sync. This can lead to incorrect adjustments being made by the ECU's closed-loop feedback system, often driving the engine rich with large positive fuel trims. Worse, the long-tube headers delay catalyst warmup and often increase emissions to a point that does not pass the vehicle's original certification regardless of what ECU calibration changes are made with them or what "high-performance" catalyst is used.

Closed-loop control systems are used in many places within the modern automotive ECU. The most prominent place that we see them is in the fuel system. A closed-loop system measures a difference between the desired system behavior (air-fuel ratio) and a measured output to calculate an error that is in turn added back into the base operation so that future events will result in actual behavior matching the desired output.

The error can be calculated a number of ways with respect to time. This may be either in the instantaneous correction that is proportional to the current error, a learned integral based on error over a period of time, or a derivative error based on anticipated errors from a rapidly moving measurement. These proportional, integral, and derivative corrections are commonly referred together as a PID loop, where not all three are always used. Fuel corrections specifically are largely done with proportional or integral corrections.

Fuel trims are used when the first guess of "open-loop" fueling did not result in stoichiometric fuel delivery to the cylinders. The oxygen sensor reads the composition of the gases

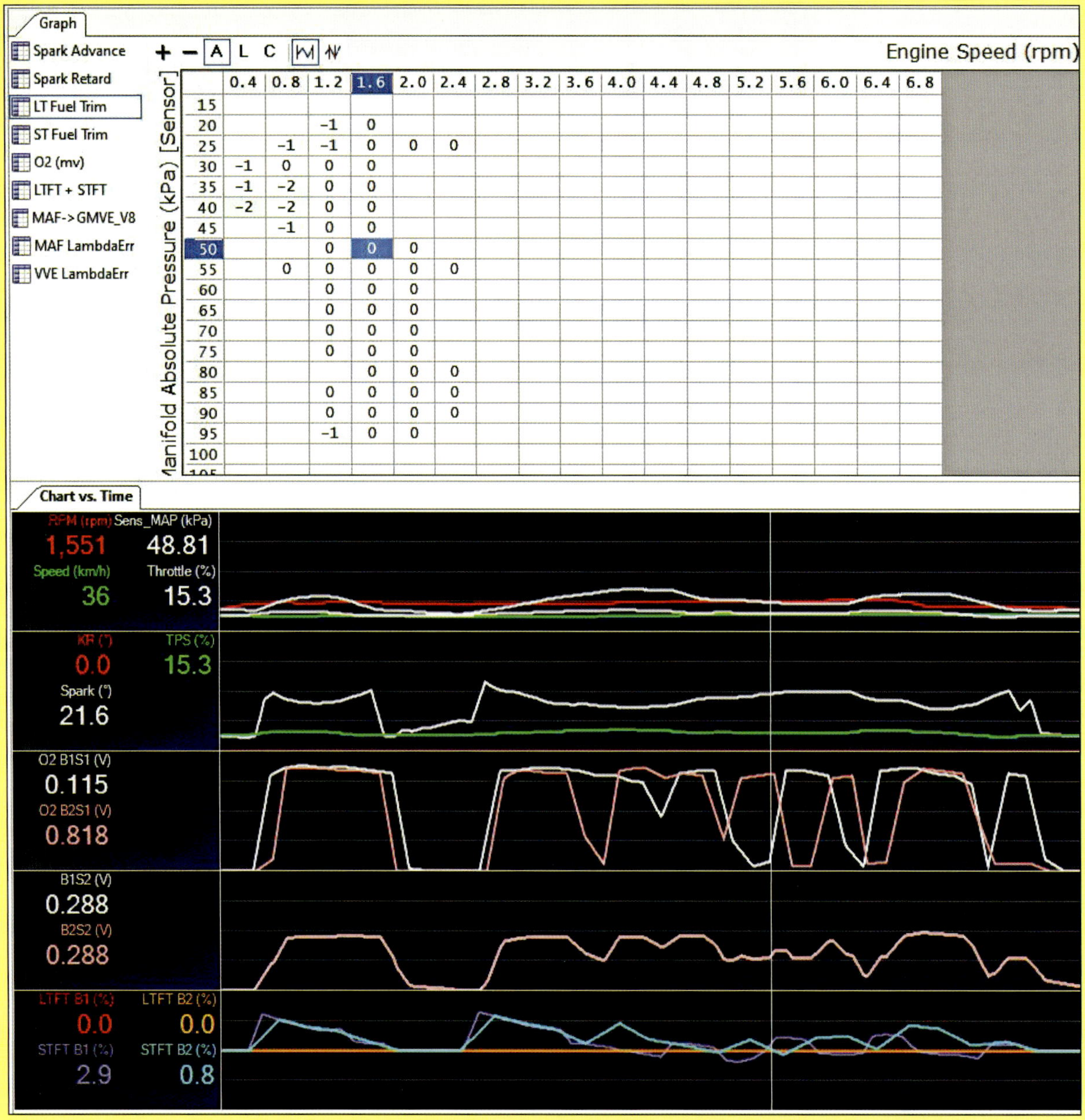

Manifold Absolute Pressure (kPa) [Sensor] \ Engine Speed (rpm)	0.4	0.8	1.2	1.6	2.0	2.4	2.8	3.2	3.6	4.0	4.4	4.8	5.2	5.6	6.0	6.4	6.8
15																	
20			-1	0													
25		-1	-1	0	0	0											
30	-1	0	0	0													
35	-1	-2	0	0													
40	-2	-2	0	0													
45		-1	0	0													
50			0	0	0												
55		0	0	0	0	0											
60			0	0	0												
65			0	0	0												
70			0	0	0												
75			0	0	0												
80				0	0	0											
85			0	0	0	0											
90			0	0	0	0											
95			-1	0	0												
100																	

A histogram (top) of average long-term fuel trims against engine speeds and loads can reveal specific areas where the ECU has been trying to correct a fuel-delivery issue. The bottom of the strip chart here also shows that this vehicle is operating close to stoichiometric without much correction required.

leaving the engine and reports back to the ECU with a signal that is proportional to the actual air-fuel ratio that was present during combustion.

To do this, the sensor must first be in a state where it can function accurately. Oxygen sensors require a hot ceramic element to work, so they are usually not available for a short time after the engine has started, especially when the engine itself was cold upon starting. They contain a heater element inside of them which helps speed up the process, but this still takes some time, depending on how close the sensor is to the engine and how hot the exhaust gases are coming out of the cylinders.

As an added complication, cold engines and exhaust systems can have condensation of the normal steam vapor that results from combustion until the exhaust temperature rises above the dewpoint. During this time, the oxygen sensor's heater element should not be operated to avoid risk of thermal shock and damage when liquid water hits the heated ceramic element. Waiting a few extra seconds can be the difference between accurate readings and failed oxygen sensors that will have the driver bringing the vehicle back with constant oxygen sensor faults.

If the sensor reports a condition that was richer than the target ratio, the ECU learns a negative fuel trim that decreases fueling over time to bring the fueling closer to the target. Conversely, if the oxygen sensor reads a lean condition, the ECU will increase fuel delivery with a positive trim in an attempt to compensate. These learned trims can be stored as either a short-term or long-term correction, often with many different corrections stored for different areas of engine operation. The same learned fuel trim will not be seen driving down the highway at 70 mph as it is in city traffic or stopped at an idle.

In closed-loop operation, the ECU will constantly toggle the fuel delivery between very slightly rich and very slightly lean to make sure that the catalytic convertor gets a steady supply of both rich side (CO, HC) and lean side (NO_x) components that will react inside of it, releasing heat and keeping things clean. If the engine was allowed to operate slightly lean for too long, the catalyst would become saturated with NO_x without any carbon monoxide to reduce them, and tailpipe emissions would show a similar "breakthrough" of emissions. Toggling between rich and lean is meant to prevent this saturation of the catalyst. This toggling is often visible in real time if one looks at the short-term fuel trims in a live scanner.

After a few seconds of constantly seeing an exhaust oxygen balance on the rich or lean side with its appropriate immediate short-term fuel trim, the ECU will begin to ratchet up the matching bank's long-term fuel trim. This ratcheting up over time is the definition of an integral correction.

Adding the correction to the long-term trim that is stored in the ECU memory allows the ECU to use this correction the next time the engine is operated in this speed-load zone. At any moment, the final ECU fuel delivery command consists of the open-loop feed forward value that was calculated based on cylinder air charge and injector models, short-term correction, and the long-term correction.

Ideally, the last two terms should be relatively small. This would be an indicator that the physical vehicle is behaving in a similar manner to those tested by the manufacturer's calibration engineers. ■

Long Term Fuel Trim Bank 1 (SAE)	9.4 %
O2 Voltage B1S1 (SAE)	0.098 V
Control Module Voltage (SAE)	14.50 V
Short Term Fuel Trim Bank 1 (SAE)	0.8 %

As an experiment, I added a known amount of E85 to the tank of this vehicle and observed the change in fuel trims. Over time, the ECU learned the long-term trim upward by an amount that matches the necessary shift to achieve stoichiometry with the new fuel chemistry.

Air-Fuel Imbalance Monitoring

Beginning in 2011, CARB added a requirement for fuel system imbalance monitoring as well. A new code, P219A/B, appeared to indicate cases where one cylinder on a bank is running significantly richer or leaner than the others. The ECU typically catches this by looking for excessive noise or "hashing" of the upstream oxygen sensor where the offending cylinder periodically spikes the exhaust with its rich or lean gases relative to the average.

Proper execution of this check requires careful design of the exhaust system and sensor placement to make sure that the gases from all cylinders actually pass the point where the oxygen sensor is installed. It's entirely possible that the gases from some cylinders flow past the opposite side of the exhaust pipe from the sensor at some speeds and loads. Making this diagnostic even more frustrating is the fact that the error must only be set when the imbalance is bad enough to make the emissions 150 percent of the allowable standard.

I once calibrated the air-fuel imbalance diagnostic on an OEM application where a single cylinder could be intentionally skewed by as much as 40 percent and the tailpipe emissions were still passing the standard on the FTP-75 test. The combination of a small, clean-burning engine and effective catalyst easily covered for any single cylinder's error in fuel delivery.

We hit the misfire limit of the fuel on that cylinder (also setting a P0300 code) before the imbalance was enough to require the MIL. CARB was not amused that P219A could not be set, but our vehicle was clean and set the MIL for all required conditions.

When it comes to fixing a vehicle with a P219A/B, the process is similar to finding a misfire on the same bank. P2019A does not need to specify an exact cylinder, so the entire bank is suspect unless you also have a cylinder-specific misfire code such as P0301 to go along with it. The exhaust should be checked for leaks near the offending cylinder, followed by a careful inspection of the fuel injector or ignition on that cylinder or bank. Corner cases may also include leaks in the intake, EVAP, EGR, or PCV systems. Be sure to check the freeze-frame data for more clues. ■

Viewed from the side, one can see the longer distance required for the gases to travel before reaching the collector and oxygen sensor on these headers. If the ECU is not recalibrated to account for this increase in signal delay, it can end up making changes that are out of sync with actual engine fueling.

Comprehensive Components Monitor

Another continuously operated watchdog is the comprehensive components monitor. This monitor covers the check for all sensor and component circuits deemed critical to emissions impact, which is essentially any device on the vehicle that has the ability to impact emissions based on the signal that it sends (or fails to send to) the ECU.

Manufacturers actually look very carefully at whether they want to allow a certain sensor to be added to a vehicle for this reason. If the ambient air temperature sensor that gives the driver a display in the cabin goes out, it is a minor inconvenience. But if that same sensor is used to trigger changes in fueling or torque delivery, then it must be diagnosed as a comprehensive component, which adds cost and complexity.

Instead, OEMs sometimes use an internally modeled value for ambient temperature based on inputs from temperature values at startup, coolant temperature, engine run time, and measured intake air temperature. The same happens for catalyst temperature, since sensors don't usually live very long in that ultra-hot environment and their constant failure would lead to MILs and fault codes on a regular basis. Again, a modeled temperature actually reduces issues here over the hassle of adding the new sensor and its required diagnostics.

Checks for comprehensive components include both OBD-I circuit integrity checks as well as OBD-II rationality checks for those same components. These checks make sure that the signal is not only within range but that it also makes sense given the other reported values. For example, an engine that has just started after being parked for a while cannot suddenly jump to 200°F without first going through a warmup profile. Likewise, a supercharged engine should not see MAP values over 100 kPa when the throttle is mostly closed.

Output actuators are also covered here. A rationality check can be performed, such as looking for an increase in MAP when opening the throttle or closing a turbocharger wastegate. Transmission shift solenoids fall into this group as well, but they can only be checked during an actual shift event. Luckily, these happen often enough that the ECU has no shortage of opportunities to look at them.

The remaining monitors are non-continuous and will pass with a single good result when ran on the drive cycle. Sometimes this is easier said than done, though. Many of these monitors require specific conditions to execute, which is why our previous discussion of what makes a valid drive cycle was so important. The idea is that all of these monitors should run any time the vehicle is driven a significant amount, and they should pass each time they are run. Some are trickier than others. The order in which they are displayed on the scan tool may vary, but here we will discuss them in a logical progression.

Oxygen Sensor Monitor

The oxygen sensor has a ceramic sensing element that changes its output relative to the chemistry of the exhaust gases passing by it. The ceramic element is covered by a protective metal shell with holes that direct a small amount of the passing exhaust toward the ceramic. Both traditional "narrow-band" and newer "wide-range" oxygen sensors

With the ECT sensor threaded into the block right next to the thermostat, this ECU can easily see the warmup profile of the engine to perform the rationality check.

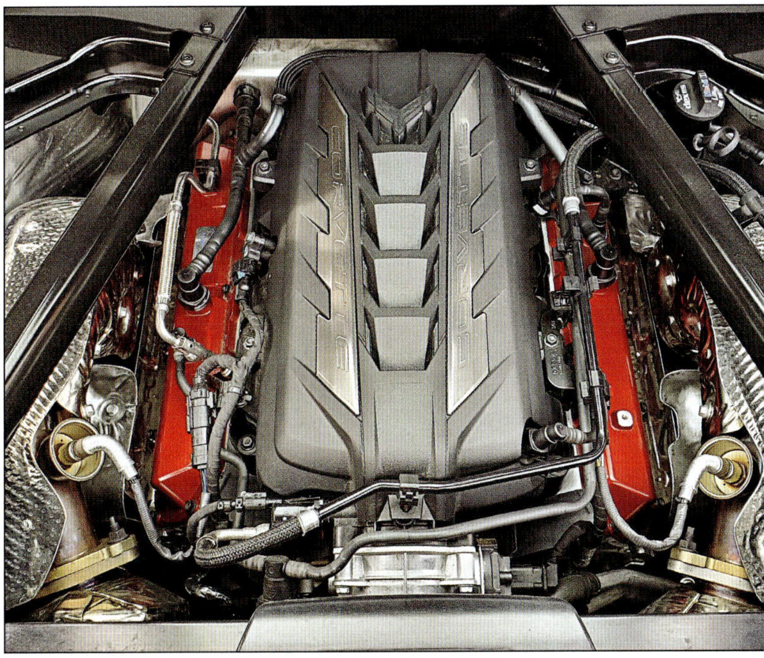

This C8 Corvette uses wideband oxygen sensors in the upstream location for feedback. The metal cups around the sensors protect the bodies from radiated heat of the upswept exhaust manifold in the tight engine bay.

> **TECH TIP**
>
> ### Nernst Cell
>
> Inside, the ceramics form what's known as a Nernst cell that reacts to the difference in exhaust oxygen content relative to a reference chamber with outside air exposure. This outside air exposure usually comes in through the wire harness itself, so a damaged or soldered lead on the oxygen sensor can compromise its fundamental operation. Any extensions added to an oxygen sensor harness should be made between the ECU and final electrical plug on the sensor, never to the wire pigtail on the sensor itself. ■

will have the same general design and diagnostics.

The big difference beyond the obvious change in accurate measurement range is that the older narrow-band sensors have a variable voltage signal based on output from the Nernst cell to the ECU. Narrow-band oxygen sensors are quickly identified by having three or four wires: two for a heater circuit, one sensing signal wire, and an optional ground. Some three-wire sensors rely on a ground through their case and the exhaust system bolted to the engine, which has its own potential issues when not continuous.

Newer wide-range sensors have five or six wires on the sensor that include a heater circuit as well as a more involved sensing circuit. Fundamentally, the signal is a variable current on one wire that the ECU must decode into a measured air-fuel ratio based on a few other variables, such as tip temperature.

To run the oxygen sensor monitor, the engine must be ready for closed-loop operation. This means that it has reached the minimum operating temperature, the sensor heater circuit has had time to warm the sensor tip, and the ECU is able to begin actively correcting the delivered fuel based on feedback from the oxygen sensor upstream of the catalyst.

Narrow-band oxygen sensors can only be evaluated when the engine is operating close to the stoichiometric mixture. Because the rapid switch from a low output voltage for any mixture lean of stoichiometric to a higher voltage for any rich mixture, they can only be monitored for this rapid switching across center.

The current-based output of wide-range oxygen sensors is more predictable as mixtures deviate from the balance of stoichiometry. They can remain active and providing valid closed-loop data even when the engine is running rich for power or component protection. This also means that a wide-range oxygen

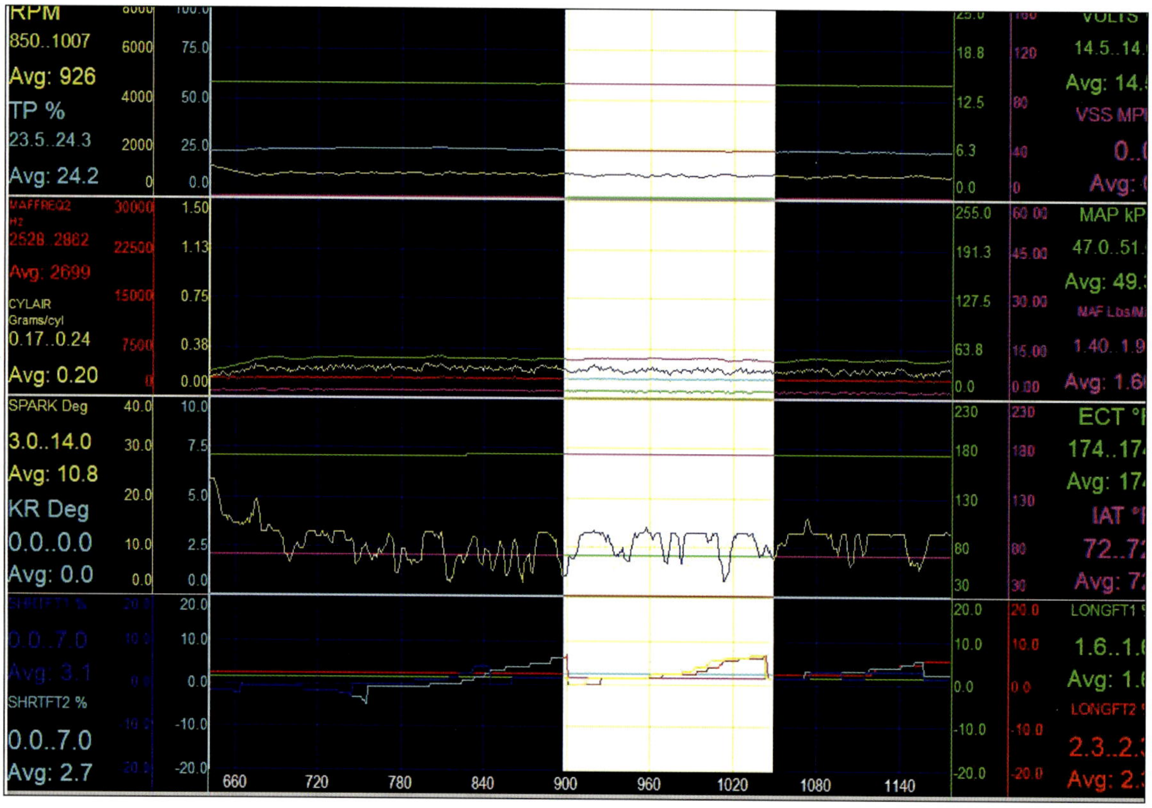

On a warmed-up engine, the short-term fuel trims should move along with the changes in closed-loop fueling. Over time, any significant drift is transferred to long-term fuel trims.

sensor's monitor can run in these conditions as well where a narrow band cannot.

The oxygen sensor monitor itself checks to see if the sensing element has the correct response to a known rich or lean condition. This type of test is known as an intrusive monitor because it disturbs what would otherwise be normal operation of the ECU to actively test the sensor. The monitor has the authority to temporarily add a certain amount of fuel to the commanded injector output so that it can look for a matching rich response on the oxygen sensors after a known amount of time.

The time portion is also critical, as some ECUs even look for cylinder-to-cylinder differences in fueling where the flight times vary. Lean testing is often done during deceleration, where fuel shutoff normally happens anyway. Again, it looks for a change in sensor response in a certain time window relative to when the injectors stopped pulsing.

Remember that the fuel system monitor relies heavily on good data from the oxygen sensors. So even if the oxygen sensor monitor has passed, its data is still being used by the fuel system's continuous monitor as well as normal ECU fueling feedback.

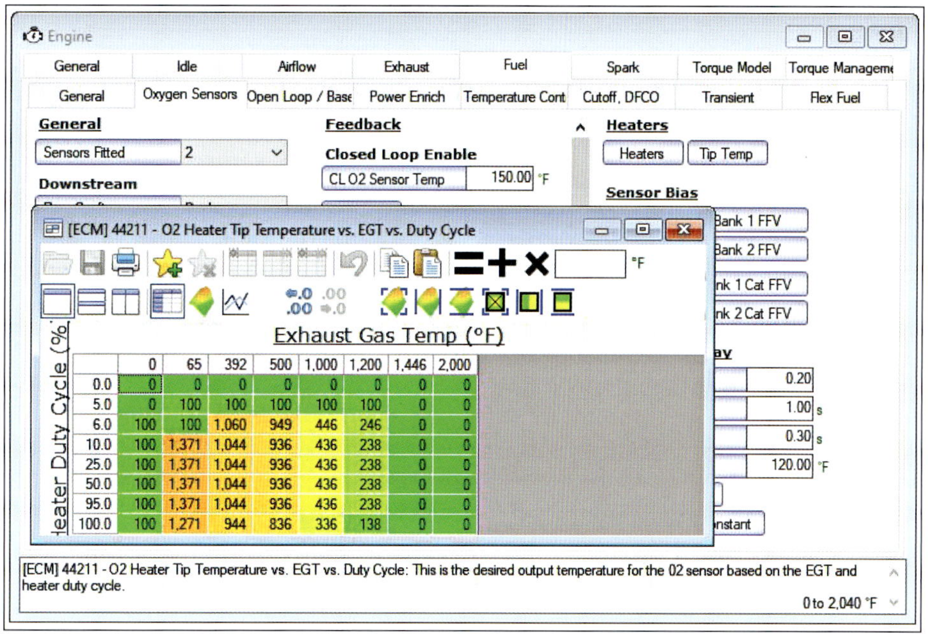

ECU tables ramp up the heater controls at cooler exhaust temperatures—but only after clearing the dewpoint. Commanding high heater output when exhaust water has condensed on the oxygen-sensor element can cause thermal cracking of the ceramic.

Oxygen Sensor Heater Monitor

This is separate on purpose because the oxygen sensor itself has two very different circuits. The primary sensing circuit that reacts to exhaust gas chemistry is covered in the previous monitor. The heater circuit gets its own monitor because it operates almost independently of the sensing circuit.

Vehicle system voltage is applied through a PWM variable circuit to a resistive heater inside the oxygen sensor. An increase in duty cycle has the effect of rapidly raising the tip temperature of the sensing element to make it more sensitive to rich or lean conditions.

The conditions for running the oxygen sensor heater monitor are similar to those for the oxygen sensor monitor. The exception is that the heater will be activated slightly before the ECU enters the closed-loop mode, so the heater circuit monitors will see action before the sensing circuit will. Remember that the heater must wait a brief amount of time after the initial engine start to let the exhaust get above the dewpoint to prevent thermal shock from condensation.

The ECU monitors the commanded duty cycle of the circuit along with voltage and current flow to verify that the resistive heater is working, usually right after startup. A short or open circuit here can mean that the oxygen sensor is slow to reach operating temperature and the ECU would have a more difficult time distinguishing rich and lean conditions.

The most common failure for this monitor is the fragile ceramic sensors and their heating elements themselves. Oxygen sensors have a finite life, and consumers should expect to change them over time. After years of shaking and rapid heating and cooling, it's not unusual to see failed heaters on a sensor that can still have a valid signal from the sensing element. The failure will be most obvious on a cold engine where the ECU is trying to use the heater circuit to bring the sensing element up to temperature.

Once warmed up, the ECU is likely commanding almost zero

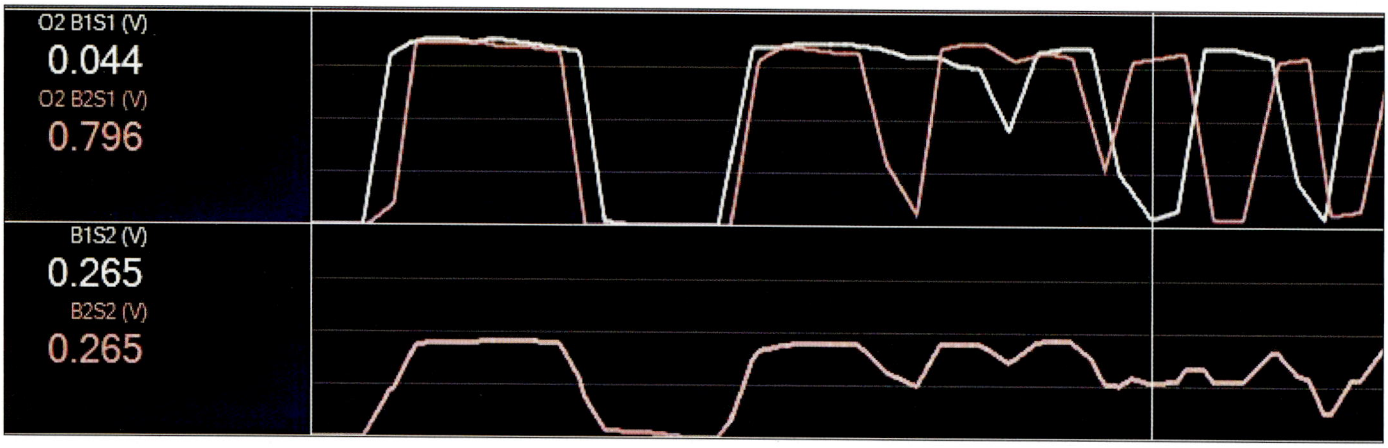

By comparing the very busy upstream oxygen-sensor signal to the slower downstream-sensor signal, the ECU can verify that the catalytic convertor is working. A slowly switching downstream signal is ideal, which means that the stored oxygen and fuel on the catalyst site is mixing with the rapidly changing raw engine-out gases.

heater circuit output, so a failed heater element becomes very difficult to diagnose until everything cools off again. It's still possible to have wire-harness and connector issues on this circuit as well as a rare condition where the driver circuits inside the ECU have failed. Always check the obvious and cheaper solutions first, though.

Catalyst Monitor

The catalytic convertor has no wires going to it. There are no sensors, actuators, or moving parts, yet it remains one of the most critical elements in the emissions system. Working completely passively, the catalyst promotes the reaction of various compounds in the exhaust to convert them into less-harmful components before heading out the tailpipe.

The only way the ECU knows that the catalyst is working is by observing oxygen sensor signals both before and after the catalyst. In a properly working system, there will be a significant difference between the noisy closed-loop upstream oxygen sensor signal and a more stable downstream oxygen sensor signal. The normal rich/lean toggling of fuel delivery around the stoichiometric mixture displays a high switching frequency in the upstream oxygen sensor signal.

As the CO, hydrocarbons, and NO_x react with each other in the catalyst, we are left with an output signal that switches between rich and lean much slower. By comparing either the switching frequency or the path length of the two signals, the ECU can verify that reactions must be taking place in the catalyst.

Even though it does not know the exact concentrations of the various constituents, the presence of a strong signal change indicates that something must be happening and that something is good for emissions. If the downstream signal looks just like the upstream signal, it is safe to say that nothing likely changes in the exhaust gases between the two measurement points and the catalyst must not be working well.

To run the catalyst monitor, the ECU must first pass the oxygen sensor monitors as well as other continuous monitors. This means that the vehicle has had an opportunity to warm up a little and enter closed-loop fueling operation. The time it takes the engine to warm up also gives the catalyst some time to reach operating temperature as well.

Ideally, the catalyst should be over 400°C, but this takes less than a minute in most modern vehicles. The engine must operate at a relatively stable speed and load so that the oscillations seen in the oxygen sensors can be attributed to closed-loop toggling rather than errors from transient conditions. The ECU will then calculate the current efficiency of the catalyst based on the difference between the upstream and downstream oxygen sensors. If this efficiency (which is usually very high on a properly functioning vehicle) drops below 50 percent, an error code will be stored. The MIL will eventually set after the second drive cycle with such a measurement.

Heated Catalyst Monitor

Although rare, there are vehicles on the road with a heated catalyst. They have a resistive ceramic heating element in the body of the catalyst that is activated upon startup to shorten the time needed to get the catalytic convertor up to a temperature where its efficiency is higher. This is usually only seen on vehicles with relatively large engines that have cold-start emissions that would be enough to fail the standard unless some heroic measures were taken to begin conversion almost immediately. It is a significant added expense in hardware, software, diagnostics, and warranty, so they are usually only present on relatively expensive vehicles too.

If the catalyst is heated, a series of tests are used similar to the oxygen sensor heater monitor to verify that the system is working as intended. Most vehicles will report this monitor as "not equipped." Instead, they rely on active controls of air, fuel, spark, and valve timing to promote a fast light-off time for the catalyst without the need for this expensive hardware and monitoring.

Evaporative System Monitor

Easily the most difficult monitor to complete for the ECU, the evaporative system monitor, serves to ensure that fuel vapors from the gas tank, charcoal canister, and vapor lines are not escaping to the outside world rather than being drawn through the intake for combustion. Modern fuel systems are so tightly sealed that they should be able to detect a single leak as small as 0.020 inch in diameter anywhere in the path. These leak checks are done using artificially created pressure differentials where vacuum is sourced from the intake manifold when the engine is running.

When the EVAP solenoid opens during part-throttle operation, the engine's vacuum pulls the pressure down in the evaporative system, drawing gaseous hydrocarbons toward the engine from the tank or charcoal canister. By keeping the system pressure slightly below atmospheric pressure, any leaks should result in fresh air being drawn in rather than hydrocarbons escaping as pollution.

The execution of the EVAP monitor requires very stable conditions for success. Because the monitor is looking primarily at the fuel tank pressure sensor and comparing it to the barometric pressure, anything that upsets the fuel tank pressure reading will instantly impact the EVAP diagnostics.

Fuel vapors are routed to the intake manifold through a control valve seen here on this Kia. When open, the engine vacuum draws the vapors in and adjusts liquid fuel injection accordingly.

The black piece of paper staked to the roof of the airbox helps absorb hydrocarbons that evaporate from the engine's intake and crankcase before they can escape through the airbox. Aftermarket cold-air kit manufacturers have had to find a way to incorporate them into designs on newer vehicles to achieve CARB EO status.

A key concern here is liquid fuel "slugging" the tank-pressure sensor, which would cause a sudden positive spike in the reading. This means that the ECU must wait until the vehicle is traveling at a stable speed on smooth, level ground so that the fuel in the tank is not sloshing around and potentially changing the vapor pressure reading. The test takes a relatively long time, 20 to 60 seconds in many cases, so keeping the liquid fuel in the tank stable for that long can be tricky.

During this time, the ECU can also look at fuel-tank level changes relative to the current average fill level to detect sloshing as well as vehicle speed or acceleration that could also result in undesirable movement of the fuel inside the tank. This extreme sensitivity is what makes for so many aborted diagnostic attempts that the monitor may not set on a particular drive cycle.

Vehicles with larger or longer aspect ratio tanks are even more susceptible to this noise factor. If you are driving a vehicle in an attempt to set the evaporative monitor, great care must be taken to avoid changes in acceleration during the drive cycle so that the ECU is less likely to abort the test due to tank sloshing.

Some vehicles employ another check to the evaporative control system after shutdown. In these cases, they look at the engine-off natural vacuum (EONV) that results from the eventual cooling of the fuel tank a while after the vehicle stops. When driving, heat from the fuel pump's operation and nearby exhaust system has a tendency to warm the fuel in the tank.

As the system cools back to the ambient temperature after the vehicle is parked, the fuel tank pressure sensor can be monitored by the ECU to verify that the sealed system creates a small vacuum. Holding a certain amount of vacuum for a minimum time is another way to check for very small leaks in the system. After this has completed, the ECU is finally allowed to go to sleep, even though the driver has long since turned off the ignition and walked away.

Secondary Air System Monitor

To fight cold-start emissions that often result from the rich condition at startup, some vehicles have a dedicated system that pumps fresh air into the exhaust for a brief amount of time after startup. Once the ECU goes into closed-loop operation and the catalyst has reached operating temperature, this is no longer needed.

Adding fresh air into the exhaust (usually very close to the engine in the exhaust manifold before the catalyst) dilutes the hydrocarbons and carbon monoxide in the exhaust with atmospheric oxygen. If the local temperatures are high enough, some of them will react and burn off together even before the catalyst becomes active, reducing emissions.

Whenever this system is active, the oxygen sensors will obviously see a leaner than actual signal compared to what was being burned in the cylinders. Special tables inside the ECU must be calibrated to allow it to compensate for this skewed signal. If the oxygen sensors do not report an appropriately lean condition when the secondary air system should be working, a fault is set specific to this monitor.

Conversely, any leaks in the system can allow fresh air to get pulled into the exhaust even when the secondary air system is not active. If a vehicle is equipped with secondary air and reports a lean condition (which comes with positive fuel trims), this system should be immediately investigated before simply replacing oxygen sensors.

EGR/VVT Monitor

For the purposes of OBD monitoring, both exhaust gas recirculation (EGR) and variable valve timing (VVT) systems are bundled into a common monitor. The reason is

The differential pressure sensor atop the EGR valve on this Ford V-6 engine is used to detect when gases are actually flowing through the EGR system. These sensors are also sometimes remotely mounted with vacuum lines, attaching them to ports on the exhaust and intake sides.

By directing oil pressure to vanes inside the phasers, the valve events can be advanced or retarded relative to the crankshaft. This mechanism is usually contained inside a large assembly bolted to the drive end of the camshaft.

The twin solenoids at the front of this engine's cam cover each control oil flow through a passage leading to a single cam phaser. Failure modes include both failed solenoids and clogged passages.

clear to a combustion engineer since increasing valve overlap increases the amount of natural EGR that results from the gas exchange cycle at lower speeds.

Instead of having cumbersome external EGR systems, engineers can simply command valve events that trap more residual gases inside the cylinder on purpose. This will get the same result as plumbing spent gases from the exhaust manifold back to the intake manifold using hardware that is already on the engine. To reduce the amount of EGR present, the cam phasing is moved to a point where there is less overlap or less trapped residual gases at the end of the intake stroke.

Adding EGR, through either an external system or careful valve timing has almost the same effect. The spent gases do not react like fresh air and fuel. Instead, they absorb heat energy as the flame front passes them, lowering overall burn temperature inside the cylinder and reducing the formation of NO_x that would otherwise need to be cleaned up by the catalyst.

Adding EGR at part throttle also means that MAP must be raised (throttle opened more). This is done to get the same amount of fresh air into the cylinders when it's fighting for a place with the residuals left behind.

Opening the throttle and raising MAP means that the engine does not waste as much energy pulling a strong vacuum, so overall efficiency improves. This is often used to increase fuel economy, which is the same as reducing CO_2 emissions. As long as there is sufficient vacuum available to drive things like a brake booster or leave headroom for immediate throttle requests without a downshift, the added EGR and lower vacuum is allowed.

On external EGR systems, the opening of the EGR valve should have some noticeable effects that can be used for diagnostics. Aside from the normal circuit checks, plausibility checks can be done by observing an increase in MAP as EGR is allowed to enter the intake manifold at part throttle. Some vehicles also have a differential pressure sensor on the EGR system to detect opening and flow.

VVT monitors focus on signals from the camshaft position sensor relative to the signal seen from the crankshaft position sensor. The phase of the camshaft can be seen by comparing where the various camshaft ring rising and falling edges are in relation to the crankshaft ring teeth. These signals will synchronize almost immediately upon cranking the engine, allowing the ECU to deliver cylinder-specific fuel injection and timing events.

Once the engine is running, the phasing of these signals is used to confirm that the camshaft phasing actuators are working correctly whenever advance or retard is commanded. Camshaft phasing is another closed-loop feedback system inside the ECU. Plausibility check of the camshaft phaser operation can be done by looking for the right change in MAP or MAF as the cam angle moves too.

A static airflow as the commanded cam angle is changed is a good indicator that either the phasing actuator or the flow of oil that drives it is compromised. You can sometimes accomplish this test by using the Mode $08 controls that allow active adjustments. Otherwise, some scan tools will have these built in as well.

If the cam phaser control is unplugged, the mechanism should return the camshaft to a safe default position. The default position for a variable cam system is called "lock-pin" and is often the position that has the least overlap between intake and exhaust events and lower resulting EGR. This is the default because lower EGR concentration in the cylinder also gives the cleanest, most stable combustion in the event of a failure. If the VVT fails, at least the engine runs okay, it will just have the MIL and a loss of fuel economy at part load.

Diesel-Specific Monitors

Although this book has focused on spark-ignited engines, it's worth noting here that diesel engines are also required to run OBD-II checks and have their own specific set of monitors. Since the diesel combustion process is inherently different than that of a premixed gasoline engine, their engine controls focus more on fuel control for torque delivery and adding airflow to clean up their emissions.

Nothing says "I don't really understand how to tune diesels right" quite like rolling coal. Visible particulate emissions are not only unhealthy but also represent wasted fuel that could have been used to move the vehicle better.

They have more concerns related to the formation of NO_x and particulates during combustion. To control this, the diesel engine uses increasing amounts of airflow to dilute the combustion chamber and some creative aftertreatment to react with the different "leftover parts" coming out of the diesel exhaust valve.

All of these strategies and hardware components are critical parts of the diesel emissions system. As such, they are tightly regulated by emissions-control bodies, such as the EPA and CARB. Disabling or removing any of these has a dramatically negative effect on tailpipe emissions. "Rolling coal" with thick black soot pouring out of the diesel exhaust is neither cool, healthy, nor the best way to actually go fast with one.

NMHC Catalyst and PM Filter Monitors

Like many spark-ignited engines, a diesel engine may be equipped with a catalytic convertor to help react unburned hydrocarbons. This may be a dedicated catalyst, with its own non-methane hydrocarbon (NMHC) monitor, or it may be a washcoat of special material on the diesel particulate filter (DPF) or particulate matter (PM) filter.

The DPF is designed as a sieve that catches particles larger than a certain size and holds them until they can be burned off later, instead of allowing the particles to exit the exhaust as pollutants. Because the DPF is large, heavy, and difficult to see through, many uneducated shops and enthusiasts immediately run to remove it as a restriction in the name of performance. The truth is that modern diesels, even with the DPF attached, vastly outperform their predecessors in almost every measure.

The primary thing seen when a "deleted" diesel without the DPF accelerates is visible black smoke coming out the tailpipe. This thick black smoke is obviously unhealthy for humans to breathe, yet I continue to be amazed at the number of shops and enthusiasts who don't seem to mind killing themselves slowly with it.

Diesel particles range from 6 to 30 nm in diameter, which is tiny but just big enough to become a serious irritant to lungs. Worse, the chemistry

A cutaway view of a Class 8 diesel engine particulate filter shows the core that looks much like an automotive catalyst. Smaller diesel engines have muffler-sized versions.

A special bypass pipe has been welded onto the case of the DPF for emissions testing. Notice that the axle is bolted to a red hub-style dynamometer as measurements are taken in the lab.

of these particles leads to formation of several types of cancer as well. Apparently, they skipped the day in history class where they would have learned about coal-mine workers dying early of pneumoconiosis (black lung disease) from almost exactly the same irritant.

Understandably, DPF delete kits are right at the top of the list of concerns for EPA and CARB enforcement. Making, selling, or using DPF delete kits is a great way to learn the hard way just how serious the government can be about protecting the environment.

There is no practical way for the ECU to pass the diagnostic monitors for DPF/PM performance with the hardware removed. So, tuners have simply turned off the tests and the vehicle then shows as "incomplete" when polled for Mode $09 data. Turning the monitor off is equally as illegal as the initial removal of the DPF, so again, it's not a good idea.

In proper operation, the DPF captures small- to medium-size particles and holds them until they either burn off naturally from exhaust heat and oxygen or an active "regeneration" event is triggered in the ECU that intentionally raise exhaust temperatures to burn and clean out the DPF. This is usually done at highway cruising speeds. However, sometimes the vehicle must execute the regeneration event while idling if it has been too long since it last happened and the DPF risks approaching capacity.

During a regeneration event, the resulting tailpipe gas temperatures also get very warm. This is why venturis are now seen on the tips of most diesel trucks that draw additional cool outside air in to mix with the exhaust gases to avoid melting or burning things near the tailpipe. Replacing one of these with a cooler-looking tip or exhaust pipe may have some unwanted effects.

NO_x/SCR Aftertreatment

Another major concern for diesel engines is that their relatively high flame temperature leads to increased levels of NO_x in the exhaust. While the ECU has careful fuel and torque control to mitigate this, there is still a need to further clean up the spent gases after they leave the engine. Since diesels do not toggle rich/lean like gasoline engines, they must take another approach.

The common solution on most diesel engines is to address the NO_x pollution after the gases leave the combustion chamber. A process called selective catalytic reduction (SCR) uses urea to react with the hot exhaust gases to trigger a series of chemical reactions that convert the pollutants to much less harmful molecules before leaving the tailpipe.

The urea injected in the exhaust is typically supplied by a separate tank of diesel exhaust fluid (DEF) that must be maintained by the driver in

Diesel exhaust fluid (DEF) is now commonly available at most auto-parts stores and gas stations. The active ingredient, urea, helps reduce NO_x in the exhaust back down to less harmful molecules.

Externally, the NO_x sensor (top) looks very much like a wideband oxygen sensor (bottom) with a few extra wires. The NO_x sensor returns values for both oxides of nitrogen as well as lambda.

addition to the normal fuel supply. Some vehicles also use an NO_x sensor in the exhaust that looks very similar to a wide-band oxygen sensor. The feedback from this sensor then becomes a key input to the NO_x/SCR monitors.

Because diesel engines run lean of stoichiometric, they require much higher airflow and turbochargers that are roughly twice as large as what would be needed on a gasoline engine of the same power level. The electronically controlled turbocharger on this engine is tucked well under the cowl near the back of the engine.

Boost Pressure

Since diesel engines run on a lean burn strategy with wildly varying air-fuel ratios, the boosting system is used to increase the amount of available extra air for this combustion process. By forcing more fresh air into the cylinder with the same amount of fuel, a leaner overall condition can be maintained even at higher fuel loads.

Doing so requires the turbocharger, wastegate, and all plumbing to be in perfect working order with no leaks since these engines also do not usually have a throttle body like spark-ignited engines do. A dedicated set of monitors watches for slow response in available charge pressure from the turbo as the wastegate position moves.

Diesel engines may be equipped with not only MAP sensors on the intake manifold but also pressure sensors immediately before and after the turbocharger's compressor. Luckily, these can all be diagnosed in a similar manner to a standard MAP sensor. If sufficient boost pressure is not available, the engine may run at a richer air-fuel ratio and also generate more particulates or visible smoke. Reducing both of these is of high importance when controlling emissions.

This diesel engine's airbox includes a multipurpose sensor (much like some gasoline turbo vehicles). Compressor inlet pressure is monitored to help estimate turbocharger speed and load.

CHAPTER 9

Use of OBD in Vehicle Inspection and Monitoring

Over the years, the process of getting vehicle emissions checked prior to renewing the annual registration has continued to evolve. In the beginning, it was assumed that all vehicles rolling off the assembly line were clean and no further testing was to be done on consumer vehicles. As concerns of ill repair, tampering, modifications, and other failures were connected to increases in airborne pollution, consumers found themselves increasingly involved in the process of ensuring that their vehicle was not actively making the air worse.

Prior to OBD-II, vehicles were often subject to a tailpipe sniffer test. These started as an idle and high-idle test and in some cases evolved to a rolls-based test where the vehicle "drove" a specific trace, such as the IM240 test, at the inspection station. These tests could catch some gross polluters, but they were anything but effective when considering cold-start emissions (where the vast majority of pollution happens) or cases where the vehicle has been tampered with and the measurement system isn't sophisticated enough to catch it.

As OBD-II became standard for all production vehicles, a whole new method of annual testing was slowly adopted across the country. Knowing the relationship between MIL illumination and allowable tailpipe emissions, local inspections worked the logic backward. They agreed that the absence of a MIL (along with proof that the monitors ran on the vehicle) meant that the tailpipe was most likely clean. This prevailing logic is now the basis for annual vehicle registration in California and most of the other "green" states that have adopted the CARB standards as well. Honestly, it is a stroke of the pen away from someday becoming a federally mandated procedure where all motorists will be forced to comply regardless of location.

This device plugs into the J1962 port to both monitor and send new CAN messages. It adds the ability to display engine control parameters in the heads-up display on the windshield.

What Do They Look At?

Once a vehicle pulls up to an OBD-II-based inspection station, the operator either directly connects a cable to the data port or uses a wireless transmitter that plugs into the same port. Either way, a series of requests is sent once a connection is made. This whole process may come to a halt if the tool is not able to connect to the ECU or other modules. Things like an aftermarket remote-start system, OBD-II-based gauges, or a stereo may interfere with the inspection tool. These should be disconnected prior to running the inspection routine.

The tool queries data from Modes $03, $06, $07, $09, and $0A. This returns all current and pending faults as well as any stored or permanent faults. The Mode $07 data is used to ensure that the ECU actually got a chance to execute the tests that would detect poor emissions. After all, not failing by virtue of not looking does not constitute a pass.

Logically, failed diagnostics mean that the vehicle is likely polluting more than it should. Failures here typically result in an immediate denial of registration until the offending condition is remedied, presumably improving the vehicle tailpipe emissions before the registration can be renewed. But this is just scratching the surface.

The Mode $09 data is the real powerhouse here. The inspection organizations have the ability to catch many more potential problems as they scour the data. Mode $09 contains data from several different modules that includes:

- Vehicle identification number (VIN)
- Module calibration number (CALID)
- Calibration verification number (CVN)
- In-use monitor performance ratio (IUMPR)

Obviously, a VIN mismatch is cause for concern, as some vehicles may be stolen or maliciously relabeled. If there is a discrepancy between the VIN on the chassis plate and that stored in the various modules, the owner will have some explaining to do. When a module like the ECU is replaced in service, it is typically reflashed with the correct VIN, so there are precious few legitimate reasons for a mismatch if nothing has been tampered with. Comparing the VIN stored in both the ECU and body control module is often a telltale sign here.

The ECU itself will report the CALID along with the CVN. The CALID is essentially the part number of the calibration that is stored in the chip. The CVN is a checksum that ensures that the calibration data is the same as what was released under the declared CALID.

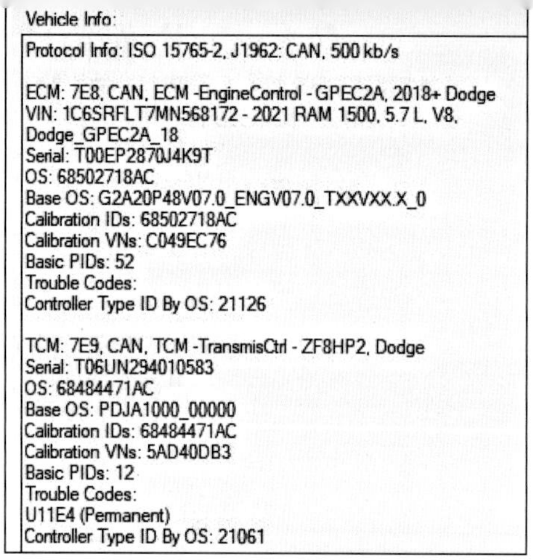

```
Vehicle Info:
Protocol Info: ISO 15765-2, J1962: CAN, 500 kb/s

ECM: 7E8, CAN, ECM -EngineControl - GPEC2A, 2018+ Dodge
VIN: 1C6SRFLT7MN568172 - 2021 RAM 1500, 5.7 L, V8,
Dodge_GPEC2A_18
Serial: T00EP2870J4K9T
OS: 68502718AC
Base OS: G2A20P48V07.0_ENGV07.0_TXXVXX.X_0
Calibration IDs: 68502718AC
Calibration VNs: C049EC76
Basic PIDs: 52
Trouble Codes:
Controller Type ID By OS: 21126

TCM: 7E9, CAN, TCM -TransmisCtrl - ZF8HP2, Dodge
Serial: T06UN294010583
OS: 68484471AC
Base OS: PDJA1000_00000
Calibration IDs: 68484471AC
Calibration VNs: 5AD40DB3
Basic PIDs: 12
Trouble Codes:
U11E4 (Permanent)
Controller Type ID By OS: 21061
```

Many professional scan tools automatically display much of the Mode $09 information upon connecting. Here, we can see the VIN along with CAL ID and CVN for both the electronic control module (ECM) and transmission control module (TCM).

Manufacturers are obligated to release both numbers (as ordered pairs) to the regulatory agencies for every legitimate calibration release made so that they can be identified in the field. If a vehicle has a valid CALID but the CVN does not match the right value for that CALID in the database, the vehicle is suspected of having a tampered ECU. This is usually the case where someone has used an aftermarket tool to "tune" their vehicle.

The only permitted exception here would be a hardware and ECU calibration package that has been certified as clean, such as with a CARB EO. In that case, the new CVN is often added to the regulatory database along with the OEM CVN for reference. Having some other value for CVN often results in either an outright failure or a trip to the referee for further inspection.

Some aftermarket tuning tools claim to be undetectable. In these cases, they may alter the reported CVN to mimic the original value. Not only is this unethical, but it's also a blatant violation of the tampering policy of the Clean Air Act. Getting caught with this is worse than just getting caught with an unauthorized calibration if it gets to the inspectors and courts. Fortunately, most aftermarket tuning software packages let the ECU calculate a new CVN when changes are made and leave it up to the user to ensure that their modifications are emissions legal or proven clean.

Finally, the IUMPR is noted for each monitor. This ratio compares the number of times that the monitor has successfully completed without faults to the number of qualifying trips driven. Ideally, it should be 100 percent, but there are always exceptions.

Admittedly, passing each monitor a single time should allow most vehicles to pass their annual inspection. What the IUMPR really does is allow the regulatory agencies to use "big data" compiled from thousands of cars daily to paint a picture of which make and model has trouble passing all monitors on a regular basis. This data is often fed back to the manufacturers along with pressure to improve their performance on future products or drive updates that will help improve existing vehicles.

A good inspector will also spend some time looking over the vehicle. A visual check for non-standard parts under the hood may drive a request for CARB EO authorization of non-OEM parts. The exhaust system is also checked to verify that the catalyst and oxygen sensors are in place and appear to be of OEM design. A "test pipe" or "delete kit" should fail here immediately regardless of what the ECU data says.

The irony here is that it's entirely possible to make ridiculously large amounts of power even through the

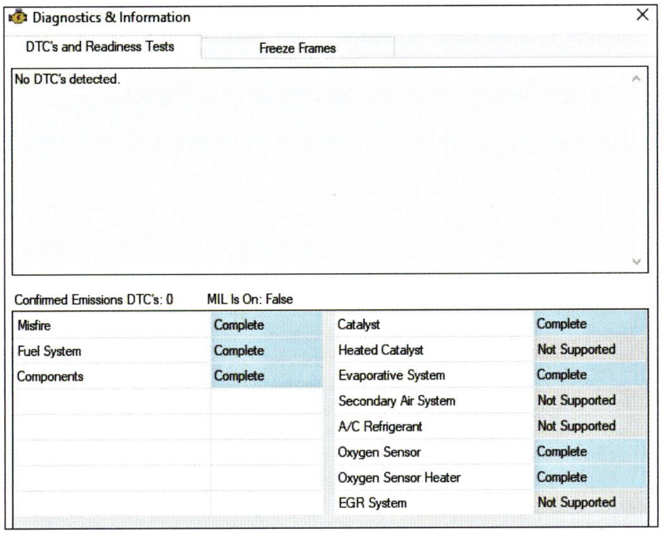

If you have a scan tool at home, this is what you want to see before reporting to the inspection station. An empty DTC list along with all supported monitors reporting complete will have you breeze through without much drama.

factory-equipped catalysts, yet some shops insist on removing them. The owners often find out the hard way that the vehicle is no longer street legal as they are in the final stages of annual inspection. In some states, a safety inspection is also required where suspension and braking systems are checked for critical issues in addition to the emissions-related items.

Pass versus Fail

The real question most vehicle owners have is, "What do I need to pass?" The inspection report typically needs to show the following criteria to earn a passing grade:

- Matching VIN
- CALID and CVN verified as correct in the database
- No MIL present
- No more than one monitor incomplete
- No monitors failed
- Passing visual inspection for catalyst and aftermarket parts

In an unmodified vehicle, this should not really be a difficult challenge as long as normal maintenance has been done periodically. As delivered, the ECU calibration (VIN, CVN, and CALID) are all correct and any updates performed by the dealership would also be perfectly normal here. As long as things such as oxygen sensors and spark plugs are working, chances are really good that all other emissions systems and diagnostics are running as intended. The presence of a MIL on the dashboard would have alerted the driver to the need for maintenance or repair long before the time comes for inspection and registration.

The visual inspection can be problematic for enthusiasts. Those new shiny parts under the hood and on the exhaust system compared to the more aged OEM pieces will tip an inspector off to a need for closer examination. The catalysts in particular will be of interest, and any deviation from the OEM configuration is likely to bring more scrutiny. If the vehicle is equipped with CARB-approved components, then the EO sticker should be affixed under the hood right next to the OEM VECI label so that the inspector sees that these are approved components that have been certified as emissions compliant.

Where enthusiasts get into trouble now that annual inspections include the mining of OBD-II data is typically the mismatch of ECU calibration to what is listed in the official databases. That, coupled with non-standard parts that may make it less likely for the vehicle to successfully complete some active monitors, can lead to situations where the vehicle fails this new plug-in inspection. In many cases, one can get by without the CALID and CVN matches, but almost no inspections will pass a vehicle that has not completed the necessary monitors.

Correcting a Failed Test

Assuming the vehicle has not been modified or tampered with from its original form, a failed inspection simply points to some form of normal maintenance that should be completed. As mentioned earlier, the stored codes point the owner or technician toward a system that needs repair. Failed monitors often expose systems that have not yet completely failed but are not running at their normal efficiency.

Either way, addressing the root cause of the trouble code or failed monitor will often improve the overall performance of the vehicle. In many cases, the customer could also expect

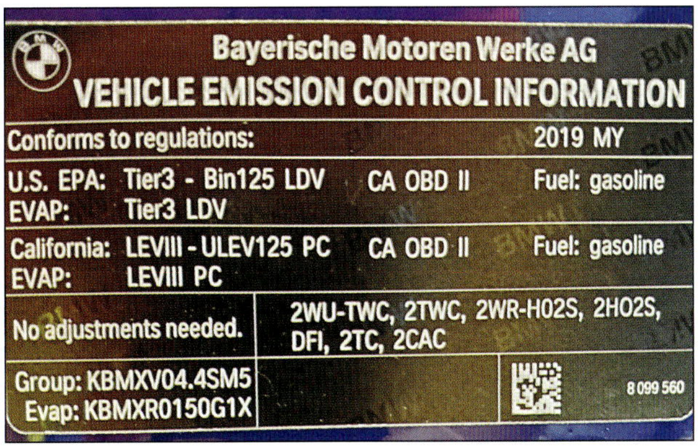

This 605-hp twin-turbo BMW M5 is certified to only make as much emissions as some 4-cylinder cars. "Tier 3 - Bin 125" means that it only makes 125 mg/mi of combined NMOG + NO_x emissions on the EPA 75 test even after 150,000 miles of use.

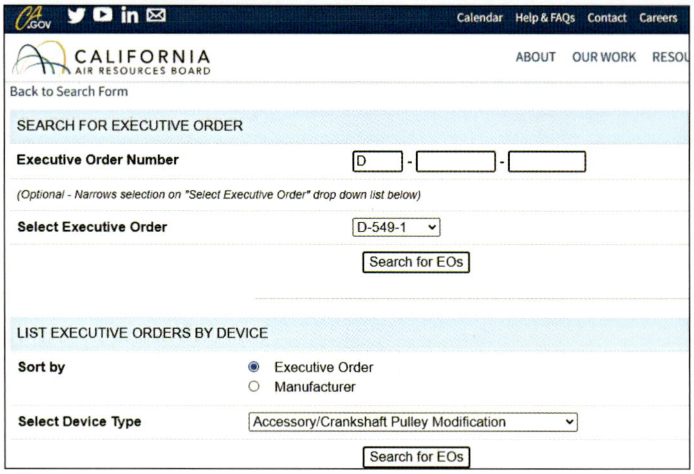

The CARB website includes a tool that allows for easy searches of current EOs. If the modifications on the vehicle are approved by CARB, there should be more information here that will help speed up approval at an inspection station.

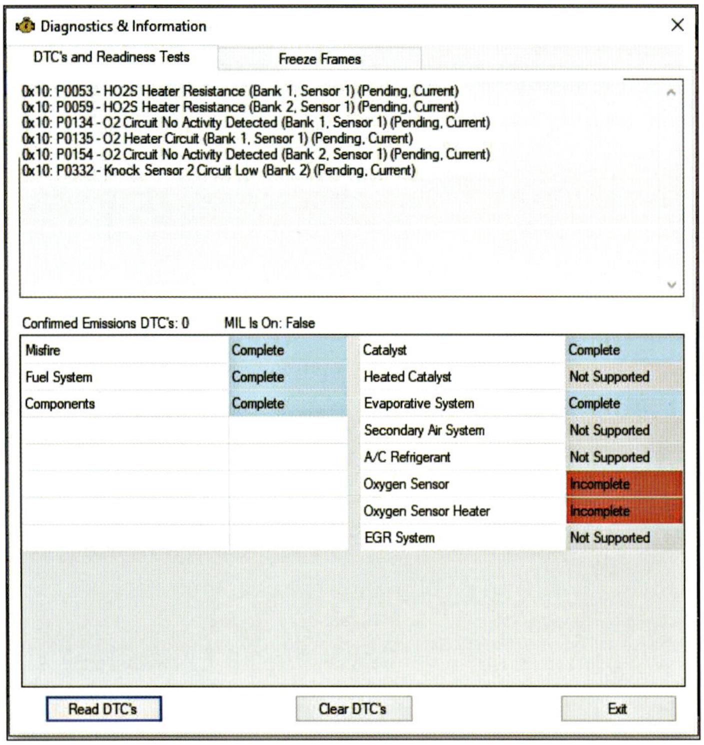

Regardless of whether this vehicle is modified or as delivered, it requires some work before it can expect to pass emissions inspection. It doesn't matter that the catalyst and fuel system monitors show complete when the oxygen sensor group obviously has a problem preventing both from executing properly.

to see an increase in fuel economy after the repair is made, so there is some additional incentive here.

After the appropriate repair has been made and stored codes are cleared, a test drive should allow the monitors to run again. A successful repair should result in all monitors reporting "Complete," setting the customer up for an easy return to the inspection station.

This post-fix test drive is often a critical requirement, as the ECU must be given an opportunity to run all of the monitors after the code-clearing process before showing up for inspection. Remember that some monitors, such as the evaporative diagnostics, can take a while to complete, depending on how the vehicle is operated on the test drive.

For a modified vehicle, the options here are a bit limited and sometimes not very appetizing. One way or another, the vehicle must pass the monitors. This may mean either a return to stock form or a significant amount of additional "tuning" time to make sure that the engine is running clean and passes each monitor when it runs. Doing so with catalysts that do not have the conversion efficiency of the original parts will prove to be exceptionally difficult if not impossible.

Any emissions systems that were turned off during the tuning process will come back to bite the user here as well. In short, leave the emissions logic alone, and make sure the engine is running clean enough all the time to pass the internal ECU tests without drama.

In locations where the CALID and CVN is not actively checked, having all necessary monitors completed will be of high importance. If the location requires the CALID and CVN to match the approved list in the database, the only way to pass will be to have either the manufacturer-supplied calibration in the ECU or one that was included with a CARB EO–approved kit with no additional modifications.

I know a lot of "it's my car and I should be able to do what I want" enthusiasts don't like hearing this, but don't shoot the messenger here. I'm only quoting the laws to which inspection stations must adhere. If the vehicle does indeed have a calibration supplied as part of an EO-approved kit, you should be able to present documentation that allows them to pass your vehicle when the CALID and CVN don't match the OEM database.

The good news for those running an aftermarket EO–approved calibration is that the vehicle should have no problem running and passing all of the necessary emissions monitors with that ECU calibration. The reason is simple: to get the approval in the first place, the kit supplier had to demonstrate the same thing. If a modified vehicle with an approved ECU calibration doesn't pass a monitor (or has a fault code), it should be diagnosed and repaired just like any other unmodified vehicle.

CHAPTER 10

OBD-Based Tools

Earlier, we looked at the history of OBD-II and saw the evolution of the standardization of how data is presented along with the interface through which it happens. Now, it's time to look at the tools of the trade. Today's professional technician, calibration engineer, shop owner, and DIY enthusiast all have some great options at their disposal now for gathering mountains of data from vehicles.

While some tools merely read and clear codes, most tools perform many different functions in addition to these basic duties. Today's tools often have laptop- or tablet-based software systems that are tightly integrated with the interface hardware. It's this software that unlocks the true flexibility of OBD-II communications. Let's take a look at some of the various interface options available on the market today.

Aftermarket tool companies, such as Innova, offer a range of options for both the DIY enthusiast and independent repair garage. These tools have become more powerful with the addition of new software interfaces that link vehicle data to internet tools and databases. (Photo Courtesy Innova)

Basic Code Readers

The simplest of OBD-II tools access only the Mode $03 and Mode $04 capability. This is sufficient for many home users who just want to know why their CEL is on and, perhaps, clear it after a home repair.

Gaining access to the fault code behind the MIL is powerful information. As we discussed earlier, a clever internet search with the right terms along with this code can often lead the user right to the necessary repair. To some, this is all they'll ever need, and a simple tool, such as the ones from Innova, does the job just fine. These tools may be as simple as a cable and LCD screen or may have a Bluetooth connection to your phone or tablet to display even more information. Some even begin the internet search to speed up the process of finding the right repair.

Dealer-Level Tools

If working at an authorized dealer for a major manufacturer, finding a good diagnostic tool is probably easy. One was probably assigned to you on the first day at the job. Their form

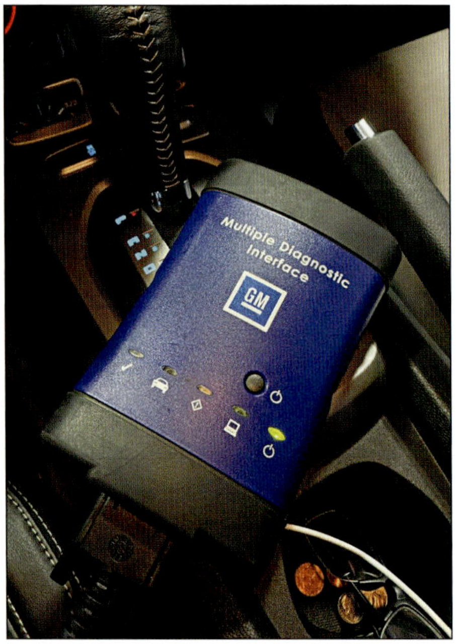

The MDI interface replaced the venerable Tech2 that so many have used since even before OBD-II. Since there is no integral display, it must be used with the appropriate GM software to access vehicle data.

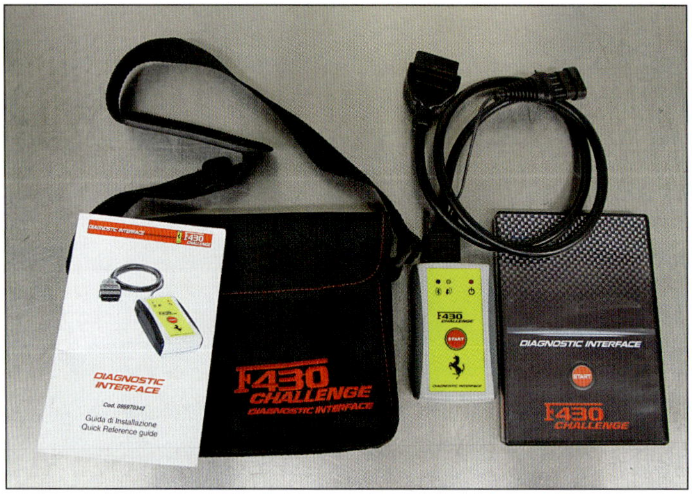

Even exotic makes, such as Ferrari, abide by OBD-II standards. This is the interface tool used to communicate with an F430 Challenge race car that runs the same ECU family as the production cars.

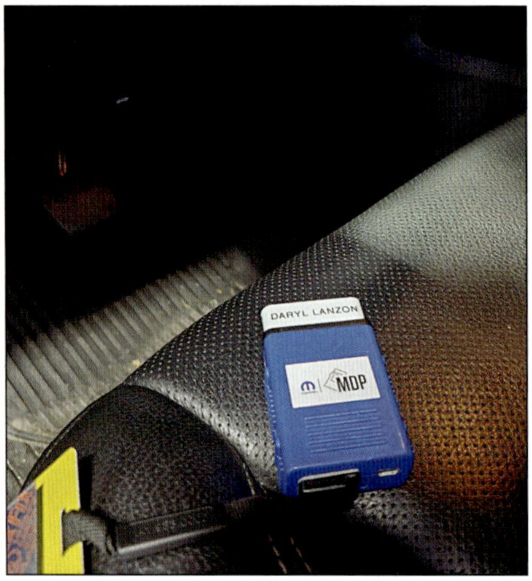

When bringing a Chrysler vehicle to the dealership for an issue, the first thing they will do is plug in a tool like this MDP dongle to the OBD port. This tool wirelessly connects to the service advisor's tablet and the local network to transmit data.

This Bosch service tool came from an international application as indicated by the Cyrillic letters. This tool can perform special service functions on its own as well as act as a J2534 programming connector.

factor may range from a laptop or tablet with a communication cable to a Bluetooth dongle. The real difference is in their software.

As issued by the OEM, the software package remains up to date with all the latest vehicle communication protocol options along with a strong library of their history. This allows the technician to plug into any vehicle of that make with ease and quickly begin gathering data.

While diagnosis and repair remain the primary use for most of these dealer-level tools, they must also support the application of field updates to the fleet. Occasionally, automakers issue updated vehicle calibrations to address emissions- or quality-related issues. Their tool must support the J2534 flash update procedures for all vehicles in question.

The good news here is that their connection to the OEM's network of data also means that they have the latest security keys needed to access and update the vehicles. The same cannot always be said for later options here. The tradeoff is that they can only update to files that are delivered by the OEM for that VIN and nothing else due to security and liability concerns.

Dealer tools will have access to all modes of SAE data, including the ability to run the two-way controls in Mode $08 and clear permanent codes stored in Mode $0A. Their library of available parameters for Mode $01 data is also very complete, again owing to their OEM software support. This lets the technician see just about everything that might be needed to find very specific failure modes.

Independent Tools

OEM- and dealer-issued tools are not the only way into the communication stream for OBD-II-equipped vehicles. Because SAE J2534 calls out a specific protocol for communication, a whole host of other tools exists on the market to perform these tasks from Drew Technologies, Debron, and others. The catch is that these access tools are often nothing more than an interface cable and chipset that allows some other user software to access the ECU in what is known as "pass-thru" communication. On their own, they typically don't have any buttons or controls on the cable or box, instead relying on software to be the user interface.

These cables alone do not guarantee complete access to all functions, as many ECUs and vehicle networks are protected by layers of security. This security must be addressed within the laptop or tablet software connected to the cable.

Some manufacturers offer a subscription-based service that provides access to a library of suitable calibration files, the security protocols necessary to flash them, and often support for additional functions, such as data collection. Many OEMs offer users the option to buy a "day pass" to their specific interface software that can access all their enhanced PIDs, specific P1xxx codes, and even reflash to the officially released calibration files for that VIN.

Some experts are able to write their own software to exploit the capabilities of these independent pass-thru cables for their own flashing and data-logging needs. However, doing so means going it alone without any support from the vehicle or interface cable manufacturers. Some of these programs are shared online, but again, one is at the mercy of available support from the online community when attempting to use them. Flashing non-OEM files is certainly possible in this configuration, but it also carries a very real risk of corrupting the ECU and turning it into an expensive paperweight.

Aftermarket Tuning Tools

For those looking for more of a turnkey solution to complete ECU interface, there are many companies that make software tools (along with their own pass-thru connector) that let the user perform most OBD-II functions. Their scan tool lets the user see trouble codes, clear them, and view a live data stream.

Their real selling point is the ability to create modified ECU calibrations and flash those into the controller to permanently modify how the engine runs. This unlocks a powerful world of potential changes that can either take a modified engine from barely running to passing emissions with flying colors or turn it into a scrap pile of broken parts if the calibration is not right. The process of this recalibration is discussed

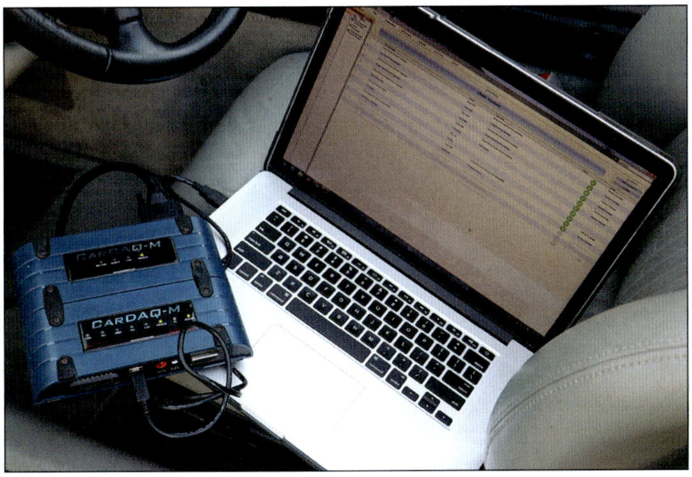

The Drew Technologies CarDaq is one of the original J2534 pass-thru devices that I often used in my OEM development engineering work. Shown here running J2534 Toolbox software, it's a hyper-flexible device that can be configured to work with almost any ECU as long as the supporting laptop software is correctly configured. (Photo Courtesy David Buckshaw)

The Mongoose cable is a more streamlined version of the J2534 pass-thru device. Many of these feature unique chipsets and transceivers to match the protocol required by a specific OEM, so don't expect one cable to work on every vehicle.

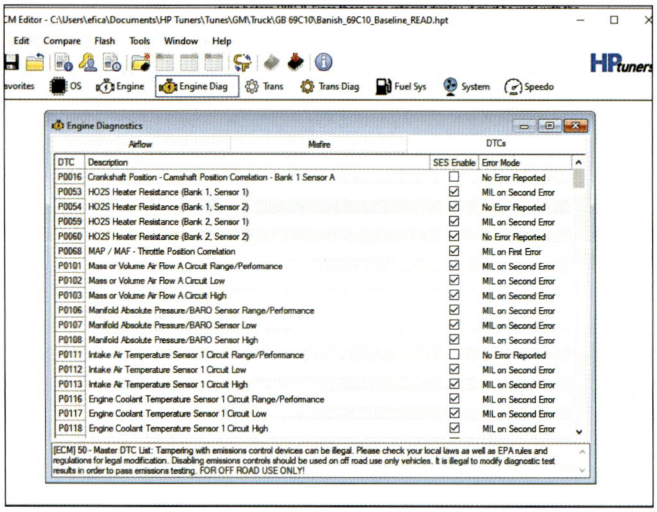

Arguably one of the most comprehensive aftermarket scanning and calibration tool suites available today, HP Tuners provides access to calibrations, live data, and special functions. Its coverage includes domestic, European, and many powersports applications.

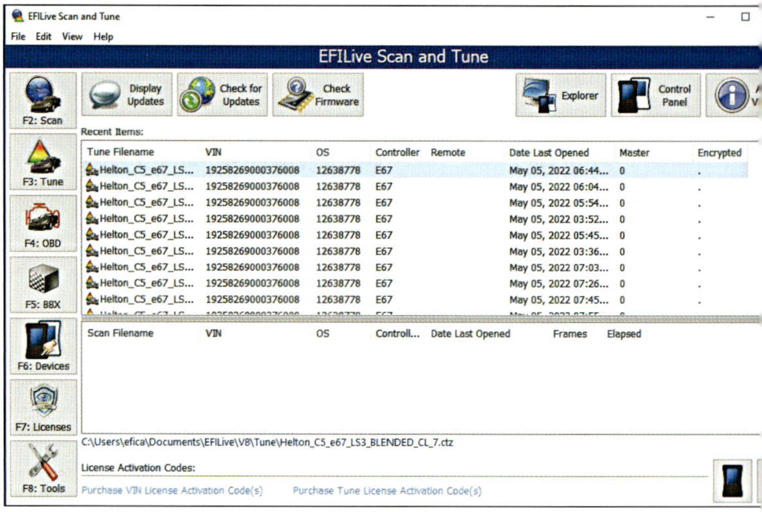

EFILive scanning and calibration tools support access to a wide range of GM family and Cummins diesel controllers. This software also includes an option for users to add their own self-defined parameters if they know enough about the specific function and ECU hex address.

elsewhere in this book, along with my two previous books and Calibrated Success training materials.

These aftermarket tool companies have spent countless hours refining their software to provide the user with what is hopefully a seamless package. It should allow the user to make changes to the calibration in engineering units without having to worry about memory address locations, hexadecimal conversions, checksum calculations, or security keys.

All of this information is contained in a special type of file (the .A2L extension is most common) at each OEM, which is held with the utmost security and digital tracking. While many in the aftermarket would love to get ahold of these "decoder ring" files, anyone who releases them without permission risks not only their job but criminal prosecution for industrial espionage. Of course, figuring all of that out in the background (without the help of the OEM, who is often not amused that someone else has access to their vehicles) is what makes their software valuable to the consumer.

Companies such as HP Tuners, SCT, and Cobb have considerable budgets and staff dedicated to the reverse engineering of factory ECU files, security, and flash requirements. It's hard to completely explain

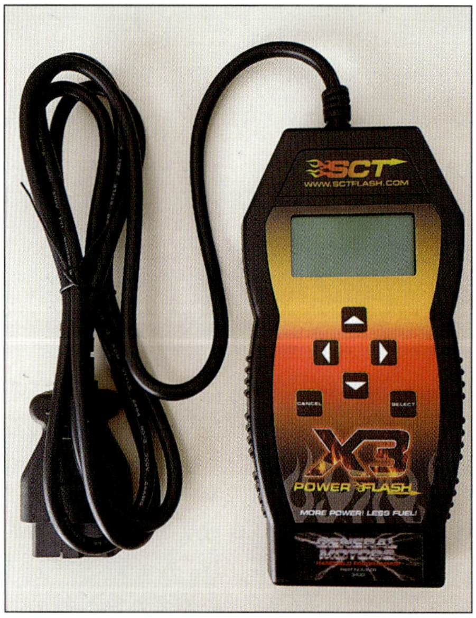

Handheld reflashing tools, such as this one from SCT, allow the user to update their vehicle remotely with one of several stored calibration files or return it to stock without the need for a laptop in the vehicle. They also have the ability to read and clear fault codes.

Older Ford EEC-IV and EEC-V modules had a special "J3" port on them that allowed an external chip module to be inserted to override the factory calibration. These Diablosport and SCT tools are used to write up to four different calibrations onto those chip modules.

just how much effort goes into this reverse-engineering process to define all the tables, axes, values, and units seen on screen for each individual ECU.

Opening their software, hundreds of different tables and values that may be modified can be seen, each potentially changing memory location and size year to year on the same engine family. Even then, what the consumer is overwhelmed by is just the tip of the iceberg. Modern ECUs have upward of 12,000 variables and tables in them.

Changing any single value in any of these tables impacts the resulting checksum, which can result in a failed write to the ECU if not corrected. This is an intentional feature of how the OEM files are built to prevent tampering that would impact how the vehicle runs, throttle-control safety, and emissions. While some users will certainly enjoy "rolling their own" with this process, using home-brewed software and a generic J2534 pass-thru device to deliver it to the vehicle, there is much to be said for being able to just purchase a complete working package that seamlessly figures out the checksums, security, and flash procedure at a reasonable price.

The majority of the high-performance aftermarket exists today based on the availability of tools like these. Across the country, dyno shops are reflashing vehicles every day using aftermarket tools. Manufacturers of performance kits, such as superchargers, also use these tools during the development phase to develop the calibrations necessary to ensure proper engine operation (and clean emissions when CARB EO certified). These same tools are then used to allow their customers to flash

Some shops, such as Redline Motorsports, specialize in reprogramming ECUs to get the most out of hardware changes that range from cold-air kits to complete new supercharged stroker motors. With a spotless floor, excellent ventilation, and data acquisition galore, this is a great example of vehicle testing done right.

HP Tuners dealers can load customer files onto devices such as this RTD for remote programming by end-user customers outside of the shop. It can be updated remotely and doubles as a data-logging interface as well.

in the calibration files as part of the installation process at home.

Some businesses also provide remote tuning services where a calibration file can be emailed to a user with the same interface and the customer does the flash update and records data for the calibrator using the software data-logging functions. Others offer preloaded programmers with performance or fuel-economy calibrations that have already been developed locally. Fleet managers often purchase these to bring fuel savings and reduce liability with lower speed limiters and less-aggressive torque requests.

In today's world of regulatory oversight, the smart companies are making sure that whatever calibration files they are sending out comply with an emissions certification that has already been approved.

Data Logging

Most aftermarket tuning software packages include an integrated data logging tool. There are also standalone options that use a generic OBD-II interface paired with their own software, such as the Torque phone and tablet app. Either way, these programs are using Mode $01 data from either generic SAE PIDs

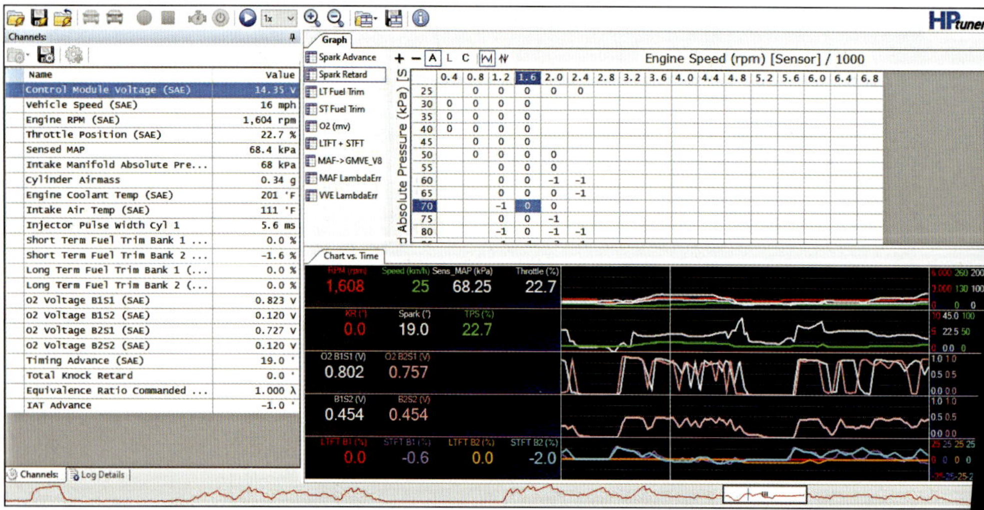

Requesting and displaying Mode $01 data in list, histogram, and strip-chart formats makes the job of data collection much more efficient. The user can collect data while driving or on the dyno and use the tool to review it later with the engine off.

The Torque smartphone application has been around for quite some time and continues to evolve. By using a common Bluetooth-enabled OBD dongle, this app can provide more data than the car's dash would normally reveal.

or more specific manufacturer data streams available on the bus.

When selecting some basic parameters within scan tools, such as HP Tuners, one is often prompted to choose whether you want to record the generic SAE value or the manufacturer's high-resolution variant of common values, such as engine RPM or temperature. Often, this doesn't matter, but there are cases where the higher resolution comes in handy.

The cool part here is that the user doesn't have to know or appreciate what Mode $01 data is or how it's requested. The tool does it all and just lets the user pick and choose which signals he'd like to include. Going a step further, the instantaneous values are recorded over time for display in moving graphs, histograms, and files for review.

The best programs will also include capability to bring in outside inputs such as a wideband oxygen sensor and overlay it with the ECU data on the same screen. This option is truly powerful since the accurate exhaust gas oxygen (lambda) reading is not available from many ECUs where the vehicle is only equipped with standard narrow-band or "switching" oxygen sensors. Feedback from the wideband sensor is key to properly dialing in airflow and fuel calibration on a running engine. Overlaying the actual measurement with an ECU estimate of where it should have been reveals the calibration adjustments that must be made to correct the situation on modified engines.

From this point, the biggest question becomes, "What should I record?" Some fundamental values should always be recorded, but specific values may vary depending on the task at hand. It's often helpful to have multiple data-logger configurations to suit basic air and fuel, spark, torque control, or transmission investigations, since the logging tools have a limit to just how many variables can be recorded simultaneously.

Tailoring a configuration to one task allows collection of more of the manufacturer's specific information under that heading. On torque-controlled vehicles, for example, there may be 20 different requestors that adjust the torque or spark advance. Keep all of them in

Name	Value
Control Module Voltage (SAE)	14.35 V
Vehicle Speed (SAE)	16 mph
Engine RPM (SAE)	1,604 rpm
Throttle Position (SAE)	22.7 %
Sensed MAP	68.4 kPa
Intake Manifold Absolute Pressure (SAE)	68 kPa
Cylinder Airmass	0.34 g
Engine Coolant Temp (SAE)	201 °F
Intake Air Temp (SAE)	111 °F
Injector Pulse Width Cyl 1	5.6 ms

"Sensed MAP" is a higher resolution measurement than the generic SAE MAP value. There are times when this extra precision is necessary when performing calibration work.

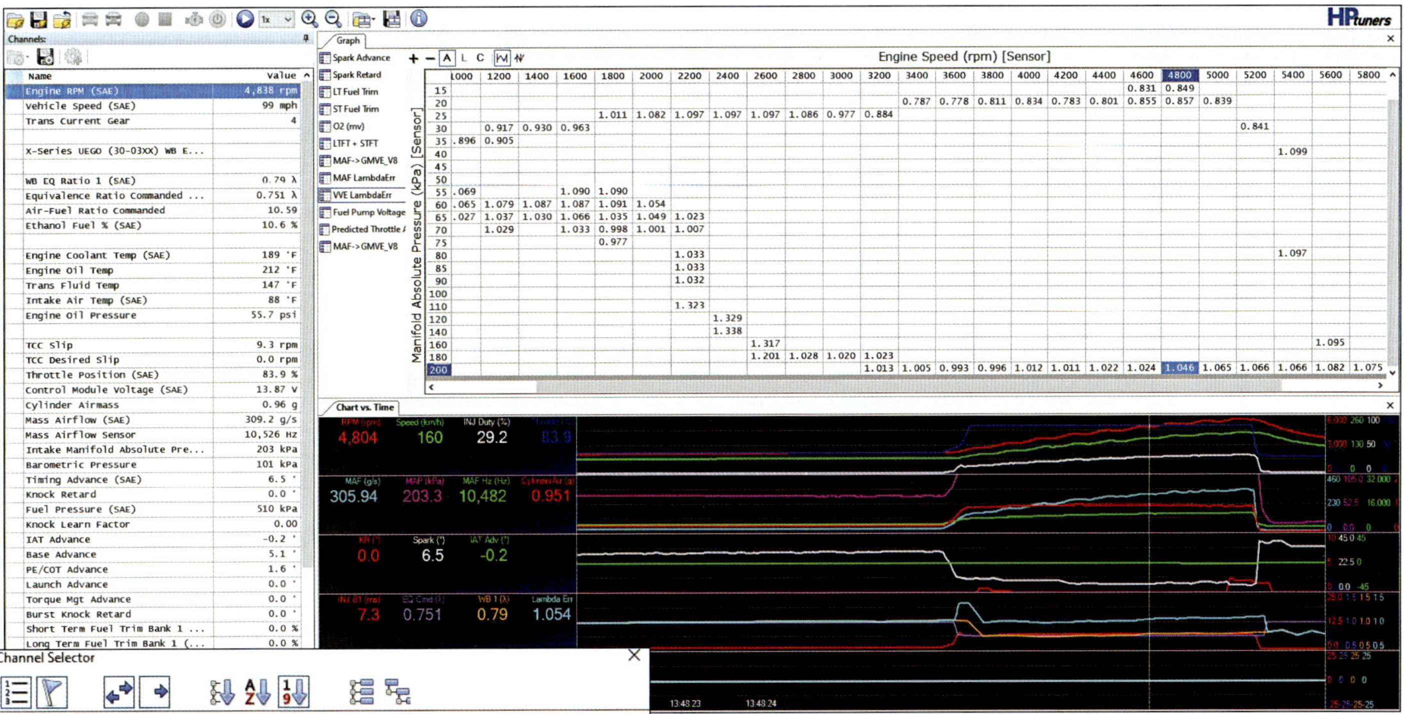

Bringing in the reading from an external wideband sensor (0.79 value in orange), it can be compared to commanded ratio (0.751 next to it in blue). As a time-saving step, I like to have the scan tool calculate the relative error between the two (1.054 in white) on the fly as well.

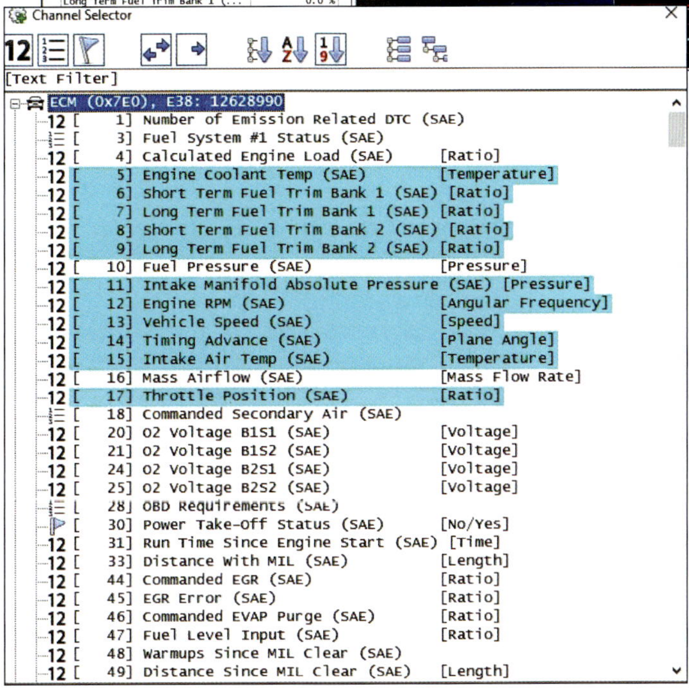

The SAE-required Mode $01 PIDs are listed in hexadecimal order on this scan tool. Users don't need to know anything other than the general name of the unit they wish to record to find it.

the recording until you're sure which ones are active during the exercise. Adding all of these often means that it is not possible to simultaneously look at all the transmission shift scheduling or pressure-control variables during that recording. That's okay, just focus on one task at a time, get things right, and move on to the next task with a different logger-channel selection.

If chasing down an elusive fault where the ECU had previously stored freeze-frame data in Mode $02, the data-logging tool becomes very helpful in the attempt to replicate the exact conditions seen during the previous failure. Simply add all the parameters in the freeze-frame data to the logging tool along with others related to the suspected failure point. For example, you may want to add individual-cylinder misfire counts in the logger here or wideband oxygen sensor data to tell you if the engine really was running rich or lean.

A more recent (and very welcome) addition to data-logging tools has been the use of histograms. A histogram allows the user to log data in a table format where the user selects the input values for the axes and another value to log at the appropriate intersection of those values. A key example is with measured lambda error plotted against engine speed and load.

The average, instantaneous, or last value can then be used to make smarter adjustments during the calibration process or quickly find issues. If plotting actual fuel-rail pressure against fuel-pump PWM command, it becomes readily apparent in a histogram if the pump cannot keep up at high demands or there is a leak in the system. When OBD-II tuning tools were new, this process required us to dump the data in Excel and plot by hand after some creative filtering and averaging. Now, it's available with just a few clicks as a serious time-saver thanks to these tools' software development.

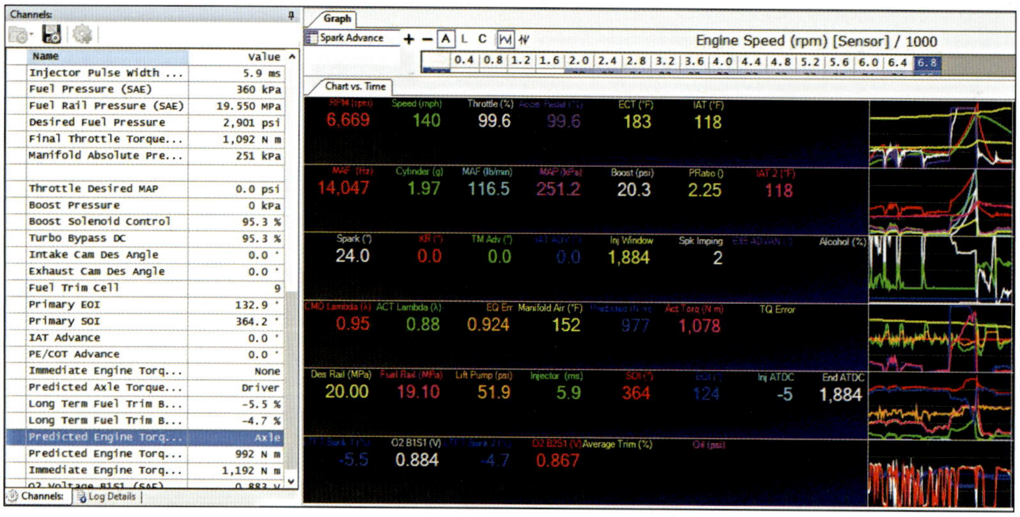

Working on torque-based throttle controls often requires the calibrator to log a large number of parameters specific to that system to catch any errors properly. Expect the page to get cluttered quickly for this task. This GM LT4 engine is making more than 1,000 hp at 20 psi of boost without complaint through the factory ECU logic after proper calibration.

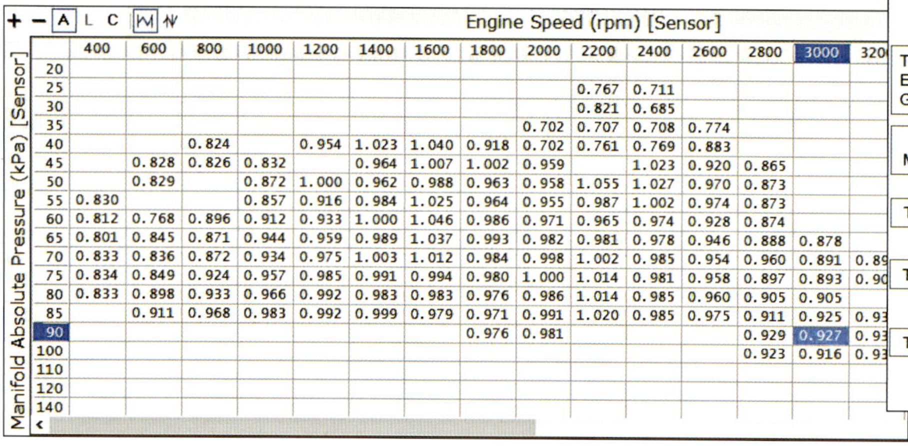

Engine Speed (rpm) [Sensor]

Manifold Absolute Pressure (kPa) [Sensor]	400	600	800	1000	1200	1400	1600	1800	2000	2200	2400	2600	2800	3000	320
20															
25										0.767	0.711				
30										0.821	0.685				
35									0.702	0.707	0.708	0.774			
40			0.824		0.954	1.023	1.040	0.918	0.702	0.761	0.769	0.883			
45		0.828	0.826	0.832		0.964	1.007	1.002	0.959		1.023	0.920	0.865		
50		0.829		0.872	1.000	0.962	0.988	0.963	0.958	1.055	1.027	0.970	0.873		
55	0.830			0.857	0.916	0.984	1.025	0.964	0.955	0.987	1.002	0.974	0.873		
60	0.812	0.768	0.896	0.912	0.933	1.000	1.046	0.986	0.971	0.965	0.974	0.928	0.874		
65	0.801	0.845	0.871	0.944	0.959	0.989	1.037	0.993	0.982	0.981	0.978	0.946	0.888	0.878	
70	0.833	0.836	0.872	0.934	0.975	1.003	1.012	0.984	0.998	1.002	0.985	0.954	0.960	0.891	0.89
75	0.834	0.849	0.924	0.957	0.985	0.991	0.994	0.980	1.000	1.014	0.981	0.958	0.897	0.893	0.90
80	0.833	0.898	0.933	0.966	0.992	0.983	0.983	0.976	0.986	1.014	0.985	0.960	0.905	0.905	
85		0.911	0.968	0.983	0.992	0.999	0.979	0.971	0.991	1.020	0.985	0.975	0.911	0.925	0.93
90								0.976	0.981				0.929	0.927	0.93
100													0.923	0.916	0.93
110															
120															
140															

Histograms are a powerful way of sorting data. Here, the same breakpoints are used in the histogram as the corresponding calibration table in the ECU so that adjustments can be made based on errors reported in each cell.

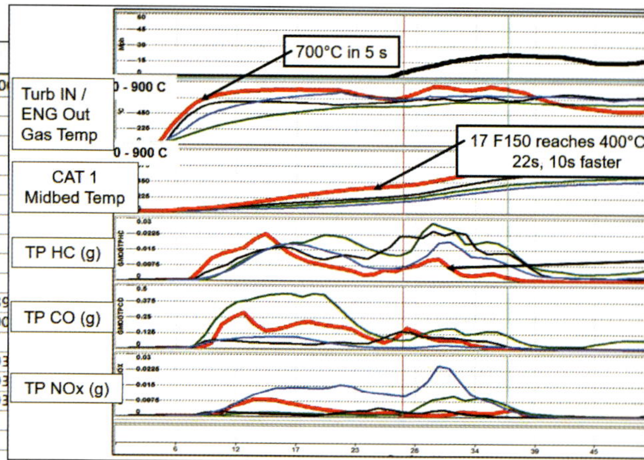

Cold-start data for several different applications reveals one that has higher carbon monoxide levels. It is the job of the emissions calibrator to reduce these events as much as possible to meet the total allowed limits of the test.

Armed with this level of data acquisition, it's possible to move from what myself and some of my colleagues only half-jokingly refer to as the world of aftermarket "tooning" into true calibration activities. Calibration implies that precise measurements are being taken, and precise changes are being made to the ECU based on math done using this data and the original ECU calibration values. Anything less these days is more like "poking it with a stick" than actual scientific work and usually makes things, such as passing emissions, difficult at best.

Modern emissions work requires high-resolution data-logging capability, as we must compare the emissions bench or tailpipe monitor readings to the values being used at that same moment by the ECU that resulted in a tailpipe reading that must be changed.

A spike in tailpipe carbon monoxide almost always means a rich condition, but understanding why the engine was rich at that moment requires the calibrator to dig in and look at RPM, spark, injector pulse width, measured airflow, fuel trims, cam position, and more. Being able to accurately compare these two data sources and make calculated changes is the only way to effectively clean up the tailpipe readings and pass today's stringent standards.

It is only after using the data logging tools to make careful decisions about calibration values that the J2534 interface should be used to reflash the ECU using the SAE protocols. At this moment, one truly begins to appreciate how simple some of the aftermarket tools suppliers have made the process of reprogramming a vehicle with non-OEM data. It doesn't alleviate the need to remain emissions compliant, though.

Modified vehicles can pass emissions, but they'll usually need to prove it, which starts with being able to pass all their original diagnostic monitors and tests. These aftermarket tools can show the results of those checks as well before ever going to an official inspection station or test lab.

Using OBD to Diagnose When an MIL Isn't Present

There are a lot of cases when a vehicle just doesn't run properly, but it somehow doesn't have the MIL illuminated. The reasons behind this disconnect can vary quite a bit. Perhaps the fault isn't bad enough to exceed the failure threshold. Remember that manufacturers are only required to report a MIL if the failure is enough to make the tailpipe emissions 150 percent of its rated standard. There can be a fair amount of daylight between "runs poorly" and "fails emissions by 150 percent" in some vehicles. Either way, it becomes an annoyance that drives many owners back to the service bay or their own garage with questions as to why the vehicle is misbehaving.

Worse, on some modified vehicles, I have seen plenty of cases where the tuner (not calibrator) has simply turned off a list of P-codes rather than make the vehicle run properly. Presumably, they didn't want the customer to bring the vehicle back and complain of a CEL that could have been prevented if they had done a better job in the first place. The lead offenders here are misfire, torque security, and catalyst and oxygen sensor monitors, which are all relatively important.

If the fault codes are turned off, the customer may be left with a false sense of security that everything is running well when he or she really should be digging into an issue or repair. Then, when the vehicle behavior is so bad that the customer notices, he is also left with no immediate clues as to where to start looking. OBD data will likely be his saving grace here.

Tools for Advanced Diagnostics

We begin by looking for the right tools. One way or another, we need a device that gets onto the ECU

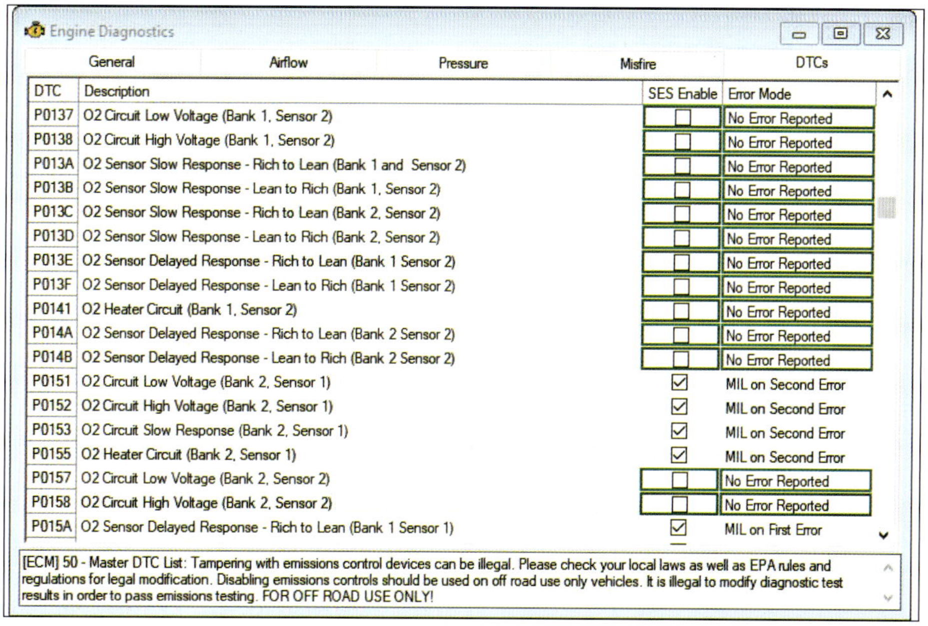

Don't do this. Simply disabling the code and diagnostic does not fix anything and leaves the tuner open to huge fines if investigated for tampering or offering defeat devices.

communication bus, whether that is CAN, serial, or otherwise. The exact method of communication is not as important as the fact that we have access to a stream of live data that can be observed. Any of the previously discussed tools should be sufficient here if they support the Mode $01 data stream, even better if they also allow us to probe the system with Mode $08 commands.

Barring that, there are also a number of CAN bus scanning tools on the market. While these are often universal and quite capable of reading all information being passed on the CAN bus, without the right "decoder ring" you may just be staring at lines of hexadecimal nonsense. Some tools will also include SAE or even manufacturer-specific conversions into engineering units. Others assume the user has their own library. Check carefully before buying something like this to scan your vehicle.

As a last resort, we can fall back to another option used long before OBD-II. A "breakout box" is an intermediate device that can be inserted into the wire harness between the ECU and rest of the vehicle. Each pin of the harness goes to an access point on the face of the box before continuing to the opposing connector. This allows the user to prove individual wires with a DMM or oscilloscope to see the raw readings as the engine is running. It's crude, but it can be a life saver when we don't trust the ECU values or just don't have access. Let's take a look at how grabbing ECU data can improve your diagnostic capability.

Misfires

Misfires represent one of the most common customer complaints. Humans can be very sensitive to changes in acceleration or vibration, especially if the cabin is not well isolated from the engine. A misfire event usually presents as a hesitation, hitching, jerking, or abnormal vibration felt by the driver caused by one or more combustion events that were less than complete.

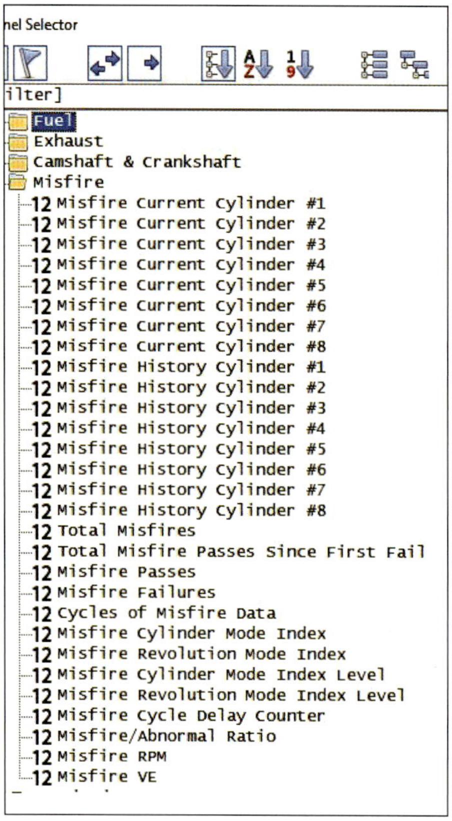

Using the scan tool to investigate which cylinders are either currently misfiring or have a history of misfires helps narrow down the source for a proper repair. These parameters are manufacturer specific and may not be supported by all scan tools.

An actual misfire event should result in some unburned fuel and oxygen going out the exhaust port. When this happens, live data should reveal a temporary lean spike in the oxygen sensor signal. If there is not a correlating change in fuel delivery shown by the average injector pulse width on that bank, we should start looking for why the fuel failed to make it to the cylinder or why the spark could not ignite it. Low system voltage may contribute to poor fuel injector opening or ignition coil charging, as both of these are coils that are sensitive to operating voltage. Some extreme cases of damage or wear can have a cylinder occasionally misfire due to poor compression or leakage when the injector and plug are both firing perfectly.

Some ECUs will report individual cylinder misfire counts. An intermittent problem on one cylinder may show up here, even if the total count is not high enough to trigger the P03xx threshold. This helps quickly narrow things down to a single fuel injector, coil, plug, or cylinder for inspection. If swapping the injector, coil, or spark plug between cylinders doesn't make the problem follow it, it's probably time to check compression and leakdown for something more sinister than the quick fix.

Fuel Contamination

Fuel contamination happens more often than some think. Gas stations are not known for being as clean as an operating room, yet we depend on them to deliver the very lifeblood our engines need. Their underground storage tanks may leak, allowing dirt or water to contaminate the fuel. Some customers have even been known to inadvertently put the wrong fuel type into their tank. Mixing up gasoline and diesel usually has an almost instant catastrophic effect on either engine type. But pouring E85 into a gas vehicle can also confuse it enough to run poorly before eventually setting a MIL, depending on the concentration of alcohol in the mixed tank.

Filling a non-flex-fuel vehicle with ethanol will confuse the ECU, resulting in poor air-fuel ratio control and torque response. Most modern ECUs can tolerate small doses of ethanol without too much drama.

The fuel rail pressure sensor on this factory supercharged Cobra has a vacuum port connected to manifold pressure. It actually reports the "delta pressure" seen across the top and bottom of the fuel injectors to the ECU for better metering.

All of these change the chemical balance that would be needed for clean combustion. While there's no good balance point for water or dirt in fuel, large blends of ethanol may require a shift of as much as 30 percent just to find the new balance point.

Non-flex fuel vehicles don't have a method to cope with this and will just ratchet up the fuel trims as they wait for the oxygen sensors to finally switch. This can be seen clearly on OBD data as the trims go starkly positive with ethanol blends. Since the trigger point for "bank lean" is often 20 percent or more, it would take a large amount of alcohol to hit it in one shot. If the driver only put half a tank or less in, he may end up with fuel trims that move a lot and a car that just runs poorly as the ECU struggles to compensate for the change in chemistry.

Low Fuel Pressure

Speaking of fuels, low fuel pressure may also be another tricky condition to find. Many cars don't have a fuel pressure sensor at all, so there wouldn't be any data on this if we wanted it in some cases. For those with a fuel pressure sensor, we have a handy indicator available to tell us if the fuel pump and regulator are doing their job.

Low fuel pressure may be caused by a failing pump (see "Fuel Contamination"), regulator, clogged filter, or loose line. Vehicles with a vacuum-referenced pressure regulator must also be checked for leaks between the intake manifold and the pressure regulator. Whether we confirm it by OBD data or a physical pressure gauge added to the rail for inspection, it's always a good idea to confirm that fuel pressure rises quickly at start and stays within range under all operating conditions before looking at injectors for issues.

If the scan tool allows you to see the fuel pump command, there should be a brief priming period right after key-on that helps build the initial pressure. Watching this is a great way to correlate with a DMM on the fuel pump wires to determine if the problem lies in the pump itself or in the relay and wiring upstream.

No Start, Hard Start

A "no crank" condition can gather a few more clues from the ECU that may be a life saver. First, is the ECU awake and communicating when the key is on? If not, we probably have either an entire vehicle or an ECU circuit–specific issue rather

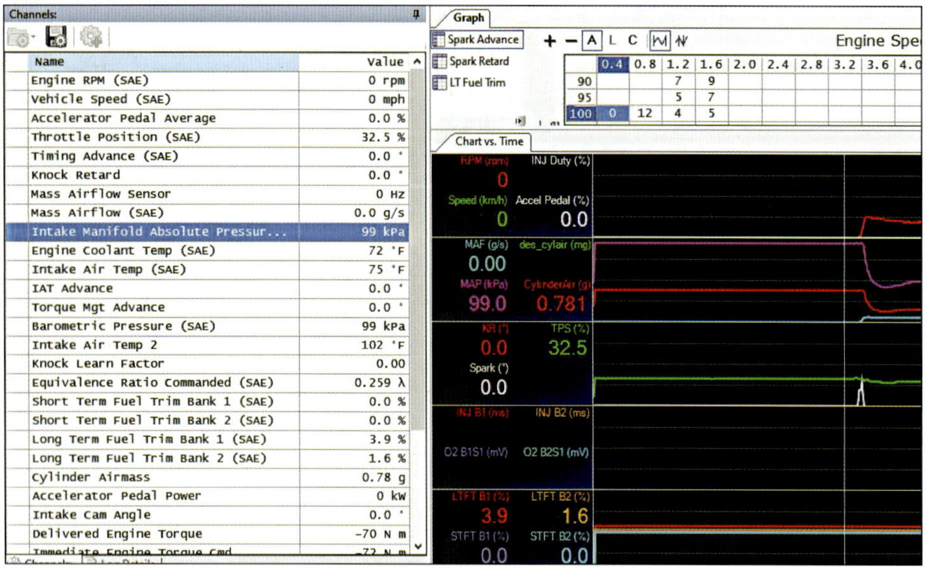

Even before the engine is started, the scan tool can show us that some sensors are working correctly by returning the same values as the current weather conditions. RPM is zero and both MAP/Baro and IAT/ECT match the garage conditions.

than a problem with the starter itself.

The first step here would be to verify that we have proper system voltage from the battery all the way to power inputs at the ECU and fuse box. Next, we can key on and query the ECU for some basic information such as system voltage, air, and coolant temperatures. This lets us know if we even have a connection at some level.

In their absence, one should begin checking to see if there is both power and ground at the ECU since the ECU is often part of the starter trigger circuit. This is essentially trying to determine whether the wiring issue is between the key and the ECU or the ECU and the starter circuit to begin the rest of the search.

When a car cranks but won't start, traditional mechanics always looked to resolve the issue to either air, fuel, or spark. During cranking, the ECU should display RPM (usually around 120 rpm, depending on available voltage). If this is missing while the engine is turning, one should take a close look at the crankshaft and camshaft position sensor circuits. Errors here often result in missing or erratic speed measurements.

Next, fuel delivery can be checked by examining injector pulse width. The initial cranking pulses are typically significantly larger than normal idle pulse width values. Where an idling engine may normally see 3 milliseconds of on-time from the injector, that same engine may be well over 5 milliseconds as it cranks. These number will vary wildly with each hardware combination and calibration, but the ability to see them in real time from OBD data still gives us some useful comparison points.

A missing pulse width may tell us that something else is wrong. A disproportionately long injection pulse paired with an ECT/ACT reading of -40 is a good indicator that either the temperature sensor has failed or is just unplugged. Since the default reading on these circuits is high impedance, the ECU reads as a very cold temperature that needs lots of extra cranking fuel. This large amount of extra fuel can quickly flood the engine. Luckily, most ECUs also have a "clear flood" mode that shuts off the injectors if the driver floors the gas pedal. This can also be observed in the recorded

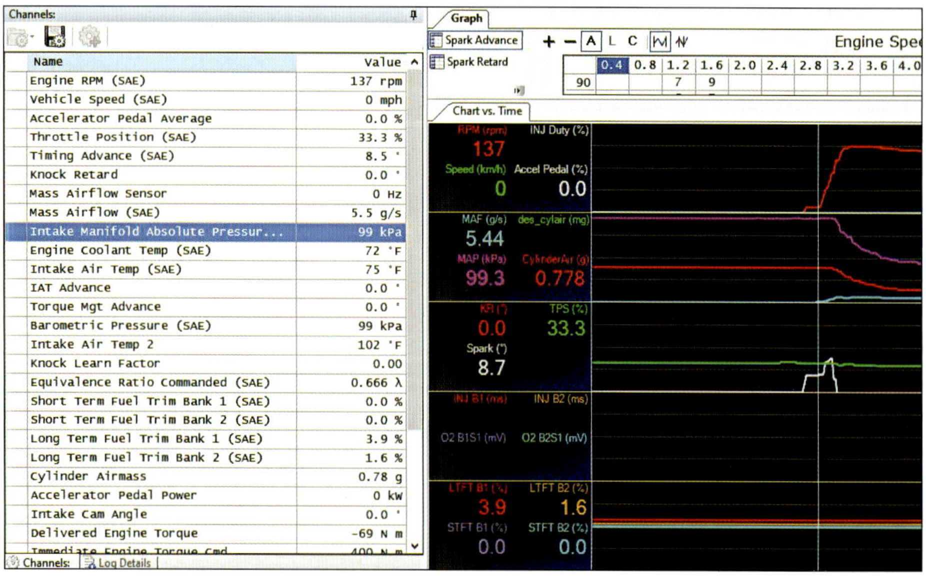

Dropping the cursor in this log during cranking right before the engine fires shows a healthy 137 rpm from the starter. The spark advance of 8.7 degrees can be verified with a timing light and the MAF output is rational at 5.4 g/s.

APP/TPS and injector pulse width values on the scanner.

Errors in spark timing can be observed in the scan tool by comparing the ECU reported values to what might be seen with a timing light. Most engines crank with relatively little spark advance (5 to 20 degrees BTDC), which should make it easy to verify against a physical timing mark on the crank damper.

In the absence of a factory timing mark, a paint mark can be added to both the damper/pulley and timing cover when the engine is brought to cylinder number 1 TDC manually with a ratchet. Even if you are off by a few degrees in finding TDC, it can be a useful tool for exposing cases where the distributor or cam sensor is 180 degrees out.

On that note, is plug number-1 even firing near its TDC or was the wiring changed, resulting in the wrong firing order? Now would be a good time to verify both the coil and the injector (using a telltale "noid light" that can be inserted into the harness connector in place of the injector works well here) firing at similar times. Remember that the injector firing should precede the ignition event here by a bit.

Finally, the cranking airflow can be checked with a number of values. SAE requires that manufacturers broadcast mass airflow, which should be a small but measurable number during cranking as seen in the OBD data. If the vehicle has a MAP sensor, it should read the current barometric pressure at key on in the scanner, with only a slight depression during cranking.

Once the engine fires, the MAP will be drawn down to the normal idle value if everything is working correctly. Throttle position should be mostly closed as long as the driver doesn't have his foot on the pedal. Engines equipped with cable throttles will also have an idle air control (IAC) valve that's position is also usually available in the scan tool. IAC and electronic throttle control (ETC) position values should not be maxed out during cranking.

Poor Performance and Economy

The most common contributor to poor performance in a fuel-injected engine is something wrong with the actual fuel delivery. Using the OBD data, we can see if the ECU has been trying to work around something for a while by checking the fuel trims. Large positive numbers here would explain poor fuel economy, as the ECU was adding fuel to compensate for something else such as a vacuum leak, an ailing fuel pump/injector, or a clogged filter. Similarly, large negative trims indicate an over-delivery of fuel that may be coming from a stuck injector, fuel pressure regulator, or EVAP solenoid.

Over time, the oxygen sensors slowly wear out from time, temperature, and poisoning. Even with a clean-burning engine, their ability to report a balanced mixture eventually becomes compromised. The result is usually a cumulative increase in learned fuel trims, as seen in the OBD data. An active request can be sent to clear these trims, but if they reappear with no other changes being made, it may be time to simply replace the oxygen sensors.

Fresh oxygen sensors in this case would quickly report a valid signal based on the actual exhaust chemistry, allowing the learn trims to quickly walk back toward center even

The number-one culprit of rapidly decreasing fuel economy is the oxygen sensor. It lives in a terrible environment exposed to salt spray, heat, and vibration that are all constantly trying to kill it.

if they were not actively cleared with a scan tool command. Since most ECUs will allow about 20 percent positive fuel trims before actually hitting the fault limit, it's easy to see why many drivers report an increase in fuel economy after replacing aged oxygen sensors. In reality, they didn't "increase" fuel economy, they just got rid of the artificial decrease that had accumulated over time in the OBD oxygen sensor data.

Vacuum and Boost Leaks

As mentioned earlier, a vacuum leak that lets an unintended additional amount of fresh air into the engine can cause a lean condition. This can often be correlated with a positive fuel trim on the engine bank nearest the leak. Cases where one bank shows positive correction and the other does not should raise this suspicion first, followed perhaps by

A loose clamp or split hose anywhere after the MAF sensor can be enough to cause a significant fuel-delivery issue, just like a traditional vacuum leak at the manifold. This turbocharged Honda CR-V also has several Helmholtz resonators between the airbox and the compressor inlet.

a check for injector performance or individual coil/plug behavior.

In extreme cases, the MAP value may also be artificially high at idle compared to normal for that vehicle. This comparison requires either some historical data or another identical vehicle configuration to know just what the normal idle MAP value should have been.

If the MAP reading is high and the MAF sensor signal is low, our first suspicion is a leak. A quick check of all fasteners and clamps followed by spraying the induction system with a fluid such as brake or carb cleaner may expose the leak as the engine draws the additional "fuel" in through the leak and audibly changes its note briefly.

Boost leaks can be a little more difficult to find since we can't see them at idle. Again, OBD to the rescue here as we look at MAP, MAF, RPM, throttle position, and wastegate duty cycle where available. An engine that's down on power may simply have a loose clamp or hose somewhere. Finding it may be tricky in the tight confines of modern vehicles, but confirming the issue can be easier with OBD data.

This is where advanced scan tools with recording or logging capability come in really handy. By plotting the values against time while accelerating on the road, one can quickly confirm if the throttle was staying open and whether boost was consistent in the MAP reading. A loose boost hose connection may briefly make a little boost at the manifold, then quickly taper off back toward atmospheric pressure at the MAP sensor as RPM rises.

If the throttle is closing or the commanded wastegate position is changing, there may be a different reason related to the torque or traction control system. With complete access to the manufacturer-specific data, one can even see which of these various requests may be limiting power.

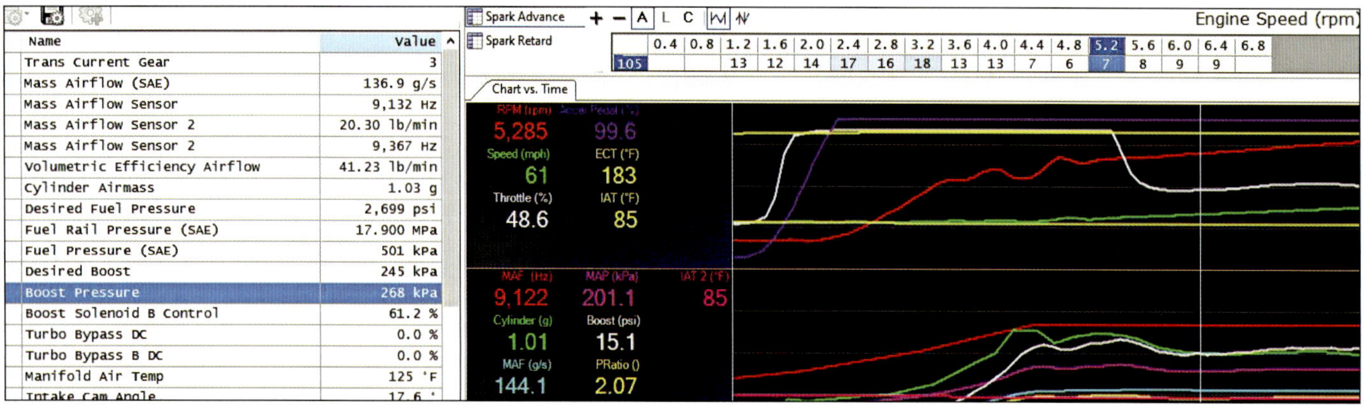

This tuner was wondering why the throttle was closing at WOT on his modified vehicle. Note the delivered "Boost Pressure" exceeds "Desired Boost." The system is working correctly, he just needed to modify the torque requests to drive it to WOT all the time.

CHAPTER 12

Special Notes for Tuners

Yes, it says "tuners," but I really mean "calibrators" here. There is a difference. The performance aftermarket has a reputation of historically doing whatever it takes to change the behavior of an engine or vehicle once they have a means to make adjustments. This could mean either adjusting the factory ECU, replacing it completely, or employing a piggyback box that has the ability to intercept and modify signals going in and out.

Piggyback Systems

Working backward, let's look at the third option. During the early days of electronic fuel injection, knowledge of the inner workings of the current control systems was very limited. There were almost no tools that look anything like what we have access to today that cleanly display the variables, tables, and functions within the ECU in normal engineering units. Worse yet, there was essentially zero data-logging capability, so it was difficult at best to know where to make precise adjustments.

The lack of access and support drove the aftermarket to make its own electronic gizmos that plugged in line between the ECU and its sensors and actuators. These would slew the reported pressure, temperature, or crank angle in an effort to get the ECU to react by adjusting fuel or spark delivery. If that didn't work, they would intercept the output pulses and modify them before they reached the injector or coil pack to deliver a different physical fuel mass or ignition timing than what the ECU had commanded. These adjustments often still shifted with moving commands from the ECU, so a simple "+1" correction wouldn't always have the same result as ambient conditions changed and the factory ECU moved with a non-linear correction.

When I owned a dyno shop years ago, I was mildly entertained watching customers insist on poking away at their "MAF translator" or "timing tricker" boxes, trying to blindly find just the right combination that yielded the best power without endangering the engine. After each dyno run, they would look at the measured lambda on the power curve

With the C8 Corvette, General Motors introduced a new level of security on the ECU that rivals that used by banks and credit cards. The initial response from the performance industry looked a lot like the piggyback boxes we saw in the 1980s and 1990s, when they could no longer break into the factory ECU.

and try to outsmart it with the twist or flick of a dip switch in hopes that the next run would hit their desired air-fuel ratio or timing. They were not always successful at protecting the engine with these adjustments.

With the evolution of security measures on some new ECUs, vehicle connectivity and security has once again locked the industry out of calibration access on some vehicles. This time, we know how the ECU is generally working, we just can't touch the calibration data. Although we can still log a fair amount of data through OBD-II protocols, making adjustments internally has proven to be impossible until once again someone else in the industry is able to circumvent the security locks keeping us out. In the meantime, what's old is new again.

A new crop of piggyback boxes is hitting the market that again are either modifying fuel and spark outputs or slewing measured inputs to the factory ECU. The controllers inside of these modern piggyback boxes also benefit from the march of technology, sporting more sophisticated controls of their own and laptop reprogramming rather than just rotary potentiometers and dip switches. They may even control additional fuel injectors while leaving factory direct-injection systems alone.

One good note here is that since they retain the factory ECU and programming, much of the original diagnostic capability remains intact. This is good news for those who need to pass a plug-in inspection that looks for modified code in the factory controller. However, it still violates the Clean Air Act clauses on tampering unless the device (and its application specific programming) has been through the certification process. It's possible to use these to get both good performance and emissions compliance, but it's not an automatic win.

This 1997 Mustang Cobra is an example of an emissions-compliant engine swap. It is equipped with the complete ECU, catalysts, and emissions controls that run a production 2012 5.0L Coyote.

Replacement ECUs

This leads us to the middle option of replacing the factory ECU with another controller altogether. While it is certainly legal to replace an older car's engine controls with a more modern ECU that complies with OBD-II requirements, doing so requires that all newer emissions functionality is employed. The engine and ECU combination must also pass the newer combination's model-year emissions standard.

One example of this is installing a 2012-model-year Chevy LSX family engine into an older Camaro. As long as the emissions monitors all run and pass, most states will allow this. That, of course, also means that catalysts, oxygen sensors, and other emissions equipment also came with the newer engine.

Some enthusiasts elect to replace a factory ECU with an aftermarket standalone ECU. This allows them to run much more wild engine combinations with a greatly simplified tuning process since most aftermarket controllers do not have anywhere near the complexity of factory ECUs when it comes to airflow modeling, torque modeling, fuel delivery, and spark control.

To many, this simplicity alone is worth the change. Throw in some extra features, such as integrated boost controllers, traction control, staged fuel delivery, and additional triggered outputs, and one can see why they are so popular. Getting these integrated with the rest of the vehicle to keep the factory dash display active and other modules on the CAN or serial bus happy can be another challenge, but there are certainly plenty of cases where those problems have already been solved with commercially available solution kits.

The biggest challenge going forward for complete aftermarket ECU replacement is that there is no way that these simplified controllers will satisfy the requirements for emissions compliance. Even if the calibrator acts responsibly, installs proper catalytic convertors, O_2 sensors, a charcoal canister, and evaporative purge solenoid, the OBD-II diagnostics are not there. Sure, they have their own diagnostics to detect missing or shorted sensors, but that is only equivalent to OBD-I detection and leaves all plausibility testing undone.

The easiest way to get complete control with a turbo kit added to this Miata is to switch to a standalone ECU. While it may drive well, make good power, and even have clean emissions with a catalyst, the lack of OBD-II reporting is problematic if it must be inspected.

Both the EPA and CARB have the authority to test random vehicles against their published certification levels for confirmation. In those tests, 100 percent of the exhaust gases are captured and run through an analyzer for measurement of various constituents.

I have yet to see an aftermarket ECU that runs the misfire diagnostic all the way to redline, as is the current requirement for all OEM applications. Worse yet, if one were to devise a way for an aftermarket ECU to report passing monitors during plug-in OBD-II testing, that would exactly fit the definition of a defeat device. I would not want to be anywhere near a person, company, or project doing such a thing once the EPA inevitably finds out that it exists. That's the kind of exceptional violation that gets jail time to go along with the steep fines.

Adjusting the Factory ECU

As a calibration engineer, the first option of adjusting the factory ECU has always been my preferred route. But this requires someone else to have cracked the security access as well as the definition of all parameters available for adjustment. It's easier said than done, but for the purpose of this discussion let's just assume that we have sufficient calibration access through commercially available tools on a laptop.

Deciding where to start making adjustments is often a daunting task for the newly initiated. This is not surprising, considering many modern ECUs may have upward of 14,000 adjustable parameters. Aftermarket-tuning software usually unlocks a few hundred of these, but that's often enough to make us dangerous. For the rest of this discussion, let's assume that we have a toolset that allows us to make intelligent changes to an already OBD-II-compliant ECU.

Linking OBD and Emissions

Keep in mind that the whole reason we have OBD is to demonstrate that our vehicles' emissions are reasonably low. By constantly testing the control system and verifying that all measured values are within a predictable range, the assumption is made that this good running condition results in a minimum of unburned fuel, clean combustion, and low generation of oxides of nitrogen at the tailpipe.

The EPA has the authority to pull a vehicle off the road and run it through testing at their state-of-the-art laboratory in Ann Arbor, Michigan, to see exactly what the tailpipe numbers are in a consistent laboratory setting. Should the vehicle fail this tailpipe sample–based testing by more than 50 percent of the allowable constituents when showing a clean OBD report, the EPA may elect to contact the OEM for further investigation. This further contact may range from a simple inquiry to significant penalties and fines, depending on what is found.

If the vehicle has been modified, the OEM is off the hook for responsibility, but that will just have the EPA digging deeper to find the root cause. Should aftermarket parts be found on the vehicle that do have some sort of emissions certification (like a CARB EO), the manufacturer of those parts probably gets the next contact from the EPA.

If the Mode $09 data shows that the ECU has been reflashed and now has data that is not covered by an approved CVN, the installer of that ECU software will find themselves under the microscope of EPA investigation. Note that this is all at the federal level, so there is no possible excuse of "they don't have testing where I live," because the Clean Air Act applies to the entire country. If this happens in California or one of the "green" states that follows their emissions regulation, the exposure may also include CARB or another state agency in addition to the EPA.

The takeaway here is that even if the OBD monitors pass on a modified vehicle, it does not guarantee immunity from regulatory oversight. The end user will often have to pass state or local monitoring that is primarily done via OBD-II inspection, but the potential still exists to get caught. Let's look at the steps needed to get to a point where there is sufficient proof that a modified vehicle is compliant.

Creating a Clean Tailpipe Measurement

Whether a vehicle or parts program is going to go all the way through the certification process or not, the first step is the same. One must put all the physical parts together on a running vehicle and calibrate the ECU to a point where the measured tailpipe emissions are indeed clean.

If we can't get the vehicle running clean, there is no point in trying to make sure that it passes the OBD monitors or state-inspection criteria. Trying to make a passing grade when we know the raw tailpipe measurements are probably bad is an uphill battle to say the least, and in all reality, ethically wrong. The proper method is to clean up the engine and vehicle performance, then have the diagnostics prove it.

So how does one get the tailpipe measurement clean? The answer starts with remembering what is measured during an official emissions test and working to ensure that these constituents are minimized in engine operation. The current standards measure a few key things: NO_x is formed at high temperatures or slightly lean conditions. Non-methane organic gases (NMOG) are essentially unburned fuel or vapors from the crankcase. Carbon monoxide (CO) is formed primarily during rich conditions.

One key thing to note here is that the old emissions standard used to measure hydrocarbons (HC) specifically. It is now sampled as NMOG, which includes many other species of organics that may be harmful to the environment. With the addition of ethanol to most pump fuel, formation of aldehydes in the exhaust became notable.

Since these are technically not hydrocarbons, they slipped past the old standard. The newer standard closes this loophole along with the old trick of doping a vehicle's fuel tank with alcohol to pass a sniffer test. There is no opportunity to dope the fuel in a certification test anyway, since the procedure requires the tank to be drained and refilled to 40-percent capacity with a specific fuel before starting. Thinking of NMOG as simply unburned fuel is probably the easiest way to resolve how we would reduce its presence in the exhaust, regardless of specific fuel chemistry.

The current LEV3 standards combine both NMOG and NO_x into a single number for comparison against the standard. This means that one cannot simply trade more of one for less of the other to bring a failing system into balance. Rather, the vehicle must emit very small amounts of both throughout the test to pass.

	A	B	C	D	E	F	G	H	L	M	N	O
1	**Test Data**	FTP75			Operator			Speed Table		Date:		
2	**Test Number**	FTP75_xxxxx			Driver			Shift Table	Auto	Cold Start		
3												
4	**Vehicle**				**Dyno**			**Fuel**		**Test Timing**		
5	VIN	*1FTEW1EG2LFxxxxxx*			Inertia [lb]	*6000.00*		CARB LEV III E10 Premium HG1921LT20		Start Time	*15:36:47*	
6					A [lbf]	*26.655*		Fuel type	GASOLINE	End Time	*17:00:06*	
7	Model	F-150			B [lbf/mph]	*-0.15707*		Density	*0.7512*			
8	Model Year	*2020*			C [lbf/mph2]	*0.049737*		NHV	17960	Soak Time	566.7	
9	Engine Family	LFMXT03.54JM						CWF	*0.8257*			
10	Displacement [l]	*3.500*										
11	Transmission	*Automatic*										
12	Odometer Start [mile]	*2909*			Flow Stream	Bag+Modal Gasoline						
13	Odometer End [mile]	*2920*			Remark	FTP MODAL Baseline Canister Load						
104												
105	**Total Result (weighted)**											
106	***Weighted***	THC [g/mile]	CO [g/mile]	CO_2 [g/mile]	NO_x [g/mile]	CH_4 [g/mile]	NMOG [g/mile]	NMHC [g/mile]	NMHC+NO_x [g/mile]	HCHO [g/mile]	***Fuel Economy***	
107	Mass per Dist.	0.0325	*0.1450*	*472.37*	*0.0190*	*0.0089*	*0.0261*	*0.0237*	0.043	*0.0005*	mile/gal	*18.33*
109	Mass per Dist. - Particulate SPC	0.0006										
117												
118	**Total Result**											
119	***actual***	THC [g/mile]	CO [g/mile]	CO2 [g/mile]	NOX [g/mile]	CH4 [g/mile]	NMOG [g/mile]	NMHC [g/mile]	NMHC+NO_x [g/mile]		***Fuel Economy***	
120	Mass per Dist.	0.0432	*0.2159*	*476.44*	*0.0269*	*0.0113*	*0.0355*	*0.0322*	0.059		mile/gal	*18.17*
121	Mass per Dist. (rounded)	0.0432	*0.2159*	*476.4*	*0.0269*	*0.0113*	*0.035*	*0.0322*	0.059		Dist. [mi]	*11.03*
125	Mass per Dist. - Parti SPC [mg/mile]	0.9505										

After running the vehicle in the lab, a report like this is generated to show its performance compared to the allowable standard. Manufacturers try to be significantly lower than the requirement, while aftermarket companies simply want to pass after their DF is added.

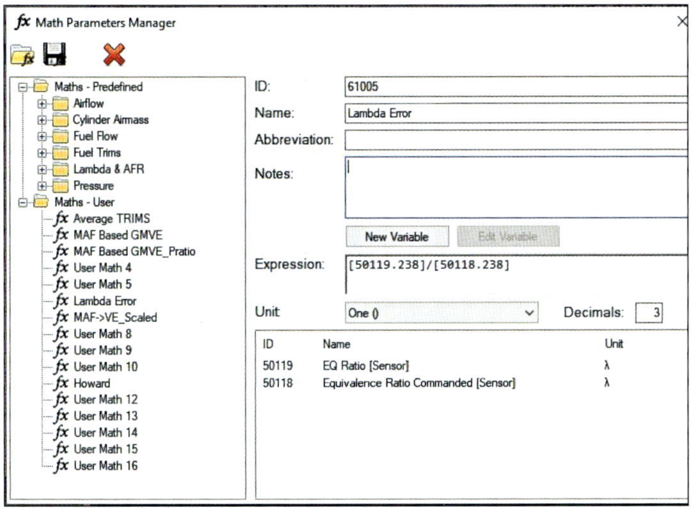

Setting up a calculated parameter based on measured and desired lambda makes the job of evaluating fueling errors much simpler. Units of lambda also take away much of the error from air-fuel ratios when alcohol is added to the fuel.

A load-bearing dynamometer is a must for taking steady-state testing. The eddy-current absorber has the ability to hold the vehicle at a constant speed regardless of engine torque so that stable fueling measurements can be made.

What is not measured on an emissions test is equally important. Although carbon dioxide (CO_2) is a greenhouse gas and we see plenty of discussion about it on TV and social media, it is not regulated as part of the current emissions limits.

CO_2 is a product of the clean combustion of hydrocarbon fuels. As such, we actually want more of it in the exhaust, relatively speaking as compared to NMOG, CO, or NO_x. In a properly running engine, the amount of CO_2 emitted is directly proportional to the amount of fuel consumed. To this end, CO_2 should be tied almost exclusively to discussions of fuel economy rather than emissions as currently measured in the United States. Since fuel economy is not regulated in the aftermarket, there is no current penalty for changing it as long as the other more harmful constituents are within the limits.

That's enough of the theory, let's get practical. From a high level, the best way to get a vehicle to pass emissions is to almost always operate the engine itself somewhere relatively close to the stoichiometric balance for the fuel being used and feed that balanced mixture to a three-way catalyst that is hot enough to convert the small amounts of "leftovers" into CO_2 and H_2O.

The most basic thing any engine controller must do to reduce emissions is be able to find and consistently deliver a stoichiometric mixture of fuel to whatever amount of air is coming into the engine. If it can't do that, there is little hope for passing any meaningful emissions test.

At a bare minimum, the engine should operate at most of the light load operating points in steady state and demonstrate its ability to show an average of lambda=1.0 in the exhaust with minimum fuel trims assisting it to get there. This sounds simple, yet I still see so many engines struggle to do this basic task, both aftermarket and OEM.

Those who have read my other books, watched my online videos, or attended one of my Calibrated Success events know that I stress this basic concept beyond anything else. I always start by telling classes that the most important job of the ECU is to accurately calculate the amount of fresh air entering the cylinder at any moment. Almost everything else going in the ECU depends on this number, including emissions as a whole.

Starting with an accurate number for cylinder air charge allows the ECU to properly determine how much fuel should be injected for each cycle as well. Doing this task in steady state takes away many of the noise factors for manifold filling, transient fueling, wall film, transport delays, feedback correction, fuel trims, and PID loop errors. By driving this initial error toward zero, there is much less correction needed in all these other factors later, which always improves emissions performance in the real world.

Once sufficient steady-state fuel-delivery control has been demonstrated, progress to transient

Transient Fueling Calibration

The difference between a passing and failing emissions test often lies within the control of the wall film or the fuel puddle's contribution to total cylinder fueling. In port fuel injection, a significant portion of the fuel takes a detour on its way from the tip of the fuel injector to the cylinder. Some percentage of the fuel spray sticks to the walls, roof, and floor of the port as well as the back of the intake valve itself.

After some period of time, this fuel is either warmed enough to evaporate or grabbed by the high-velocity air speeding past. It eventually joins the fuel that is going directly from the injector to the cylinder inlet. Modern port injection puts the fuel injector relatively close to the intake valve compared to some older designs, central port injection, or even a carburetor.

In the case of the carburetor, quite a large portion of the delivered fuel passes through some sort of puddle as the entire interior of the intake manifold is effectively wetted with fuel when running. This is the key reason why fuel delivery has moved ever closer to the cylinder itself over time, as the need to precisely control total fuel mass delivery for each valve opening event is increased as emissions regulations continue to tighten.

At the far end of this spectrum lies direct fuel injection. In this system, the tip of the injector has been moved inside of the combustion chamber, effectively eliminating intake port wall film and the need to compensate for it.

Once we understand a physical attribute of the engine, next we need a way to control it or at least recognize its effects and adjust other parameters accordingly. In the case of intake-port wall-film contribution, manufacturers have each developed their own method of compensation. Some are rather simple adders based on rate of change for throttle position or MAP.

Others have adopted a physics-based "X-Tau" approach that can accurately model the rate of fuel deposition and evaporation to and from the walls. In this case "X" represents the percent of fuel that lands in the wall film, rather than going directly into the cylinder on each shot, which largely changes with temperature for a given injector spray pattern. The "Tau" is the time constant for evaporation, which is again a function of temperature but also airflow and local pressure.

This is what the port-mounted injector sees as it attempts to deliver fuel to the cylinder. Each of these surfaces can temporarily hold a small amount of fuel on its way toward the combustion chamber.

Still others hover in between the two, with layers added on over the years to give the calibrators just enough flexibility to make it work. As one of the guys who had to work on them, I can appreciate the physics-based approach for its ease of calibration with predictable response, but we often to have to work with what we are given.

Any meaningful hardware change to the engine often affects the transient fuel controls. This means that if drive quality and/or emissions are on the list of goals for engine operation, these transient fuel control tables will probably need to be recalibrated to match the new hardware's needs.

The best way to actually calibrate transient fuel addition models is to perform a simple step test. The top graph on the next page shows a throttle input step (blue line at top) where the engine begins at a light load and throttle angle is quickly moved up toward WOT. The engine should be at a stable λ=1.0 (orange "wideband" line on strip chart) condition prior to the step and it should track the commanded EQ ratio (light blue "EQ Cmd" line) as it transitions from λ=1.0 down to its final power enrichment of about λ=0.86 at full load.

These two conditions demonstrate good base airflow mapping accuracy and allow the calibrator to concentrate on what happens between them. The "Lambda Err" calculated value (white line) shows the instantaneous difference between the two.

Any deviation in the middle of the step event can now be attributed to either too much or too little compensation for wall-film effects as fuel is stripped away from the port walls as airflow increases. Transient fuel models help reestablish the wall film and make sure that the total fuel delivered to the cylinder remains balanced with the incoming air charge all through the event and afterward.

The typical modern multi-port injected engine may have an "X" value of as much as 15 percent of the fuel being added to the incoming air charge from the wall film on a fully warmed-up engine. Cold engines with more fuel condensation on the ports may easily have triple this amount.

Changing the injector flow rate, spray pattern, or targeting can have a profound impact on this balance as well. If one

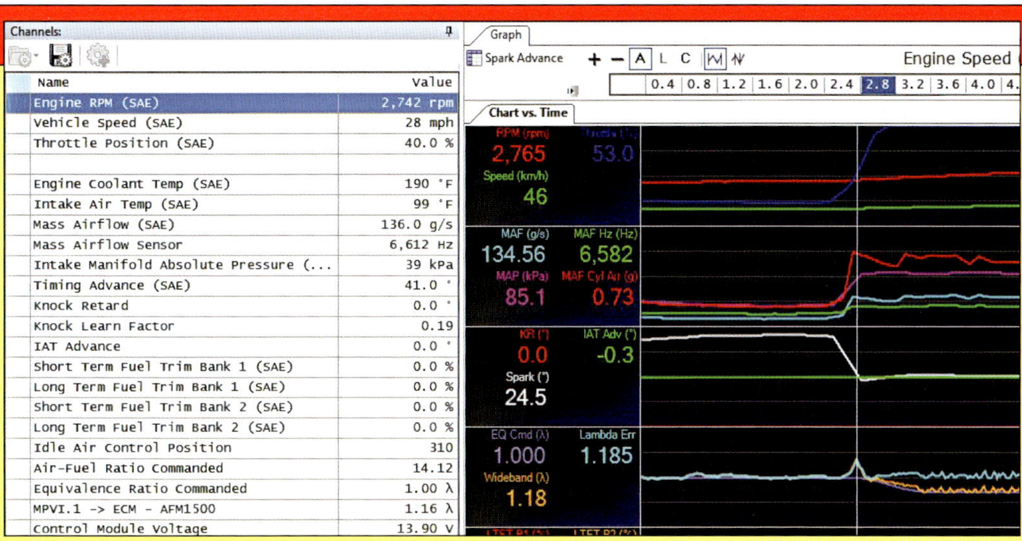

The spike of lean fuel delivery during the tip-in event can be fixed with transient fuel calibration. This engine tracked well to commanded fueling both before and after the throttle change, it just needs more help as the wall-film contribution is changing.

changes from a narrow-to a wide-spray-pattern injector, it can be expected that the X component or wall impact factor will need to be significantly raised to compensate, even though almost none of this shows up in steady-state measurements or typical WOT dyno runs.

If the airflow side of the intake system changes significantly, it may either aid or hamper the rate at which fuel is stripped from the port walls during transients. Changes (such as new intake manifold geometry, port cross-sectional area, or camshaft duration) that may affect port velocity can contribute to a change in the evaporation rate of fuel from the port walls.

The only way to know for sure which way all of these factors stack up to shift things is to test. In some cases, positive change may be found at one engine speed or load and a negative change at another relative to the baseline values. Again, test, test, test, and then recalibrate based on data.

In steady-state conditions, the amount of fuel trapped in the wall film will reach equilibrium with the amount evaporating, but during transients the amount contributed to total cylinder fueling is heavily impacted by this film or puddle. Modified engines with new injectors or radically different airflow characteristics often require these tables to be modified to bring transient fueling back on target. In cases where both injector targeting and intake airflow have been altered, expect multiple changes to the transient fueling model.

One general tip is that most immediate fueling errors are usually based on the "X" or impact factor, where lingering smaller errors are often the result of evaporative errors over time. Start with global changes to the entire wall-film model rather than one cell at a time since most OEM tables are already shaped to follow the general trend of what the engine needs. It is ultimately up to the calibrator to experiment with both impact- and evaporation-based tables to deliver a consistent delivered lambda as a result of the various compensation tables.

Once the step test can be passed at one temperature and amount of change, the test can then be repeated for various engine speeds and loads. I often find that the global changes to the wall-film model from a single-step test take care of most changes that would be required here.

If conditions still deviate too far from the desired air-fuel target during a transient, you can now start making changes to specific rows/columns or cells of the transient model with the confidence that the nominal condition has already been optimized. Repeat as needed until you find it difficult to get any significant lambda error during step transients. At this point, you should be ready to attempt a drive cycle–based emissions test. ■

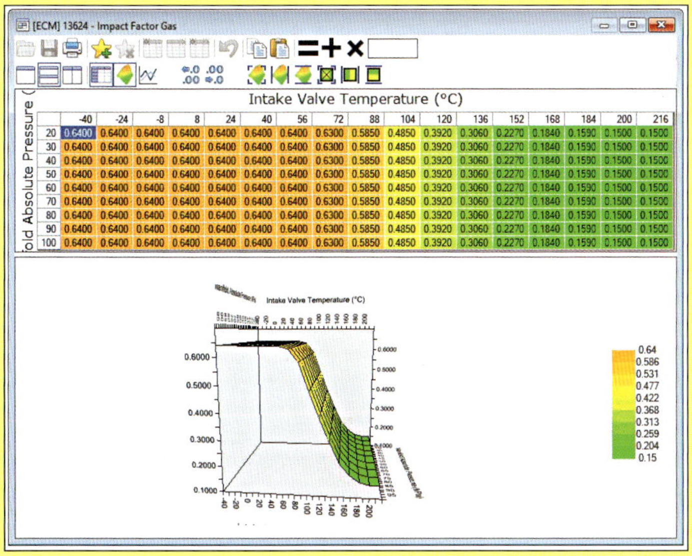

The ECU model of the wall-film contribution versus intake-valve temperature closely mirrors the fuel-distillation curve shown earlier. These values are heavily dependent on injector spray pattern and targeting.

fuel correction for simple step inputs. This can be changing throttle from a steady 20 percent to a steady 40 percent in a single event. Using this one directional change, it becomes easier to calibrate transient fueling and wall-film models for any hardware changes.

Things such as injector spray pattern or intake port geometry have the largest impact here rather than the steady-state testing that would have been previously performed. If the spray pattern has significantly more fuel impinging on the port walls, it would have eventually reached an equilibrium state of deposition and evaporation during the steady-state test. So, the eventual fuel delivery to the cylinder would be the same as that leaving the injector.

But in the case of the step transient, we now see the effect of running some of that through the puddle on the port wall and must make corrections so that the delivered lambda does not change too much during the step event. This data is used to correct the transient fuel models until step inputs can be done at various speeds and loads with minimal disturbance to measured lambda.

If the engine is able to consistently feed an exhaust mixture near lambda=1.0 to the catalyst whether at steady state or during transients, the tailpipe emissions numbers will be generally good. Most emissions concerns can be root caused to cases where these basic functions are not keeping the engine operating at stoichiometry as the vehicle is driven.

Once we have an engine that can stay near stoichiometry on its own in open loop, closed-loop feedback from the upstream oxygen sensors can be enabled. At this point, the closed-loop corrections should be rather small. Ideally, fuel trims should be less than 5 percent everywhere.

In practice, many OEM applications have significantly higher variability. This is largely due to build tolerances across an enormous fleet of engines, fuel injectors, and sensors that all have their own variability. Random production vehicles with fuel trims inside of 10 percent either direction are generally considered good by OEM calibration teams.

Now, I did say, "almost always operate near stoichiometry" for a reason. Whenever the engine transitions from normal operation to fuel shutoff (which is common during deceleration or stop-start events), we inevitably have some lean operation in that transition. This lean period creates some NO_x, which is hopefully stored in the catalyst to be later balanced by an intentional rich offset that feeds some carbon monoxide to the catalyst. Provided the catalyst is at a good working temperature and condition, the NO_x and carbon monoxide react to break back down to raw nitrogen (N_2), CO_2, and water.

In a similar fashion, engines often require a little bit of extra fuel to assist the starting process as they transition from cranking to normal running. This effect is exaggerated at lower temperatures. For this reason, factory calibrations add significant amounts of fuel at startup and low temperatures. This additional fuel is the primary source for most emissions accumulated during testing and when the vehicle is operated on the road. OEM engineers spend countless hours determining just how much extra fuel is to be delivered here to provide good starting quality on a wide range of fuels while still avoiding the creation of excess carbon monoxide and NMOG emissions on startup.

When attempting to optimize an aftermarket calibration for new engine hardware, startup fueling should also be of key importance before showing up to the emissions lab for testing. While the factory enrichment functions are a great starting point, we have a couple of advantages in the performance

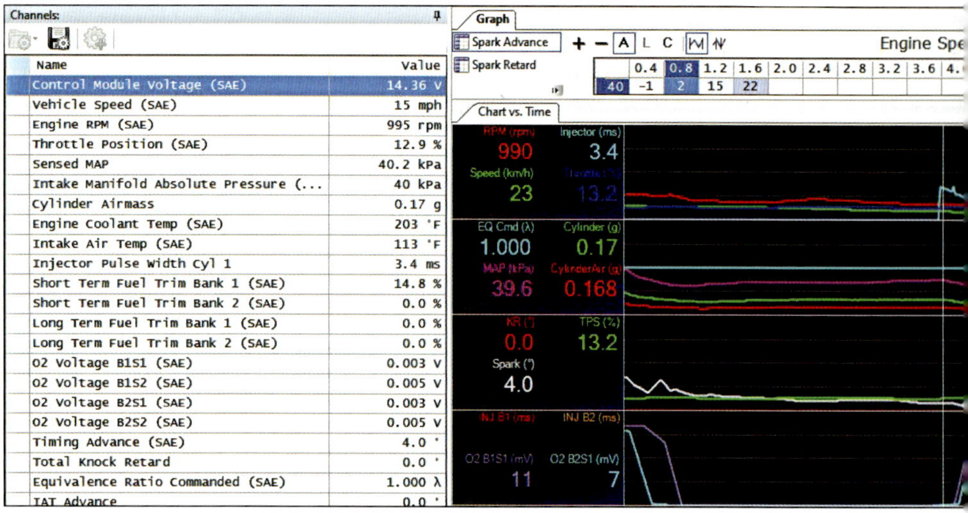

The catalyst gets saturated with oxygen during an extended fuel shutoff event on deceleration. To offset this, the ECU will add a little more fuel during the initial tip-in event (white line at top) to help balance the tailpipe emissions before settling into the normal pulse width required for stoichiometry.

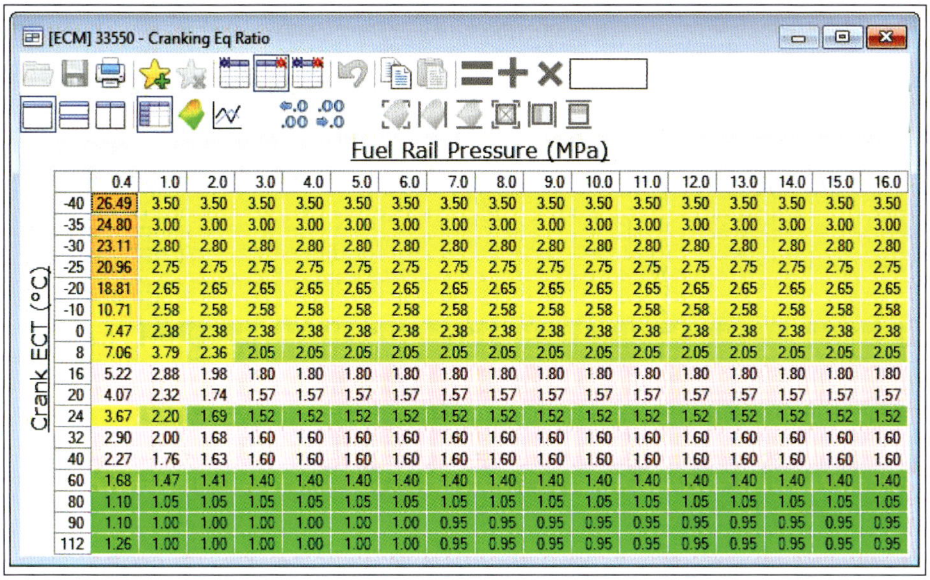

[ECM] 33550 - Cranking Eq Ratio

Fuel Rail Pressure (MPa)

Crank ECT (°C)	0.4	1.0	2.0	3.0	4.0	5.0	6.0	7.0	8.0	9.0	10.0	11.0	12.0	13.0	14.0	15.0	16.0
-40	26.49	3.50	3.50	3.50	3.50	3.50	3.50	3.50	3.50	3.50	3.50	3.50	3.50	3.50	3.50	3.50	3.50
-35	24.80	3.00	3.00	3.00	3.00	3.00	3.00	3.00	3.00	3.00	3.00	3.00	3.00	3.00	3.00	3.00	3.00
-30	23.11	2.80	2.80	2.80	2.80	2.80	2.80	2.80	2.80	2.80	2.80	2.80	2.80	2.80	2.80	2.80	2.80
-25	20.96	2.75	2.75	2.75	2.75	2.75	2.75	2.75	2.75	2.75	2.75	2.75	2.75	2.75	2.75	2.75	2.75
-20	18.81	2.65	2.65	2.65	2.65	2.65	2.65	2.65	2.65	2.65	2.65	2.65	2.65	2.65	2.65	2.65	2.65
-10	10.71	2.58	2.58	2.58	2.58	2.58	2.58	2.58	2.58	2.58	2.58	2.58	2.58	2.58	2.58	2.58	2.58
0	7.47	2.38	2.38	2.38	2.38	2.38	2.38	2.38	2.38	2.38	2.38	2.38	2.38	2.38	2.38	2.38	2.38
8	7.06	3.79	2.36	2.05	2.05	2.05	2.05	2.05	2.05	2.05	2.05	2.05	2.05	2.05	2.05	2.05	2.05
16	5.22	2.88	1.98	1.80	1.80	1.80	1.80	1.80	1.80	1.80	1.80	1.80	1.80	1.80	1.80	1.80	1.80
20	4.07	2.32	1.74	1.57	1.57	1.57	1.57	1.57	1.57	1.57	1.57	1.57	1.57	1.57	1.57	1.57	1.57
24	3.67	2.20	1.69	1.52	1.52	1.52	1.52	1.52	1.52	1.52	1.52	1.52	1.52	1.52	1.52	1.52	1.52
32	2.90	2.00	1.68	1.60	1.60	1.60	1.60	1.60	1.60	1.60	1.60	1.60	1.60	1.60	1.60	1.60	1.60
40	2.27	1.76	1.63	1.60	1.60	1.60	1.60	1.60	1.60	1.60	1.60	1.60	1.60	1.60	1.60	1.60	1.60
60	1.68	1.47	1.41	1.40	1.40	1.40	1.40	1.40	1.40	1.40	1.40	1.40	1.40	1.40	1.40	1.40	1.40
80	1.10	1.05	1.05	1.05	1.05	1.05	1.05	1.05	1.05	1.05	1.05	1.05	1.05	1.05	1.05	1.05	1.05
90	1.10	1.00	1.00	1.00	1.00	1.00	1.00	0.95	0.95	0.95	0.95	0.95	0.95	0.95	0.95	0.95	0.95
112	1.26	1.00	1.00	1.00	1.00	1.00	1.00	0.95	0.95	0.95	0.95	0.95	0.95	0.95	0.95	0.95	0.95

Just a 2-percent change to the pink highlighted cells was enough to move this vehicle from failing emissions to passing. Precision is required here, and the resulting table should still be smooth in shape to pass any scrutiny from regulatory inspectors.

aftermarket. The biggest of these is that the high-performance engine packages are often only rated for higher-octane fuel. So, if the vehicle was originally calibrated for regular-grade gas, chances are good that there is more startup enrichment than we may need when we don't need to protect for some of the worst-case fuels out there.

The OEM engineers had to play a delicate balance between NMOG and carbon monoxide emissions and a potential no-start condition when starting with bad fuel. Nothing is worse for NMOG emissions than a failed start that dumps raw fuel out the exhaust and blows the test completely.

Customer satisfaction based on crank time and engine speed run-up smoothness are also negatively impacted if there is not sufficient evaporated fuel ready for combustion. Leaning out the fuel tables associated with this function can be a great way to improve emissions during the critical first 20 seconds of run time. Just avoid getting too greedy with it. Otherwise, it will have the same issues the factory guys had with low-quality fuels.

Be sure to check with both summer and winter blends of pump gas if working on something that will be driven year-round. Winter fuels have a significantly higher vapor pressure and evaporate more quickly at the same temperature than summer blends. Ideally, the vehicle should work with either fuel in either season without noticeable issues to the casual driver.

Catalyst Lightoff

While we're on the topic of starts, it's time to discuss one of the most critical emissions functions in modern ECUs. The catalytic converter is a wonderful device that has an almost magical effect of cleaning up tailpipe emissions compared to the raw engine-out readings. To do this, it must be at a very hot temperature.

As shown earlier, catalyst efficiency is a function of temperature.

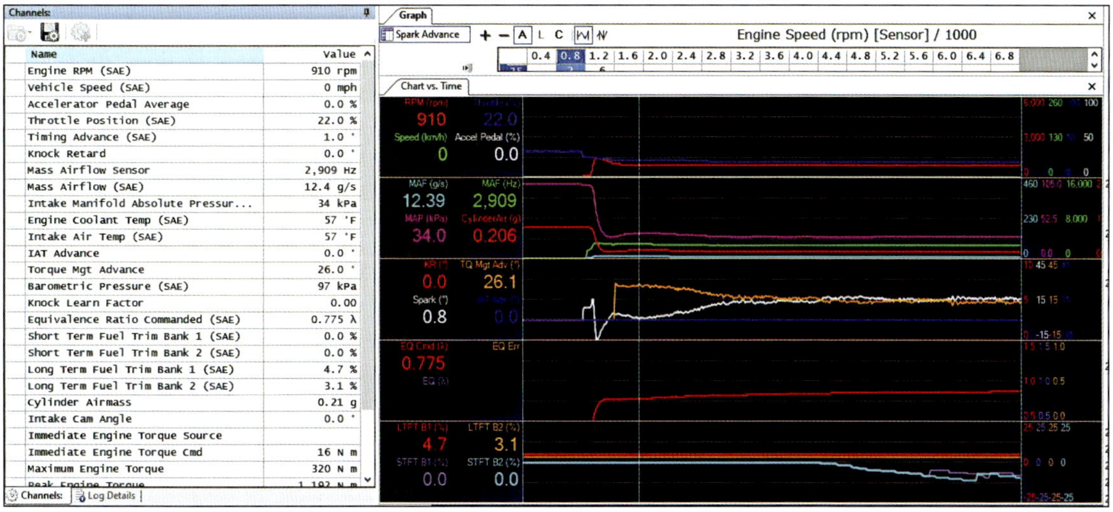

Immediately after startup, spark advance (white line on center strip chart) is significantly retarded to help raise exhaust temperatures quickly. This truck normally idles with around 17 degrees of advance, but it runs close to 0 degrees initially.

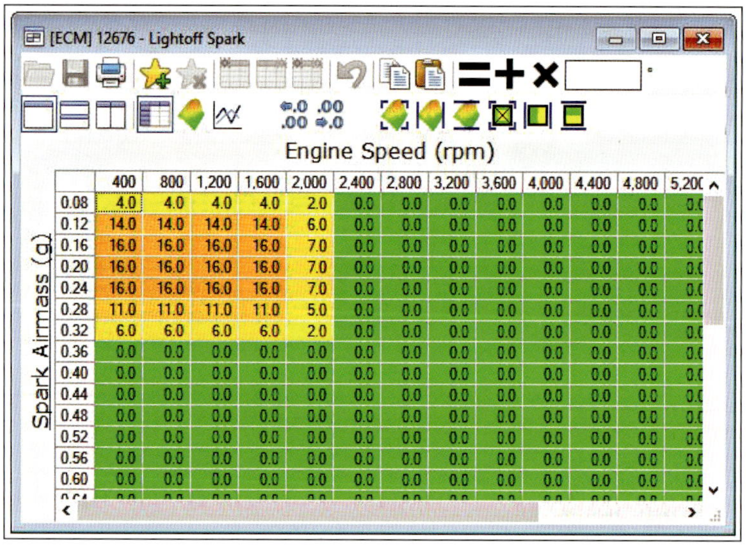

[ECM] 12676 - Lightoff Spark

Engine Speed (rpm) / Spark Airmass (g)

	400	800	1,200	1,600	2,000	2,400	2,800	3,200	3,600	4,000	4,400	4,800	5,200
0.08	4.0	4.0	4.0	4.0	2.0	0.0	0.0	0.0	0.0	0.0	0.0	0.0	0.0
0.12	14.0	14.0	14.0	14.0	6.0	0.0	0.0	0.0	0.0	0.0	0.0	0.0	0.0
0.16	16.0	16.0	16.0	16.0	7.0	0.0	0.0	0.0	0.0	0.0	0.0	0.0	0.0
0.20	16.0	16.0	16.0	16.0	7.0	0.0	0.0	0.0	0.0	0.0	0.0	0.0	0.0
0.24	16.0	16.0	16.0	16.0	7.0	0.0	0.0	0.0	0.0	0.0	0.0	0.0	0.0
0.28	11.0	11.0	11.0	11.0	5.0	0.0	0.0	0.0	0.0	0.0	0.0	0.0	0.0
0.32	6.0	6.0	6.0	6.0	2.0	0.0	0.0	0.0	0.0	0.0	0.0	0.0	0.0
0.36	0.0	0.0	0.0	0.0	0.0	0.0	0.0	0.0	0.0	0.0	0.0	0.0	0.0
0.40	0.0	0.0	0.0	0.0	0.0	0.0	0.0	0.0	0.0	0.0	0.0	0.0	0.0
0.44	0.0	0.0	0.0	0.0	0.0	0.0	0.0	0.0	0.0	0.0	0.0	0.0	0.0
0.48	0.0	0.0	0.0	0.0	0.0	0.0	0.0	0.0	0.0	0.0	0.0	0.0	0.0
0.52	0.0	0.0	0.0	0.0	0.0	0.0	0.0	0.0	0.0	0.0	0.0	0.0	0.0
0.56	0.0	0.0	0.0	0.0	0.0	0.0	0.0	0.0	0.0	0.0	0.0	0.0	0.0
0.60	0.0	0.0	0.0	0.0	0.0	0.0	0.0	0.0	0.0	0.0	0.0	0.0	0.0

While running this much spark retard shortly after startup may make the engine run noticeably rougher, it can have a huge impact on catalyst heating and total emissions. Zeroing out this table may feel better, but it certainly won't help cold-start emissions.

Starting with effectively zero conversion at room temperature, as the catalyst approaches about 450°C, it begins to exhibit a tremendously high conversion efficiency for hydrocarbons, CO, and NO_x when those elements are fed to the catalyst in relatively equal amounts over time. This conversion creates a good deal of heat because it is effectively combustion. This heat release helps keep the brick at a good conversion temperature once it has been reached, but getting there from a cold start takes some work.

The older emissions standards were loose enough that many vehicles passed by letting the catalyst passively warm up from whatever exhaust gas was fed to it over time. As vehicle emissions limits became tighter, it also became obvious that something had to be done to reduce the large amounts of tailpipe emissions that were being generated in the time between engine start and when the catalyst finally got to a good working temperature.

Calibration engineers began to employ strategies that would reduce the time needed to bring the brick up to temperature. If the conversion efficiency can be increased sooner, it follows that tailpipe emissions during this time can be greatly reduced. Strategies were implemented that may have what some customers call poor running characteristics that are actually quite effective at increasing the rate at which the catalyst temperature rises.

These strategies intentionally trade either fuel efficiency or noise and vibration during the first few moments after a cold start for a dramatic improvement in emissions over the whole driving cycle. When this happens, the engine is not running poorly; it is doing exactly what it is supposed to do.

The first strategy used is ignition timing. Normally, ignition timing is selected to match maximum brake torque timing (MBT) for whatever engine speed, cylinder load, and charge temperature is present. This results in the best mechanical efficiency between combustion pressure and crankshaft torque.

At high load, we are often knock limited and forced to run lower ignition timing in an effort to avoid knock and potential engine damage. Whenever we do this, we typically see an increase in exhaust-gas temperatures. The temperatures rise in this case because the combustion event was started so late that it cannot complete during the power stroke. This leaves a notable amount of combustion heat being generated as the gases are exiting the cylinder into the exhaust port on their way to the catalyst. Further, heat that would otherwise be absorbed by the water-cooled cylinder liners is also pumped out the exhaust port.

Having recognized this, calibration engineers applied the concept to cold-start operation, where they were looking for a way to increase temperatures. So, catalyst lightoff spark retard was born. Tables were added to the ECU that allow the calibrator to intentionally retard the timing after start based on engine temperature. The assumption here is that if the engine is starting from ambient temperature, the catalyst is probably also cooled off and would benefit from some additional heating to reach a higher conversion efficiency sooner. These tables may be layered with multipliers or decay values to help them taper away smoothly as temperatures rise to normal for the catalyst.

A decision must then be made by the calibrator as to just how much catalyst heating spark retard is to be used. It becomes a delicate balance between adding heat to the exhaust and increasing engine roughness. The more spark is retarded, the more inconsistent the combustion events become.

In the extreme case, misfire results can be more detrimental to emissions than a longer lightoff time for the catalyst. Keep in mind that misfires on a cold engine and catalyst result in unfiltered loss of unburned hydrocarbons going right out the exhaust because there is not yet any meaningful secondary reaction hap-

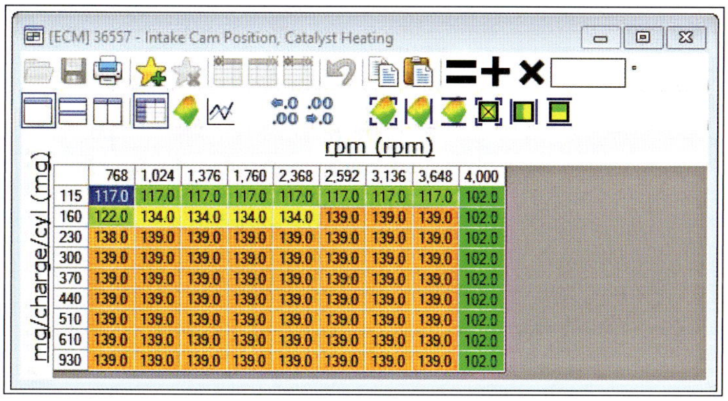

[ECM] 36557 - Intake Cam Position, Catalyst Heating

rpm (rpm)

mg/charge/cyl (mg)	768	1,024	1,376	1,760	2,368	2,592	3,136	3,648	4,000
115	117.0	117.0	117.0	117.0	117.0	117.0	117.0	117.0	102.0
160	122.0	134.0	134.0	134.0	134.0	139.0	139.0	139.0	102.0
230	138.0	139.0	139.0	139.0	139.0	139.0	139.0	139.0	102.0
300	139.0	139.0	139.0	139.0	139.0	139.0	139.0	139.0	102.0
370	139.0	139.0	139.0	139.0	139.0	139.0	139.0	139.0	102.0
440	139.0	139.0	139.0	139.0	139.0	139.0	139.0	139.0	102.0
510	139.0	139.0	139.0	139.0	139.0	139.0	139.0	139.0	102.0
610	139.0	139.0	139.0	139.0	139.0	139.0	139.0	139.0	102.0
930	139.0	139.0	139.0	139.0	139.0	139.0	139.0	139.0	102.0

Some ECUs employ specific cam-angle strategies during catalyst heating. These values are used briefly after a cold start and then phased back toward a different normal-cam-angle target table as the engine warms up.

pening in the catalyst to help clean it up. Just a few misfires on cold start can blow the entire amount of allowable emissions for the whole test in the first few seconds. Add to that, limits for NVH based on quality metrics, and it becomes a tricky tradeoff in many cases.

I have seen a lot of aftermarket tuners simply zero out these cold-start spark-retard tables to improve idle quality or just simplify the calibration. In today's emissions-conscious world of high performance, this no longer has a place.

The factory cat heating spark functions are actually a great starting point, even for heavily modified engines. If the vehicle has a catalyst, you might as well make it work as soon as possible. Some trimming may be necessary to avoid misfire where cam overlap has increased, but one should always strive to use this function as intended to make sure the warmup profile is good.

Cam timing is another variable that modern engines can use to help shorten the time needed to bring up the catalyst efficiency. During normal engine operation, variable camshaft phasing is often used to either reduce pumping losses, improve scavenging of exhaust gases at high load, or improve volumetric efficiency through better intake filling.

During a cold-start event, our priorities are different. By advancing the exhaust valve opening event into the tail end of the power stroke, calibrators can once again allow still-burning mixtures to exit the cylinder and head toward the catalyst. This takes some of the power away from that stroke, as pressure pushing on the piston drops very quickly once the exhaust valve opens.

Another trade-off is created between pushing on the piston and heating the catalyst, but this can be mitigated by adding more total air and fuel charge to the cylinder. Increasing the idle airflow brings the magnitude of potential torque up, knowing that some fraction of that will be lost to the intentional early blowdown as the exhaust valve opens.

In an aftermarket application without a variable camshaft phasing system, this may still be a consideration factor for manufacturers who are looking to pass emissions with their product. Keep in mind that as engine speeds rise, the ideal phasing may change. So, picking a cam phasing that assists in catalyst warmup at idle may not necessarily hurt top-end power as much as one would think in some applications. To be more blunt, if the product is not able to pass emissions going forward, it may end up with no place in the market anyway, as enforcement actions continue to tighten.

Minimizing Emissions After Warmup

If the vehicle made it past the initial warmup phase on the engine without blowing right past the allowable emissions limits for the test, the remainder should be much easier. While the back end of the test can't necessarily be used to fix an early failure, there can still be issues later that could ruin an otherwise clean run. The key here is to stick to the basics.

Once the catalytic convertor is up to a good working temperature, it becomes a great "cleanup tool" for small deviations from the target balance of lambda=1.0. Remember that the whole way a catalytic convertor works is by combining small amounts of one bad thing with small amounts of another to react and only have CO_2 and water going out the tailpipe.

In normal closed-loop operation, the ECU logic uses feedback from the oxygen sensors to constantly toggle engine fueling rather tightly on either side of the stoichiometric mixture. This quick and shallow switching provides the catalyst with a steady but small stream of both carbon monoxide and NO_x that keeps it heated with continuous reactions inside. The trick is to avoid overloading the incoming stream of exhaust gases to the catalyst with too much of either.

During transients, or poorly controlled steady-state operation, we have the potential to bias either one way or the other and saturate the catalyst with more carbon monoxide (rich) or NO_x (lean) than it can react with the current amount of stored material. In these cases, we get breakthrough of the offending constituent and ratchet up the tailpipe count for emissions.

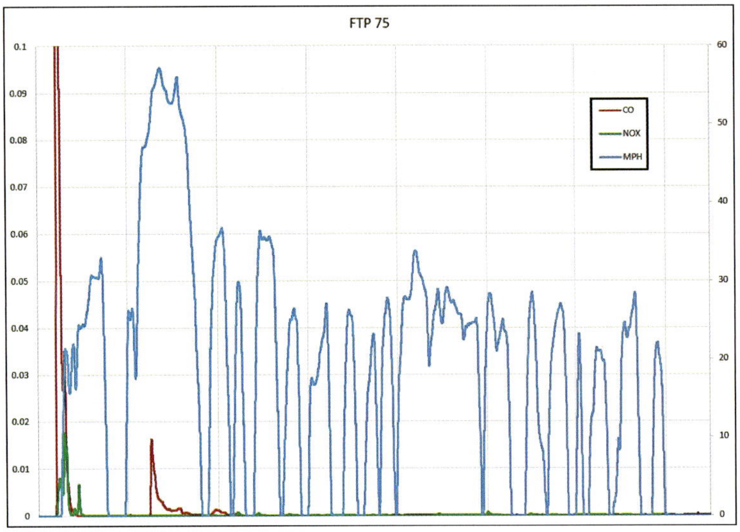

Most tailpipe emissions slip past the cold catalyst in the first couple hills of the FTP-75. After that, we barely see much tailpipe activity as long as the engine stays close to lambda=1.0 and the catalyst is at a good working temperature.

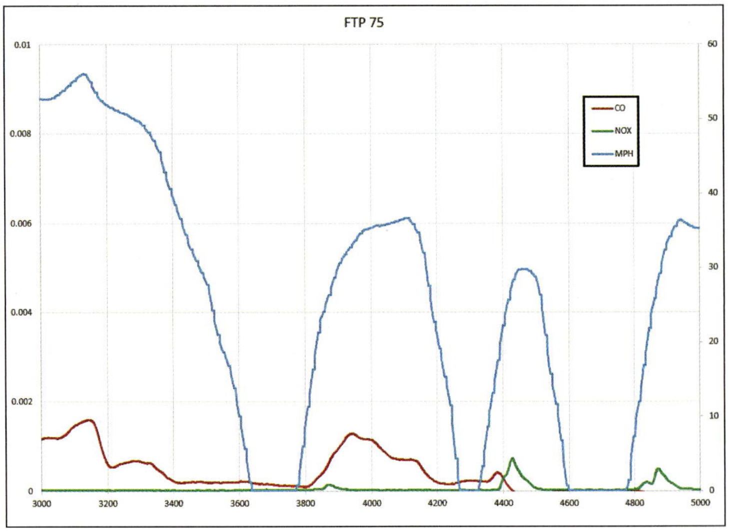

Zooming in on the same FTP test, we can see events where there were NO_x and carbon monoxide breakthroughs measured by the emissions bench. These likely correlate with points where the delivered fueling varied from the stoichiometric target.

The best way to prevent these breakthrough events is to eliminate them at the source. This means always making sure the engine is operating very close to the stoichiometric air-fuel ratio so that there is a minimum of cleanup needed at the catalyst. This is easier said than done in many cases.

Keeping the engine lined up with lambda=1.0 fueling in steady state should be easy, but it doesn't always happen. If the closed-loop trims keep walking to numbers larger than 10 percent or so, it's a good indication that the base engine calibration needs work.

If the reference fuel and airflow calibrations are correct, one should not see significant adjustments in learned fuel trims. This all starts with good injector data and accurate modeling of the MAF curve and/or volumetric efficiency model. If the engine is relying on large fuel trims to get back to a balanced mixture, then either the base calibration was off or the closed-loop trims are being generated by poor feedback from bad oxygen sensors or a bad location for them. This should all be addressed prior to going any further in emissions development.

Once the steady-state fueling is in line, transients can be investigated to reduce the amounts of accumulated emissions from each event. While they may look like small events, they add up over the course of the emissions test and can be enough to fail when working toward today's extremely tight emissions standards.

In a perfect world, an engine experiencing a part-throttle tip-in event that does not go to WOT should see a delivered lambda=1.0 measurement before, during, and after the event. How far it deviates from this largely determines the emissions generated.

With too little transient fuel compensation, the engine may hesitate from the loss of torque associated with a leaner mixture, but it also creates more oxides of nitrogen. Adding transient fuel delivery often fixes both the drivability and the emissions problems simultaneously. The key here is to only add this fuel in the transient model and not in the base airflow model.

Transient fuel corrections should not be done by increasing the VE table or the MAF curve values at all. Depending on the logic structure of the ECU, there may be something as simple as "acceleration enrichment" or a full physics-based wall-film model that controls the additional fuel delivery. "Additional" is the active word here, as the base fuel delivery is already being handled by the normal airflow model, and this transient model adds to whatever that base was. This is why it's so important to have an accurate base fuel and airflow model before beginning so that there is less math left to be figured out during transients.

If the tuner simply adds to the VE in these cases, he or she will end up with a telltale "blister" in the VE surface right where most tip-in events happen. This can be seen in a

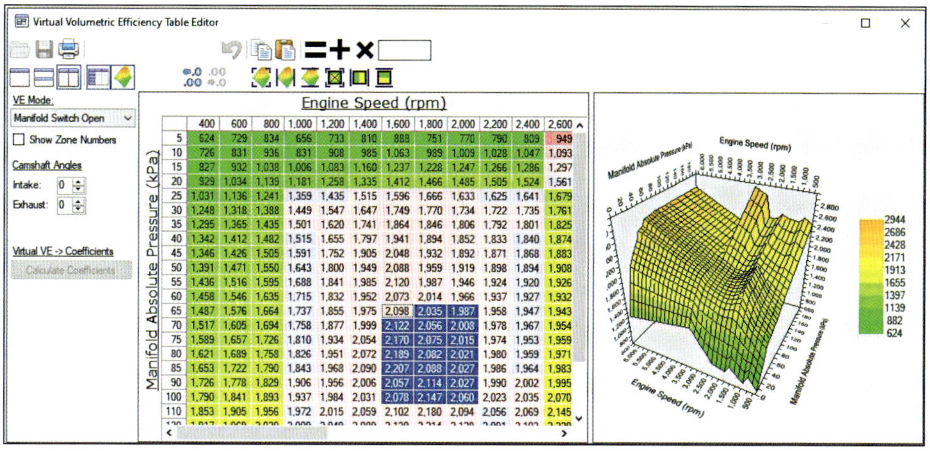

A common calibration error for less experienced tuners is to "bake in" the correction for poor transient fuel compensation into the base VE model. Although the engine may have been lean here in the data log, the root cause was not steady-state cylinder filling.

three-dimensional view of the table where the otherwise-smooth progression is interrupted between 1,200 and 2,000 rpm below 80 kPa.

The problem with this blister is that when the vehicle is operated steadily in that same region, a rich condition occurs that would require the learned oxygen sensor trims to dial out the extra fuel. This learned trim is then remembered next time the engine goes to this same condition on tip-in, and we have a circular problem of fueling accuracy where it is lean again.

I know I sound like a broken record here, but the only robust fix is to make sure that steady-state fueling is on target with base tables and that transient controls are used to add just enough extra fuel to stay on target during changing conditions.

So, if adding fuel fixes the drivability concern and avoids a generation of NO_x emissions, why not err on the rich side during most events? From a drive quality standpoint, the slightly rich condition is indeed the winner most of the time. But once we factor in emissions (and fuel economy), all those little rich excursions add up and bite us.

Every time the engine goes rich of stoichiometry, carbon monoxide emissions rise sharply. Along with increased CO, we can also see larger amounts of unburned fuel in the exhaust as well. The unburned hydrocarbons show up in the HC trace for older standards or NMOG in the current standard, which are effectively similar when it comes to calibration work. Once again, the solution is to keep the engine as close to the stoichiometric balance of lambda=1.0 as much as possible to reduce the intensity and frequency of these events.

While allowing delivered lambda to dip down to 0.92 or richer on tip-in may feel great to the driver, it just won't cut it here. In a perfect world, transient events should have no more than the usual 2 to 3 percent closed-loop variation that we see driving in steady state. Short excursions to 0.95 are not awful but should be limited to very brief duration since the total tailpipe emissions count is a function of both richness and exhaust flow.

By being only slightly rich for a very short amount of time, a minimum of rich flow is passed to the catalyst that can hopefully all be stored for subsequent reaction before going out the tailpipe. Breakthrough events can be mitigated by both intensity and duration limits to transient fuel addition.

Oxides of Nitrogen

If we have a tailpipe NO_x measurement, we may also see spikes in that particular emission that should be addressed. An NO_x measurement

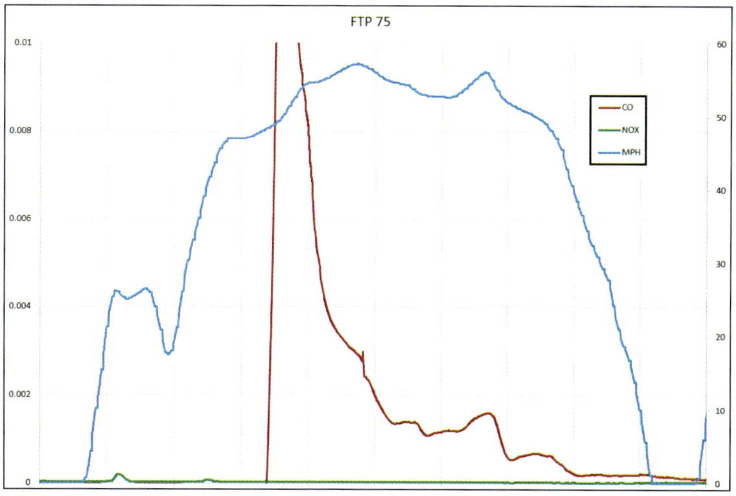

This carbon monoxide spike during hill number-2 of the FTP 75 was caused by a rich condition during the acceleration event. There can be a slight delay between when the event actually happened and when the gas bench records the measurement.

may be obtained from either a PEMS, five gas, or an emissions bench modal port.

NO_x can be generated even at lambda=1.00, but it can be more difficult to identify and reduce. Gasoline engine controls do not currently use NO_x sensors, so there is no direct feedback that such emissions are occurring (as may be seen on some diesel controllers). Instead, the factory ECU assumes that NO_x emissions must be within allowable limits by confirming that lambda controls, EGR, and variable-cam-position systems are all in good working order.

Since EGR and cam phasing have such a large impact on combustion temperature, they are the secondary methods to control the production of NO_x emissions. Assuming the unmodified vehicle is operating in the same conditions as it was submitted for emissions testing from the manufacturer, the absence of any faults here make the argument for a likely clean tailpipe NO_x number.

For aftermarket recalibrations, we see EGR valves and variable cams as tools that can be used to improve emissions. Generally speaking, anything that reduces flame temperature inside the cylinder helps to also reduce formation of NO_x emissions. Introducing more exhaust gas into the cylinder accomplishes this by slowing the burn rate and absorbing some amount of heat during combustion.

While exhaust gases may seem hot at first, making this counterintuitive, they are actually much cooler than the flame temperature. Because the inert exhaust gases have mass, they are able to absorb heat from subsequent combustion events that are a higher temperature. By keeping the flame and post-combustion in-cylinder temperatures below the threshold that breaks the nitrogen bonds, less NO_x is formed.

Adding cooled EGR is one of the most effective methods of reducing NO_x emissions. Adding the cooling to the recirculated gases greatly increases the amount that can be introduced to the engine before combustion quality suffers.

The good news is that the flame and cylinder don't really care how those exhaust gases got into the chamber. Residual gases left in the cylinder from poor scavenging, reversion of exhaust gases up the intake port during overlap, or external EGR valves that introduce spent gases into the incoming charge all have the same net effect. They all dilute the final combination of gases present immediately prior to combustion with some amount of inert exhaust. Granted, they have different magnitudes of effect and are dependent on different conditions, but they can all be used to the same final effect.

The key limiting factor to how much EGR can be introduced to an engine is roughness and potential for misfire. As previously mentioned, diluting the incoming air and fuel charge with spent gases that slow combustion reduces temperature. With too much of this, the flame has trouble cleanly traveling from the kernel near the spark plug all the way across the chamber to an even wall quench. Disturbances in flame travel can lead to irregular generation of pressure, which is felt as uneven application of torque to the crankshaft.

Engineers measure engine roughness by looking at the statistical covariance of the indicated mean effective pressure (CoV of IMEP). This number represents how much the measured cylinder pressure is jumping around relative to the average. Measuring the IMEP requires in-cylinder pressure measurements that have to be taken with special transducers that go into new holes drilled through the cylinder head to the chamber from the outside. The cost of these probes and their necessary electronics make their use mostly prohibitive for the casual engine tuner.

For them, a well-trained "butt meter" is usually the indicator of how rough is too rough. The scientist in me hates that we don't get a good measurement with a real number, but it is what it is when resources are limited.

Some modified spark plugs are available that include pressure

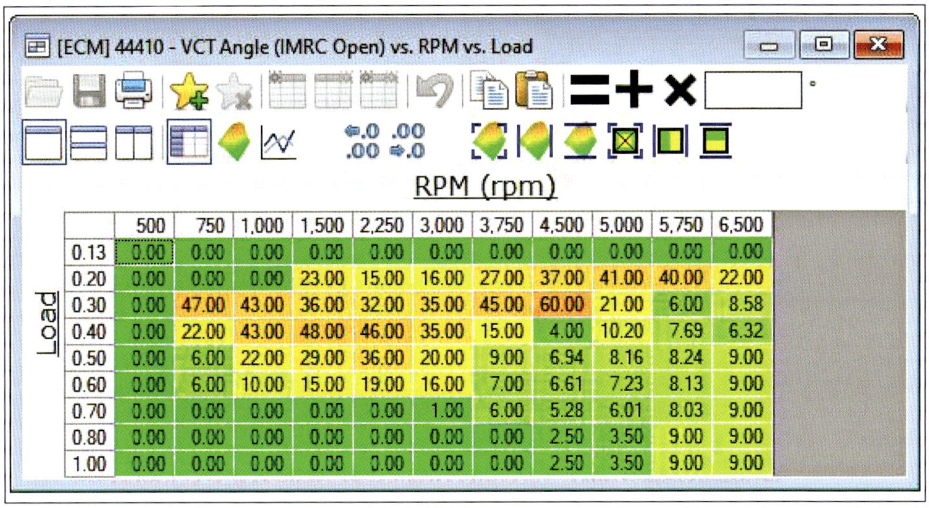

Load \ RPM	500	750	1,000	1,500	2,250	3,000	3,750	4,500	5,000	5,750	6,500
0.13	0.00	0.00	0.00	0.00	0.00	0.00	0.00	0.00	0.00	0.00	0.00
0.20	0.00	0.00	0.00	23.00	15.00	16.00	27.00	37.00	41.00	40.00	22.00
0.30	0.00	47.00	43.00	36.00	32.00	35.00	45.00	60.00	21.00	6.00	8.58
0.40	0.00	22.00	43.00	48.00	46.00	35.00	15.00	4.00	10.20	7.69	6.32
0.50	0.00	6.00	22.00	29.00	36.00	20.00	9.00	6.94	8.16	8.24	9.00
0.60	0.00	6.00	10.00	15.00	19.00	16.00	7.00	6.61	7.23	8.13	9.00
0.70	0.00	0.00	0.00	0.00	0.00	1.00	6.00	5.28	6.01	8.03	9.00
0.80	0.00	0.00	0.00	0.00	0.00	0.00	0.00	2.50	3.50	9.00	9.00
1.00	0.00	0.00	0.00	0.00	0.00	0.00	0.00	2.50	3.50	9.00	9.00

The amount of allowed cam retard on this 4.6L 3V Ford engine was limited by roughness requirements. Further increasing the values a bit around 30-percent load would yield slightly better fuel economy but at an engine roughness amount that was deemed unacceptable for quality.

transducers. These integrated pressure-sensor plugs are expensive. Their accuracy does not match dedicated probes, and they often change the heat performance of the electrode, which may alter combustion compared to the normal spark plug for that application. They can be used, but take the data with a grain of salt.

Since the cylinder pressure jumps are usually negative in this case, deviations are felt and measured as losses of torque followed by a return to the normal value. A CoV of IMEP value of 3.0 or greater risks having customer complaints on most OEM applications.

The aftermarket has a notably higher tolerance for engine roughness, so some degradation in the name of performance, fuel economy, or bringing a high-performance application into emissions compliance is often acceptable. This means that dialing in a little extra EGR either directly through a valve or by changing cam timing can be used to tame the emissions of an otherwise-borderline vehicle. An added side benefit is that more EGR at part throttle often yields an improvement in fuel economy as well. I have yet to have a client complain about improved fuel economy after calibration.

Final Cleanup and Spotting the Problems

By this point, both base calibration and simple transients have been addressed by either steady-state or step-change testing. Getting to the point where one has confidence in tailpipe emissions now comes down to looking for deviations from the norm.

Minimizing NMOG, CO, and NO_x emissions starts with keeping the engine on target for stoichiometric air-fuel balance at all times. Throughout any drive cycle, any excursion of more than about 5 percent from lambda=1.00 is now of interest to the calibrator. Any such event can be quickly spotted by plotting lambda against time along with other common engine-operating parameters such as RPM, vehicle speed, throttle position, cam position(s), and temperatures.

Peaks above 1.05 or dips below 0.95 lambda should alert us to an area of concern that can then be isolated into specific speed, load, and operating condition. Does the engine always deviate from lambda=1.0 at this operating point? If so, an investigation into the base fueling should be restarted.

One special note here on air-fuel ratio. While the engine targets a

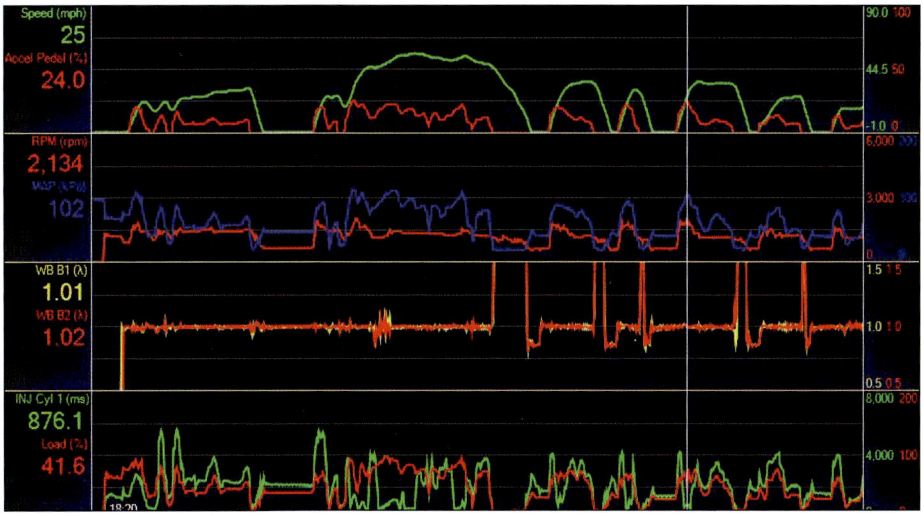

This engine stays very close to lambda=1.00 after it's warmed up. The only deviations are the lean spikes during deceleration fuel shutoff followed by a brief rich period to rebalance the catalysts.

stoichiometric ratio most of the time, this does not include power enrichment or component protection fueling. Ideally, neither of these should become active during normal driving, especially at the lighter loads seen on emissions tests. Extra fuel is added to increase torque and sometimes prevent knock, but in the lighter-load region seen during normal driving and emissions test cycles, this should not be necessary.

The FTP-75 tests particularly light loads and low speeds that simulate stop-and-go traffic, so the engine should not be anywhere near its capacity limit to justify excess fueling to make the required torque. The supplemental FTPs of US06 and SC03 were later added to test the vehicle under higher loads, but even these should be easy to manage on most performance applications where there is a much more favorable power-to-weight ratio. This favorable ratio means that the engine doesn't have to work very hard to meet the acceleration rates defined by the test.

SFTP NMOG+NOx and CO Stand-Alone Exhaust Emission Standards for 2015 and Subsequent Model LEV III Passenger Cars, Light-Duty Trucks, and Medium-Duty Passenger Vehicles						
Vehicle Type	*Durability Vehicle Basis (mi)*	*Vehicle Emission Category*[1]	*US06 Test (g/mi)*		*SC03 Test (g/mi)*	
			NMOG + NOx	*CO*	*NMOG + NOx*	*CO*
All PCs; LDTs 0- 8,500 lbs. GVWR; and MDPVs Vehicles in these categories are tested at their loaded vehicle weight (curb weight plus 300 pounds).	150,000	LEV	0.140	9.6	0.100	3.2
		ULEV	0.120	9.6	0.070	3.2
		SULEV	0.060	9.6	0.020	3.2
		SULEV	0.050	9.6	0.020	3.2

The supplemental FTP tests have their own g/mi standards separate from the FTP-75. Notice the higher carbon monoxide limits since higher engine loads are expected on these drive cycles. (Photo Courtesy CARB)

Performance applications with a good power-to-weight ratio should make it all that much easier to run the emissions cycles without the need to trigger additional fueling. Almost all of the test should be performed at a measured lambda=1.0 condition.

Many OEM applications today remain at the stoichiometric mixture even at WOT until thermal protection is needed because they are capable of delivering the rated power without excess enrichment. Some systems employ a delay logic that only activates power enrichment after some time of keeping the load beyond the

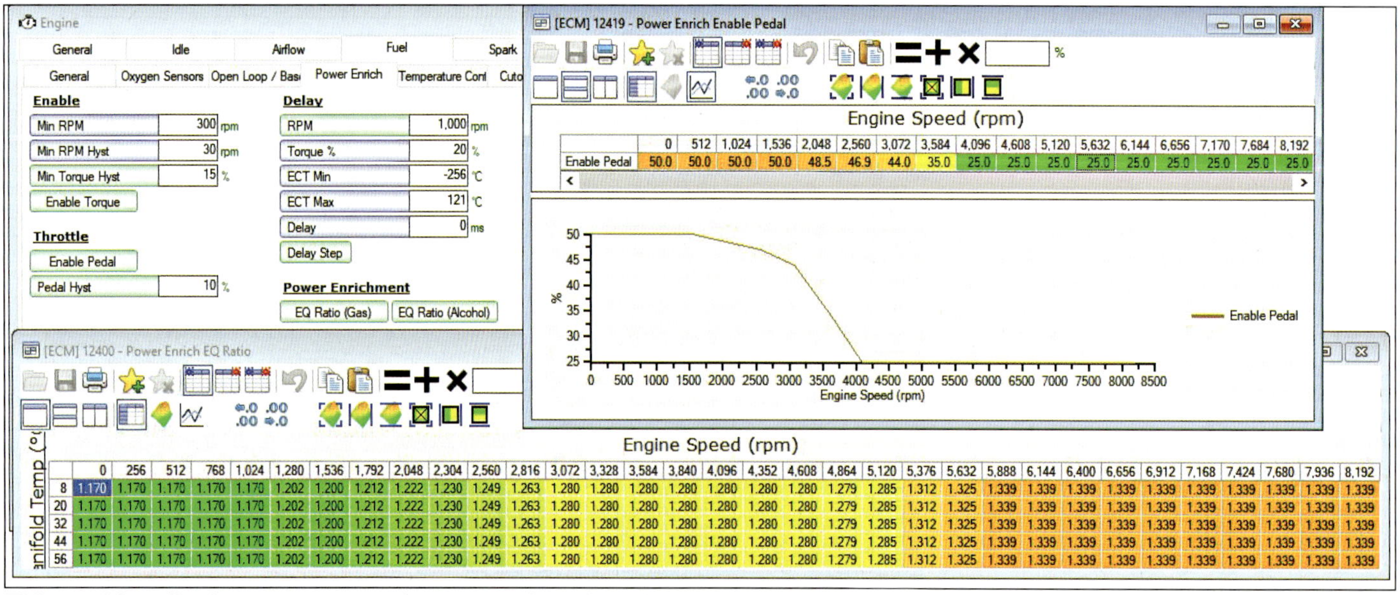

This positive-displacement supercharger-equipped truck has new enabling criteria for enrichment along with a new target ratio. The values were chosen to follow either lean best torque (LBT) fueling or the enrichment necessary to protect the catalyst from overheating.

qualifying threshold for enrichment. This is done partially to avoid triggering enrichment on emissions tests as well as normal driving. They also don't usually get the exhaust components anywhere near hot enough on an emissions cycle to require extra fuel for thermal protection.

Special care should be taken when setting the enrichment thresholds to avoid their activation during testing. I have seen plenty of aftermarket calibrations that enable power-enrichment fueling much earlier than stock, particularly on supercharged applications. One or two small excursions into power enrichment can create enough carbon monoxide to blow the whole test if airflow was high enough. This is to be avoided.

If a rich excursion is seen on the lambda trace, and it can be attributed to a commanded enrichment triggered by these strategies, it warrants some additional work to revise the thresholds and clean up the emissions. It's also important to note here that OEMs are not allowed to operate more than 4-percent rich of lean best torque (LBT) fueling under power enrichment unless they are actively protecting components from thermal damage. This drives what many outsiders see as "crazy" target WOT air-fuel ratio tables in some applications.

Another common error that I see is the disabling of the catalyst temperature control fueling. This feature will add a significant amount of fuel during extended high-load operation to reduce exhaust gas and catalyst temperatures.

A similar logic may also be employed for turbocharger inlet temperature control. The vast majority of turbos and catalysts have functional temperature limits set by their manufacturers of 950 to 1000°C. Adding fuel beyond LBT reduces the bulk flame temperature and has a knock on effect to EGTs.

With catalysts, there is the added benefit that continuous rich operation saturates all sites on the brick with CO. This stops the active conversion that generates its own heat inside the catalyst until more oxygen or NO_x is added.

Beware, our saturated catalyst can also be damaged by enabling fuel shutoff immediately after high-load enrichment as a large shot of oxygen hits a very hot fuel-charged brick. OEMs often delay deceleration fuel shutoff for a short period of time after component cooling enrichment has been used to allow the brick to cool to a safe temperature before resuming exothermic reactions.

While it may be convenient to eliminate one additional, somewhat unknown source of fuel enrichment, this protective logic should remain intact if at all possible. There is no direct measurement of the catalyst temperature by a sensor, so all of this is based on a complex model. Most aftermarket tuning software does not unlock all of the parameters used in this model, so the best advice here is to make sure that it is being fed accurate numbers for airflow, fuel delivery (injector model), and MBT spark reference.

Retaining the overtemperature protection logic helps to greatly extend the life of the catalyst or turbo. The failure of either of these would lead to catastrophic increases in emissions later in life, so a small, intermittent increase in carbon monoxide from richness is still better for the environmental impact than a vehicle operating with a failed or burned-out catalyst that is no longer able to do any cleanup work for the engine.

Was the variable cam achieving the correct target position? If not, the VVT controls may need to be adjusted to allow better tracking or limit the movement of the target to unreasonably quick changes that cannot be achieved. One should also avoid commanded camshaft-angle tables with large peaks and valleys in them. Although this may optimize cam position for one particular operating point, it becomes very difficult for the ECU to execute in normal

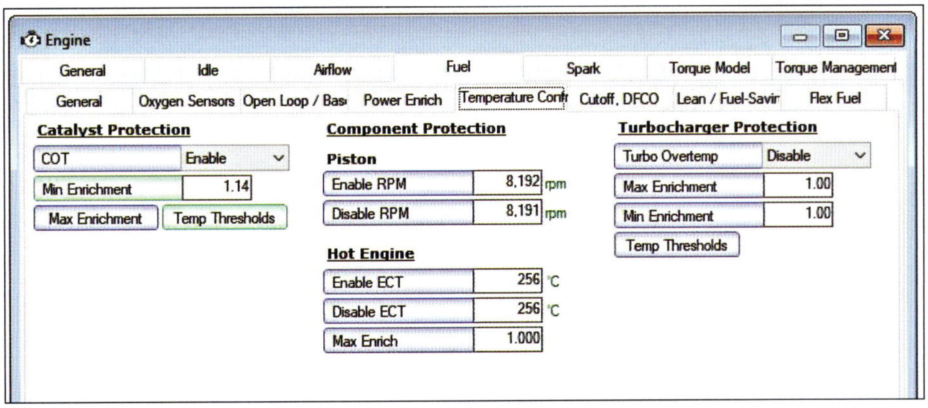

The factory strategy employs a model of exhaust gas and catalyst temperatures that are used to trigger additional fueling to keep them cool. Thermocouple data on this supercharged application showed that we needed to allow intervention sooner than the original calibration.

operation. Instead, cam-angle-target tables should be smooth and progressive, much like a VE surface. This allows the ECU to remain in constant control of the camshaft phaser to have minimal error between commanded and actual position even as the target moves in real time while driving.

Are there more transient events than necessary? In normal driving, transients are inevitable, but if their frequency can be reduced, we also see a reduction in emissions as more time is spent in the well-controlled steady-state operation state than trying to constantly compensate for changes.

Continuously changing gears forces significant engine-speed changes that each require some amount of transient compensation and have imperfections in fuel delivery. By widening the hysteresis between gears, these events can be reduced often at the cost of fuel economy. A similar argument can be made for variable-displacement or cylinder-shutoff mechanisms, as these radically shift the cylinder load and MAP required to make the same torque before and after a transition. Filtering of the driver-input request also falls into this discussion.

A rapidly reacting throttle may feel very sporty to the driver, but these rapid changes each require individual compensations too. Numbing the throttle response may be a bitter pill to swallow for the performance calibrator, but modern drive-by-wire controls often let us have a different response rate at low versus high pedal inputs to maintain good response if the driver genuinely requests larger amounts of additional power.

Since the overall power capacity is usually very good in performance applications, I find that it's not as much of a penalty as one might think to soften the low pedal-input responses on powerful engines to make them less "twitchy" on initial tip-in. No one likes trying to parallel park a car that is trying to prove it has 500-plus hp right off idle anyway.

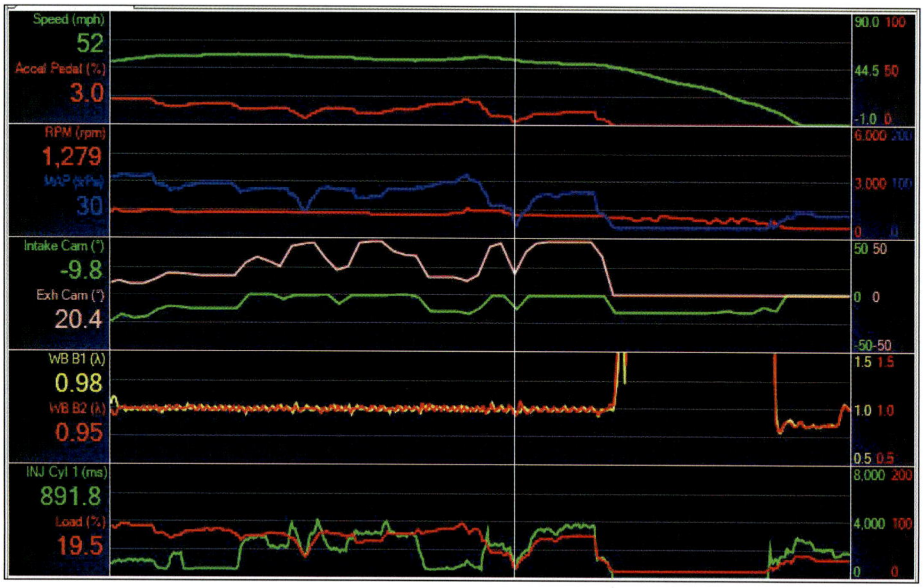

Requests that have the cam position rapidly moving back and forth may be difficult to execute in reality. The result can be that neither position was achieved in time and ECU estimation of cylinder filling could also be incorrect.

Most normal driving occurs below 40-percent pedal input. By maintaining smooth and predictable engine response at lower pedal inputs, we can improve both fuel economy and emissions while still having the option for very lively response if the driver uses the far end of pedal inputs for strong acceleration requests. Eventually, the driver learns the pedal response to suit their driving style, and keeping a smooth rate of response in the normal driving range helps reduce the number and intensity of transient events.

Every transient event comes with some small amount of imperfection in fuel control at best. Each has the potential for significant impact if it doesn't match the modeled behavior in the calibration. The single events may not be enough to make the difference between a pass or fail for the emissions test, but reducing a large number of them throughout the test can add up to a significant change in accumulated emissions over the whole test duration.

If all of these concerns are properly addressed, the result should be a vehicle that's tailpipe emissions should be fairly clean on any emissions cycle. This is easier said than done, but once clean engine operation has been achieved, the remainder of the emissions certification process gets much easier in comparison.

Passing OBD Monitors

A properly running vehicle that can pass tailpipe-emissions tests in a lab should not have too much trouble passing its own internal monitors within the ECU. These monitors are all there to help diagnose conditions that would lead to increased

Narrow longitudinal fuel tanks are particularly susceptible to sloshing during acceleration or braking. The moving wave inside makes it impossible for the tank pressure sensor to get a valid reading and execute the leak diagnostics.

emissions, so a vehicle with clean emissions very likely passes all monitors without too much trouble.

Actually, passing them at this point should merely be a formality. In fact, at the OEM level all monitors should be able to run and pass during the normal course of emissions testing. The "five cycle" emissions tests are usually enough to give the ECU a chance to see all the conditions necessary to execute.

Many of these happen so fast, they are easy to miss. Right after startup, checks are made for comprehensive components, O_2 sensors/heaters, and misfire. If the engine makes it to closed-loop operation, it should quickly pass the O_2-sensor checks. A few moments later, the catalyst should hit a temperature at which it begins converting with high efficiency.

At this point, the downstream O_2 sensors and catalyst monitors should also have passed. A vehicle that fails to pass these monitors by this point usually has something wrong enough to fail the lab test.

The evaporative system diagnostic is usually the last to complete. This one can be tricky because it requires very stable conditions to run. These conditions must be present throughout the test, which can take a minute or two. Aside from an average fuel level somewhere between 15 and 85 percent, the ECU also wants to make sure that the fuel is not sloshing around inside the tank. It detects slosh by looking at the instantaneous fuel level to see if the float is moving up and down too much. Large amounts of fuel slosh inside the tank can "slug" the fuel tank pressure sensor with a wave that is far more intense than the slight pressure changes it is trying to detect from engine vacuum being applied to the tank through the evaporative control solenoid near the intake manifold and vapor feed line.

This test often completes easily on the highway fuel economy test (HWYFE), where speeds are in the right range and being strapped to the dynamometer prevents most sloshing inside the tank. Since the HWYFE isn't always tested in aftermarket checks, the evaporative monitor is often left to be found during real world driving.

On the road, this stable condition is a little more difficult to reproduce. It may take several attempts to get all the way through the monitoring period without upsetting the tank slosh from road conditions, traffic, or driver inputs. Patience is key here. As long as the fuel tank, charcoal canister, and the rest of the evaporative system is in good working order, it should eventually pass. Even the OEMs sometimes struggle with this one.

With all of the tailpipe testing and internal monitors passed, the hard part should be over. The only thing left to do with this

SEMA offers its members not only a great place to perform testing but also some excellent guidance on submitting paperwork to CARB for approval.

now-demonstrated clean-running vehicle is organize the paperwork that proves it. Whether submitting to CARB, the EPA, or just keeping good internal data on a development program, complete and organized paperwork is important.

If seeking a CARB EO, CARB will have already supplied a list of information that it needs to process the submission. It is important to check every line, as a single missing piece of information can hold up the approval of an otherwise passing test by months. This is one place where working closely with the right test lab can save lots of headaches and precious time.

The SEMA Garage offers great testing facilities and will also submit the final paperwork to CARB on behalf of their testing clients. The team at SEMA is very experienced, and it has a great working relationship with the inspectors at CARB. SEMA goes over every line of each submission to make sure that nothing is left out. This means that when the CARB inspectors get a submission from SEMA Garage, they are confident that it is complete and can be handled much more quickly than most independent submissions.

Having a guide like the team at SEMA Garage (or some other third-party consultant who also specializes in these paperwork submissions with CARB) can often pay for itself in potential lost time to market with a product that is already proven clean but not yet legally approved. I have been nothing short of impressed with the speed at which programs can be approved in this manner when testing with SEMA Garage. Of course, I also had to make sure I gave them a vehicle that ran clean enough to pass on the first try.

Notes for Smaller Shops

Manufacturers of components and large kits should already be well aware of the need to get CARB testing and EO approval to make sure they are compliant with both local and federal laws. The receipt of an EO is really the best option for an aftermarket concern. Anything less quickly falls into the gray area that may lead to enforcement actions. When the stakes are large with potential enforcement actions for violations of the Clean Air Act, there really isn't much room for discussion for manufacturers.

What about the vast majority of the high-performance industry that isn't a manufacturer that has the luxury of just making a handful of part numbers that can be emissions certified? What about the thousands of shops that are distributors and installers for these brands? What about the independent installer's end users? For every major manufacturer, there are thousands of smaller workshops across the country that must also be aware of their potential exposure here.

Both the EPA and CARB have a history of going after not only large manufacturers but also smaller businesses that simply cannot afford to pay giant fines and stay in business. A single enforcement action has the potential to financially ruin a small family-run business that took years or decades to grow. Because the language of the original Clean Air Act is so broad with respect to offenses based on manufacturing, offering for sale, installing, or using defeat devices, shops and installers everywhere should be aware of the situation.

Don't shoot the messenger here. I didn't write the law, and I'm only repeating what has been said for decades. The enforcement agencies will not entertain any discussion of ignorance of this law.

Finding complete legal compliance at the working shop level can be tricky in the performance aftermarket. In the strictest terms, any vehicle that is able to drive to the shop cannot have any part of its engine, controls, or emissions system replaced with anything other than a direct OEM replacement part of identical design and function—unless the new component comes with sufficient paperwork to prove its compliance.

A CARB EO sticker/number is

What kind of vehicles are you working on? If it has a license plate and even occasionally gets driven on the road, there is potential concern about emissions liability.

Building a solid combination of working parts with a known good calibration is basically the same thing OEMs do. It saves tons of time on each subsequent vehicle since each one starts with the benefit of all the hard work done developing the first calibration for an identical vehicle.

the most common solution here. While there are a large number of products out there that have successfully completed the EO process, the performance industry thrives on the American individual spirit and the need each vehicle owner feels to truly personalize his or her vehicle.

As a former shop owner, I can clearly recall the never-ending string of customers who came in asking for their own dream build based on a unique combination of parts to be fitted to their car. You can guess how rarely the conversation started with, "What parts do you have that meet all federal emissions requirements?" Living outside of California, this was pretty much a non-event. But having dealt with other friends who owned shops across the country and countless clients nationwide since, I can assure you that the winds of change have come to the performance industry.

The single biggest piece of advice that I give to most shop owners is to communize some of their offerings. I call this my "Number 3 with a Coke" strategy. At a glance, fast-food restaurants don't seem to have too much in common with your average speed shop. But they do a couple things really well, and we should pay attention.

The vast majority of orders at a fast-food chain are simply given by number rather than the customer asking for a specific combination of items. In these cases, the business has put together a known combination that not only satisfies the customer's desires but also improves the efficiency of delivery and profit. Combining key items results in a package with known results that can be consistently duplicated time and time again. Because the business also knows that it is likely to sell these things in similar quantities, it makes it much easier to plan on how much to order and cook for each shift. Are you starting to see the parallels here yet?

If a speed shop can put together a known group of parts for a specific vehicle package, it can much more confidently tell the customer ahead of time what is to be expected regarding both performance and pricing. After all, this is exactly what the OEMs do with their own vehicle packages. The discussion turns from "It will probably make around 500 hp" to "These consistently make just over 500 hp," which inspires much more confidence in the customer.

The idea of packaging known combinations is great from a marketing standpoint, but there is another more important benefit behind the scenes. Each vehicle package installed goes together just like the one before it. This makes the technician's job more routine, and the home installer is more likely to see their project closely follow the instructions.

When it comes to ECU tuning, we see the real benefit. The tuning process can be quite involved. By the time we properly go through the mapping of fuel delivery, air charge determination, torque control, and emissions, we can have a lot of hours in the project. Starting all over from scratch on every new vehicle means that much of this must be repeated every time if we are to get it right. But if we start with a familiar hardware package, the calibration process gets to take some very powerful shortcuts.

Using the same airbox means a common MAF transfer function. Running the same supercharger, spark plugs, and injectors on similar engines means that tons of fueling, spark, and torque values can be retained from job to job. Sure, the first one may take several weeks to really nail down the ECU calibration, but the second one may be done in 10 minutes! Job number-three is done in another 10 minutes and so on.

Since tuning can be one of the most time-consuming tasks on many speed-shop projects, being able to turn endless hours of dynamometer mapping into a simple reflash and cursory power check to generate a pretty graph for the customer is a real game changer. The value is still there for the consumer, and he or she actually benefits from the large amount of time invested in job number-one every time the car is driven.

This common tuning process should not only include basic fuel, air, and spark mapping. It should also include torque-based throttle controls

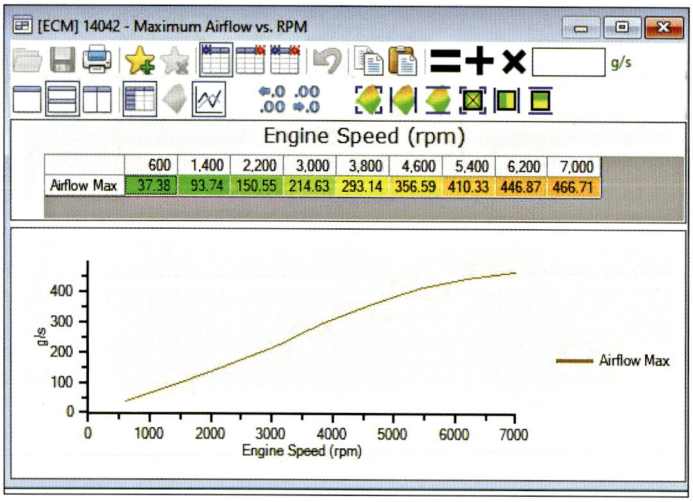

One of the last steps in the calibration should be to adjust the ETC airflow limits. This should be populated with new data recorded on the vehicle with some modest safety margin added to detect potential runaway throttle events.

Even if by some miracle the vehicle passes initial emissions testing with this catalyst, it should not be expected to have anywhere near the effective lifespan of an OEM unit. Sadly, items like this are on the endangered species list in the performance industry.

where equipped. Runaway-throttle detect for safety on electronic-throttle engines is a must in today's litigious society. Emissions compliance has become more important than ever.

Think of how easy a calibration job would be if you were working with a familiar engine that is running a camshaft and intake combination that you've mapped previously. Simply copy and paste the VE data into the new ECU and it fires up on the first try. Fuel trims are within just a few percent of zero, as they were on the original test subject. All emissions monitors and diagnostics are able to run and complete without issue. The throttle response is crisp and predictable, and the power at WOT is right in line with expectations.

The good news here is that if job number-one included collecting passing emissions data for a new combination, all subsequent builds of that same variety can now be covered under the same data or certification. Some smaller shops may even use this logic now to justify going the extra mile toward CARB EO certification for their most popular packages, as this is the best-known way to prevent any enforcement action from the "alphabet agencies." Even without a complete EO certification, I still recommend collecting some emissions data to verify that our packages really are being environmentally responsible.

The more common the packages are, the more data can be shared among projects. Always starting with known fuel injectors and their complete characterization data should be a no-brainer today. If a customer comes in with an unknown set of injectors, just think about how many different tables and functions will be impacted by any errors before accepting such a challenge.

Throttle bodies are another similar concern. Again, being a stickler for accuracy here prevents a lot of issues toward the end of the tuning process when it becomes difficult or impossible to iron out the mismatch. Finally, the factory catalysts are at least proved to work on a stock vehicle for well over 100,000 miles when properly protected.

Aftermarket "high-flow" catalysts not only have lower conversion efficiency leading to worse tailpipe emissions but they also usually just don't last as long. It's no fun to have a customer come back only a few months later after an install to have you diagnose their P0420 (catalyst performance) code only to figure out that the ECU diagnostic is right and the catalyst really isn't working properly anymore. Simply turning off the code at this point is irresponsible and illegal.

Make sure that any custom ECU tuning includes leaving all emissions monitors active along with their related P-codes. It is a good idea to actually go one step further and check to see if the monitors have run after completing the calibration work. Most calibrators will take a quick street drive after dynamometer work. During this time, they get a chance to see if they missed anything from a drive-quality perspective. It also presents a great opportunity to make one last check for codes and monitor completions before delivering the vehicle back to the customer.

Document your work here. Whether it's a log file or a screenshot, anything is better than nothing if there are ever questions in the

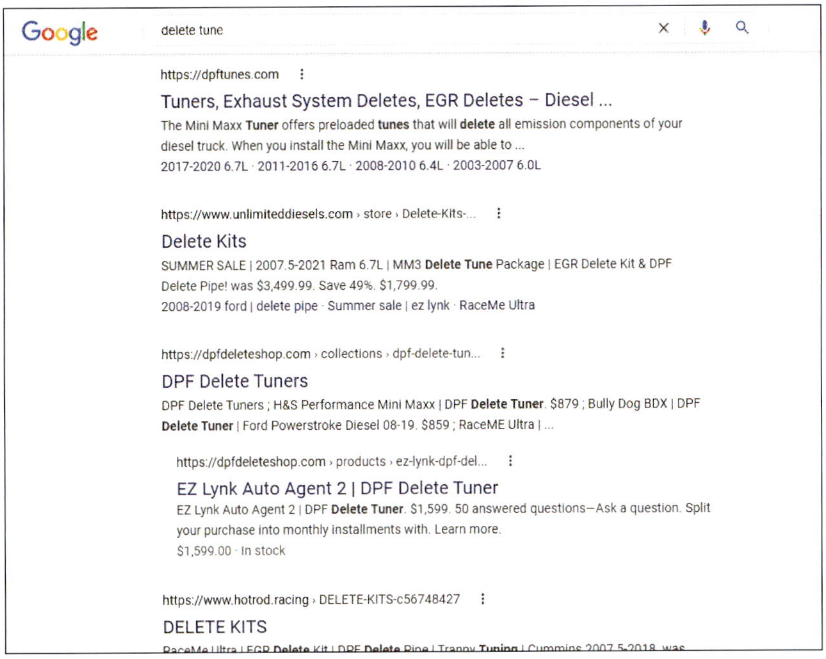

Advertising federally illegal products and services online falls squarely under the "stupid criminal" category. Quietly offering them for sale over the counter at your shop isn't much smarter these days.

Some swaps are easier than others. Getting this 2017 GMC powertrain (complete with all emissions) running again inside a Divco milk truck took a lot more hours than anticipated when it came to troubleshooting various wiring concerns.

future. Having some proof that the vehicle was working correctly when it left your possession may make all the difference in the world if you are being questioned by an agency.

Don't Break the Law

There are a number of "don'ts" worth mentioning here as well. The first should be obvious: don't break the law. The Clean Air Act specifically covers a wide range of offenses related to tampering with emissions-control systems. Among these are "manufacturing, offering for sale, or installing" defeat devices. The most obvious of these are anything with the words "delete," "eliminator," or "off-road only" in the description.

Parts intended to replace a key piece of the emissions control system with an otherwise empty connector fall right on the top of the pile of things the EPA is looking for when it searches for violations. It doesn't even have to look very hard to find these. Shops that are replacing catalytic convertors, DPFs, GPFs, SCR systems, or EGR systems with block-off plates or empty pipes are practically begging to get caught these days. Some shops are even dumb enough to advertise it on their web page or post it publicly to social media. Just assume that Big Brother is always watching and remember how big the fines get before tossing the man an easy open-and-shut case.

While we're at it, defeat devices aren't just physical. Using a programming tool to shut off catalyst monitors, downstream O_2 sensors, EGR, or other emissions functions is just the same as physical removal in the eyes of the law. Turning off codes to avoid having the CEL on may bring some short-term relief from the customer, but it certainly doesn't meet the regulations and leaves you responsible. Given enough samples, investigators will begin tracking where these changes are being made and can potentially find their way to your doorstep. The liability cannot be understated here.

Another "don't" for shop owners is the "all it needs is a tune" job. Rarely is this the case. Take the time to thoroughly look over the physical build before strapping the car to the dyno. For car owners reading this, ask ahead if the tuning shop has a checklist that you can go over before arriving. Nobody wants to deal with pending or active P-codes, vacuum leaks, bad wiring connections, insufficient fuel supply, or other issues when it's time to concentrate on the ECU.

Your car won't pass emissions with these problems, so don't think the tuner should be able to work around them. Time is money here, and some jobs just don't pay for the time required to complete them correctly. I have fired customers before who consistently brought a vehicle that could not be calibrated due to mechanical or electrical issues.

CONCLUSION

Hopefully, this book clarified the connections between driver observations, repair needs, emissions compliance, and calibration responsibilities. Coming from OEM experience, these are all the same discussion, and we simply can't have one without the others.

It's improper to approach more complex repairs without taking a moment to think about the "how" or "why" behind the diagnostics that tripped the code and started the process for the customer in the first place. The more we understand what the ECU is looking for when running a particular diagnostic routine, the easier it becomes to identify where things went wrong and execute the correct repair the first time.

No customer likes paying a repair bill only to have to return a week later with the same problem, or worse yet, fail their mandatory inspection needed to renew their registration. It is the responsibility of the technician or DIY enthusiast to use the powerful tools at their disposal to gather the right information and narrow down the repair to the correct solution. Using the OBD-II system actually makes this process much easier than it ever was before as long as the user understands the information.

Here, I am speaking to a class of engineering students at my alma mater, Kettering University.

It's easy to be overwhelmed by the mass of information available on OBD-II systems. The goal of this book was to provide a practical breakdown with just enough buzzwords to impress your friends at the shop next time. Joking aside, no one is likely to quiz you on the various data modes, but knowing things (such as the fact that you have the option to grab freeze-frame data to better replicate an elusive failure) sure does help.

Understanding that fuel slosh in the tank makes it almost impossible for an evaporative diagnostic to run clean also helps drive different driving behavior when trying to get that last monitor to complete before a plug-in test with the state. These are the practical lessons that I hope you take away from the book.

On the performance side, we have also discovered that power and emissions compliance are not completely at odds with one another. Modern engines meet emissions standards that allow only a tiny fraction of the pollutants of their predecessors while making record levels of power and delivering comparable fuel economy.

Even adding tremendous amounts of power through the use of aftermarket parts remains possible while maintaining the same

I (far right) am meeting with Congressman David Trott (center) as part of the SEMA Washington Rally. Advocating for the RPM Act was part of helping our lawmakers understand and protect our hobby.

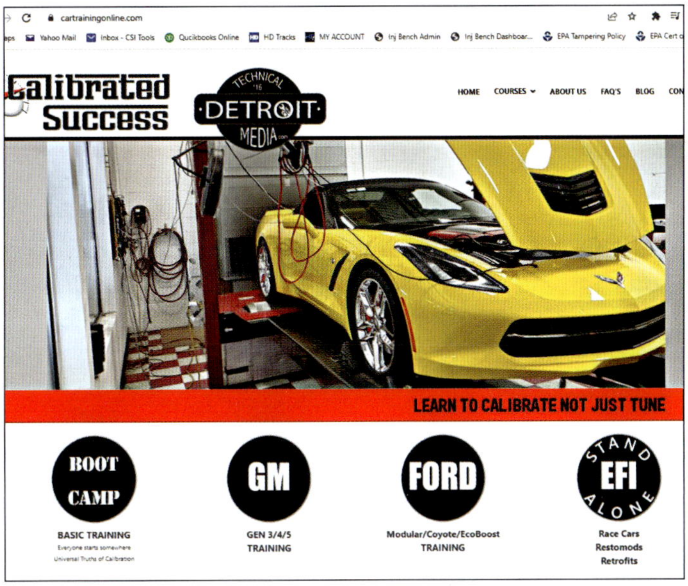

All of my EFI training videos are available directly through the streaming site cartrainingonline.com.

emissions compliance as long as the fundamental rules of combustion and diagnostics are observed. The only real change here is that with inspections becoming increasingly more common, fewer violations slip through the system. As such, more and more enthusiasts are choosing parts and calibrations that have proven clean emissions, making it a cleaner world for everyone even as they enjoy their added power.

Over time, the gross violations of running defeat devices on public roads will erode to near zero, but the responsible power junkies will continue to thrive. Gone will be the days of "off-road" pipes and delete kits, but we will watch together in awe as some deliver astounding power levels through fully functioning catalysts and clean tailpipe numbers. At Calibrated Success, I have been proud to help many clients deliver these clean emissions numbers on their products and see a bright future ahead for the street-performance market.

Performance and emissions are not mutually exclusive. It's just going to take a little more effort on the part of those willing to push the envelope to make sure that they are doing their part to remain environmentally responsible.

For those still looking to learn more, don't forget to grab my earlier books or check out Calibrated Success for videos, classes, and additional materials. There are also endless online resources regarding almost every detail of OBD-II functionality. This book represents only the tip of the information iceberg. With all of the constantly updated information from automakers and required diagnostics, remember to exercise good internet searching habits whenever investigating a vehicle issue or fault code, as this really is a moving target today.

More information about upcoming events and projects from Calibrated Success are also available at calibratedsuccess.com.

Appendix

Fault Diagnostic Examples

While it remains impossible for this book to provide examples for every possible fault on every possible car, let's take a look at some of the high-percentage issues that one may encounter. I can already see the complaints about how this book "didn't teach me how to fix my specific car." I know, and that's not the point here. Smart readers can look at these examples and see a thought process for confirming a diagnosis along with a workflow that ensures a proper repair rather than a complete step-by-step guide to a specific repair.

If you are looking for that vehicle-specific process for repair on your exact vehicle, I suggest starting with an internet search as previously described. There is a high likelihood that someone out there has already done a writeup on it online. What we have here is a sanity check that allows you to add up the clues to confirm a diagnosis and verify a completed repair.

Many aftermarket induction kits require the removal and reinstallation of the MAF sensor element. If the installer doesn't get things reconnected properly, the ECU will probably set an MIL and have all kinds of trouble keeping control of the air-fuel ratio as well as many other critical functions.

Unplugged MAF Sensor

One of the most common occurrences after installing a part, such as a cold-air kit, new air filter, or other part, is to accidentally leave something unplugged. This will trip one of the OBD-I circuit diagnostics pretty quickly as long as everything is working as intended. In this example, the airbox must be removed along with the MAF sensor to replace it with a more streamlined induction package and conical high-flow filter element. When reassembling, it's easy to get distracted and either completely forget to plug in the MAF sensor or not get the connector seated all the way into the sensor body. Either way, we end up with an open circuit to the critical air-measurement device for the ECU.

When we start the vehicle without the MAF sensor plugged in, we notice a longer cranking time followed by rough engine operation. Something is definitely wrong. Luckily, the ECU is running continuous checks on the important circuits, including that for the MAF sensor. It has detected the open circuit and immediately registered a P0102 code into Mode $03 memory along with illuminating the MIL. The engine is able to run, but barely—thanks to a background airflow model inside the ECU. This is usually based on throttle position and RPM, so don't expect much precision since it's literally limping along with limited inputs. During this operation, the fueling may not be ideal, and we may also see fuel trims walk out to some unrealistic values.

Seeing the MIL, grab your trusty scan tool and check for codes. Among a potentially longer list of faults, we see the P0102 related to the MAF along with a P0113 for the intake air-temperature sensor that is also housed in the MAF meter. Now, shut off the engine, open the hood, and look at the MAF sensor.

At this point, the failure should be obvious if a connector is laying near the open sensor. The pins on both the connector and the sensor should be inspected for damage along with the retaining clip feature on the connector. There's no use trying to force bent pins back together, so repair them if necessary. Plugging the wire connector back into the sensor with a positive click indicates a good connection. A quick tug on the connector to verify that it won't drop loose again is also a good idea.

Now, restart the engine. Cranking time should return to normal along with idle quality and engine roughness. The MIL may not yet be gone if we check our scan tool, as these sometimes require a couple drive cycles to self-heal. We can speed up

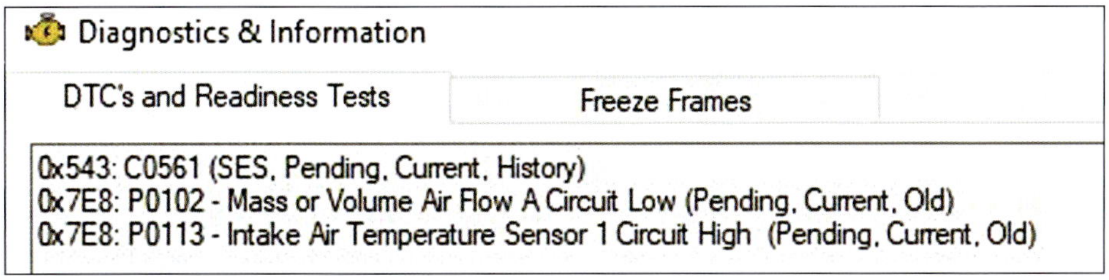

With the MAF sensor unplugged during engine operation, the ECU should almost immediately register a P0xxx code as seen here. This OBD-I level check is run continuously due to the importance for proper engine operation.

the process by issuing the Mode $04 Clear Codes command. If all is well, we should not see the P0xxx return now that the connection is secure. A quick test drive will confirm this as well as give the ECU a chance to unlearn any bad O_2 corrections that may have piled up during the faulted operation.

Aging Oxygen Sensor

If you've ever wondered why auto-parts stores claim up to a 20-percent improvement in fuel economy from installing new oxygen sensors, this is it. What they forget to tell you is that this repair doesn't necessarily increase your fuel economy over what it had when new, but rather brings your very poor fuel economy that resulted from an old oxygen sensor back closer to normal.

As oxygen sensors age, they slowly get poisoned and lose their ability to register the correct air-fuel ratio in the exhaust. In response, the ECU typically increases the fuel trim (adding more fuel to the engine) until it sees the switch in oxygen sensor signal that it wants.

Over time, this manifests as a large positive fuel trim until the ECU either trips a fault for Bank Lean code (P0171/P0174) as part of the fuel system monitor or one of many codes directly related to the sensor itself. There are also a number of codes related to "slow response" (P0133/P0153) or "no activity detected" (P0134/P0154) that may also appear with aging sensors. Any of these telltale conditions should trigger a close examination of the oxygen sensors along with an inquiry as to their age and history.

If the MIL is on, this process is sped up quite a bit when looking for the cause. In some cases, we may just have a sluggish engine that gets poor fuel economy because it's getting more fuel than it really needs for clean combustion. After ruling out leaks (fuel, vacuum, and exhaust) for obvious issues that would change the delivered fuel or measured exhaust chemistry by the oxygen sensor, the next step is to look at the sensor itself.

Even if the sensor is connected and appears to be free of damage, it may still have an accumulation of poisoning or damage to the internal sensing element. If the vehicle has large positive fuel trims or an oxygen sensor–related fault and the sensor has been on the vehicle for 50,000 miles or more, it's smart to replace it with a fresh one. In the case of an engine with multiple oxygen sensors, a complete new set might not be a bad idea, since the aging happens to both banks and sensors at the same rate.

Arguably, the hardest part of this job will likely be removal of the old sensor from the exhaust system. Sometimes, these sensors are easily accessible, other times the technician will curse the name of every engineer on the program getting to them. Years of road grime, corrosion, salt spray, and heat cycles are a recipe for anger when trying to break them loose. The right tool helps immensely. Although one can theoretically remove most oxygen sensors with a 7/8-inch wrench, that doesn't always work. Having a few options, such as an O_2-sensor socket or wrench can be a lifesaver. Don't forget to apply a thin coating of anti-seize lubricant to the threads of the new sensor before installing as well.

With the sensor swapped, the engine can be restarted and codes cleared using Mode $04. Being able to use the Mode $08 function to re-zero the fuel trims is a big help. Otherwise, you will have to wait for the ECU to hopefully recognize the rich condition and slowly walk the trims back toward the normal range to restore proper fueling. This may take a while, since there are sepa-

Short Term Fuel Trim Bank 1 (SAE)	8.6 %
Long Term Fuel Trim Bank 1 (SAE)	-4.7 %
Short Term Fuel Trim Bank 2 (SAE)	30.5 %
Long Term Fuel Trim Bank 2 (SAE)	-0.8 %
Injector Pulse Width Avg. Bank 1	1.4 ms
O2 Voltage B1S1 (SAE)	0.523 V
O2 Voltage B2S1 (SAE)	0.453 V

A large positive fuel trim number is common with aging oxygen sensors. If the sensor is not able to generate sufficient output signal, the ECU will typically keep adding fuel in the trims over time in an attempt to bring the oxygen sensor signal into the normal range. Errors will initially show up in the short term, but they will likely be transferred to long-term trims over time.

Removing oxygen sensors that have been installed in the vehicle for a while can be tough on a normal day. If you are fighting corrosion or bad access angles, tools such as these that wrap around the sensor for more positive contact allow more torque to be applied without damage compared to an open wrench.

rate trim "cells" for idle and various driving conditions that must all be relearned. Again, resetting the trims via Mode $08 command is a big time-saver. Watching the live stream of Mode $01 data for fuel trims after installing the fresh oxygen sensor shows if the ECU likes the new input from the fresh sensor. Ideally, fuel trims will stay under 10 percent. Persistently small fuel trims will be the confirmation you're looking for to validate the engine operation with the new oxygen sensor.

Coil Fault

Ignition systems present some unique failure modes. One could write an entire book on all the possible ways vehicles can suffer under them. Again, catching them all here is just not practical. That said, the most common issues are usually aging spark plugs, wires, or coils that result in intermittent delivery of spark to the cylinder. It's quite common for the flexible boots on spark plug wires or coil-on-plug modules to deteriorate with age and heat. Small cracks or gaps can present a lower resistance escape path for the spark energy than the plug itself, sometimes creating a visible arc to a new ground path outside of the cylinder.

When this type of failure occurs, the engine experiences either poor combustion quality or a misfire. Older, less-sensitive control systems may not catch this misfire event, but many newer ECUs will. Better yet, they correctly identify which cylinder in the firing order had the event by counting the crank teeth from the gap and correlating with which one was near TDC at that moment.

Getting a P0301 for misfire on cylinder number-1 is far more specific than a P0300 general misfire. It also helps point us toward a specific spark plug, coil, wire, or injector as the root cause. Better yet, a P0351 points toward Ignition Coil A, indicating that an issue was found with the wiring circuit of the first coil in the firing-order sequence. In this case, the ECU has narrowed our search for the engine roughness down to a single component for inspection. Keep in mind that presence of some specific faults, such as the coil circuit failure, may prevent the execution of other diagnostics, such as fuel system or misfire.

As a case study, I had a newer 2012 Ford 5.0L engine swapped into a 1997 Mustang chassis. The conversion to an engine that was never native in that chassis led to many potential failure points for both hardware and electronics. Upon starting, the engine just didn't feel right. Connecting the scan tool started to explain why, as there was not yet an MIL on the dash to illuminate. Worse, a bug in the scan-tool software did not display the list of fault codes in the usual location on screen, so I was misled for a moment into thinking, "Nothing is wrong."

Oxygen sensor readings told another story. While Bank 2 was showing right on Lambda 1.0, Bank 1 showed approximately 1.2 (20-percent lean). This significant leanness on one bank correlated with the lazy engine response and roughness I was seeing, so I knew more digging was required with the data. I began adding more fuel and misfire-related channels to the scanner, looking for the smoking gun. Misfire counts were zero on all cylinders. Both oxygen sensors

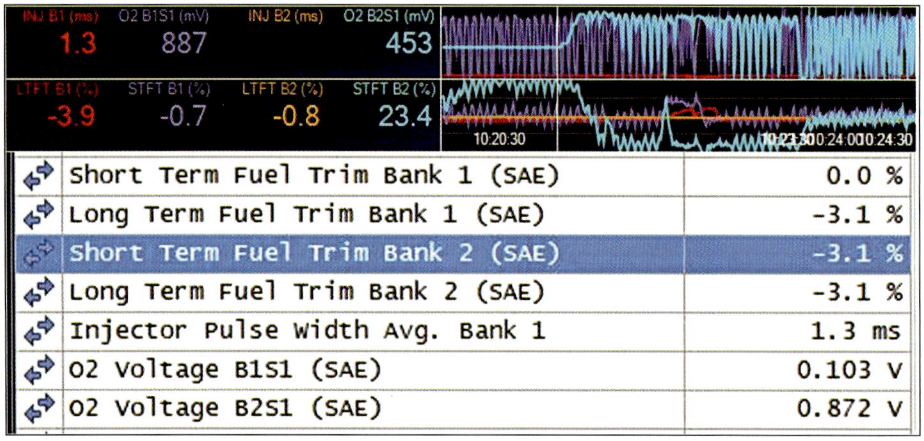

Short Term Fuel Trim Bank 1 (SAE)	0.0 %
Long Term Fuel Trim Bank 1 (SAE)	-3.1 %
Short Term Fuel Trim Bank 2 (SAE)	-3.1 %
Long Term Fuel Trim Bank 2 (SAE)	-3.1 %
Injector Pulse Width Avg. Bank 1	1.3 ms
O2 Voltage B1S1 (SAE)	0.103 V
O2 Voltage B2S1 (SAE)	0.872 V

After the failed oxygen sensor reading (white) is returned at the vertical cursor in the top strip chart, output signal to the ECU should be greatly improved and oscillate like the other working sensor (blue). As a result, the ECU should return to fueling that is much more tightly driven by the base calibration values and no longer require significant fuel-trim values to get to the stoichiometric balance of air and fuel as shown in the tabular data with trims much closer to zero.

Vehicle Info:

Protocol Info: J1962: CAN, 500 kb/s

ECM: 7E8, CAN - Copperhead 2048K, Ford
VIN: 1ZVBP8CF1C5238821 - 2012 Ford Mustang GT Coupe, 5.0 L, V8, Ford_Copperhead
OS: FPFD32A.H32
Calibration IDs: FPFD32A.H32
Basic PIDs: 42
Trouble Codes:
P025A - Fuel Pump Module Control Circuit/Open (Pending, Permanent)
P0351 - Ignition Coil A Primary/Secondary Circuit (Pending, Permanent)
P0446 - Evaporative Emission System Vent Control Circuit (Pending, Permanent)
P0453 - Evaporative Emission System Pressure Sensor/Switch High (Pending, Permanent)
U0109 - Lost Communication With Fuel Pump Control Module (Pending, Permanent)
P0605 - Internal Control Module Read Only Memory (ROM) Error (Permanent)
Controller Type ID By VIN: 11080
Controller Type ID By OS: 11080

This powertrain-swapped vehicle has a long list of errors at first glance, mostly because the evaporative system hardware has not yet been adapted to the older vehicle. More importantly, we see the critical failure that we were looking for, explaining poor engine running with the P0351.

Mass Airflow	19.54 g/s
Air Load	0.141
Desired Load	0.148
Injector Pulse Width	1.3 ms
WB EQ Ratio Bank 1	1.25 λ
WB EQ Ratio Bank 2	1.01 λ
O2 B1S1 Ready	Yes
O2 B1S1 Htr Fault	OK
O2 B2S1 Ready	Yes
O2 B2S1 Htr Fault	OK
Closed Loop Active	No
Effective Throttle Area (ETC Model)	0.139 in²
Manifold Vacuum (ETC Model)	12.736 inHg
Torque Source	Driver Demand
Fuel Source	Injector Cut
Spark Source	Base / MBT
VCT Schedule Mode	Best Fuel E...

Using a scan tool that can display Mode $01 live data tells us a lot about what is going on during a failure. Here, we can see the highlighted air-fuel ratio difference on Bank 1 as well as another clue in the reported fuel source that will lead us to the proper diagnosis and repair.

reported as ready, but the engine was locked in open-loop fueling with a peculiar fuel source labeled "Injector Cut." Cutting an injector would certainly explain the lean raw lambda reading on Bank 1. The question became, "Why?"

With lots of experience with this particular ECU's torque-control system, it was easy for me to dive into the specifics of which torque-control mode allows such a fuel cut and perhaps experiment with disabling individual options in the calibration, but the solution proved to be much simpler. Just because we have access to some of the finer points of the ECU calibration data does not mean that we should jump there so easily. Instead, it was back to the basics on this one.

I contacted the technical-support team for my scan tool and eventually discovered that there were indeed stored P-codes in the ECU that I was not seeing on the screen I usually check. Instead, the bug had them only visible in a less-obvious place (which was of course fixed for the next update).

All of a sudden, seeing the basic information of Mode $03 fault codes, I saw the P0351 in the list and immediately knew where to start looking under the hood. Coil A is the first coil in the engine firing order, which is also cylinder number-1. I opened the hood expecting to need to remove this coil and inspect the spark plug itself for damage too. I had my trusty DMM ready to start measuring voltage supply at the coil as well as ground resistance and resistance across the primary and secondary windings, looking for an open circuit or short somewhere.

I slapped my forehead after popping the beauty cover off the coils on Bank 1. The wiring harness connector was ever so slightly backed out from the proper seating location on the coil. This was just enough to not have a solid connection, failing the diagnostic checks as well as preventing ignition on that cylinder.

Look for the difference between the left and right coil connections. The coil on the left is properly seated with the red locking tab in the correct position. The coil on the right is cylinder number-1, where we were looking for a root cause of the coil fault and lean condition.

All it took was being backed out a tiny bit for the pins inside the connector to no longer have the necessary clean and complete contact required for the coil to work. Had this connection been solid, we would have been removing the coil to test continuity and impedances before proceeding.

The ECU was luckily smart enough to detect this, and part of its mitigation routine was to disable the corresponding fuel injector for cylinder number-1 to limit engine and catalyst damage when ignition was not possible in the cylinder. This was the reason behind the mysterious "Injector Cut" fuel source seen earlier.

A simple push and click of the connector fixed the issue. Somewhere during prior work, the coil had been removed for inspection and it was not properly reconnected with the locking tab in place. Indeed, the simplest solution was the right one here again. Restarting the engine revealed a different exhaust note that now matched what we would expect from a healthy 5.0L, and the scan tool immediately showed both banks operating in closed-loop fueling with readings tightly centered around lambda=1.0 from the oxygen sensors. Checking the fault code list now shows that the P0351 has gone, and we are able to confirm a proper repair for the vehicle.

The major lesson here is that although there are corner cases we read about from time to time, the vast majority of engine faults turn out to be something rather simple. Always check the simple items first before getting roped into some crazy research project.

GLOSSARY

Acronym	Meaning
ADAS	Advanced Driver Assistance System
AFR	Air-to-Fuel Ratio
ANN	Artificial Neural Network
AEB	Automated Emergency Braking
AECD	Auxiliary Emissions Control Device
CAL ID	Calibration ID
CVN	Calibration Verification Number
CARB	California Air Resource Board
BAR	California Bureau of Automotive Repair
CAN FD	CAN Flexible Data
CEL	Check Engine Light
CAA	Clean Air Act
CID	Component Identification
CVS	Constant Volume Sampling
CAN	Controller Area Network
DF	Deterioration Factor
DTC	Diagnostic Trouble Code
DEF	Diesel Exhaust Fluid
DPF	Diesel Particulate Filter
DPFE	Differential Pressure Feedback
DMM	Digital Multimeter
DI	Direct Injection
DMRs	Direct Memory Reads
ECM	Engine Control Module
ECT	Engine Coolant Temperature
ECU	Electronic Control Unit
EO	Executive Order
EONV	Engine-Off Natural Vacuum
EGR	Exhaust Gas Recirculation

Acronym	Meaning
ETC	Electronic Throttle Control
EV	Electric Vehicle
FTP	Federal Test Procedure
FID	Flame Ionization Detection
FOTA	Flash over the Air
FTIR	Fourier Transform Infrared Detection
FUL	Full Useful Life
HWYFE	Highway Fuel Economy Test
IMEP	Indicated Mean Effective Pressure
IAC	Idle Air Control
IUMPR	In-Use Monitor Performance Ratio
IAT	Intake Air Temperature
LBT	Lean Best Torque
LIN	Local Interconnect Network
MIL	Malfunction Indicator Lamp
MAP	Manifold Absolute Pressure
MAF	Mass Airflow
MBT	Maximum Brake Torque
CALID	Module Calibration Number
MID	Monitor Identification
NDIR	Non-Dispersive Infrared Detection
NMHC	Non-Methane Hydrocarbon
NMOG	Non-Methane Organic Gases
OBD	On-Board Diagnostics
NO_x	Oxides of Nitrogen
PIDs	Parameter Identifiers
PM	Particulate Matter
PEMS	Portable Emissions Monitoring System
PCV	Positive Crankcase Ventilation

Acronym	Meaning
PID	Proportional, Integral, and Derivative
PWM	Pulse Width Modulated
SCR/ DEF	Selective Catalyst Reduction or Diesel Exhaust Fluid Dosing
SHED	Sealed Housing for Evaporative Determination
SCR	Selective Catalytic Reduction
SENT	Single Edge Nibble Transmission
SAE	Society of Automotive Engineers
SEMA	Specialty Equipment Market Association
SD	Speed Density
SFTP	Supplemental Federal Test Procedures
TCM	Transmission Control Module
TID	Test Identification
TIAP	Throttle Inlet Air Pressure
TPS	Throttle Position Sensor
TDC	Top Dead Center
TCU	Transmission Control Module
EPA	United States Environmental Protection Agency
UDDS	Urban Dynamometer Driving Schedule
VPW	Variable Pulse Width
VECI	Vehicle Emissions Control Information
VIN	Vehicle Identification Number
VVE	Virtual VE
VE	Volumetric Efficiency
WOT	Wide-Open Throttle